Insights

Behind early childhood pedagogical documentation

Edited by
Alma Fleet
Catherine Patterson
Janet Robertson

Pademelon Press

Published in 2006 by
Pademelon Press
7/3 Packard Avenue
Castle Hill, New South Wales, 2154

Editing and Project Management by Persimmon Press
Design and Production by tania edwards design
Index by Olive Grove Indexing Services
Printed in Australia by Ligare Pty Limited

Insights : behind early childhood pedagogical documentation.

Bibliography.
Includes index.
ISBN 1 876138 20 3.

1. Teaching - Methodology. 2. Early childhood education -
Evaluation. I. Fleet, Alma. II. Patterson, Catherine.
III. Robertson, Janet.

372.21

Foreword

Insights: When the gaze turns inward

Rebecca S New

What does it mean to have insights? The very meaning of the word describes a private act—the result of looking deep inside to explore one's [pre-] conceptions of things. Insights are often characterised by surprise and sometimes provoke a reckoning of formerly held ideas and ideals. I experienced these sensations and more as a result of reading this volume of essays, each rich in detailed descriptions of what it means to educate other people's children in a way that promotes social justice. I had anticipated stories of how documentation has helped to reveal the vast and untapped potentials of children. I was hoping for more examples to support my own views of documentation as a mediating tool for collaborative inquiry and respectful relations among adults [parents as well as teachers]. What I had *not* anticipated was the use of documentation as an unflinching process of re-search into the 'deep politic' of early childhood education. This new *insight* was slow in coming, coming into focus as I slowly turned the pages.

Drawing upon work in classrooms in Australia and New Zealand as well as North America, educators share their *insights* into their work. I read most of these essays while in Italy, and was struck by how the responses to children resonated with the Italian verb *educare*-to care for and care about. Throughout the volume, there is a deep and abiding affection for the children being described—children with real names who are determined to make sense of the world they live in, even when it means that they must resort to various forms of subterfuge in order to play out their fantasies, their fears, and their developing understandings. And yet, it is not this image of children that stayed with me as I turned the pages; it is the image of the adults—early childhood educators willing to take risks in the classroom, in telling their stories, and in asking difficult questions about the value and ethics of their work.

In my mind, therefore, the most remarkable feature of this book is its profound humility. As much as they proclaim to have learned about the children they teach, the authors repeatedly remind us of how little we know about those we presume to care for; they underscore the uncertain nature of our professional goals and understandings. Not once do these authors presume to be fully in charge of what they uncover in the process of documentation and discovery. Students once confessed their resistance to documentation as a fear of 'going public'. Authors in this volume have publicly 'gone private' in their critical self-examination of their motives, their methods, and the meanings of their work with and on behalf of young children. The principle of social justice as a guiding force seems to have served not only as a source of inspiration; it also sowed seeds of doubt. Thus, authors openly display their struggles to differentiate between children's rights and adult responsibilities; between carefully detailed observations and the denial of children's rights to privacy; between the terrors and the thrills of risk-taking and rule-breaking; between an interpretation of education as a preserver of culture or an impetus for change.

The editors describe the terrain of early childhood as rich with interpretive possibilities and they make reference to 'roadmaps for possible journeys'. I would argue for a different metaphor, one that more aptly describes the provocation found within these pages and was suggested to me in a recent article on 'inquiry, imagination, and the search for a deep politic'. In this article, the author (Gitlin 2005) describes the critical need for an epistemic stance—what he refers to as a 'deep politic that does not ignore what is taken for granted' (p 17). He goes on to urge teachers to let go—to move out 'beyond efficiency, standardization, and obedience' to achieve a state 'where equity is in the air we breathe' (p 23). How to get beyond the *status quo*? Langston Hughes' poem *Emancipation* invites us to 'turn the telescope around' and 'look through the larger end' (Hughes 1994; cited in Gitlin 2005, p 23). It is just such a use of documentation that is in evidence in this volume—as a process of both purposeful inquiry *and* open-ended curiosity, as a means of looking inward as well as out, as a demonstration of 'the human potential to interrogate and (re) imagine the known world' (Ibid, p 15). This volume thus illustrates the potentials for documentation to serve as a heuristic—a manifestation of a commitment to re-search for new and more equitable ways of living with, learning from, and teaching young children.

Rebecca S New, Ed.D
Associate Professor
Eliot-Pearson Department of Child Development
Tufts University, USA

References

Gitlin A (2005) Inquiry, imagination, and the search for a deep politic. *Educational Researcher*, 34 (3), pp 15–24.

Hughes L (1994) Emancipation: 1865. In A Ramsersad (Ed) *The collected poems of Langston Hughes*, p 547. New York: Vintage Books. [cited in Gitlin (2005), p 23].

Contents

Acknowledgments

This book would not have been possible without the support of many colleagues, friends and family. In particular we would like to thank each of the authors of chapters and responses who have created this project. Each in turn would like to thank professional colleagues, children and families whose ideas and experiences are at the heart of the matter. We would like to recognise our fundamental humanity, and note that life's inevitable complications accompanied us on this journey.

As is always the case, the work behind the scenes shapes the final product. In this case our heartfelt appreciation goes to Christine Baxter, our editorial consultant. Her persistence and thoughtful attention to detail enabled a more coherent and professional presentation than would otherwise have been the case. Any errors or unclear statements that remain are in spite of her careful efforts.

We would also like to thank the staff of Pademelon Press for their assistance and support in enabling us to offer these ideas to the larger community for consideration and the helpful exchanging of ideas and inspiration.

Finally, we acknowledge our debt and gratitude to the educators of Reggio Emilia for the provocations of pedagogical documentation.

Alma Fleet, Catherine Patterson and Janet Robertson

About the Authors of Chapters

Biographical details about commentators
are contained within their responses.

Chris Bayes

Chris Bayes is a professional development facilitator who works with early childhood centres in Auckland, New Zealand. Chris has an interest in creating curriculum with teachers, children and parents that engages them intellectually, emotionally and spiritually. She was granted a Winston Churchill Fellowship in 1999 that took her to Melbourne, Reggio Emilia, Germany and London, to study the implementation of the theory and practice of Reggio Emilia in different cultural settings. Since then, she has been working alongside a number of teachers to provoke their thinking about teaching and learning and curriculum implementation.

Joanne Burr

Joanne Burr currently teaches nine and ten-year-old children in a public school in far western New South Wales, Australia. She has been teaching children in primary school since she graduated from university four years ago. Joanne is a strong advocate for public education and is very interested in how teachers can support students and families who, due in part to their social circumstances, have not experienced a feeling of empowerment in their lives. Her interest in pedagogical documentation and associated teaching strategies is ongoing and constantly evolving. Joanne lives in a small, warm community with her husband, Tim, and blue cattle dog, Elsie.

Sandra Cheeseman

Sandra Cheeseman is currently combining work and postgraduate study at the Institute of Early Childhood, Macquarie University, Sydney (Australia). She has worked previously in a range of children's services as a teacher, director and in senior management positions. Most recently, she has worked in the area of professional development with children's services staff considering the NSW Curriculum Framework as a tool for re-thinking early childhood curriculum.

Belinda Connerton

Belinda Connerton currently teaches three to five-year-old children in a community-based long day care centre on the mid-north coast of New South Wales (Australia), after seven years teaching in a Municipal centre in a culturally diverse area in inner Sydney. The culture shock of this sea change has been a challenge. Belinda has begun implementing an emergent curriculum program, which is also inspired by Reggio Emilia philosophies. This has been done with a team who had no experience with these philosophies, but one which has embraced new ideas wholeheartedly. Belinda's current challenge is introducing cultural diversity in a context which is relevant to the centre community, and to implement a focus on pedagogical documentation which explores social justice issues.

Danielle Crisafulli

Since graduating in both Arts and Early Childhood Education, Danielle has been teaching children from three to five years of age. Currently in her fifth year of teaching, she spent two years at a Municipal long day care centre in south-western Sydney, then moved on to a position at a community-based preschool in Sydney's inner west.

Sarah Felstiner

Sarah Felstiner taught four and five-year-olds at Hilltop Children's Center in Seattle, Washington (USA) for nine years, and now serves as the school's Office Manager. Before coming to Hilltop, Sarah worked with young children and undergraduates at the Bing Nursery School of Stanford University. Sarah treasures deep connections with children and their families, and the privilege of adventuring with children by facilitating and documenting their passionate pursuits. She particularly enjoys designing classroom environments that are both functional and aesthetic, and sharing her love of music and sense of humour with young children.

Alma Fleet

Alma Fleet is passionate about educational change. She has taught young children, primary grade students and adults in California, Scotland and Australia. Formerly Head of the Institute of Early Childhood, Macquarie University, Sydney (Australia), she teaches its undergraduate and postgraduate students as well as people working in schools and early childhood settings. Recently, she was given a University award for outstanding contribution to Community Outreach work related to professional development. She is involved in a nationally recognised Bachelor of Teaching program for Aboriginal and Torres Strait Islander student teachers, contributing to research with the first graduates of this program. While she has a background in literacy development, and her doctoral work related to the practicum, she is influenced by ideas from Reggio Emilia, her own family and by colleagues.

Miriam Giugni

Miriam Giugni has been working in early childhood education for 13 years. She has worked in both urban and rural areas in New South Wales (Australia) including a wide variety of culturally diverse communities. She is passionate about equity and social justice which she undertakes in her daily practice with children, families, staff and students. Miriam enjoys activism and advocacy for early childhood educators and is part of the Social Justice in Early Childhood Group in Sydney. Her other professional interests include lecturing, training, consultancy, curriculum facilitation and action research. She also has a passion for creative arts—painting, poetry, dance and music. Miriam is currently doing a PhD in early childhood studies at the University of Melbourne (Australia) where she is exploring the troubles and enchantments of everyday practice for equity in early childhood education.

Kiri Gould

Kiri Gould currently works as a lecturer in early childhood teacher education at Unitec, Auckland (*Aotearoa*/New Zealand). Formerly the manager of an early childhood centre, she has had a variety of experiences teaching in different early childhood centres. She has had a growing interest in social justice issues relevant to early childhood education and enjoyed exploring these issues with student teachers at Unitec. She is also interested in exploring issues related to leadership in early childhood education and effective professional development for early childhood teachers.

Margaret Hammersley

Margaret Hammersley has had extensive experience managing a wide variety of Australian early childhood services in a career spanning 30 years. Inspired by the philosophies of Reggio Emilia, she is implementing them in her own purpose-built centre, completed in early 2005 on the New South Wales mid-north coast.

Alexandra Harper

Alexandra Harper began working as a primary teacher in a parent-run school in Sydney (Australia). She has also lectured in teacher education at the University of Western Sydney, University of Newcastle and the Institute of Early Childhood, Macquarie University. In addition, she has presented at an international and many national conferences. She is currently Assistant Principal at Willoughby Public School, Sydney (Australia).

Laurie Kocher

Laurie Kocher has been a public school kindergarten teacher (four, five and six-year-olds) near Vancouver (Canada), for over 20 years. Recently, she has joined the team of the Institute for Early Childhood Education and Research at the University of British Columbia (UBC). Her doctoral research, completed at the University of Southern Queensland in Australia, focuses on how Reggio-inspired pedagogical documentation provokes change for both practitioners and the audience. Laurie considers her encounters with the preschools of Reggio Emilia to be an ongoing source of inspiration and hope for children and for teachers—and for us all.

Jill McLachlan

Jill McLachlan is a storyteller who lifts people's expectations of children and increases people's respect for children's thoughts and the value of dialogue as part of the learning process. By creating opportunities for children to engage in meaningful and 'real' learning experiences, Jill aims to impart a passion for thinking. She teaches five, six and seven-year-olds at a small school in Sydney (Australia).

Catherine Patterson

Catherine Patterson currently teaches undergraduate and postgraduate students at the Institute of Early Childhood, Macquarie University (Australia). As a teacher educator, Catherine's interests include curriculum decision-making, the professional experience of student teachers, and qualitative research methods. Her recent research has focused on the professional lives of early childhood practitioners.

Ann Pelo

Ann Pelo is the Mentor Teacher at Hilltop Children's Center, a full-day child care program in Seattle, Washington (USA). Before embarking on that journey into nurturing teachers' learning about pedagogical documentation and anti-bias practices, she taught three, four, and five-year-old children for 12 years at Hilltop. She is the co-author, with Fran Davidson, of *That's Not Fair: A Teacher's Guide to Activism with Young Children*.

Lesley Pohio

Lesley Pohio was the Head Teacher of Akarana Kindergarten and has extensive experience in the early childhood sector both as a practitioner and as a professional development facilitator. She currently lectures in Early Childhood Teacher Education at Unitec, Auckland (*Aotearoa*/New Zealand). She is particularly interested in the visual arts in the early childhood context and the impact of documenting children's experiences utilising a narrative framework, and incorporating Information and Communication Technologies.

Janet Robertson

Janet Robertson has been teaching, directing and advising for more than 20 years. Her interest in the challenges that Reggio Emilia's educational experience poses, drew her to return to teaching. Currently she is the two's and three's teacher, and part-time outdoor teacher at Mia-Mia, the Child and Family Centre at the Institute of Early Childhood, Macquarie University, Sydney (Australia). Endeavouring to re-conceptualise early education in both the indoor and outdoor learning environment within the Australian context has been a driving force in her work.

Lisa Schillert

Lisa Schillert has been lucky to share the lives of the many children, families and colleagues, who have enriched her teaching experiences in Australia and overseas, in her 15 years of working in early childhood education. She is consumed in the magical world of motherhood and is passionate about helping all to see the potentials and capabilities of young children.

Pamela Silversides

Having completed her Early Childhood Education degree in 2000, Pamela was a targeted graduate to Cammeray Public School in Sydney (Australia) in 2001 where she taught Kindergarten for four years. Currently she is teaching Year 3 and is the Technology Coordinator and head of web design for the school. As part of this role, she developed (with Joanne Burr) and maintains the school's website and intranet, including a forum on which photographs and samples of children's work are displayed. Pamela hopes to use this technology as a springboard to document children's learning and share this with children, fellow teachers, families and communities on the intranet.

Edith Stanke

Edith Stanke has worked in the early childhood field since 1995. Prior to this, she worked in the areas of psychology and social welfare. She is motivated by the knowledge that the quality of education provided to children in the early years is critical to the development of balanced individuals, who are a fundamental component of a balanced society.

Lesley Studans

Lesley Studans is currently teaching five to seven-year-old children in a Catholic systemic school in western Sydney (Australia). She also works with teachers in her system developing their skills in working with children and their families in the first years of school. She has been teaching for 20 years and first came into contact with Australian thinking about Reggio Emilia during four years teaching in a before-school setting. In her struggle in a school setting with the provocations from Reggio Emilia, Lesley has found pedagogical documentation to be a most powerful aid to developing understandings about herself as a teacher, the children and their families, and the curriculum. She is currently exploring children's spirituality through pedagogical documentation. Through all her endeavours, Lesley has been supported by the RE-Search group at Macquarie University, Sydney (Australia).

Introduction

Alma Fleet, Catherine Patterson, Janet Robertson

Several years ago, when this collection had its genesis, the idea of creating a book about work being done in the area of pedagogical documentation seemed a useful contribution to make. It seemed a simple enough proposition at the time. Early childhood educators were asking for support in exploring newer ways of working and, in particular, being fascinated with the provocations such as pedagogical documentation emerging from the town of Reggio Emilia in Northern Italy. That is still the case. The stage, however, is not the same. The scenery changed constantly and the previous script is unrecognisable. The book has evolved, shaped by rapid shifts in circumstances and is now constructed to reflect the ongoing conversations that are taking place in professional early childhood communities.

This book introduces the novice to ways in which adults and children explore possibilities for investigation together, but it does more than this. It is also a site for those who have been thinking through relationships between social justice issues and pedagogical decision-making. There are many ways into the conversations that are taking place and multiple definitions of the topics being considered.

Considering social justice

Increasingly, there is interest in the importance of social justice in the early childhood professional community. For example, in Australia, the Social Justice in Early Childhood group, based in New South Wales, held its second annual conference in 2005 and in Melbourne, The Centre for Equity and Innovations in Early Childhood (located in the University of Melbourne) had its fourth annual conference in 2004. Recent publications by Australian authors provide further evidence of this growing interest. For example, MacNaughton (2005) and Yelland (2005).

Nevertheless, it is interesting that many current early childhood textbooks do not include definitions of 'social justice'. In some cases the term, and possibly the construct, is overlooked; in other cases, understanding is assumed. A web search reveals that the term itself is contested, with discussions related to the extent to which governments should, or could, ensure equity of opportunity for all citizens (see for example, Wikipedia, 2004). From an early childhood perspective, Cannela (1997, p 162) writes strongly about 'social justice as a human right':

Younger human beings are poor, hungry, familiar with violence, and subject to institutionalized assaults on their families, cultures, and values. We send some of them to schools that are dirty, rat infested, and have very few materials while others have all the resources and every opportunity that anyone can imagine... Further, even those 'children' from privileged groups are placed in the margins of society as inexperienced, immature, innocent, and needing protection from the real world. Our construction of 'child' silences a group of human beings, removing all possibility for social justice for them.

This confronting statement may seem distinct from issues of pedagogical documentation and everyday practice in environments for young children, including the inspirations from Italy. However, the Italians in Reggio Emilia have had a key role in providing provocations and examples of documentation that have inspired many of the authors in this book. Sergio Spaggiari, Director of the preschools and infant–toddler centres of the municipality of Reggio Emilia has commented about the city (2004, p 12):

> ...though not physically a border town, [Reggio Emilia] has intentionally situated itself in a transit zone of ideas and people, where diversities can be the essential resource for cultural exchange and civil enrichment.

In general, the dialogue in the English-speaking educational community about the experience of the municipal child care centres of Reggio Emilia has overlooked the centrality of social justice in that experience. Perhaps in an attempt to make the challenges of Reggio Emilia more politically and educationally palatable in the United States, the socialist politics of the city and Emilia Romagna region, and the social justice agenda running through the schools, was downplayed in the initial interpretations in North America. To us, this silence is deafening. It is as though an entire perspective of the Reggio experience is expunged in the English language texts that promote 'Reggio ideas'. The municipal infant–toddler centres and preschools of Reggio Emilia are politically active and have a very 'out there' social justice profile, so much so that some centres are named after important political events or people. For example, the preschool Neruda was named after a Chilean political martyr and poet, Pablo Neruda; and another centre, Iqbal Masih, was named after an eleven-year-old child worker murdered in Pakistan after speaking out about child-bonded labour. Pedagogical documentation from work with children in the Diana School in Reggio Emilia has explored the 'Rights of the child' (Malaguzzi, Castagnetti, Rubizzi and Vecchi, 1995), racism, poverty and war. As Carlina Rinaldi (2001a, p 42) puts it:

> The reoccurring question is whether the school is limited to transmitting culture, or can be, as we in Reggio Emilia strive toward, a place where culture is constructed and democracy is put into practice.

Furthermore Reggio Children (2004) note that:

> Over the years, in collaboration with the Municipality of Reggio Emilia and the Friends of Reggio Children Association, Reggio Children [a support organisation for the schools]…has carried out cooperative initiatives with educational institutions in a number of countries and territories, including Albania, Bosnia, Kosovo, Cuba, and Senegal. Educational projects are now underway (focusing on improving environments and teacher professional development) in Egypt and the Palestinian Territories…

This work was made possible by using part of the profits made from publications and the international delegations that visit the municipal schools of Reggio Emilia. More recently (March 2005), Reggio Children appealed to the friends of Reggio Emilia to become part of a 'project of solidarity' for the countries affected by the Boxing Day 2004 tsunami. The President of Reggio Children (Giordana Rabitti, 2005, p 12) wrote:

> We are thinking of helping in building anew, or restoring a place for childhood, be it a school or a children's hospital or a place of the children or for the children. This enterprise should be accomplished in collaboration with those who are living in that place and are more capable than we are to listen to the needs, the wishes, the dreams of those who suffered so much, or those who have lost the hope their life can begin again.

It is this commitment to democracy and equity which intrigues and encourages us.

Considering pedagogical documentation

What is pedagogical documentation? For many people, the image that will come to mind with this term will relate to wall panels developed in line with the Italian experience or collections of photographs, drawings, conversations and analysis of experience. However, a straightforward definition would be misleading as the possibilities are complex; aspects of the concept will unfold throughout this book. While artefacts are certainly inherent in pedagogical documentation, more is implied by this term than the creation of products. For example, Carlina Rinaldi (2001b, pp 85–7) writes that:

> …education is seen not as an object but as 'a relational place'…It is a construction of relationships that are born of a reciprocal curiosity between the subject and the object…where the children can give new identity to the object, creating a relationship for the object and for themselves that is also metaphorical and poetic…

Documentation is thus a narrative form. Its force of attraction lies in the wealth of questions, doubts and reflections that underlie the collection of data and with which it is offered to others…They are three-dimensional writings, not aimed at giving the event objectivity but at expressing the meaning-making effort…

Provocations from Reggio Emilia are ongoing. In addition, other voices are contributing to the conversations that are unfolding. The notion of 'pedagogical documentation' emerges in association with the Scandinavian use of the term 'pedagogue' in relation to adults who work with pedagogy, the exploration of teaching and learning. The term 'pedagogical documentation' came to the attention of Australians visiting Scandinavia in 1997; it was coined originally by Gunilla Dahlberg and is now being used worldwide (personal communication).

In countries where 'pedagogue' is not a common term, would it not be simpler just to use the terms 'teachers' and 'teaching'? Perhaps, but that would be misleading. For as well as other problematic issues related to cross-cultural translations, there are debates related to the notion of teaching that get entangled with definitions of qualifications. It is clear that the greater the knowledge of qualified staff in group settings, the better the outcomes for children. Nevertheless, it is also clear that all staff working in teams in children's services can consider these newer ways of working and make a contribution to them. The language used can sometimes exclude people unintentionally or obscure meanings. We are trying to avoid those mistakes.

Exploring the book

There are many ways of working that are associated with similar starting points. Ideas move so quickly that the type of documentation that was envisaged when this book began, is now only one of many possibilities. To reflect some of these possibilities as well as the range of viewpoints associated with the discussion, this book is organised as a series of reflections. They are not interactive enough to be called dialogues, but the format is intended to invite readers to be part of the unfolding conversations.

To enable the linking of issues and ideas, the chapters are grouped under headings: *Part 1—First Principles*; *Part 2—Beginnings*; *Part 3—Engaging the Hard Questions*; *Part 4—Looking Deeper, Seeing More* and *Part 5—Pulling Together, Reaching Out*. Groups of chapters are followed by invited responses. This flow of voices is intended to provide a dialogic frame for the ideas; that is, a style of presentation that emphasises multiple viewpoints and possibilities associated with the ideas being explored.

The provocation for this book emerged from conversations amongst the editors at the Institute of Early Childhood (IEC), Macquarie University, Sydney, Australia. Subsequently, authors were invited to consider the ideas being raised in the context of social justice issues. The world's complexities have become increasingly obvious through the immediacy of technology. The births and deaths of people and nations become part of daily discussion, radio commentary and visual backgrounding for breakfast tables and computer screens. Differences between individuals and groups of people become elements in the enacting of power relationships and inequity, as well as springboards for opportunity and possibility. The realities of poverty and terrorism are as much a part of children's lives as play and wonder. Discussions about pedagogy can no longer take place under an isolated heading of 'curriculum'; they have become recognised as integral to philosophies of practice and approaches to personal decision-making. These ideas will be unpacked as the book unfolds.

Considering some of the issues raised in each chapter may highlight ways in which the major threads are woven throughout the book. These brief comments about the chapters will not provide the power of the original and may focus on elements different from those identified by the readers. These mentions just serve as an overview. In their comments regarding each section, the respondents have highlighted points of interest for each reader to consider.

The first chapter orients the reader to the main definitions and debates that currently surround the concept of pedagogical documentation. It will support those who are completely new to the topic, exploring ways that photographs and excerpts of conversations help give insight to children's worlds, to the learning and growing that is taking place, to planning possibilities, to conversations with families and other adults, to professional self-reflection. It will help to highlight other authors who have written about various forms of related professional practice and it will introduce some of the pragmatic and philosophical threads of current discussions. It is a useful place to start in order to contextualise the rest of the debate.

The chapters that follow may be read in any order. They are written mostly by people who are working with young children. Sometimes, colleagues in colleges and universities who are involved in thinking about these ideas have collaborated with these authors. The authors work in a range of settings and systems (author information is included in the book).

Each chapter includes a context summary as the authors are from several countries and terminology varies with the geography. In the tension between recognising accomplishments and honouring privacy, pseudonyms have been used for adults and children unless permissions have been provided for the use of real names.

The pieces contain stories of experience that include children from the youngest through to those in the early years of school. Adult thinking, interactions and shifts in perception are represented through the voices of early childhood staff and children's families. While the ideas may be of interest to families and to those working with older children, most examples are drawn from the period of early childhood (birth to age eight).

In *Part 1*, the first group of chapters begins with Chapter Two. In this chapter, Jill McLachlan raises issues of teacher power, including complexities related to giving children space and knowing where to challenge them, while acknowledging and engaging with previously invisible content. Recognising the importance of treating children's hurts as part of curriculum relates directly to social justice.

In the next chapter, Janet Robertson offers provocations regarding the images of children that we hold as demonstrated in our interactions with them. For example, her account of a toddler becoming a 'dancer' rather than a 'hitter' underlines the importance of consciously seeking positive perspectives when interpreting behaviour.

In the North American consideration of 'the disposition to document' in Chapter Four, Sarah Felstiner, Laurie Kochler and Ann Pelo raise challenges related to emotional and intellectual risk-taking. These authors give insight to work in practice and invite us to be puzzled by the unexpected. In Chapter Five, Kiri Gould and Lesley Pohio reflect on experiences in New Zealand and critique narrow definitions of assessment. This chapter has a focus on assisting teachers to work with an empowering national early childhood curriculum, especially through the use of narrative writing and 'Learning Stories' told from multiple perspectives. With a focus on problem-solving and empowerment, Kiri and Lesley incorporate elements of the processes involved as well as maintaining commitment to creating pieces (both large and small) of pedagogical documentation.

As commentators, Jan Millikan, Margie Carter and John Nimmo reflect upon the chapters in Part 1, adding their reflections to the dialogue. This pattern of a commentary after a group of chapters is intended to highlight the slippery and complex positions that teachers take in constructing curriculum.

Chapter Six begins *Part 2*. It includes many illustrations of the meaning of a learning community where all members are valued and curiosity is rewarded. During an interview with Catherine Patterson, Belinda Connerton recalls provocations for joint exploration. These include children's reconstructions of the Twin Towers after September 11th in New York, and Belinda's interpretation of their efforts as children attempting to re-create a history in which more people might have survived. These stories reflect one teacher's journey towards more insightful seeing, listening and recording.

There is an exploration in Chapter Seven of aspects of early childhood teacher education, with perspectives from novices beginning their differing journeys with pedagogical documentation, in widely varying circumstances.

Joanne Burr, Danielle Crisafuli and Pamela Silversides tell of their work in a program with Alma Fleet and Catherine Patterson. Recommendations are made for starting slowly with small projects, listening to a range of voices and recording in a variety of ways. The impact of differing work contexts is also highlighted.

In Chapter Eight, Lesley Studans writes from the perspective of a school teacher about the importance of 'teacher voice' in pieces of pedagogical documentation. She also recognises the importance of integrated investigations for meeting school or system prescribed outcomes across many learning areas.

Janet Robertson presents Chapter Nine through a lens of relationships with a focus on 'gaze'. She writes about the importance of 'children's presence' and of seeing children's exchanges as 'gifts' (Rinaldi, 1999) to each other as well as data to help adult understanding. Following Janet's chapter, Margaret Clyde and Wendy Shepherd emphasise the importance of not underestimating children and of the need for infrastructure support in pursuing this goal.

Beginning *Part 3—Engaging the hard questions*, Ann Pelo writes from Seattle, Washington, extending the context presented in Chapter Four by highlighting the intersections between pedagogical documentation and social justice. In exploring 'documentation as a verb', she foregrounds the role of a 'mentor teacher', recasting to the local context while acknowledging her intellectual debt to the '*pedagogista*' of Reggio Emilia.

In Chapter Eleven, Sandra Cheeseman and Janet Robertson raise issues of privacy, purpose and consent in documenting children's work. This chapter is not a provision of answers, but rather a foregrounding of the importance of asking the questions. Queries are raised about the place of staff in the process which are reminiscent of the 'image questions' raised about adults in Chapter Three.

Miriam Giugni in Chapter Twelve, raises challenges related to popular culture as a contested context in early childhood settings and as a rich site for reconceptualising identity work as relevant early childhood curriculum. She raises provocations about 'Barbie'-related behaviours and the social power of the 'suits' worn by super heroes.

In Chapter Thirteen, Alma Fleet challenges narrow definitions of diversity and illustrates the value of connecting with often-ignored curriculum. Through mini-stories and three extended narratives, these experiences provide examples of entry points into a more sophisticated discussion about interpreting diversity. Following these chapters, Anthony Semann and Anne Stonehouse engage with the relevance and authenticity of curriculum in the context of social justice imperatives.

Part 4 brings us to *Looking deeper, seeing more*. Janet Robertson's narratives emphasise moments when adults become learners, in listening to and thinking about children's experiences. Again, three stories create sites for understanding possibilities—seeing a teacher think through events over time helps readers share in the act and art of interpreting interactions.

Alex Harper considers potentials for confronting social justice issues in a formal school framework in Chapter Fifteen. She portrays a teacher doing things 'differently' in a context of accountability. Alex notes that there are times when capturing a photograph is less important than living an investigation with children. At the same time, she is confronting teacher power in selecting avenues for exploration and in accepting or rejecting the temptations of sanitised versions of world events.

This section ends with two perspectives from New Zealand. In Chapter Sixteen, Chris Bayes highlights the importance of acknowledging local sociopolitical contexts and gives an example of thoughtful, holistic curriculum. Her examples illustrate that, in the use of 'Learning Stories' within a 'community of learners', there can be tension between either a focus on individuals, or on individuals within a wider frame of reference. Following this chapter, Diti Hill also comments from a New Zealand perspective with a focus on participatory democracy. Jenny Porter concludes this section on *Looking deeper, seeing more* with the journey of transforming learning in one school context.

Part 5 has a focus on *Pulling together and reaching out*. In Chapter Seventeen, there are snippets of conversations heard in a range of places, as the speakers struggle with pragmatics and evolving personal philosophies. Conversations with Alma Fleet, Margaret Hammersley, Catherine Patterson, Lisa Schillert and Edith Stanke reflect differences in attitudes to documenting due to changing perceptions over time. The potential of portfolios is raised, leading again to the question of language use. What exactly do people mean in contrasting a portfolio with a piece of pedagogical documentation? Does one focus on an individual's activities or development while the other is a working document seeking insight and understanding? Are there times when these purposes overlap? This chapter also explores the roles associated with being a 'gatherer' of information, as well as the delicacies of 'being documented' as an adult.

Chapter Eighteen concerns the ethics of an exhibition, again raising the difficulties of language use, communication subtleties, and the essence of responsive relationships. This account of the creation of *Exhibit-on* by Alma Fleet and Janet Robertson reveals key elements of decision-making in the creating of an exhibition, intending to celebrate and provoke—all within a frame of behaving ethically. In her response to these chapters, Sue Groom echoes the difficulties that many practitioners have with pedagogical documentation in shifting from 'what it is' to 'what it does'.

Finally, in the Conclusion, we reflect on where the dialogue has taken us thus far and muse about where discussion might propel us in the future. We emphasise that the onus is on each reader individually to construct and collaboratively co-construct meanings from the provocations that are offered.

While the intention of these chapters is to be accessible, the approach is not simplistic. The ideas are too important and the issues too complex to be dealt with in ways that are transparent to every potential reader. Work that we have been doing suggests that people who choose to work in early childhood, irrespective of qualification or compensation, are hungry for ideas. They want to explore their own practice and improve the work they are doing, learning from children, the community and each other, as the journey unfolds. We designed this book both to help the newer members of the professional community to gain access to the discussion, and also to engage those who have been thinking around these ideas for a longer period of time. Some people might enter this book as part of a course of study while others might dip into it individually or in groups to further their own thinking.

Ideas are gifts in a thoughtful world community. Thinking with others is a supportive way to explore 'big ideas' (Oken-Wright & Gravett, 2002). We look forward to further discussions with readers as these ideas contribute to evolving discourses and become part of wider debates.

References

Cannella GS (1997) *Deconstructing early childhood education: Social justice and revolution.* New York: Peter Lang Publishing.

MacNaughton G (2005) *Doing Foucault in early childhood studies: Applying poststructural ideas.* London: Routledge.

Malaguzzi L, Castagnetti M, Rubizzi L & Vecchi V (1995) *A journey into the rights of children: As seen by children themselves.* The unheard voice of children series. Reggio Emilia: Reggio Children.

Oken-Wright P & Gravett M (2002) Big ideas and the essence of intent. In VR Fu, AJ Stremmel and LT Hill (Eds) *Teaching and learning: Collaborative exploration of the Reggio Emilia approach.* (pp 197–220). New Jersey: Merrill Prentice Hall.

Rabitti G (2005) Letter from Reggio Children. *Challenge: Reggio Emilia Information Exchange Australia*, 9 (1), p 12.

Reggio Children (2004) Listserve discussion. Retrieved 12 December 2004, from <http//www.reggiochildren.it>. Reggio Emilia: Reggio Children.

Rinaldi C (1999) Presentation to the Municipal infant-toddler centres and preschools of Reggio Emilia Study Tour from Australia and New Zealand. (April 7–14). Reggio Emilia, Italy.

Rinaldi C (2001a) Documentation and assessment: What is the relationship? In C Giuduci, C Rinaldi & M Krechevsky (Eds) *Making learning visible: Children as individual and group learners.* (pp 78–89). Reggio Emilia: Reggio Children.

Rinaldi C (2001b) Infant toddler centres and preschools as places of culture. In C Giuduci, C Rinaldi & M Krechevsky (Eds) *Making learning visible: Children as individual and group learners.* (pp 38–46). Reggio Emilia: Reggio Children.

Spaggiari S (2004) Crossing boundaries. *RE Child: Reggio Children newsletter.* Reggio Emilia: Reggio Children.

Wikipedia (2005) *Definition of social justice*. Retrieved 25 October, 2004 from
<http://en.wikipedia.org/wiki/social justice>.

Yelland N (Ed) (2005) *Critical issues in early childhood education*. Berkshire,
England: Open University Press.

Chapter One

An Overview of the Terrain: Roadmaps for Possible Journeys

Alma Fleet
Catherine Patterson
Janet Robertson

Alma, Catherine and Janet have been professional colleagues for more than ten years at Macquarie University in Sydney, Australia. During this time they have had the opportunity to visit Reggio Emilia several times, to visit Scandinavia as part of an international delegation exploring the impact of ideas from Reggio Emilia and to work together in professional contexts.

Introduction

Much is happening in the terrain of early childhood, in the world of education, in the lives of educators, children and their families. This chapter includes roadmaps which offer opportunities for intellectual engagement, for both teachers and children. As Laevers (2004) points out, it is our responsibility to be 'looking for the full reality of the child before you'. He also noted that the single way of knowing the effectiveness of what we are doing is to consider the children's wellbeing, involvement and sense of agency.

As we live our lives, we find joy in our work and puzzlement in how to always, always work to think more deeply, connect with the challenges that surround us, and to improve our professional practice. To help meet these goals, we begin this chapter with one of those everyday voices which happened to slide into our lives.

Dear Alma,

I am sure that you will not remember me, but I was a student at IEC [Institute of Early Childhood, Macquarie University] graduating in 2000. I am now a teacher in a two-to-threes room working in long day care. I have recently under-taken several courses relating to the Curriculum Framework (New South Wales, 2002) which I have embraced and believe is a wonderful tool. However, I am finding it difficult to implement programming and documentation changes, as a query has been raised in relation to the confidentiality of the children and their families, as stated in the regulations…

My main question relates to journals which we have implemented, as a way of recording the children's development, since the beginning of the year. All of our observations, many of which are social, include the first names of all the children and are usually supported with photographs. The observations are written in the positive. The suggestion has been made that only the full name of the child, in whose journal the observation appears, should be included and all others should be in first initial format only. My gut feeling is that this detracts from the documentation, particularly in terms of social competence and the importance of the children's friends. There was also a suggestion made that the faces of others in the photograph should be blocked out!

I feel that I am struggling with what I am being taught at these training courses and then what is being quoted from the regulations. I am hoping that you can provide me with a little insight as my interpretation of the Curriculum Framework is that our portfolios are appropriate.

Here is a small sample of a written inclusion in Martin's journal which is accompanied by three photos of the children.

Today we made a fire engine using the box, a ladder, fire hats, hoses and the steering wheels. Martin was very interested in the 'fire-engine' and sat at the steering wheel upon his arrival in the morning. As more children arrived, the play became more dramatic and complex. Gerry, Tod, Melissa, Jim and Ross were all wearing hats and carrying fire hoses. They moved about the yard together putting out imaginary fires by pointing their hoses and saying 'shhhhh'. The children discussed their ideas amongst themselves using words such as 'all gone', 'fire's out!', 'need to climb the ladder' and 'over here!'. They then moved onto the bikes and rode around the yard making fire-engine noises 'nee nar, nee nar' putting out more fires. They stayed in the group and continued this play for approximately 15 minutes.

Yours sincerely,
Briony

This email is an example of discussions in staffrooms regarding issues emerging from the provocations of new ways of working with young children. The confusions of language and concern about regulations are prevalent. When is a journal a portfolio? Is the documentation being referred to here the same as 'pedagogical documentation'? Where does privacy intersect with pedagogy? What about the children and voices we aren't seeing and hearing?

The reply to the email query included the following:

Good grief! Thanks for this…My immediate response is that your gut feelings are absolutely correct. If we believe in the social construction of knowledge and that children grow in interaction with each other and the things around them, then those relationships should be evidenced in documentation, both as a source of celebration and a basis for planning. Families are also interested in the life of the centre, not just of their child in isolation…Perhaps there has been a local misinterpretation? To me, Martin's example is most appropriate with photos, for public viewing and discussion.
All the best,
Alma

While these discussions relate to the nature of staff work, the rich possibilities inherent in learning alongside children, and the sociopolitical contexts in which children's centres are situated, they also include the perspective of families. The value of keeping various forms of documentation about the nature of children's experiences with each other and their environments is clear in these following two testimonials from parents (originally British) of children in centres in Reggio Emilia, Italy. Firstly, Caroline writes of her daughter's experience in an *asilo-nido*, or infant-toddler centre called *Arcobelano* (Rainbow). In describing the warm relationships with staff and the nature of life in the centre, this mother comments (Hunter, 2001, pp 39–40):

There was a very natural feel to the way that the children's activities developed and changed. The apparent lack of formal structure to the activities belied the careful selection of materials and situations that were offered for the children to respond to. My impression was that my child was being very carefully 'listened' to and that each avenue explored was a new voyage of individual as well as collective discovery. Beautifully displayed large panels illustrated the children's activities and development clearly; at the end of each year we were given a thick volume of photographs, commentaries and creative work which Sunniva [now 16 years old] looks at to this day. I am particularly grateful to the infant–toddler centre for these lasting records; as I was working more than full-time I never had as many opportunities as I would have liked to document Sunniva's first years myself.

Similarly, another parent describes her experience of her son's time at the Anna Frank preschool in Reggio Emilia. Jenny writes (Leask, 2001, p 46):

The parents' meetings are always illustrated by slides or videos of the children involved in work-in-progress, projects or outings. Statements of intent for the week, the term and the year, are pinned up in the classroom alongside a daily plan and a daily diary showing how the plan may have changed course or been adapted according to what the children have come up with. Examples of the children's work are up on the walls together with written explanations of the starting point, fragments of dialogue, photos of the children at work and their own explanations of what they are doing. As a parent, I find that all these various types of documentation provide a vivid, clear, exciting and at times very moving understanding of, and access to, Sam's life in the school, as well as opening my eyes to the idea of children as navigators in their own learning.

These excerpts are both inspirational and challenging. Novices might be asking, how could I do all of that? What is it exactly that I might be doing? Well, many things that will depend on local contexts. For the moment, we wish to focus on the role of pedagogical documentation in an educator's professional repertoire.

Young children: thinkers and researchers

So, what might be included under the umbrella of the term *pedagogical documentation*? In 1999, Dahlberg, Moss & Pence wrote (pp 147–8):

When we use the term 'pedagogical documentation', we are actually referring to two related subjects: a *process* and an important *content* in that process. 'Pedagogical documentation' as *content* is material which records what the children are saying and doing, the work of the children, and how the pedagogue relates to the children and their work. This material can be produced in many ways and takes many forms…This material makes the pedagogical work concrete and visible (or audible)…This *process* involves the use of that material as a means to reflect upon the pedagogical work and to do so in a very rigorous, methodical and democratic way.

This chapter builds on that conceptualisation, exploring the possible meanings of a range of thinkers who are writing about, or trying to create, pedagogical documentation. The intention is to describe thinking processes in association with thoughtful ways to approach decision-making and recording.

In describing pieces of pedagogical documentation or people's approaches to the topic, does that mean that there is a particular process or strategy that can be followed in order to 'do' this kind of work? Definitely not! The issues are philosophical as well as practical. Confusing though it may be, this book will not advocate one way to document experiences or even one way to approach work with children. It will share experiences of people working in several countries along with their attempts to theorise their practices. These theories are often 'grounded' in that they emerge from reflections about the experiences that have been unfolding. The theories will sit within the philosophical positions held by the authors, but may not be clearly identifiable under one of the 'Grand theories' recognised in the literature such as social constructivism. More about this notion of practical theorising will emerge throughout the book and may be useful to people who are wondering about the endless debates regarding the relationship of theory and practice.

There are extremes of what is meant by pedagogical documentation, including small examples of works-in-progress, various types of folders, wall panels, videos or even an approach to practice. This way of working may be informed by having thought about the processes associated with a particular set of beliefs and procedures. Many people relate their conception of the nature of pedagogical documentation to the work done in Reggio Emilia during the second half of the last century. As a major spokesperson for 'the project of Reggio Emilia' (as that extraordinary enterprise is often called), Carlina Rinaldi (2001) has made the following observations about the contexts of pedagogical documentation (p 79):

> I believe that documentation is a substantial part of the goal that has always characterised our experience: the search for meaning—to find the meaning of school, or rather, to construct the meaning of school, as a place that plays an active role in the children's search for meaning and our own search for meaning (and shared meanings)… We cannot live without meaning; that would preclude any sense of identity, any hope, any future.

She then goes on to clarify the nature of the undertaking (Rinaldi, 2001, p 88):

> So what is the secret? There is no secret, no key, if not that of constantly examining our understandings, knowledge, and intuitions, and sharing and comparing them with those of our colleagues. It is not a transferable 'science', but rather an understanding, sensitivity to knowledge.

As can be seen from Carlina's comments, the words to describe what we call 'pedagogical documentation' are elusive. This may contribute to an apparent desire in some teachers to want a recipe, a diagram, a format or a series of steps on how to 'do' pedagogical documentation. We ponder this, and think it can be laid at the door of the belief that teaching comes from a manual that can be followed. Dahlberg, Moss & Pence (1999) refer to the great 'project of modernity' —a particular systematic way of thinking about the world. In this conceptualisation, measurable progress and the concept of 'one right way' ruled not only the world of education, but most western human endeavour. While there is a sense that 'modernity' happened at a time in the past, there are elements of that conception which are on-going. In that conception, there was a belief that measurement and standardisation would ensure the certainties of quality. There is a shift that is gathering momentum which challenges these traditional notions of education and teaching. In postmodern theories, where multiple viewpoints are held, issues of power and social justice inherent in the everyday workings of institutions such as schools are questioned. The position of teacher is recognised as complex—with the teacher as moral agent and critical thinker; no longer a transmitter of knowledge but, with children, a collaborator, researcher and knowledgeable 'other' in the educational endeavour.

To return to the question at hand, what is pedagogical documentation? Maybe if we describe what we think it is not, things may become clearer. It is not purely display of either children's or teachers' work, but at times has elements of display. It is not simply a document, but often resides on paper, disk, and book. It is not a running record of events which unfold, but can take that form and role during the course of the experience. It is not a checklist or planning format, but there will be times when such organisational elements are used to propel the experience forward. It is embedded in the actions, learning, research and collaboration among a group of children and an educator.

Perhaps to highlight the complexities, it will be helpful to unpack an extended investigation that a group of three, four-year-old children and Janet undertook in 2004 at Mia Mia.

Hoppy's letterbox

In the early morning before school opened, a wild rabbit was seen disappearing into the garden. Later in the morning, I mentioned this sighting to Oliver and his mates and they had a conversation about what kind of rabbit, what it was called and where it might be now. There was already a pet rabbit in the school called Fizzy, whom Oliver had adored since infancy. Mei Mei, her interest piqued by Oliver's animation, joined in the conversation. They poked about near the last sighting by the tree, calling out to each other and the rabbit.

At this point, the investigation was born. As yet it had no name, no goal and no direction, but I was alerted to the possibilities by their excitement. Abandoning their fruitless search, partly hastened by voiced concerns for a frightened rabbit possibly cowering in the garden, they sat on a nearby seat and chatted further. They asked a lot of questions, such as 'what is its name?'; 'what sort of house does it have?'; 'why is it here?'; 'where is its mum?'; and so on. These questions arose from the context of knowing a great deal about rabbit husbandry from their experiences with Fizzy. Rather than answering their questions, I redirected them, asking in turn what the children thought, suggesting they could draw their ideas. With alacrity, they set to the task. During this interlude at the outdoor drawing table, the rabbit gained a name: Hoppy; and age: three years old; and a reason for being on the playground: wanting to play with Fizzy.

Children looking for the rabbit

They chose, however, to draw what they thought the rabbit's house would look like. Predictably, the house drawings included very human items, kitchens, spas and beds. I became aware that Mei Mei would smile at some of the more extravagant interior decoration ideas from Oliver, or the other children now engaged in drawing. It is possible to surmise she knew that this was fanciful, but kept it to herself; rather like a child who suspects Father Christmas is not really true, but is unprepared to disabuse others or herself just in case. The morning drew to an end, and the children left to go to lunch wondering how they could ask the rabbit the remaining unanswered questions, but not before they left a bundle of drawings beside the tree, a gift for Hoppy.

Now, with time away from the children, it was possible to explore what pedagogical opportunities their interest could offer. Where could this interest go and was it worth the trip? Making the decision it was worth following, I ran through the potential pathways. The rabbit could represent the 'unknown other' in need of succour and help—a potential relationship which could enrich our outdoor lives. The children could extend help in forms of food or housing. Or it could meld with a focus on literacy (bearing in mind the gifts they had left were, in part, letters). It is at this point the investigation gained momentum beyond anything the children or I could imagine.

I incorporated some of these possibilities by writing a reply to the children from Hoppy on a leaf (thanking them for their concerns), and took the children's offerings away, leaving the leaf letter on the ground near Hoppy's bolthole. On discovering the letter after lunch, the excitement reached fever pitch and Hoppy received more mail in return. It is at this point that the issue of a letterbox arose. Several children were not satisfied with the temporary and vulnerable status their treasured letters endured prior to Hoppy's collection. They clamoured to make a letterbox, and so a quick one was devised out of cardboard and decorated with love tokens and numbers.

For several weeks the letterbox survived and letters passed to and fro. Then it rained and the letterbox became a crumpled puddle of wet paper. It was at the same time that the children saw Hoppy late one afternoon scampering across the playground. Even the doubting Mei Mei was once again galvanised into believing there was a rabbit, but reserved judgment about whether the rabbit actually wrote the letters.

Kate proposed that they make a new letterbox, which would not fall apart. The focus of the investigation shifted—no longer centred on Hoppy, but something Hoppy needed. Endeavouring to step aside from the 'powerful teacher', I asked them to draw their own letterbox as a design starting point. All three watched and discussed their drawings. Then Oliver asked me to draw mine. Perusing this, and its fourth interpretation of what a letterbox could look like, gave Kate an idea; she suggested that they ask all the staff in the centre. At this point, I offered the word 'survey' as a description of what they were proposing. So a survey was designed for staff.

The cardboard decorated letterbox

The three struggled with the appropriate words to use when asking an adult the question. It became clear that diction, correct word order and manners were essential. After several rehearsals, they were each able to 'ask' the question in a way that an unknowing adult would understand. If a momentary stumble occurred, the others would prompt, 'please'. Soon all the staff had responded, drawing their letterboxes. As they were heading back to the playground, Kate suggested they ask people 'out there', pointing to the adjacent lecture theatre and courtyard dotted with undergraduates. Oliver agreed, but Mei Mei was reluctant. Oliver took her hand and Kate said she would not have to 'ask'. How well children know each other! Mei Mei was indeed overwhelmed with speaking to strangers but, relieved with the transfer of responsibility, was able to nod and go outside the gate. They approached students, asked the question and proffered the clipboard. I was a close support, but clearly let the children lead the way. The response from students was positive and they willingly drew their letterboxes, engaging the children in further discussion about why this information was required.

After ten minutes I realised the children were mostly approaching and asking white women standing on their own.

They bypassed men. I started to intervene, pointing out groups or individuals who were not white females, as potential respondents. They complied, but then the choices became mine from then on. When I stood back, they floundered, uncertain whom to ask, constantly checking back with me if a possible choice was 'ok'.

An image of how children are taught 'stranger danger' flashed through my mind—of how 'difference' can equate with danger; of skin colour, gender and looks—as indices of 'bad guys'. At that point, an older man, also black, walked out of the lecture theatre. I suggested approaching him, and the three stepped back, shaking their heads. Taking the clipboard and leading the way, I intercepted the man, asking the question and handing him the pen. The three children trailed after me, slowly warming to the task.

The investigation had thrown up a huge issue, one not anticipated. After all, they had been designing a letterbox for a rabbit. Returning to the playground to resume the design process, I looked down at the sheets of survey drawings. They were all letterboxes, but they were all different.

A comment

We have been offered a powerful narrative of emergent curriculum (Nimmo, 2002) intersecting with social justice. This story enables us to pause to consider the definition of 'social justice' that is being used here. As mentioned in the Introduction, few early childhood textbooks include a definition of the term; it has become a catch-all for whatever the user intends, whether the context is

Interviewing a student teacher

political, educational, legal, or in the welfare system. Basically, the concept highlights equity: a right to fair treatment for individuals and groups regardless of personal characteristics, circumstances or origins; a right which includes the need for action where inequities exist. There is rarely a linking of discussions related to social justice and pedagogical documentation; that is the challenge for this book.

Unpacking the process of an investigation

Having painted a backdrop, we can now return to the letterbox story to tease through the decisions that Janet made as the teacher in the middle of an evolving opportunity. This sequence provides a frame for thinking about the other stories in this book, but is not intended as a script for being a documentor.

Charting the progress

The process of documenting pedagogically can highlight a narrowing of focus in the way an experience with children transpires. The choice in this case was a moment of serendipity—the chance meeting with a wild rabbit—which led to a group of three, four-year-olds designing a letterbox for a rabbit. It also created an opportunity for a teacher to witness covert racism. Pedagogical documentation captures, changes, decides, reminds, informs, illustrates, prompts and supports the investigation as it proceeds. 'It' is not the folder, or the glimpses of work in progress, or the computer on which the information is held. 'It' is the process of collaboration and the momentum of the experiences of teachers with children.

A reminder, a history

Pedagogical documentation is also a tool to aid reflection, during the investigation, on what has happened and how changes might be made—a memory in process of all the little things said, drawn and photographed, so that the momentum is supported by the fabric of the final piece. Because these aides de memoir are retained, becoming a reflective diary for both teacher and children, they can provoke further thinking and decision-making. Externalising thinking in this way makes it accessible to others.

Drawing it together

During daily life, whole stories of potential interest to children are always emerging. As decisions are made, a small part of a whole story becomes the central focus for an investigation. This process is different from many forms of webbing or thematic mapping in that it enables the unexpected to emerge. In reviewing what was said and drawn, there will always be enough rich material to sustain the topic. In this case, in the beginning there was the children's counterpoint between the wild rabbit and the domestic rabbit—they wanted the wild rabbit to be like Fizzy and for them to play together. Looking back, the focus became one of diversity and fairness. The documentation was able to initiate this discussion again with these children even though, for them, the focus was on a rabbit-accessible letterbox. Multiple purposes always co-exist and thus choices are always involved.

Pedagogical documentation, in part, has a large functional role, helping to keep practical issues on the boil, enabling planning for what will be needed. The need to go and buy wood, or to reschedule when one of the key children is away, has to be tracked, recorded and allocated time. Provisioning the child care environment or school as a space for relationships and thinking, rather than a place for entertainment and containment, is central to pedagogical documentation. Even with the best will in the world, thinking with children in spaces which detract from thinking, becomes problematic.

Tensions

There is always a tension within pedagogical documentation, in being a tool to assist organisation and at the same time being flexible enough to shift direction if something monumental evolves. This tug between fluid ideas and concrete organisation is evident in the arrangements prior to the first design session with the three Hoppy lovers. Janet had to be ready to accept the many ways they could approach the problem of the letterbox. For example, they might have suggested buying one, rather than designing and making one. What could be the possibilities for this suggestion and thereby altered focus? At another time, placing everything on hold as design problems arose (such as how can the rabbit reach the letterbox if it is installed on a post?), makes a mockery of time lines. In addition, the environment needed to be provisioned; for example, providing clipboards enabled the survey to happen.

Simultaneous multiple perspectives need to be juggled and respected. From the first sighting of Hoppy to the construction of the letterbox took four months. Mei Mei's doubts, Kate's leadership, the uncomfortable lump of racism, the natural momentum of the design, the design detours (at one point they doubted a rabbit could walk up the stairs they had designed, so they trialled stair climbing with Fizzy to see if their theory was plausible), negotiation with other staff, time management, and the physical creation of the box, all need to be accommodated under the umbrella of pedagogical documentation.

Complexity in completion

At the end, a sprawling piece can be assembled; re-telling it all as if the story had a beginning and end, when really this is just a moment in a continuum, an excerpt that has been taken from a larger piece. Fizzy has been at the centre for five years—as long as the children have been there, so she's an expected part of the centre environment; they know a lot about rabbits and have parties for her and so on. This rabbit fragment is part of having an ongoing life with a rabbit. People ask how a piece ends. Well, it has not necessarily ended. The work may just stop, a letterbox might be made or there might be a plague of rabbits, or other children will want to use the letterbox for another purpose, but the story continues. The investigations or stories or pieces of pedagogical documentation are not discrete; the events have unfolded in an ongoing context where conversations continue after the story has been told. Other things happen invisibly—we're just not a witness to them. When you look at part of something through a magnifying glass, it doesn't mean that the whole has ceased to be. It is, like all curriculum decisions, a case of selective focus.

After time, the large collection of material may be whittled down to the short story, of which a fragment might be shown and shared with a larger audience. Rather than a simple narrative of what happened, it is the analysis of the processes which occurred, for both teacher and children, that is important. It is also essential to remember that the entire re-telling is subjective. There is no 'truth' in pedagogical documentation; there are 'understandings'. The players, writers, and readers all have their own understanding of what happened, and what might happen. The vehicle of pedagogical documentation makes these understandings visible, for further 'understandings' to be made.

Unfinished business

Pedagogical documentation related to experiences with children informs further teaching, research and relationships within the school environment and beyond. Immersion in intensive theory making and life with a small group like these four (teacher and children), leaves them with a more detailed script with which to live their lives, both in the immediate future and beyond. These three children gave Janet an intellectual gift; they showed her how pervasive 'whiteness' is. The issue of whiteness (see for example MacNaughton, 2005; Jay, 2005 or Oldstein, 2001) and how to engage with it, remains with her forever.

Others too have these kinds of encounters. In a presentation about an experience around 'witches' in her north England nursery school, Kath Bedingfield (2004) describes how she was caught up in the construction of a large wooden witch with a group of energetic boys over several weeks. She became aware of a subtext for one boy who seemed determined to kill the witch and enacted rescues from evil. At last, pausing to listen, it emerged he was attempting to deal with the war in Iraq. The witch was completed, but the war continues. It remains the same for all of us, whether witches or rabbits; there are subtexts of which we must be aware and which need to be interrogated.

Revisiting this current example, the element of potential racism is sitting on the back burner as rabbit fever has the current priority. Later, because Janet knows now that these children behave in this way, she may be able to go back in through the photographs, revisiting the experience. 'Tell me whom you talked to? What was happening here?' There might be discussion about fairness, skin colour, gender and so on. At some point, Janet had written in her reflections:

> I was angry with them, well not them, but the world that makes young children make intrapersonal decisions made on images of skin and gender, and thought, 'that's not fair', but when you're on the run, it's not always the moment to respond in depth. I intercepted, this time as a moral agent and 'took over'. I took their power from them because I made a judgment about the appropriateness of their choices. Could I have trusted them to stop asking white women? You live this piece as it unfolds; the teacher is inextricably living with the children with these things. Those things that are bonuses to us, like time, can be a problematic tool. I must find a way I can ask them without accusing them. They're complicit in something they don't understand. I have to help them to see how that complicity is unfair, but at the same time I can't tell them that it's OK to go talk to anyone in the street. This moment can be retold in the staff room and meetings with parents, used as a way to propel the arguments that young children are already making meaning of the implicit racist overtones in this white-centric world. There is a knotty problem of how to manage the interceptions of keeping children 'safe' (stranger danger) and responding to popular culture's superhero racist overtones. I have to instil these concerns within my teaching rather than having an approach where a study of racism can be 'ticked off', although that may be effective for some people. It's very much an unfinished story. There's more that's yet to happen which may or may not take the form of a long piece with those three children, or a moment may come up for a conversation that just ends this piece. In the traditional ways of working, I still have a goal and an objective, but I wish to confront apparent complicity in racism. These three children and their families come from three corners of this round earth and now the children are in this space, which I need to engage. If racism is all around us, we can interrupt it whenever we are aware that it is happening. Others would plan and engage this concern differently but, in this case, an unexpected event has raised an issue and a responsibility that must be pursued.

After the story: Looking around

This collection of recounts and analytic reflections helps to illustrate the power of pedagogical documentation as defined by Gunilla Dahlberg (Dahlberg, Moss & Pence, 1999). It demonstrates that the focus is not on the photograph or the cutting and pasting, but on listening, pausing and engaging in the unexpected. Vea Vecchi (1998), *atelierista* in Reggio Emilia, expresses this as follows (pp 141–2):

> All of this documentation…becomes an indispensable source of materials that we use every day to be able to 'read' and reflect critically, both individually and

collectively, on the experience we are living, the projects we are exploring. This allows us to construct theories and hypotheses that are not arbitrary or artificially imposed on the children.

So how did this concept of pedagogical documentation develop? A clear statement comes from Edwards, Gandini & Forman (1998, pp 10–12):

> Early in their history…the educators realised that systematically documenting the processes and results of their work with children would simultaneously serve three key functions: It would provide the children with a concrete and 'visible' memory of what they said and did in order to serve as a jumping-off point for next steps in learning; provide the educators with a tool for research and a key to continuous improvement and renewal; and provide parents and the public with detailed information about what happens in schools, as a means of eliciting their reactions and support. This bold insight led to the development of documentation into a professional art form in Reggio Emilia, involving the use of slide shows, posters, short books, and increasingly, videotapes to record children's project experiences.

Some of these large projects from Reggio Children are internationally renowned (such as *The Little Ones of Silent Movies*, Reggio Children, 1992; *The Amusement Park for Birds*, Reggio Children, 1996), adding to the understanding of pedagogical documentation and simultaneously suggesting that everyday staff in everyday places might not be able to create work of this complexity, richness and power. These anxieties are inevitable. Yet we would be wise to accept these gifts from the educators in Reggio Emilia and then think through ways that our own work can build on these gems of stories embedded in philosophical discussions. Rinaldi (1997a) said to a visiting delegation in Italy, 'Please be patient—not everything is possible immediately. Everything in any case isn't possible because it means there is an end, and there is not.' Amelia Gambetti, the executive coordinator of Reggio Children, writes (2004, p 7):

> …our experience, which has never been offered as a model or an example to be copied, has instead been proposed as an educational project to which reference can be made for raising the quality not only of early education but also of the values of life and the society.

Recognition of both the uniqueness of the Italians' offerings and the need for re-interpretation in local contexts is a critical component of this discussion of pedagogical documentation (see, for example, Clyde, 1994).

Hill, Stremmel & Fu (2005) add to the philosophical and pragmatic efforts to wrap definitions around the concept (p 178):

Viewed as 'an act of love' by Rinaldi (1997b) and 'an act of courage' (Goldhaber & Smith, 2001), documentation can be the supportive link to truly understanding the child's curiosities and to crafting a curriculum that is then meaningful and joyful. In this way then, documentation can be seen as a 'search for understanding'.

It is no wonder that people find it difficult to understand what is often viewed as a teaching tool, when Rinaldi (1997b) defines it as 'an act of love'. In highlighting the complexities associated with trying to understand this concept, Millikan (2003) reports on a discussion by Australian educators exploring concerns related to pedagogical documentation (pp 101–2):

> Participants in the discussion group said they had found that the pedagogical documentation in the Reggio Emilia context was difficult to explain to others. This is largely because the purpose of observation and documentation for many educators in Australian preschools is to contribute to the developmental records of individual children. The many possibilities inherent in the Reggio Emilia documentation, such as leading an inquiry forward, being a tool for children's own reflections, enabling parents to view and contribute to the process of children's learning, for teachers' professional development, and as an advocacy for children, can be a daunting prospect to contemplate.

New (1998), from an American perspective, reiterates these roles (p 268):

> Documentation provides children with feedback about their work, and serves as a 'springboard' from which they can continue in their pursuit of an idea or the representation of an experience, often in a partnership with other children. As teachers view each other's efforts, they are encouraged to collaborate in the exchange of ideas and materials. Such thoughtful evidence of children's schoolwork also engages parents in discussions of children's school lives in a way that is conducive to further involvement...

Discussions in New Zealand similarly reflect this range of purposes for pedagogical documentation (Mitchell, 2003). Fraser (2000) agrees with these potentials for documentation and adds a rider from a Canadian perspective. She draws on her experiences with local early childhood services to explore some of the practicalities of documentation. Challenges related to finding time, finding funds and finding space are all considered. It is important to note, for example, that large pieces are less possible without appropriate levels of staffing and supportive environments.

Listening to children

In trying to establish the essences of pedagogical documentation, one of the key elements is listening. Writing from England, Peter Moss (1999) has commented that (p 5):

> Knowledge is co-constructed, in relationship with others, both children and adults, and in this process listening is critical, listening both to others and to ourselves.

He continues to write in this area, extending the conversation in a book with Gunilla Dahlberg from Sweden (Dahlberg & Moss, 2005), in which they write (p 107):

> In a pedagogy of listening and radical dialogue, the teacher has to dare to open herself or himself to the unexpected and to experiment together with the children in the here-and-now event…the teacher and children become partners in a process of experimentation and research, in which the children invent a problem before they search for solutions.

In defining the 'pedagogy of listening' (p 80) from the perspective of the educators in Reggio Emilia, Rinaldi (2001) wrote that (pp 83–4):

> To ensure listening and being listened to is one of the primary tasks of documentation…as well as to ensure that the group and each individual child have the possibility to observe themselves from an external point of view while they are learning...

Each of these perspectives highlights the centrality and the everydayness of this basic human act. For example, Shafer (2002) explains the significance of listening to the children and documenting 'the complexity and brilliance of ordinary moments' (p 185). She goes on to comment (pp 194–5):

> Uncovering the extraordinary within the ordinary is, to a large extent, a matter of listening. Considering with colleagues and parents the implicit assumptions or questions that lie just below the surface has been the key to finding meaningful, self-sustaining material for exploration.

In this context, 'listening' encompasses recognition of the importance not only of hearing, but of reflecting thoughtfully on what is being seen and heard.

Listening in the context of 'the everyday' is highlighted also in Fleet & Robertson (2004) in foregrounding the richness beneath daily interactions and events (p 5):

> From a social justice perspective, the view of a child working effectively in a group, of children learning ways of being together, is part of a solutions-oriented world. These approaches have the potential to empower those who may not usually have a voice.

'Listening' is thus seen to be reflecting a philosophical position. Seeking to provide the opportunity for all voices to be heard in every early childhood setting could be seen as an instance of seeking socially just practice. Janet's example encourages us to consider the interplay between the achievement of socially just outcomes and the presence of socially just practices. This relationship is complex and underlies many of the chapters in this book.

Possibilities for future conversations

As part of the broader goal to listen to children, it is also essential to listen to the milieu in which you and the children reside. These contexts for curriculum decision-making and recording include wildly varying influences ranging from:

- political environments, where elections are won and lost on the basis of refugee policies and perceptions of global threats;

- regulated environments, where children's services are responsible for a range of quality assurance processes that impact on approaches within services and where schools are framed by outcomes-based syllabus documents;

- family experiences and expectations which are so diverse that within one site the perspectives may contradict each other and confront the positions held by staff;

- living situations that are so unique that commonalities can be difficult to locate;

- school accountability contexts where narrow definitions of literacy and mathematical curricula limit the possibilities for recognising learning in everyday investigations; and

- sites where staff have such divergent views and understandings that beliefs interfere with efforts to build a community of learners.

The idea of pedagogical documentation is, therefore, both local and global (Greishaber & Hatch, 2003). An exploration of pedagogical documentation can clarify a way of working which has been robustly supported by the Italian experience but firmly grounded in local soil. One piece might be a one page fragment of an evolving query from young children in the local setting, while another piece of pedagogical documentation may intersect with global concerns or initiatives. There are also intersections with government documents such as *Te Whāriki* (1996) from New Zealand and the *New South Wales Curriculum Framework* (2002) or the *South Australia Curriculum Standards and Accountability* (DETE, 2001) framework from Australia. None of these require the use of pedagogical documentation, but all of them incorporate philosophies enabling benefits from pedagogical documentation.

Finally, at both the local and global level, the emphasis here is on the link between pedagogical documentation and social justice. Making this link is absolutely essential if people are considering current sociopolitical contexts as sites for pedagogical decision-making. If three and four-year-olds are faced with images on the news of blindfolded people with guns to their heads, or of children swept away by a tsunami, there's no point spending time colouring in yellow duckies. Bigger issues must be addressed. Given an opportunity, children insist on engaging with important issues, AND it's the thinking that goes with making the choices in documenting pedagogically (if you like) that can empower staff in all children's settings to engage with social justice.

Seeing children differently and listening with more intent (a la Oken-Wright & Gravett, 2002) as a basis for decisions about what's worth pursuing, can be stymied at basic levels (such as concerns with formatting photographs). Pragmatics can be explored in workshops, but the philosophies involved have to be interrogated in staff rooms, over time, in order to help people understand why the effort is so important. If the matter is simply record-keeping for accountability, it doesn't matter much whether you use checklists, portfolios or flow charts. BUT, that is not the case. The bigger picture matters a great deal, reflecting societal power, inequities, opportunities, curiosities, knowledges and so on that are always present in daily events.

The focus in this landscape is on complexity and grappling with the unknown, in changing unproductive practices and growing into ways of being with children and families that are empowering for all participants. Once the terrain becomes familiar, there are many possible journeys to be made, some of which are not yet on any charted map. Making a start is a good place to begin.

References

Bedingfield K (2004, October) *The witches project*. Paper presented at the Introduction to Reggio's Approach conference. Kendal, UK.

Cannella G (1997) *Deconstructing early childhood: Social justice and revolution?* New York: Peter Lang Publishing.

Clyde M (1994) Opening address presented at the conference *The challenge of Reggio Emilia: Realising the potential of children*. Melbourne: University of Melbourne.

Dahlberg G, Moss P & Pence A (1999) *Beyond quality in early childhood education and care: Postmodern perspectives*. London: Falmer Press.

Dahlberg G & Moss P (2005) *Ethics and politics in early childhood education*. London: Routledge Falmer.

Department of Education, Training and Employment (2001) *South Australia curriculum, standards and accountability framework*. Adelaide: DETE.

Edwards C, Gandini L & Forman G (1998) Introduction: Background and starting points. In C Edwards, L Gandini & G Forman (Eds) *The hundred languages of children: the Reggio Emilia approach—Advanced reflections*. (2nd Ed). (pp 5–25). Greenwich, CT: Ablex.

Fleet A & Robertson J (2004) *Overlooked curriculum: Seeing everyday possibilities*. Research in practice series. Canberra: Early Childhood Australia.

Fraser S (2000). Documentation. In *Authentic childhood: Experiencing Reggio Emilia in the classroom*. (pp 77–99). Ontario: Nelson Thomson.

Gambetti A (2004) Exchange and the value of the encounter with others in the Reggio experience. In *REchild: Reggio Emilia newsletter*. December. Reggio Emilia: Reggio Children.

Gandini L & Goldhaber J (2001) Two reflections about documentation. In L Gandini & C Edwards (Eds) *Bambini: The Italian approach to infant/toddler care*. (pp 124–145). New York: Teachers College Press.

Goldhaber J & Smith D (2001) *The choices we make: Documentation as an act of courage*. Paper presented at the conference: Recasting the Reggio Emilia approach to inform teaching in the United States. Virginia Tech. Blacksburg, Virginia.

Grieshaber S & Hatch JA (2003) Pedagogical documentation as an effect of globalization. *Journal of Curriculum Theorizing*, 19 (1), 89–102.

Hill L, Stremmel A & Fu VR (2005) *Teaching as inquiry: Rethinking curriculum in early childhood education*. Boston: Pearson Education.

Hunter C (2001) Sunniva's extra pocket—a parent's reflections. In L Abbott & C Nutbrown (Eds) *Experiencing Reggio Emilia: Implications for pre-school provision*. (pp 38 –42). Buckingham: Open University Press.

Jay G (2005) *Whiteness: Deconstructing (the) race*. Retrieved 28 January 2005 from <http://www.uwm.edu/People/gjay/Whiteness/>.

Laevers F (2004) *Using curriculum to inform quality.* Keynote address presented at the European Early Childhood Education Research Association conference, Malta.

Leask J (2001) Sam's invisible extra gear—a parent's view. In L Abbott & C Nutbrown (Eds) *Experiencing Reggio Emilia: Implications for pre-school provision.* (pp 43–47). Buckingham: Open University Press.

MacNaughton G (2005) *Doing Foucault in early Childhood Studies: Applying poststructuralist ideas.* London: Routledge.

Millikan J (2003) *Reflections: Reggio Emilia principles within Australian contexts.* Sydney: Pademelon Press.

Ministry of Education (1996) *Te Whāriki: He Whāriki: mātauranga mō ngā Mokopuna o Aotearoa: Early childhood curriculum.* Wellington: Learning Media.

Mitchell L (2003) Shifts in thinking through a teacher's network. *Early Years,* 23 (1), 21–34.

Moss P (1999) Difference, dissensus and debate: possibilities of learning from Reggio. *Modern Barndom OM.* Stockholm: Reggio Emilia Institute.

New R (1998) Theory and praxis in Reggio Emilia: They know what they are doing and why. In C Edwards, L Gandini & G Forman. *The hundred languages of children: The Reggio Emilia approach—Advanced reflections.* (2nd Ed). (pp 261–89). Greenwich CT: Ablex.

New South Wales Department of Community Services. Office of Childcare. (2002) *New South Wales Curriculum Framework for children's services: The practice of relationships—Essential provisions for children's services.* Sydney: Office of Childcare.

Nimmo J (2002) Nurturing the spirit to teach: Commitment, community and emergent curriculum. *Australian Journal of Early Childhood,* 27 (2), 8–12.

Oken-Wright P & Gravett M (2002) Big ideas and the essence of intent. In VR Fu, AJ Stremmel & LT Hill (Eds) *Teaching and learning: Collaborative exploration of the Reggio Emilia approach.* (pp 197–220). New Jersey: Merrill Prentice Hall.

Oldstein T (2001) 'I'm not white': anti-racist teacher education for white early childhood educators. *Contemporary Issues in Early Childhood* 2 (1), 3–13.

Reggio Children (1992) *The little ones of silent movies.* Reggio Emilia: Reggio Children.

Reggio Children (Producer) (1996) *The amusement park for birds.* [Video]. Reggio Emilia: Reggio Children.

Rinaldi C (1997a, January) Closing presentation to The Winter Institute: The experience of the municipal infant-toddler centers and preschools of Reggio Emilia. Reggio Emilia, Italy.

Rinaldi C (1997b) *The fine art of listening.* Paper presented at the Second Annual Summer Institute, Columbus School for Girls. Columbus: Ohio.

Rinaldi C (2001) Documentation and assessment: What is the relationship? In C Giudici, C Rinaldi & M Krechevsky (Eds) *Making learning visible: Children as individual and group learners.* (pp 78–89). Reggio Emilia. Italy: Reggio Children.

Shafer A (2002) Ordinary moment, extraordinary possibilities. In V Fu, A Stremmel & L Hill (Eds) *Teaching and learning: Collaborative exploration of the Reggio Emilia approach*. (pp 183–95) New Jersey: Merrill Prentice Hall.

Vecchi A (1998) The role of the *atelierista*. In C Edwards, L Gandini & G Forman (Eds) *The hundred languages of children: The Reggio Emilia approach—Advanced reflections* (2nd Ed). (pp 139–47). Greenwich, CT: Ablex.

First Principles

Chapter Two

No, It's Not Okay:
Drawing a Line in the Sand

Jill McLachlan

Jill McLachlan is a classroom teacher presently working in an independent school in Sydney, Australia. The school caters for children from three to eight years old, with approximately 180 students in total. Most of the children attending the school are from upper-middle class families, with many of the parents working in executive positions. The story you will read in this chapter relates to a Year One class at that school. The children were aged between six and seven when the conversations took place. It is with the support of both the children and their parents that the story is published.

Introduction

One of my favourite experiences in the last two years was seeing the movie *Spider-Man*. I was glued to the screen from start to finish, coming out of the cinema quite inspired to actually be Spider-Man. Visions of grandeur overtake us all from time to time! At this point I imagine that you may be bewildered by this fairly foolish admission, but there is a link between this movie and the purpose of this chapter. The connection comes in the form of a saying that runs as a theme through the movie: 'With great power comes great responsibility' (Raimi, 2002, n.p.); and it is that thought that I present for reflection.

Issues of power and control face teachers every day. I believe that in the landscape of children's lives we cannot underestimate the powerful role we play with each group of children that we teach. Teaching is powerful, and with that power comes a need for great responsibility. How we use the power we have is the subject of this chapter.

From the first day I stood before a class to teach I recognised the tangible power that comes from working with young children. I began teaching with a Year One class at a public school in New South Wales. I had very little idea where we were going, but the children were following and I was thrilled to have the chance to 'be a teacher'.

In this first and formative year of my teaching I began to explore the scope and nature of my power and influence in the classroom. I chose the way the children sat, the way the classroom looked and the consequences for 'inappropriate' behaviour. I even chose when it was okay to laugh. I began to learn the art of 'classroom control'.

In that same year I also began to question my power. My influence was obvious. What would keep me accountable for the way in which I used my power and my influence with the young hearts and minds that made up my class? I have been pursuing this question ever since.

On a very practical level, our decisions and directions often reveal an underlying belief that children's experiences at school should be controlled and pre-determined by the teacher. We set ourselves up as the major decision-maker in our classrooms—choosing the tone, the timing and the content of each school day. Frequently, children say that their favourite time during the day is lunch or morning tea. It is worth reflecting on the fact that during these times in a day, children often have the most autonomy in their school lives.

Although time constraints are a major factor that can deter teachers from following up incidents, insights or interests brought forward by the children, I believe there are other influences at work. One significant factor can be found in our discomfort investing in learning that is process-oriented rather than outcome-focused. In other words, one of the reasons we avoid diversions in our programs is because we are uncomfortable relinquishing control of the outcomes in learning. Trusting that something will come of an unplanned event or discussion can sometimes be seen as a 'waste of time' or even a dangerous habit to get into.

Following the interests of children is not a predictable process, no matter what the context. Children see differently, walk differently, care differently and talk differently from adults and from each other. Walking beside children, rather than leading them, requires constant and committed reflection with every step. It means getting down low, adjusting your pace regularly, and following through to completion. It requires negotiation, questioning and risk, recognising and respecting the differences that exist among a group of thinkers.

Engaging with children's real concerns and thoughts requires careful and intentional decision-making on the part of a teacher. When the question asked or the situation that has occurred touches on issues we don't have clear answers to, we begin to ask ourselves many questions:

- Is this discussion worthwhile?

- Is it okay for me to share my opinion?

- When do I challenge the group?

- When do I choose to stay silent?

- How can I relate within the group without exerting control over the process?

- How can I create space for the children to have a voice?

- How can I protect all of the children if I can't control the direction of the responses?

In other words, this list might be simply put: 'How do I facilitate meaningful learning in this moment?'

Some challenges that arise are easier to navigate than others, but what do you do with the tricky questions? How do you respond appropriately to the deeper issues that inevitably rise to the surface in any social group? What would you do in the face of cruelty, rejection or other forms of injustice? What do you do with the issues that a bandaid, a wink and a smile could not even begin to resolve?

I am reminded of Italy and the schools of Reggio Emilia. They seem to touch the 'untouchable'. I admire and respect them for the risks that I so often fear to take. How have they come to navigate so confidently through such unexplored territory? Why are they open to risk, adventure, questioning and open-ended experiences in a way that I have only dreamt about? There is such power in the way they 'see' and therefore relate to children. They seem to carry with them an almost mystical faith in children; faith in the sense that they pursue the unseen, confident of a goal that can only be described in retrospect. It seems to me that their faith in the children themselves is what frees them to share their power.

They see a child, who is:

> Rich in resources, strong, and competent… unique individuals with rights rather than simply needs. They have potential, plasticity, openness, the desire to grow, curiosity, a sense of wonder, and the desire to relate to other people and to communicate… children are also very open to exchanges and reciprocity as deeds and acts of love that they not only want to receive but also want to offer (Rinaldi, 1998, p 114).

Who wouldn't take this child's lead? So the journey towards shared power and control has begun for me. Children are powerful; I am learning to give some of my power away.

Choosing partners: A story

The story that follows invites you into a set of exchanges that altered permanently my perceptions of control and my image of myself as a teacher. I was challenged and transformed by my journey with this particular class. What began as a 'risk' in my mind, transformed into a miracle. I experienced the child that Rinaldi saw. I met a child I would follow anywhere.

This experience took place in 2003 with a group of Year One children I was teaching at a small independent school in Sydney, Australia. I had been teaching this group for over a year, having been their teacher in Kindergarten and now in Year One. There was a strong rapport in the group and a real sense of connection between the children.

I feel small in the face of trying to retell this story. One should tread lightly in the presence of the sacred. I hope my footsteps are not too loud.

The children had lined up outside the classroom after lunch. To add a bit of interest to the not very exciting routine of heading into the classroom, I asked the children to group themselves into pairs. I asked each child to choose a friend who was wearing a matching shirt but different pants. I called the children one by one and asked them to consider the selection process I had outlined and select an appropriate partner.

What eventuated was a determined pursuit by the children to make sure they could match with someone who was their own gender. The tactics of avoidance amazed me. Faces were pulled, whispering began, some boys hid behind each other to avoid eye contact with the girls, seemingly showing through their actions a distinct desire to *not* be chosen by a girl.

This *moment* challenged me. Why did the children feel they needed so forcefully to exclude themselves from each other? How did the avoidance serve them? I found the behaviour unsettling and surprising.

Perhaps you might say, 'That's kids for you. What do you expect? They see gender stereotyping everywhere. It's not their fault. It's modelled to them and they simply repeat the behaviour.' But I knew these kids. I had taught them for almost two years. I knew their families and I knew that they loved being together as a group and that they respected each other deeply. I could not contain within this chapter all of the phenomenal moments where these children upended my expectations. The ways in which they spoke to each other, supported each other and protected each other was uncanny.

For example, earlier in the year Sally had become quite teary and anxious about a spelling test. Anna noticed Sally's concerns, but chose not to address her directly. Instead she turned and addressed me: 'Mrs McLachlan, I remember that last year Sally was a very good speller.' Anna kept eye contact with me the whole time and intentionally created a platform for Sally's skills to be publicly affirmed. I responded, 'I remember that too.' A smile crept across the teary face, and Sally picked up a pencil, ready to 'have a go'. A six-year-old friend had transformed the anxious moment.

This was the 'culture' of our classroom. It was a place where we worked together. We built each other up. We celebrated each other's successes and stood alongside each other when situations were difficult. It was a place of acceptance and inclusion. Perhaps that is why alarm bells started to ring in my mind when during a simple transition into the room we were being robbed of our 'culture', that which made us 'us'.

What made it acceptable (and even funny) to exclude each other because of gender when the same children would be up in arms if someone even dared to criticise another child's work? I was surprised that the children seemed unaffected by the actions of their peers. No one reacted to the rejection openly. No one cried over the exclusion. I wondered why children who would stand up for each other's work in the classroom would not stand up against these behaviours.

I reflected on a question that was asked at a recent conference. The question to the panel in a closing session was actually more like an appeal for advice. It went something like this: How do you provide an environment that does not allow or encourage racism, gender stereotyping and other forms of prejudice whilst still giving children free choices about who they do or do not play with. Is it okay to let children choose? It was a poignant question at the conference that was still swimming in my mind as I watched the children make their way into the classroom.

At the conference, I was wondering who would address this educator's query when Miriam Giugni, a colleague, stood up to respond. Miriam (see Chapter Twelve) is an educator who loves to push boundaries and is thoroughly committed to children's rights and empowering children as decision-makers and independent thinkers. How would she respond? How would she balance the rights of the individual with the rights of the 'other'? Would she dare to draw that so-elusive line in the sand?

Her response floored me. 'No, it is not okay'. I sat up and took notice. It was not the response I expected. With her simple statement, 'No, it's not okay',

Miriam had confronted my views about children's free choice, my role as a model to children and my role as an advocate for social justice in the classroom. Miriam put herself into the picture, not as a commentator or an analyst, but as a human being—a social being. She invested her humanity into her response that day. I did not know how to respond. In fact, I did not know if I even agreed with her point of view. The thoughts brewed quietly in the background as my life and my teaching continued on.

It wasn't until weeks later, as the children in my class determinably chose partners, overtly choosing friends based on gender that the thoughts consciously stirred in me again. I found myself stirred by Miriam's 'line in the sand'. In response to the children's reaction, I altered the selection criteria for selecting a partner. This time I asked the children to pair up with someone who had different coloured socks to them. Sock colour clearly divided the girls and boys and I wondered what the children were going to do if they had no choice but to choose a partner of the opposite sex. This time with less choice, a couple of the children were willing to have a go, but as they approached the room did not make eye contact with each other and ran away from their 'partners' as soon as they got inside.

The words, 'No, it's not okay' were bubbling in my mind. What was I going to do? Karen, my teaching partner, had now come and sat with us, so I decided to call all the children back again. I sent them for a walk around the playground track while I updated Karen on what I had seen. She too, was surprised and gave me the go ahead to follow up what was happening and postpone what we had already planned for the afternoon.

The children came back from their walk and gathered outside the classroom. I explained that we were going to play another partner game but this time the children were to find a spot on the playground with their partner and find out the answers to three questions: Do you have any brothers and sisters? What is your favourite food? Where do you live?

Anticipating the way the children would most likely partner themselves, I asked the girls to come and stand out the front. I then asked them to choose a partner from one of the boys. Just as before a number of the children hid and became very silly about the possibility. Enough was enough. I couldn't contain the statement. 'This is not okay' sprouted from my lips. 'There are some times when it is okay to say no to being someone's partner. And there are times when you can choose to play with a particular friend. But saying you don't want to be someone's partner just because they are a girl or a boy is not okay.'

I couldn't believe I had said it. I wondered what in the world Karen was thinking about my determined response. I wondered if she felt as I did when I first heard Miriam make a similar declaration. My next steps were more cautious. I decided to proceed with the paired activity and got the girls to stand up again. This time the children promptly chose partners and went to the playground to find out the answers to their questions. I worried that my voice had led the children to change their behaviour, simply 'because I said so'. Time would tell.

After about ten minutes I rang the playground bell and invited the children to join me inside the room to share what they had found out about their partners. Each pair had the chance to share at least one thing they had found out. Everything was going along as you might expect until Kate and Cameron stood up. What they said floored me:

Cameron: Well, we found out quite a bit actually.

Kate: Yeah, because we found out we both have little sisters who are the same age.

Cameron: Yeah we never knew that. I didn't want to go with a girl but I'm glad I did because otherwise I would have never known about Kate's sister.

Kate: They are both really annoying sometimes.

Cameron: We got to talk about how they are both annoying.

Kate: I'm glad Cameron was my partner.

Cameron: Me too.

Partly stunned and partly relieved that something positive had eventuated, I decided that perhaps standing up for something had its benefits. The rest of the children shared their thoughts, and then Anna put up her hand: 'Mrs McLachlan, once someone said that they didn't want to play with me and I laughed and I said I didn't really care. But when I got home I was really sad.' Anna's face told a story as significant as the words that came out of her mouth. I found myself at a loss for a response that could honour the significance of what she had shared. I only wish you could have seen and heard that statement. Karen and I were the only ones that did. In that brief moment I realised the injustice of our seating arrangement. I had never before considered that when children are grouped to face a teacher at the front, the only person privileged with their whole message (words, facial expression and body language) is the teacher. Is it any wonder that children get fidgety in discussion time or their minds start to wander?

I have often felt exhausted at the end of a day after feeling the pressure to constantly perform in front of the children to keep them focused or get them motivated. Without knowing it, I had positioned myself as the entertainer or the 'presenter'. Anything else shared by the group was heard, but not necessarily seen. Often whatever I found engaging about the children's ideas was being lost to the children themselves. Is it any wonder that children vie for the attention of the performer, yearning for a connection with the one face they can see and hear clearly?

This moment also gave me insight into why children, excited about what's happening, will turn and begin to talk to a person alongside them. I began to recognise the instinct to connect. It was deep within the children I taught and if

I wasn't going to offer it to them in a group time, they would find it somehow. Moved by the power of what I saw in this moment of Anna's sharing, I apologised to her and the group explaining that I knew it would be hard to share again but that I felt her words, and particularly the way she shared, was so important that we all needed to be able to see how she was expressing herself, to really 'hear' what she was saying. Anna agreed to do so. The class sat up and took notice of her statement in a dramatically different way now that Anna was 'within view'. The tone shifted immediately.

Feeling that I needed to address this situation of power and connection, I asked the children if they could position themselves in such a way that they could see each other more clearly. The children moved themselves into a sort of circular cluster and the conversation took off.

I reminded children of the earlier discussion and repeated the suggestion that perhaps there were times when it was not okay to say 'no' to someone who wanted to play. I reminded them of my statement that it was not okay to 'say no' to someone just because they were a boy or a girl. The children flooded the conversation with other situations when they believed it would not be okay to 'say no':

Like if your mum was from another country.
If you spoke a different language.
Just because you looked funny.
If you were dirty or something.
If you're different from other people.
Yeah like if your skin was different.

The ideas kept coming. At one point, concerned that the children could put themselves into inappropriate or potentially dangerous situations in the name of accepting others, I decided to add another perspective. I thought it was necessary to shed light on when it is appropriate and at times important to 'say no' to someone. Examples of times it was 'okay to say no' were: playing a game that was meant for only two players, having a special quiet time with just one friend, someone being rough or violent or touching inappropriately. I spoke to the children about the differences between playing and touching, and we talked openly about the kind of touching that was okay and not okay.

At one point the children began to giggle about silly nicknames. On one level I understood the need for some light relief in the discussion, but on another level I wanted to encourage the children to think about the impact of their silliness and how it might impact others. I decided to tell a story about my own experience.

When I was at school I used to love playing sport. But every time I would play sport I would get so hot and my face is very sensitive. And so whenever I was playing sport my face would go really red. And I mean really red.

At this point, one of the children interjected, 'Like it did the night before Bug Night when all the clay models crashed on the floor.'

'Yes', I chuckled before continuing, 'a bit like that, but a bit different.'

Because we were now sitting in view of each other, the children could benefit and connect with this child's reflection. They smiled and had a little laugh in response and were then back in focus with my story:

> Well my face would go so red that one day someone called me tomato face. And do you know what? I just laughed. I didn't want to get upset because it was very important to me that people liked me. So I pretended it didn't matter to me.

I paused before sharing the reality of my experience:

> But it did make me sad. Do you know I used to go home and run into my room and I would cry and cry because the children had been so cruel? I'm not mad at those children because they did not know it made me sad, but I wished that I had told them to stop.

After a moment, Susana looked at me and began to share quietly, 'I do that when children make jokes about my last name. Sometimes they call me meanie, meanie, meanie. I think next time I'm going to tell them to stop.' The room was silent. The tone had become heavy and weighty in its significance.

Gabe began to speak slowly, 'Some people call me Gay and some people call me Gabrielle just because they think it's funny.' Tears welled up in his eyes and in many of our eyes for that matter, 'But it's not funny.' Another child in the class immediately connected, 'No, it's not funny Gabe and it's not okay.'

Another child added, 'I don't think we should make fun of people's names. I think we should protect each other's hearts.'

Other stories now rose to the surface and each of the children who wanted to share had the chance to do so. The sharing was eventually interrupted by a simple request: 'Mrs McLachlan, I want this to stop.'

> We can stop, but would you be willing to tell us why you want us to stop. This has been an important conversation for us all and if we're going to stop it would be good to know why.
>
> Because it's too sad. I know what people are saying is important but it's all too sad. It's about what we don't want to be like. Maybe we could talk about the kind of people we do want to be like.

And so we did.

With great relief I began to record on the whiteboard all that the children shared about, 'the kind of people we want to be'. There was an intense shift in the conversation and the statements speak for themselves. There was an electric commitment in the room to set a high benchmark. The children shared with an intentionality and a passion in their voices that I would find nigh on impossible to record. This is what they decided:

The kind of people we are going to be...

We are going to be people who are positive, honest and willing to 'have a go'.
We are going to be problem solvers.
We are going to be people who share.
We are going to be people who are generous.
We are going to be careful people.
Careful with our voices.
Careful with our bodies.
And careful with what we say.
We are going to use words that make people happy.
We are going to think before we speak.
We are going to make people laugh.
We are going to speak with words that are kind.
We are going to be the kind of people who SAY NO to being mean.
We are going to help people and watch out for our friends.
We are going to respect and protect each other's property.
We are going to include people in games.
We are going to ask people to play.
We are not going to say no to someone because they are a boy or a girl.
We are going to do the right thing at the right time.
We're not going to tease.
We are not going to make jokes about people's names.
We are not going to make jokes about love.
We are not going to make jokes about what people look like or where they come from.
We're not going to make jokes about violence. Because violence is not a joke.
We are not going to play war or pretend games with guns. Because guns are real and people do die.
And we don't want any heart breaking.
We are going to protect people's hearts.
We are going to stand up for our friends.
These are the kind of people we are going to be.

Afterwards I felt as if we had just taken part in a group therapy session. The sincerity and passion that was expressed by the children was impressive. Their trust of each other and their choice to be active in a pursuit of 'justice' was chilling. I would never be the same. We would never be the same.

Later that week I asked the children if they would like the opportunity to share what they had discussed in a school assembly. They unanimously agreed. We divided up the lines and each child read a part of this powerful vision statement to the school. I had goose bumps as the children invested what they believed beyond the boundaries of our classroom. I was so proud of the way in which they offered themselves to the other children with such pride and a sense of worth.

There was an immediate change in the children. Playground times became opportunities to play with a range of children. Never again did the children fuss about a partner or about working or playing with someone different from themselves. We were different.

A wonderful situation eventuated a couple of weeks after the children had presented their ideas in the assembly. Some Kindergarten children had been playing together and pretending to shoot each other with guns. One Kindergarten child was distressed by their choice of play and went to tell a teacher. The teacher said: 'Would you like to write or draw about your feelings and then talk it over with the other children?' The child drew a picture depicting her sadness about the game and wrote almost the same words that Year One had presented at assembly: 'I don't think people should play pretend games with guns, because guns are real and people do die.' I shared this story with Year One. They had made a difference.

Conclusion

We need to constantly underpin the decisions we make as educators with a deep faith in the students we teach. Belief in the innate drive within humanity to explore and understand frees us to journey without a predetermined destination, where learning is a recognised by-product of life, not an added extra. Teaching needs to move from something we do to something we are in relationship to children. In this way, teaching becomes a way of describing the journey we walk with children—a journey of learning through experience, through relationships and from each other.

What I am connects me to a child; what I do sets me apart. Connecting with children and responding to the issues that arise in any classroom inevitably introduces more 'grey' topics into our curriculum. It requires us to reach beyond pre-determined plans and meet face to face with the children we teach, honouring their right to be heard, to exert influence and to follow their passions meaningfully. It honours children's desire to connect with each other and encourages them to persevere with friendships and challenges when life does not present a simple and straightforward answer. In practical terms, this means not always knowing where the road will turn and choosing at times to release control over the direction of a learning experience. Listening, observing, questioning and clarifying become essential tools of the trade. Talking, drawing, constructing, designing and wondering become an essential part of the learning partnership built between teacher and child.

It means engaging with all of the questions, queries, experiences and actions presented by the children in the class, lending our experience, specific skills, knowledge and power as they are needed. We must begin to engage with the whole child, not just the 'parts' that are easiest to influence or relate to. Learning becomes an issue of growth not outcomes, and the person is elevated above the products we can assess. Are we willing to let children influence the decisions we make and directions we choose? Are we willing to give them a voice along the way? Are we willing to share our power? Are we willing to go where they want to go, and often need to go, no matter how uncertain the nature of the path or the 'academic' validity of the outcome? Is it too risky to listen and follow a child's lead?

Or is it too risky if we don't?

References

Raimi S (Director) (2002) *Spider-Man*. [Motion Picture]. California: Columbia Pictures.

Rinaldi C (1998) Projected curriculum constructed through documentation—progettazione. An interview with Lella Gandini. In C Edwards, L Gandini & G Forman (Eds) *The hundred languages of children: The Reggio Emilia approach—Advanced reflections* (2nd Ed). Greenwich, CT: Ablex.

Chapter Three

Reconsidering Our Images of Children: What Shapes Our Educational Thinking?

Janet Robertson

Following early exploration of the challenges of Reggio Emilia's pedagogical experience to Australian education, in 1992 Janet took the position of toddler teacher at Mia-Mia, a not-for-profit child care centre attached to the Institute of Early Childhood, Macquarie University in Sydney, Australia. It was here she began to explore 'the image of the child' from a practical as well as theoretical position, becoming a researcher with children. An earlier version of these ideas was presented as a keynote address at a conference (Robertson, 1996).

Central to the educational experience in the municipal infant–toddler centres and preschools of Reggio Emilia is a philosophical image of children which underpins all their work. This is an image of a strong, powerful child, rich in potential; endowed with rights, desirous of relationships and a co-constructor of knowledge (Rinaldi, 1993). 'The image of the child' is so apt a phrase, typical of Italian educators in Reggio Emilia, and one layered and rich in meanings. To English-speaking educational communities, the concept that philosophy, theory and practice can be bundled into a phrase to be used in everyday teacher talk is (and was to this Australian educator) rather perplexing. What did they mean? When I first heard it, in 1991, I thought it was about how I as a teacher looked upon children. But I soon quickly understood it to be much more: I was a participant and complicit in the gazing (MacNaughton, 2000; Robertson, 2001) or creation of that image and the forces were as compelling upon me as they were upon the child. We were both actively engaged in creating meaning out of the social sculpting going on about, and upon us. I realised that we were not passive in this exchange, that resistance, silence, compliance, negotiation and compromise are undertaken in our daily teaching lives, and that these exchanges are shaped by cultural images of children, childhood, teaching and the purpose of education.

I have found over the years that by looking at how other cultures create their images of education, I can see my own images more clearly. The approach that early education takes in communities often reflects strongly held values within that community. For instance, in Hong Kong, preschool children aged between three and four years wear a school uniform. The image of the uniform spells out that academic education is highly prized and will be the focus of learning within the institution. As children dress in the morning, the clothes create the 'pupil' and differentiate the expectations of this part of the day from the rest. There is little emphasis on outdoor play; a consequence of high land prices and perhaps a culture that may not regard outdoor play as educationally important. On the other hand, in Denmark, Germany and Norway, there is another style or manner of education reflecting those communities' strongly held values about nature and physical wellbeing. Translated into English, they are known as the 'Forest schools'. These are sites within the community on which there may not even be a building, places which have streams, meadows, rocky outcrops, caves and marshes where children, three to six years old, spend a major portion of the day outdoors with little or no equipment besides nature, a back pack, friends and their teachers. Both the Forest schools and the preschools of Hong Kong are manifestations of education from communities who dearly love their youngsters and hope to give them the best start. These two examples of early education— polar opposites—illustrated for me how images of children and education are culturally bound.

So what does this mean? Over the years of writing and speaking about 'the image of the child', I have used various phrases to convey my meaning. I've coined the 'notion or idea of the child' (Robertson, 1996). I've made postmodern references to the 'gaze upon the child' (Robertson, 2000). In all, I've never been sure I actually get it. Firstly, it's not about a child, as children in education are not alone. Secondly, they are not without the whole bucket of goodies which come with them—parents, carers, teachers, neighbours, media, history, past parenting and future experiences, political manipulations and social sculpting. Thirdly, nor do I come without my baggage, my own enculturation in education and society. Lastly, as we—the child and I—journey through our educational days, we in turn shape each other and change, creating an 'other', a third space (Soja, 1996).

We need to look at what shapes our educational experiences wherever we're living. With five states and two territories in Australia, education is not homogenous. For example, in the state of New South Wales (NSW), university qualified teachers are legally required within child care centres when 29 or more children attend at any one time. Teachers are not required in other states. What image of child care education does NSW hold that is not held by other states?

So, what are our images here in Australia? Are they different to those in Reggio Emilia? We can expect that they would be (Millikan, 2003; Robertson, 1996). In the schools and community of Reggio Emilia, they have spent 40 years refining, articulating, and practising their philosophy in action. We too have been labouring in education with an image of children. It is not, however, an image that we clearly spell out. The challenges offered to the Australian early childhood community by the educators of Reggio Emilia are to reassess the influences on our imagery, articulate our image of the child and define the way it drives our educational experience and theories. In doing so we may encounter what Ben Mardell calls, 'false dichotomies' (2001, p 282). Taking an either–or perspective makes for an apparently simple clarification. But nothing is simple, 'there are times when something is not one thing or the other, but both' (Mardell, 2001, p 283).

Using stories from my own experience with children, this chapter attempts to examine our images of children and those from Reggio Emilia. In doing so, it raises these questions:

- Do we have an image of children endowed with rights?

- Are our educational philosophies, theories and practices predicated on an image of what children are able to do?

- Do we see children as researchers, testing hypotheses and co-constructing knowledge and meaning?

- Is our image one of children greedy for knowledge and meaning?

- Is our image one of children as a group of individuals or one of individuals within the group?

- Does our image of children alienate them from their contexts?

- Do we see the role of teacher as one in which uncertainty drives the path of learning or do we see certainty as the crucible upon which teaching is forged?

- Does our image of children require us to make their thinking visible to others?

Do we have an image of children endowed with rights?

The image of a child endowed with rights and therefore entitled to the best, as compared to a needy child getting the crumbs from the table (Bredekamp, 1993, p 13), is powerful. Viewing children as needy permits us as a community to offer children second best. To me this is the foremost challenge Reggio Emilia gives us—to do our best. In many ways Australians would claim they endow children with rights. I think the question is, which rights and for whom?

Australian community values are changing from the collectivism of the 'we', to the individualism of the 'I'. Is an individual right different from a collective right? To clarify: a collective right for all Australian children to the best education possible is different from the right of each individual child to avail themselves of the best education their families can afford. In Reggio Emilia, the collective 'we' exists. As a city with strong socialist values and communist politics, the collective rights and therefore responsibilities for the 'unknown other', are strong. The prevalence of the individualism that we encounter in Australia would not endure in Reggio Emilia. An example of the Reggio Emilia collective 'we' is the right of every child identified with a special need (or as the Reggio Emilia educators call it, 'special right') to be automatically offered a place, and additional resources (including a teacher if necessary), in the council child care centres. These additional teachers would be responsible for a maximum of four children.

It would seem to me that a 'right' has a corollary—responsibility. Children require us to support their fundamental rights. Without adults taking responsibility for the protection and provision of these rights, children are powerless to access them. In an individualistic paradigm, the circle of those who carry the weight of the responsibility shrinks. Typically in Australia, we see the responsibility for children (and the provision of their rights) as the province of the family. One family can make little difference to educational funding policies when both major political parties operate within an 'individual rules' paradigm. As Richard Eckersley (2004) says, we are seeing the 'withering of collective effort' (radio broadcast).

As increasing numbers of Australian children are parented with individualism foremost, we are seeing a trend towards a culture of indulgence, appeasement and entitlement (Carr-Greg, 2004). Too simplistically have we understood that the child has rights and not added the partner—responsibility. If we believe children are capable and entitled to have rights, then we must grant them the capability and entitlement of taking on responsibility. For example, children have a right to play. For the purposes of my argument, we can assume that children are within a context which is conducive and appropriate for play. Each child then has a responsibility for the play to be fair, mutually beneficial and not hurtful. An adult must intervene when unfairness, hurt and harm occurs and support children in learning how to be with others without tears and distress. Once these values are present, the child has the responsibility in play of recognising the right of others to play too. The notion of rights as interdependent and not individual is then established. The Italian phrase, 'Io chi siamo'—'I am who we are' (New, 1998) or 'we are who I am', illustrates this interconnectedness and points out how culturally bound notions of rights are.

At this point I would like you to reconsider the very typical Australian early childhood phrase 'free play' and wonder whom it is free for, and is it fair? Picture a playground, the less physically inclined children clinging to the fringes as happy gangs of others range across the space, unheeding of their trampling of others' rights. Whose problem is it? It is ours—our pedagogy which enshrines rights without responsibility. However, I am wary that my argument then can make the faults of the system a child's responsibility. This is not my intention. Perhaps to put it another way, a child has the right to learn responsibility and the responsibility to honour rights, while adults have the right to teach responsibility and the responsibility to honour rights. The question we may need to ask ourselves is, do we have an image of children endowed with rights and responsibilities or do we have an image of children as needy and incapable of responsibility?

Do we see children as rich in potential? Once again I am mindful of how the Reggio Emilian image can be interpreted. The image of the child, rich in potential, is powerful and dangerous. I say 'dangerous' because if children's rights to the best are not being fulfilled, then are we going to expect them to manage anyway because they are seen as 'rich in potential'? Children living in Australian Aboriginal settlements without running water, adequate health care or education cannot be held responsible for their loss of rights and potential, even though they are one and the same—still rich in potential and entitled. In an individualistic society it becomes possible to blame children for their circumstances and for the responsibility to fall upon those with the least resources.

Are our educational philosophies, theories and practices predicated on an image of what children are able to do?

In the first month of Mia-Mia's operation, Rob gave me a gift. Rob, at two-years -one-month, was a slight, small child, his premature birth still impacting on his health and wellbeing. He had almost no verbal expressive language. However, he clearly indicated he would like to investigate leaves. His determination and persistence in seeking out leaves, looking at them, arranging them and drawing them was all conveyed to us by gesture and eye contact. Whenever we guessed his intent correctly, he would nod. Amid the babble and chat of the toddler room, his silence was obvious. One day he sat with a leaf and drew a shape.

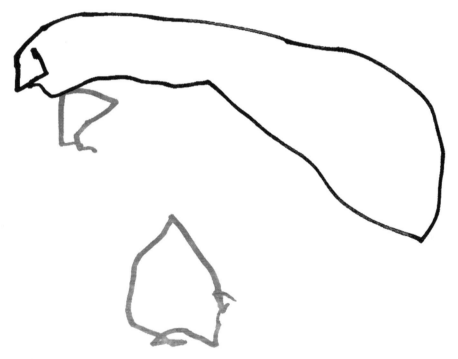

Rob's first leaf drawing

When asked if it was a leaf, he nodded. The following day, after a walk collecting yet more leaves and some research with a magnifying glass, Robbie clearly demonstrated his increased knowledge about leaves in a subsequent drawing 24 hours after the first.

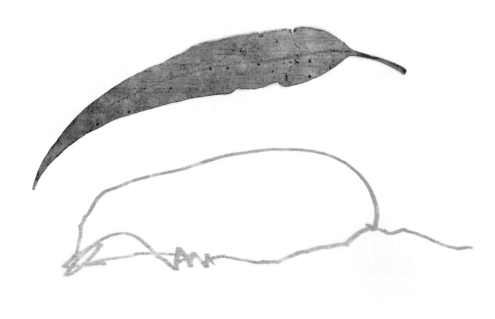

Rob's second leaf drawing

It was then that he uttered his first word on the subject—'leaf'. His intent, desire, and ability are all demonstrated here. By holding an image of Rob as capable, we were able to see what he wanted to know and support him in his ability to express this to us. If, however, we had persisted with what he was unable to do, that is talk, we may have missed seeing how competent he was. His gestures and visual thinking enabled us to speak with him, when he remained silent.

Do we see children as researchers, testing hypotheses and co-constructing knowledge and meaning?

Lillian Katz (1994), speaking of the quality of early childhood programs around the world, wearily suggests '…that many are missed opportunities to significantly enhance young children's physical, social and intellectual development' (p 9). She also describes many American preschool and primary programs as a 'serious waste of children's minds' (p 9). One of the implications arising from our experiences in Reggio Emilia is that we must seriously consider whether the curriculum we offer our children is wasting their time and minds. The experiences offered young children in Reggio Emilia are a far cry from those scathingly mentioned by John Nimmo (1994)—'the canned curriculum, embalmed curriculum, accidental curriculum, or unidentified curriculum'—or, from my own offerings—'the test curriculum, this'll do curriculum, the activity based curriculum, the preparation for school curriculum and lastly, the thematic curriculum' (Robertson, 1996).

To provide a simple illustration of curriculum content derived from first-hand problem solving, where children were working as collaborators and co-constructing knowledge, rather than acquiring it in isolation from others, I turn to the story of the snails. Children in the playground at Mia-Mia proposed solutions to the problem of snails eating the peas in the vegetable garden. Firstly they moved the snails, but this proved ineffectual. Then they gave them something else to eat in another place, and this failed as the snails ate this repast as well as the peas. Eventually the children decided to make a hotel for the snails to live in. It is possible here to see children as researchers. The flow of ideas that coalesce, divide, and make a third idea which is then put into action, is typical of the fluid way in which hypotheses are tested, adapted and then accepted through manipulation of everyone's ideas and actions. Unexpectedly, the hotel worked, as the children chose to make it out of a cardboard box and the snails happily munched their way through the interior decoration, ignoring the peas.

Is our image one of children greedy for knowledge and meaning?

Do we have an image of children grappling with and thinking about difficult uncomfortable topics, or do we see them as naïve and innocent about the perils and inequities of the world? If we see them as innocent, we miss many opportunities to engage with them about the way they are constructing their understandings of justice, fairness and danger—for it is without doubt that children are making constructions. The media is omnipresent and children over-hear, and are party to, conversations about what is going on around them. Topics that have arisen from the children at Mia-Mia include:

- What happens when you die?

- Why did the bomber blow up the people?

- Is there a difference between real violence and pretend violence?

- How do you grow up to be an adult?

- Why is your skin dirty?

- What would it feel like to live in a detention centre?

- Why do children cry?

Engaging with children in troublesome thinking is problematic, but important. Ignoring the hard stuff and only engaging in the fluff and fun from curriculum choices is to keep underground issues of social justice and to further silence and compound the inequity. If we see ourselves as functional teachers, teaching specific skills, we may find it challenging to accept our role as moral agents. I would argue that we are moral agents even if we do nothing. If we ignore knotty issues when they arise, it is then that our silence speaks volumes. Doing something places an issue in the open, and the uncertainty of dealing with complex problems becomes a joint effort. Do we see or hear our silences?

We have all witnessed youngsters grappling with concepts well out of their depth, though I say 'out of their depth' advisedly. Take an apparently simple example—writing and two-year-olds. Over the years I have seen many toddlers 'writing', already engaging in the complex task of unravelling script. I see their efforts as purposeful and worthy of response from adults. Our response has been to provision the toddler's book area with about a hundred books. Responding to their interest in text means we must provide them with more than cardboard lift-the-flap books. The shelves are groaning with car repair manuals, music books, books in many languages, road atlases, catalogues and anything else which sates or piques their interest.

I, too, still puzzle over some texts and scripts. I use a dictionary and a thesaurus to remember the meaning of words I have forgotten, and a phrase book when in another country. If we see ourselves as life-long learners, then we, too, are often keen to acquire knowledge, regardless of how difficult it may be.

Perhaps a story involving the use of books—a cultural tool useful to us all—will make my meaning clear. Several very young children (two years ten months to two years eleven months) were investigating electrical storms. The reference texts we used included diagrams of clouds, electrical build up, water absorption and so on, plus rather dramatic photographs of lightning strikes and storm damage. These pictures captivated them. They frequently asked adults to explain them, puzzling about the diagrams and material. As Forman, (1997) notes, 'Children chew over the information in books, they present children with things they do not understand and will work hard to construct, until they do understand' (personal communication, 25 January).

Indeed, this was the case here. These children learned how to find their favourite pictures in the large coffee-table books, memorising the sequence of pictures as a guide to where they were in the book. I might add the book was almost too heavy for the children to carry. Furthermore, I discovered that lightning is not yellow, it is pink. At first I thought the photograph of pink lightning slashing through a dark sky was a misprint, but as I leafed through the book, each one was pink. Apparently it has to do with heat. I now can puzzle over why we thought it was yellow.

As members of a family and community, children bring to our educational settings a wealth of knowledge. I wonder what would happen if we tried to discover what they already knew, before we started to 'teach' them. In a nameless infants class of twenty-four children during the first week of term, the curriculum consisted of the number one, the letter A, the colour yellow and a shape—the circle. Week two was the number two, B, red and a square. On the way home on Friday, Lara's mother, hoping to bolster her daughter's flagging enthusiasm for school, wondered aloud 'what will happen next week?' Lara, five years old and world weary said, 'three, C, blue and triangles'. Lara already knew all her colours and shapes, could count to fifty, write the names of her family and understood the nature of the alphabet. Two weeks into school and she was bored. The school's image of the child had constrained her possibilities.

Examples of prior knowledge that children bring to new situations are many. Mapping and knowledge of cartography occur frequently in my toddler class. Two-year-olds show sophisticated understandings of graphics and symbols (Robertson, 2000)—reading the street directory, deciphering the legend and seeking symbols within the pages. They clearly understand what a map is for and can demonstrate this knowledge in drawn maps depicting locations using agreed symbols. I don't teach them mapping—they know it from their life experiences.

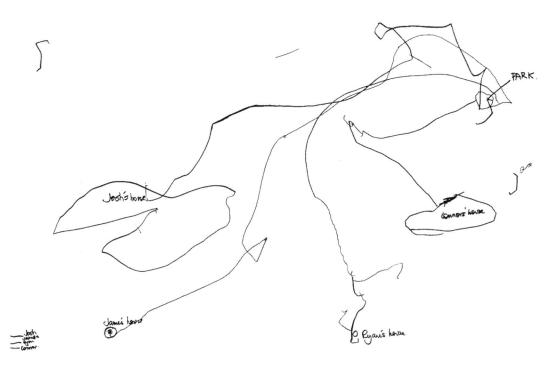

Toddler mapping

Is our image one of children as a group of individuals or one of individuals within the group?

Are we teaching community, the 'we', or are we teaching the 'I' of individuality? If we hold an image of children solely as individuals, we will find it difficult to place them in the context of the group within which knowledge is organised and learned. We will find it problematic to acknowledge the depth of learning constructed within the group if we are focusing on the teacher–child dyad or a child alone. Simple examples from the toddler's room illustrate this point. Georgia smelt flowers by blowing on them until her friend, Thalia, showed her how to sniff. Melanie copied Pip's careful management of her painting palette, and therefore mixed colours with more finesse.

If we take the stance that we teach a group of individuals, we are not able to focus on how the group has created the knowledge (Rogoff, 2003), or as Mardell (2001, p 285) puts it, 'we need to rethink our notions of human cognition as residing inside the heads of individuals and consider a view of knowledge as socially constructed'.

Consider the problem of a phone conversation. A group of four, four-year-olds is attempting to organise a party to launch a boat and they wish to invite the boat builder. One child remembers there is a phone number on the side of the dinghy on a label and copies it. Armed with the number, another of the group rings it. When the phone is answered, Matt says, 'Come to the party' and hangs up. With some help from another in the group who knows Matt should have at the very least, said 'hello', the children realise the predicament in which they have placed themselves and the shipwright. One of the children came up with the strategy of working out what needed to be said, memorising it, rehearsing it together then making the call again. Once again, several hours later, the number was dialled and a successful invitation delivered. Matt, with little experience of real phones (it was perhaps to him a surprise that the phone was answered) and no experience in the structure of a phone conversation, which includes niceties (hello) and pragmatics (date, time and place of party), managed the call. The invitation could not have been conveyed without all four children, their differing expertise and personalities. One knew where the number was and could copy it on a bit of paper; another how to dial; and Matt was the only one who would make the initial call. Undeniably, Matt learnt how to make a call on the phone, but so did those who did not actually use the phone. In the rehearsals, turns were taken to be either the boat builder or the caller. All of them can now recognise the pragmatics of an invitation and they all learnt they needed each other's minds, courage and drive, to complete a difficult task. Thereby they 'also learn with others—modifying, extending, clarifying, and enriching our [their] own ideas and those of others' (Mardell, 2001, p 286). It was the individuals within the group which assisted the group to achieve a 'collective body of knowledge' (Mardell, 2001, p 292).

If our curriculum choices are driven by a belief in 'worthy' educational outcomes, then we miss opportunities to engage in the richness of group learning and being. Furthermore, the dimensions of our perception of learning alter. The excitement, fun and irony of the phone call to the shipwright are as important as the cognitive aspects such as copying and dialling the number. I would argue that this bundle of complex emotions actually drove the group on.

As a footnote here, you will have noticed that many of the stories I tell— making a phone call, reading books and playing—are grounded in simple everyday experiences. I believe we rely too much on curriculum materials and educational truisms to illuminate and guide our practice. For example, my image of the child is one who will learn shapes, colour and size through real experiences solving real problems encountered while living within learning communities. The reductionist image of children as only capable of understanding the primary colours, is one I do not accept. Experience has shown me that children are passionate about colour in all hues, tones and shades. Stepping aside from truisms, catalogues and curriculum materials, allows an image of competent children to shine.

Does our image of children alienate them from their contexts?

Are our images of children constrained by our context of work? The physical separation of our educational settings, the distance travelled by staff, children and families, is very different from the close-knit city of Reggio Emilia. How many of us live near our centre or school, or live in the same housing complex? This separateness creates an educational image of a child de-contextualised from home and community. On entering the door of educational settings, children are in some way altered (G Dahlberg, personal communication, Stockholm, November, 1997). They become pupils, subjects of the theories and practice of an institution (I use the word 'subjects' in the postmodern sense), which holds an image of children determined by the institution's knowledges and truths. Furthermore, the vision of teachers is limited to the time-span children are in their class. We do not have an image of them as adults who will vote, drive, parent, create homes, love partners and inevitably grieve the death of loved ones. We often do not have a long relationship with children—the year in 'our' class may be as far as it goes. I'm privileged to work in child care and have a prolonged time with families and their children, seeing them everyday for 48 weeks of the year in some instances for nine years. The notion that we are living, learning and growing older together is easier to hold onto when this is the case.

Another illustration of the alienation of educational settings in NSW is the physical separation from the rest of the community, compounded by fences and prohibitive notices. They sit, islands of 'education' in the middle of communities, but sequestered like monasteries. Without an invitation, folk are not allowed in, nor are children allowed out, without permission. It is small wonder the role of education (beyond teaching the alphabet) has become diminished in the eyes of the community. The image of education becomes that of acquiring skills, rather than learning, and the image of teaching as that of transmitting skills, rather than supporting learning and research.

Do we see the role of teacher as one in which uncertainty drives the path of learning? Or do we see certainty as the crucible upon which teaching is forged?

Do we unpack the tools we use in observing and planning for children (Robertson, 1997)? Undeniably in our early childhood community, the socially, culturally and politically created, agreed image of children is passed onto us through various channels. One such conduit is through our early childhood tertiary institutions. One particular tool given to aid our collective, agreed understanding of children's image is 'observation'. In fact, this tool and the method by which we use it are enshrined in NSW state government regulations (DOCS, 2004) and in the federal government's National Quality Improvement System (NCAC, 2001).

In no way do I wish to discredit or dismiss these regulatory mechanisms. However, I do think they deserve critique. Do we see within them, powerful and competent children? Observational tools as they are often used, are implemented because they are required and are geared towards deficit models, individual children, teaching evaluation and behaviour management. I want to provoke us as a profession, to shift elsewhere in our thinking. The question 'who reads our observations?' is revealing. Is it possible that the only person reading the observation is the observer who wrote it? The individual observes the individual.

The belief that an observation can be 'objective' is a fallacy. All observation is subjective, and as such has more validity if what is written is made visible to others, who may interpret it differently. Asking children if they agree with what you have written, asking families and other teachers or using multiple media, are all ways of taking the subjective from an 'I' perspective to a 'we'. It is essential we pose the question, 'what are we seeing?' In Reggio Emilia, observations are unpacked, discussed, repeated and analysed in collaboration with colleagues and families. In some cases, the teachers physically repeat the actions a child has taken in, say, clay, to see if it is the material suggesting a solution to a problem or the child manipulating the material to get a solution. In such a re-creation, the teacher is trying to get into the child's mind. Further observations are made, using varying forms of media—photos, tape, and video. Children are asked what they think is happening and what their understandings of their experience were. In addition, observations pay particular attention to the setting, the medium, placement of children, gestures, body language and time span. If we take on board the idea of children and teachers as researchers, observations become only one tool of data collection. Needing an 'optimum level of detail to communicate' (G Forman, personal communication, 25 January 1997), further material is brought to the research collaboration including samples of work, conversations and multiple points of view. This can lead to a greater understanding of the experience and to the questions: 'Is what I saw believable?', 'Is what I saw believed by others?' and, more to the point, 'What else can we see?'

Do we question our certainties when we observe, or confirm them? I suspect that we often observe to find proof of what we already know. As early childhood educators we are well versed in child development theory and fit the observation to this knowledge. Currently there is critique of child development theory, as racist and narrow (Dahlberg, Moss & Pence, 1999), and so the very knowledge which informs observations is flawed.

It is also apparent that, for many, the perception—'I saw what I believed'—blinds them to other possibilities within the observed moment. For example three girl toddlers are playing a pretend cooking game. Two of them argue about who will be the 'Mummy', the heated conversation smouldering even when a resolution of sorts, 'well two mummys then', has been reached. After a period of ten minutes, Lara boils over and hits Robyn on the head with a pair of tongs. At that moment, all movement in the area ceases. Katsu and Robyn freeze and Lara slowly lowers the tongs to her side. I could choose to view Lara's behaviour as a deficit, or see how she restrained herself from another blow. I can also see how the other two assisted her to regain her equanimity and composure by their stillness. Katsu, who appeared (to me) to be on the fringes of play, rebutting their earlier suggestions of being the 'baby' in favour of a princess, broke the ice by twirling through the tableaux of Lara and Robyn saying, 'let's dance'. I could conjecture that Katsu has not read the situation right, and is indeed not even on the same page in terms of the 'mummy plot', or I could choose to see her ice breaker as a deliberate gift to the others, a peace making gesture. I am able to report that the others picked up her gesture and all sense of dispute evaporated as they pirouetted away together, Katsu at last part of the gang.

Within a paradigm of developmental theory and individualism, I would miss the interconnected experiences of each of the children, none possible without the others. Without Robyn to hit on the head, Lara would not have had the opportunity to not hit her again. Without Lara, Robyn would not have had the opportunity to argue her case about who was going to be the mummy, and make a solution (albeit temporary). Katsu would not have been able to make her gift, have it accepted and change the emotional mood of the play. In choosing to see powerful, competent children, together creating social meaning, the observation takes a different slant.

Do we shackle our observations to our teaching intentions and vice versa? Are we open minded enough when observing, do we actively seek another's opinion, take a different stand, and critique what it is we 'see'? Or are we focused on what it is we are teaching and fit the observation to the outcome (what an odious word, so full of sanctimony and closed possibilities) as the curriculum requires. 'I know what I am going to see' is dangerous, taking the child and teacher down a prescribed path, eliminating the sort of surprises we see occurring in Reggio Emilia.

Are planning and observation formats based on a deficit image of children? If planning is predicated on what the child cannot do, and we construct goals accordingly, then yes, our formats will be based on deficit images of children. Rather, finding out what children can do, and what they want to do, can drive the way we look at our formats. Checklists of skills skim the surface of what is important to know about children. Observations taken of children as individuals miss their rich and complex intellectual and emotional entanglements with others. The opportunity to see children as researchers, as philosophers and as powerful within groups, is lost when 'running records' are taken of a child alone. Consequently, the planning which then follows is still determined by individual experiences of the child and by perceived deficits. Consider the story of Lara and the tongs. Planning for her inability to refrain from hitting loses sight of the times she did not hit. It becomes easy to see her hitting as a problem, to see her in isolation from her friends, as a wild child unable to restrain her impulses. As we have seen, without her friends, she would have had the opportunity neither to hit, nor not hit.

Does our image of children require us to make their thinking visible to others?

A further implication of our images of children is how we show and describe each child to the 'outside world'. If we hold an image of children as remarkable thinkers and learners, then we are obliged to make this visible to others. If we hold a notion of children as learning what we teach them, we are not accountable to the child, only to our employer or to the test. How do we describe a powerful child to others?

In Australia, we in the early childhood profession have not articulated to each other or to the wider community what it is we actually do with children, or what children do. 'Most of us do early childhood practice much better than we talk about it' (Stonehouse, 1989, p 117). Those crumpled paintings in lockers at the end of the day can't possibly tell the whole story. We display children's work, but usually without comment, or possibly accompanied by a commentary such as 'painting teaches eye–hand co-ordination and allows children to express themselves'. Such comments indicate that we have decided what is going on, and thus we validate our teaching to families and ourselves.

Pedagogical documentation goes beyond display. To move from display to pedagogical documentation is a choice. Essentially, making public ideas about how children (and the adults) are learning and making meaning is scary. It would be much easier to our keep our files private, our professional judgment in the cupboard and our subjectivity to ourselves. The question is, is this fair? Whether or not we agree with the concept of pedagogical documentation, information about children's learning is not the property of the adult staff. Nor is it the property of the child, for no child at an educational setting learns alone. How to present this learning respectfully with multiple voices and meanings is the issue. Our knowledge, our subjectivities, our theoretical paradigms drive every decision we make about how a child will learn in our settings. Making that at least visible to others so they may agree or not, is what children are entitled to. Choosing to use pedagogical documentation has been for me exciting, challenging and affirming. I am able to work in respectful uncertainty, creating new theory with children and colleagues. As we examine and critique our practice and theory via pedagogical documentation, we become a community of learners.

Conclusion

Each of the eight questions asked in this chapter could also be asked in a different way. If we are attempting to conceptualise what shapes our educational thinking, we cannot leave out the teacher's role. Therefore we can ask:

- Do we have an image of children and teachers endowed with rights?

- Are our educational philosophies, theories and practices predicated on an image of what children and teachers are able to do?

- Do we see children and teachers as researchers, testing hypotheses and co-constructing knowledge?

- Is our image one of children and teachers greedy for knowledge and meaning?

- Is our image one of children and teachers as a group of individuals or as individuals within the group?

- Does our image of children and teachers alienate them from their contexts?

- Do we see the role of teacher as one in which being uncertain (Rinaldi, 1993) drives the path of learning? Or do we see certainty as the crucible upon which teaching is forged?

- Does our image of children and teachers require us to make their thinking visible to others?

When we reflect on our image of children, we are reflecting on our own image as educators, parents, neighbours, consumers and citizens. In this chapter, I have tried to question our Australian image of children within education and therefore our place within education. As these are stories from my own experience, the chapter necessarily reveals my own reflections. I hope, however, the point that our images impact on children and education, is not ignored. As I look at learning and education, the metaphor of the image of the child, once for me a simple question of how I looked at children, has become redolent with purpose, challenge and opportunity. I am no longer silent or submissive in my understanding of the forces behind, around and beyond us, as we embark on this endeavour called education.

References

Bredekamp S (1993) Reflection on Reggio Emilia. *Young Children*, 42 (1), 13–17.

Carr-Greg D (2004) (Presenter) *Breakfast show*. [Radio broadcast]. ABC Radio 702, 10 February, Sydney: Australian Broadcasting Corporation.

Dahlberg G (1997) Personal communication. November, Stockholm.

Dahlberg G, Moss P & Pence A (1999) *Beyond quality in early childhood education and care: Postmodern perspectives*. London: Falmer Press.

Eckersley R (2004) The science of the self. *Okhams Razor*. [Radio Program] ABC Radio National, Sunday 30 May. Australian Broadcasting Corporation.

Forman G (1977) Personal communication. Reggio List, 25 January.

Katz L (1994) Images from the world: Study seminar on the experience of the Municipal infant–toddler centres and pre-primary schools of Reggio Emilia, Italy. In L Katz & B Cesarone (Eds) *Reflections on the Reggio Emilia Approach* (pp 69–88). ERIC Monograph Series No 6.

MacNaughton G (2000) *Rethinking gender in early childhood education*. Sydney: Allen and Unwin.

Mardell B (2001) Moving across the Atlantic. In C Giudici, C Rinaldi & M Krechevsky (Eds). *Making learning visible: Children as individual and group learners* (pp 278–83). Reggio Emilia, Italy: Reggio Children.

Millikan J (2003) *Reflections: Reggio Emilia principles within Australian contexts*. Sydney, NSW: Pademelon Press.

National Childcare Accreditation Council (2001) *Quality Improvement and Accreditation System*. Canberra: NCAC.

New R (1998) Theory and praxis in Reggio Emilia: They know what they are doing, and why. In C Edwards, L Gandini & G Forman (Eds) *The hundred languages of children: The Reggio Emilia approach—Advanced reflections* (2nd Ed). (pp 261–84). Greenwich, CT: Ablex.

New South Wales Department of Community Services (2004) Children's Services Regulations related to the *Children and Young Person's Care and Protection Act* (1998). DOCS: Sydney.

Nimmo J (1994, September) *Building community to realise the potential of children: The challenge of Reggio Emilia in the USA*. Keynote address at the conference: The challenge of Reggio Emilia: Realising the potential of children. Melbourne, Australia: University of Melbourne.

Rinaldi C (1993) The emergent curriculum and social constructivism: An interview with Lella Gandini. In C Edwards, L Gandini & G Forman (Eds) *The hundred languages of children: The Reggio Emilia approach to early childhood education* (pp 101–12). Norwood, NJ: Ablex.

Robertson J (1996, May) *Unpacking our Australian images of children*. In *Unpacking Reggio Emilia: Implications for Australian early childhood practice. Conference Proceedings*. North Ryde, NSW: Institute of Early Childhood, Macquarie University.

Robertson J (1997, May) Seeing is believing. In *Unpacking Reggio Emilia: Further implications for Australian early childhood practice. Conference Proceedings*. North Ryde, NSW: Institute of Early Childhood, Macquarie University.

Robertson J (2000) Drawing: Making thinking visible. In W Schiller (Ed) *Thinking through the arts* (pp 154–61). Harwood Academic: Amsterdam.

Robertson J (2001, July) Unpacking the gaze: Shifting lenses. In *Unpacking Interpretation: De-constructions from Australia, America and Reggio Emilia. Conference Papers*. North Ryde, NSW: Institute of Early Childhood, Macquarie University.

Rogoff B (2003) *The cultural nature of human development*. New York: Oxford University Press.

Soja E (1996) *Thirdspace: Journeys to Los Angeles and other real-and-imagined places*. Massachusetts: Blackwell.

Stonehouse A (1989) *Parents and caregivers in partnership for children*. Sydney: Community Child Care Co-operative Ltd.

Chapter Four

The Disposition to Document

Sarah Felstiner
Laurie Kocher
Ann Pelo

Like many small child care programs in the United States, Hilltop rents space in a Church—in our case, a large Lutheran church with brick walls and a copper roof. Hilltop Children's Center is a private, not-for-profit program offering full-day care for children aged three to five, as well as after-school and vacation care for those aged six to ten. There are about 70 children enrolled at Hilltop and most of them are preschoolers. Since 1971, Hilltop has been located on the top of Queen Anne Hill in Seattle, Washington. The seven small rooms on the top floor of the church house our classrooms and art studios for preschool aged children as well as our program's administrative office. The 'Big Kids' use one large room in the basement of the church.

Ann, Sarah and Laurie

The majority of families and staff at Hilltop Children's Center (with a handful of exceptions) reflect the dominant European American culture of the urban neighbourhood in which the center is located. The parents at Hilltop are mainly professionals, working full-time in law offices, architecture firms, computer software companies, and other high-income fields. They are typically politically liberal, religiously unaffiliated, and 'culturally hip'.

Ann Pelo and Sarah Felstiner, core teachers at Hilltop Children's Center, have been incorporating elements of the philosophy from Reggio Emilia into their teaching practice for nearly ten years. Ann and Sarah have both participated in study tours to Reggio Emilia and have engaged in independent study of the ideas from the educators of Reggio Emilia. Inspired by these ideas, they have developed their own style of documentation, a style that is culturally relevant for their own community. During their years of documenting children's work, they have created an extensive collection of project history books detailing various investigations and experiences. Ann and Sarah are frequently asked to share their teaching experiences with other educators in North America.

Laurie Kocher has been a teacher of four, five, and six-year-olds in the Canadian public school system for over 20 years. After first encountering the work of the preschools of Reggio Emilia, she also was inspired to adapt many of the principles of the approach into her Kindergarten program. Her doctoral research is based on taking a close look at the practice of pedagogical documentation at Hilltop Children's Center, and specifically at Ann's and Sarah's work.

In this chapter, as we three weave our thoughts together, we'll discuss our understandings of pedagogical documentation from a theoretical perspective, and then move into a description of what documentation looks like in practice at Hilltop Children's Center.

Laurie: A particular place—the parts and the whole

Hilltop Children's Center is a particular and remarkable place filled with dedicated, passionate teachers. It is important, I think, to point out that Ann and Sarah work within the context of a whole system of support and professional development. While my doctoral research specifically focused on the work of these two individuals, their work represents a part of the whole, and must be considered in this context. Margaret Wheatley's (1999, p 143) words come to mind:

Seeing the interplay between system dynamics and individuals is a dance of discovery that requires several iterations between the whole and the parts. We expand our vision to see the whole, then narrow our gaze to peer intently into individual moments. With each iteration, we see more of the whole, and gain new understandings about individual elements. We paint a portrait of the whole, surfacing as much detail as possible. Then we inquire into a few pivotal events or decisions, and search for great detail there, also. We keep dancing between the two levels, bringing sensitivities and information gleaned from one level to help us understand the other. If we hold to the awareness of the whole as we study the part, and understand its relationship to the whole, profound new insights become available.

Laurie: What is pedagogical documentation?

We, and our children, have been raised in a culture of documentation. Cameras and video cameras appear almost anywhere there are children. Proud parents save school report cards, greeting cards, diplomas, crayon drawings, and photos—all artefacts of childhood. These artefacts only begin to tell the stories, however. 'Without words, without a narrative, there is only a shadow of an anecdote with no particular shape, without substance' (Burrington & Sortino, 2004, p 225).

Pedagogical documentation, as developed by educators in Reggio Emilia, is a way of making visible the often otherwise invisible learning processes by which children and teachers work in early childhood centres and schools (Cadwell, 1997). This documentation may be presented in many formats, such as videotapes, books, display panels, or slide shows. Usually, the documentation, regardless of format, includes anecdotal observations, samples of children's works, photographs that illustrate a process, transcripts of children's voiced ideas, all accompanied with a teacher's reflective commentary. It is this interpretive piece, this narrative, which sets pedagogical documentation apart and makes it a viable tool for reflection.

From early on in the educational project of Reggio Emilia, educators recognised the rich potential that pedagogical documentation offered in several areas. Firstly, the artefacts of photographs and transcribed conversations provide children and teachers with a tangible record that can be revisited, inviting further opportunities to extend the learning. Secondly, documentation serves as a tool of research for the educators, encouraging on-going evaluation and renewal of the educational experience. And thirdly, the detailed information collected and displayed for parents and the public serves as a means of eliciting their reactions and support, and thus a way of advocating for high quality early childhood programs (Kocher, 1999).

Pedagogical documentation is not primarily about creating beautiful panels or displays, but about following and shaping the knowledge building process (Guidici, Krechevsky & Rinaldi, 2001). As Reggio pedagogue Carlina Rinaldi (1998, p 120) describes it:

Documentation sustains the educational process (teaching) in the dialogue with the learning processes of the children. Documentation is a point of strength that makes timely and visible the interweaving of actions of the adults and of the children; it improves the quality of communication and interaction. It is in fact a process of reciprocal learning. Documentation makes it possible for teachers to sustain children's learning while they also learn (to teach) from the children's own learning.

Dahlberg, Moss & Pence (1999, p 144–5) capture the essence of what it is to be a reflective practitioner when they respond to the question: 'How can we practice a reflective and communicative pedagogy?':

It presupposes, first and foremost, a reflective practitioner who, together with his or her colleagues, can create a space for a vivid and critical discussion about pedagogical practice and the conditions it needs. It also requires certain tools. With inspiration from the early childhood institutions in Reggio Emilia, in northern Italy, many pedagogues around the world have begun to use pedagogical documentation as a tool for reflecting on pedagogical practice.

Krechevsky and Mardell (2001, p 289) suggest that the very act of documenting changes teachers' understanding of what goes on in the classroom, causing them to slow down and 'encouraging them to reflect on and understand the deeper meaning and value of a learning experience'. This reflection informs their decisions about where to go next. 'Rather than trying to tell the whole story of an experience or putting up the work of every child, teachers become selective about what to document' (p 289), continually making decisions about the moments and experiences that are most meaningful to record. Often, these may be the 'ordinary moments' that occur spontaneously, in addition to thoughtful exchanges that take place during complex project work. 'Instead of simply describing the experience of the learning group, this view of documentation involves a deeper analysis of the purposes behind it and behind the related learning processes and products (p 289).'

Australian educator Jan Millikan (2003, p 102) points out that pedagogical documentation:

…provides for many inherent possibilities, such as leading an inquiry forward, being a tool for children's own reflections, enabling parents to view and contribute to the process of children's learning, for teachers' professional development, and as an advocacy for children.

She cautions that this can, indeed, be a daunting process and so we must proceed slowly. In the following section, we'll talk about the role of documentation as it is evolving at Hilltop Children's Center in Seattle.

Laurie: 'coming home'—a sense of the possible

Upon first viewing *The Hundred Languages of Children* exhibition (a travelling collection of children's work documented and compiled by the educators in Reggio Emilia), I was overwhelmed by the depth and complexity of the children's work and by the multiple 'languages' with which children expressed themselves —with words, movement, drawing, painting, building, sculpture, shadow play, collage, dramatic play, and music, to name only a few. Particularly impressive was the reflective, profound, and sometimes metaphorical text that accompanied these documentation displays. Transcribed recordings of children's conversations were paired with the reflective commentary of their teachers. The image of the child as strong, resourceful, curious and competent was everywhere evident in *The Hundred Languages of Children* exhibition. Indeed, children's thoughts and feelings were offered in such a deep and respectful way that I came away changed, determined to attempt to document the work of children in my own classroom following along the lines of the work of educators in Reggio Emilia. This effort led me to seek out other educators who were also incorporating the practice of documentation into their work, and ultimately to Hilltop Children's Center where my doctoral research was located.

In conversations that took place with teachers as I was conducting my research, Sarah and Ann also identified a powerful sense of connection upon initial exposure to the work of Reggio Emilia educators. Referring in particular to viewing the video *To Make a Portrait of a Lion* (Commune di Reggio Emilia, 1987), which portrays one project undertaken by Reggio educators with young children, Ann's comment reflects this experience:

> The heart and soul piece, the way of being with children in the world, the pedagogy that grows out of the image of the child, the image of the teacher, the image of the family, is so deeply resonant for me. Watching the video 'Portrait of a Lion', I had this experience of weeping, just weeping—weeping both from being so deeply moved with this joy at what children and families and teachers were experiencing together in Reggio, and weeping with this yearning for my own work to continue to deepen in those sorts of ways of building relationships with children and families, and supporting children's thoughtful collaborations.

Both Ann and Sarah speak of a sense of resonance, of a heart-felt connection with this portrayal of living with children in an authentic, intentional way. It is almost as if each woman articulated an experience of coming home, of arriving, metaphorically, in a place where the lived experience meshes with the dream of what could be possible. Canadian researcher Max Van Manen's seminal work, *Researching Lived Experience* (1990, p 5) comes to mind as he describes phenomenological research:

From a phenomenological point of view, to do research is always to question the way we experience the world, to want to know the world in which we live as human beings. And since to know the world is to profoundly be in the world in a certain way, the act of researching—questioning—theorizing is the intentional act of attaching ourselves to the world, to become fully part of it, or better, to become the world. Phenomenology calls this inseparable connection to the world the principle of 'intentionality'.

The vehicle of pedagogical documentation is what makes these experiences in the schools of Reggio Emilia, this principle of intentionality, visible and shareable.

Ann, Sarah and Laurie: the role of documentation at Hilltop—'Documentation is a verb'

The word 'documentation' is a familiar one amongst families and teachers at Hilltop, and is understood to represent the writing and photos posted on the curriculum boards in the school hallways or on project panels. In addition to documenting on-going project work, teachers attempt to daily post a page or two of observations, unfolding project work, recorded conversations, or spontaneously captured 'ordinary moments' (Shafer, 2002). Often digital photos are included in these postings. Each teacher has his or her own style of writing and presenting the documentation; this in itself is a conscious effort to embrace diversity. Different headings on the curriculum board—such as community happenings, anti-bias learning, social learning, socio-dramatic play, stories and emerging literacy, art and symbolic representation, sensory knowledge, logic and mathematical thinking, and on-going projects and emerging interests—provide a way to organise these pieces of writing. Copies of these writings are made for children's individual journals. Over the course of time, a fairly comprehensive picture is painted through these stories of life lived in community at Hilltop.

But documentation represents a more active, vibrant practice—the practice of deep engagement by adults in the lives of children. Documentation means a way of being with children with intentionality—a habit of paying attention, watching and listening closely, reflecting together about what we see, planning from our reflections and understandings, and telling the stories in ways that enrich our community.

Teachers at Hilltop are working to reclaim this vibrant, vital understanding of documentation, embracing documentation as an active verb rather than an inert noun. We're re-invigorating our understanding of written documentation, seeing it not as a static piece of paper, but as a series of love letters about the children, exchanged between teachers and families, traces of our shared lives.

Documentation holds many elements. It could be replaced with more descriptive and specific words: observing closely and making notes, studying the observation notes, and telling the story. These are the key practices that, woven together, become our practice of documentation. For further discussion on this, see Chapter Ten, 'At the crossroads: Pedagogical documentation and social justice'.

Ann and Sarah: Pedagogical documentation and emergent curriculum

At Hilltop, curriculum 'grows' out of teachers' observations of children's play activities in an emergent, organic sort of way. We strive to be close observers, paying careful attention to the passions that underlie children's work. Documenting helps us to attend more carefully to children's work—to their actual words, and to the intricacies of their play. In so doing, we often notice themes or patterns or repeated ideas that help us to identify not just what children are playing, but to speculate on why they are playing it. In various projects, careful note-taking and transcription helps us hypothesise that there are strong, serious emotional themes underlying children's fast and light-hearted play. In carefully observing and recording children's play, we have the opportunity to wonder, 'what are these children trying to figure out?' Looking back over collections of drawings, words, and photographs, often in collaboration with our co-teachers, we can trace the strain of a developmentally critical theme. We may see elements of the same powerful themes—identity, relationship, self-expression, and scientific inquiry, to name just a few—emerge each year, but always embedded in a new topical context that is specific to that particular group of children.

It's through the habitual practice of capturing children's work that we discover potential or unfolding study projects. We laugh, and talk, and interact with children all day long, but also watch for moments to snap a photo or jot a note about play that seems to stand out for one reason or another. Some of these seeds-of-ideas blossom slowly over time, while others burst forth and play themselves out in an hour or a day. Rarely do children propose turning their spontaneous work into a short-term or long-term project. Rather, we take responsibility for noticing opportunities that seem rich with possibilities to investigate further, or to bring children together, or to provoke development of particular skills, or to emphasise issues of bias or cultural relevancy. Documenting this rich play is part of what turns on-going work into projects. By documenting each relevant work session or play sequence and gathering that documentation, we demonstrate the purposeful process of discovery that children and teachers undertake together, this process of 'reciprocal learning' that Rinaldi (1998, p 121) describes.

Pedagogical documentation is critical in extending and deepening children's involvement in on-going project work. Recording their conversations provides a wealth of potential ideas to pursue, and lets their own brainstorming sessions be the source of their plans rather than depending on outside encouragement from teachers. We use tape-recorded conversations to help anchor children's work by continually directing them back to decisions they have made as a group. Photographs create a pictorial history of where we've already been in the course of a project, and looking back over those photos with children often reminds them of previous intentions or sparks new ideas. Saving their drawings and other artwork also provides a tool for sustaining project work by identifying particular aspects that children may want to learn more about, or providing models to use in re-representing an object or idea in another medium.

At Hilltop, our documentation practices have grown hand in hand with our expanded and clarified techniques for facilitating an emergent curriculum. We have discovered how integral and critical documentation is in bringing the spirit and ideals of emergent curriculum into actual practice. We have come to believe that emergent curriculum is essentially an attitude, a commitment to put children and their pursuits at the heart of the curriculum. That philosophical goal is translated into practical reality by the art, skill, and disposition to document children's work.

Laurie: a culture of research

The documentation process allows each teacher to become a producer of research and to examine his or her own development as a reflective practitioner. As teachers examine the children's work and prepare its documentation, their own understandings of children's development and insights into their learning are deepened. On the basis of the rich data made available through documentation, teachers are able to make informed decisions about appropriate ways to support each child's development and learning (Beneke, Harris-Helm, & Steinheimer, 1998). A significant component is the teachers' own reflective text, which is an integral part of the documentation. Most importantly, documentation provides a focus for concrete and meaningful adult and child reflection on children's learning processes.

Practising the art of pedagogical documentation while living school days with children fosters a culture of research at Hilltop. Gandini and Goldhaber (2001, p 143–4) believe that the process of documentation can be an agent of change. Pedagogical documentation:

> …has the potential to change how early childhood educators see ourselves as professionals. It certainly requires that we expand our identity from nurturer and caregiver to include theoretician and researcher. We have found that documentation demands a high level of intellectual commitment and curiosity and a passionate engagement in our work.

Having incorporated pedagogical documentation into a nearly daily practice, there is a very high level of intellectual engagement for these teachers, which is made manifest in the process of interpretive writing. Sarah speaks of the intellectual vitality she finds in the process:

> I'm so engaged by the intellectual piece, and so engaged by the professional development inherent in active documentation…Is the documentation what keeps us intellectually linked in to this daily work? Here we are, smart, thinking, intellectually curious people who are attracted to work with young children, and is documentation part of what lets us be both of those things at the same time? Sure, there are moments of living with kids that aren't intellectually rewarding or fulfilling, unless we really come at the question of 'Who is this kid?' with curiosity, or 'How do I know this family?' or 'What is the meaning of this interaction?' If we take in the message that we can be really curious about everything that happens, it's completely intellectually fulfilling work, which so many people just don't understand. That's a message that belongs in the work…

This 'culture of research' invites constant discussion and making of hypotheses and predictions about the on-going work with the children, and is closely linked to the other aspects of the teacher's work involving documentation—namely listening, observing, gathering documents, and interpreting them (Rinaldi, 1998). Engaging in continuous self-reflection imposes high requirements on teachers, but also functions as a challenge and inspiration for a deeper engagement (Dahlberg, Moss & Pence, 1999).

Laurie: Reflective commentary

Many have been intrigued by the process of pedagogical documentation developed by the educators in Reggio Emilia. What makes the work of these teachers at Hilltop particularly inspiring is the insightful reflective commentary that is paired with their observations of children's experiences. For example, during an investigation launched by play around Disney's 'Lion King', Sarah wrote:

> Thinking back on this first gathering with this group of children, I'm struck by two things. First, it seems that one of the main jobs for this group will be grappling with and working on the interpersonal dynamics of how decisions get made in their play. These girls have been learning all year about the power struggles of inclusion and exclusion, and this work team may be an opportunity for them to think through these issues. Second, I heard some ideas emerge in this first conversation about good lions and bad lions, light lions and dark lions. I will be curious to see how these distinctions and classifications play out in our next meetings… Though my primary intention for the Lion Work Team is that they

have a chance to explore the Lion King story in a wide range of symbolic languages, it seems this work may also be a rich opportunity for them to play about issues of race and bias… My role as a teacher continues to be that of watcher, listener, documentor. I don't plan to do much overt provocation around issues of racial difference until I better understand what internal questions and wonderings these girls really have.

During another investigation, Ann wrote:

In their play, children work actively, explore and understand themselves, their friends, their world. They are asking questions, constructing knowledge, extending and deepening their understandings. When we observe their play, listening carefully, we can see 'underneath' the topical content of their play to the development themes at its roots. Our note-taking about and transcribing of children's play helps us uncover these themes. Our sense of these developmental themes guides our work with children, as we seek to support, enrich, and extend their work around these themes. It's tempting for adults to stick with kids' topical themes, and certainly easier than digging deep for the themes underneath. When we notice the themes under kids' play, though, we honour their authentic work, and we can meet them there. Our curriculum, then, becomes driven by the children—a respectful, engaging, fascinating approach to curriculum for us adults and for the children.

Documentation, such as that collected and collated by Ann and Sarah, is focused on what Seidel (2001, p 307) describes as:

…the 'stuff' of understanding—ideas, theories, hypotheses, feelings, experiments, deductions, notions of cause and effect, imagination, intuitions, 'performances', and the relationship of experience, skill, knowledge, and insight—cognitive processes involved in coming to know something… Recording and presenting children's actions and interactions can reveal the genesis of ideas and then, in being shared, can lead to new thoughts, questions, and discoveries.

The work of Hilltop teachers exemplifies the ideals of Zeichner (1999), who suggests that critical reflection incorporates moral and ethical criteria into the discourse of practical action. Here the major questions are, 'which educational goals, activities, and experiences lead toward forms of life which are more just, equitable and so forth?'.

Laurie: Writing as a native language

A significant component of sophisticated pedagogical documentation is the teacher's reflective commentary, and so it's not surprising that someone who is a competent writer would be drawn to this practice. Ann and Sarah have both commented that their comfort level with professional writing helps with this aspect of documentation. As Ann expressed it:

> Writing…it's my native language, really. To really sink into the experience, or a moment that I'm watching unfold, and to write about it… I mean, writing is something that I do anyway, so this way of being, that we call documentation, it's a really great fit. So there's that personal piece for me, of feeling sustained by documentation, because it is going to this native language place. And feeling like it's a place where I really practice and deepen my writing skills, and become a better writer—that can only be a good thing. When I write, I feel able to do more nuanced thinking about children and learning and able to dig deeply as well as to see broadly what's the heart and soul of learning and play. It is research and writing, and I'm living it all day every day…

The writing process itself helps to deepen one's own thinking or, as Richardson (2000, p 923) says, 'writing is a way of "knowing"—a method of discovery and analysis'. Van Manen (1990, p 36) suggests that in phenomenology, one studies the obvious: a phenomenon that is right before us but that is not well documented or described. He also writes that the aim of phenomenology is to 'transform lived experience into a text that expresses something essential in re-living and a reflective appropriation of something meaningful'. Ann and Sarah are able to think 'out loud' in their documentation, to be transparent in their thinking, thereby inviting the reader into the reflective process.

Laurie: Infinite attention to the other

Carlina Rinaldi has put forth the challenge that 'the best environment for children is one in which you can find the highest possible quantity and quality of relationships' (Cadwell, 2003, p 136). Bill Readings (1996, p 16) says: 'I want to insist that pedagogy is a relation, a network of obligation…[in which] the condition of pedagogical practice is an infinite attention to the other.' The primacy of relationships is a strong theme that pervades the work at Hilltop. As Ann describes it:

> That's sort of the heart of the whole relationship piece…the whole heart of the beginning and sustaining piece for me of this work. Documentation is the practice…that reflects and cultivates relationships… Certainly I'm so engaged by the intellectual piece, and so engaged by the professional development, I mean, all of that is definitely there, but the living, breathing meaning of it for me is being in relationship, being in community.

Hilltop teachers have worked hard to effectively develop systems where collegiality and collaboration support relationships among the children, educators and parents, relationships with the community, opportunities for learning and the co-construction of knowledge. Working with an emergent or responsive curriculum that is negotiated with all the stakeholders is a dynamic process that generates documentation and is re-generated by documentation. Building and maintaining relationships is the guiding thread. As Rinaldi (1998, p 122) puts it:

> …documentation influences the quality of relationships among and between teachers, children, and parents… documentation becomes the heart of each specific project and the place for true professional training of teachers.

With relationships at the heart of their daily lived experience with children, Ann and Sarah tend to have their eyes wide open and riveted on the learners, taking up Ayers' (2002, p 42) call for 'honest and righteous teachers to stay wide-awake to the world, to the concentric circles of context in which we live and work'. Having a strong belief in children who are capable, competent and creative, with a fierce interest in a sense of fairness (a belief or image of the child also held by educators in Reggio Emilia), Hilltop teachers are committed to fostering opportunities for children to be active protagonists in their worlds. By so doing, teachers invite students to become (Ayers, 2002, p 42):

> …capable, more thoughtful and powerful in their choices, more engaged in a culture and a civilization, able to participate, to embrace, and, yes, to change all that is before them.

Ann and Sarah: embracing difference and working for justice

Ann and Sarah write that:

> For us, the practice of documentation, coupled with the principles of emergent curriculum, fit 'hand in glove' with social justice work. By studying our documentation notes, we can see underneath the words of the children to the themes and issues under-girding them. With that understanding, we can respond in meaningful ways, taking an active role in shaping an activism project.

Expanding on this, Ann says of her social justice work with children:

> It's my core, my spine to my work, that's been the sort of deepest anchor. That's what drew me to working with young children in the first place… If, in fact,

we're paying such intimate and close attention to children and building deep relationships with them that deeply respect who they are individually and culturally, we can't help but do anti-bias and diversity work… There's no way to do that work without paying close attention to children, and hearing from them what their passions and pursuits are, and meeting them in that place, and letting that be the curriculum that we live with children. Bringing those two pieces together…feels really important to me.

For many years, each Hilltop teacher brought his/her passions (or his/her lack of passion) about anti-bias issues to the classroom, and each teaching team found its own way to integrate anti-bias work and activism into the life of the classroom. More recently the staff began to talk together about issues of diversity and anti-bias work, exploring what a centre-wide commitment to anti-bias work might mean for the program. They have been reflecting on ways to involve parents in creating a school as dedicated to anti-bias work as to an emergent curriculum. Throughout the year, teachers engage with families in dialogue about their anti-bias work and what they're doing about diversity issues at Hilltop. A pamphlet that provides an overview of anti-bias practices with children is included in the initial registration package for families.

Hilltop teachers devote part of our team meetings each week to discussing current anti-bias efforts and opportunities in the classroom. A deliberate attempt is made to introduce meeting topics, thinking games, teacher skits and other activities to provoke conversations about bias and fairness. In addition, teachers support in-depth study projects that contain elements of activism for social justice. Though perhaps not immediately visible on the walls and shelves in the form of commercially produced 'multi-cultural' posters and props, all of these anti-bias efforts are recorded in on-going documentation of classroom work.

Our teachers are committed to nurturing within each child a disposition to speak and act for peace, tolerance, and justice. With that as a base, the teachers create an environment for learning that has multiple entry points. Such an environment must be abundant with opportunities to practice justice; to display, foster, embody, expect, demand, nurture, allow, model, and enact inquiry toward moral action (Ayers, 2002).

One of our main objectives at Hilltop—our mission, even—is to support children's social development, and help them learn how to be in the world with each other. Some of this learning happens naturally in the course of children's play, but occasionally we also seek out ways to do some gentle coaching about the skills needed for getting along with each other. A particular thread we've observed from one year to the next is the question of inclusion and exclusion. For example, what do you do when you're playing a fun game with somebody, and then another child comes along and wants to join? Or, conversely, what do you do if you see some children playing a fun game, and you want to join it?

A scene from Teacher Theatre

To invite children into conversation about just these questions, we sometimes use a tool called 'Teacher Theatre' at our morning meeting. 'Teacher Theatre' has been a part of Hilltop culture for a number of years.

It's a way of introducing a topic for discussion without drawing direct attention to the people or incidents that inspired the need for a conversation. Sometimes two teachers will replay a disagreement that they saw happen earlier in the morning, or a few dollhouse figures or plastic animals will have some kind of a problem that needs to be resolved. For example, once two teachers acted out stealing pieces from each other's block structures. Another time, two small lion figures had a problem about excluding a third lion from their game. In 'Teacher Theatre', children watch the scenario unfold, and then offer suggestions as to how the teachers (or dolls, or animals) might solve their problem. Then the scenario is replayed several more times, trying out children's suggestions.

We have found 'Teacher Theatre' to be a gentle but effective way of including the whole group in the process of clarifying class agreements, and in the process of creating a classroom culture that is safe and fair and happy. These sometimes impromptu performances are always photographed, tape-recorded and transcribed, so that teachers and children can refer back to them, and also share them with families. Often, children will replay a 'Teacher Theatre' scenario days or weeks after it was first presented. And more importantly, they often refer to the scenarios in the context of their own social play—'we're having the same problem that those lions had!'—and then use the ideas they had brainstormed for the 'Teacher Theatre' characters to solve their own conflicts.

Another tradition at Hilltop is to invite children to create self-portraits as one way of helping them extend their understandings and conversations about skin colour. Building on other colour-mixing practice done earlier in the year, this self-portrait work focuses on creating the colours of children's skin, hair, eyes, and lips.

Here are excerpts from Sarah's write-up of a session of self-portrait work, which included many photographs of the children at work. She noted:

I began by inviting each child to look into the small mirrors placed around the table. Children talked as they looked, making quiet observations to themselves and each other: 'my skin is a little bit brown and a little bit pink', and 'I have freckles, like my daddy', for example. One child said, 'I have brown eyes, brown to match my hair.' After a bit, I gave each child a plastic plate with four separate sections, and asked them to start by mixing the colour of their skin.

Child mixing colours

Researching a portrait: looking in mirror

I moved around the table, giving children squirts of whichever colour they requested from the many bottles of commercially available 'people colour' paints. They soon noticed that there was no bottle labelled 'Emily' or 'Kenji' or any other name. Each child clearly needed a mix of many shades to reach a skin colour that they felt matched what they saw in the mirror. Once children began mixing, they became quite particular about the colour they were creating. 'It's still too dark!' or 'I need more brown', they said as they worked. 'This is a lot about mixing!' one child declared.

I noticed a few kids holding their paint-soaked brushed up near their faces to compare colours, and they often needed to make more adjustments (stirring in yet more paint) once they'd looked into the mirror to check if it matched. Once each child was done, I gave her or him a small piece of paper to paint on, suggesting that they 'look in the mirror to notice the shape of your face, and then try to make that shape on the paper'. As each child finished painting their basic face shape, I collected the small pieces of paper and set them aside to dry for a bit while we worked on mixing colours for hair.

We repeated the whole process described above—pouring, stirring, testing, pouring and stirring some more—until each child had a match for her or his hair colour. Then they looked closely at their hair in the mirror, and painted that part onto their self-portrait. I set the self-portraits aside again, and we repeated the whole process for eye colour, and yet again for lip colour. Finally, I took a digital photo of each artist, and printed them out to display alongside the portraits.

This was a painstaking but satisfying process. I was impressed by the intense concentration each child showed in carefully mixing the colours they wanted. I was proud of the hard work they did to make such artful and sensitive reflections of themselves. And I was fascinated by the spontaneous, easygoing conversations about appearance that children had with each other while they worked. For example:

'I need some black and some brown for my hair, because my mom has brown hair, and my dad has black hair'.

'I need more brown, 'cause my skin is darker'.

'My skin is white'.

'Mine is peach'.

'Your skin is pinker, like mine. You can use this pink when I'm done'.

This hard work children did creating self-portraits offered them a new medium to explore and understand their own appearance, and to think again about the conversations we've been having about race and skin colour. We're often looking

Self-portrait

Playdough provocation set up for thinking about skin colour

for opportunities like this—ways to extend children's thinking by helping them revisit their own big ideas again and again, in as many different media, or 'languages', as possible.

Ann and Sarah: pedagogical documentation is the cornerstone

Reflecting on our individual experiences of developing a personal style of pedagogical documentation over a number of years, we both describe the practice as having become the cornerstone of our pedagogical work with children. Ann expresses it this way:

> The process or way of being in the world, is really what it is, a way of understanding our work, or understanding our relationships with children and with each other that is about mindful presence and authentic engagement and curiosity and delight. How that all gets lived out or made tangible is the form of this thing we call documentation, this paper we put up on the wall, this document we send out to the web-page, whatever form it takes…documentation is an expression of a way of being with children. I think of documentation as growing out of deep listening and close observation, so that's not anything that necessarily shows, it's not any tangible piece. I'd say that's a core piece of documentation, really being

present to what the children are experiencing, doing, saying, playing about, arguing about, collaborating about, feeling about. So, that is a central component of documentation, that mindful presence…

Sarah describes documentation as a really close description of what teaching an emergent curriculum looks like:

> It's the main activity, if you take documentation in its biggest description that includes the reflective part, and the use of what you've collected to be thoughtful and playful about what you might want to do next. To me, documentation is that something to hang onto…the anchoring structure in a very organic curriculum.

She considers her collection of documented projects incredibly treasured items. They provide really solid evidence or traces of doing rich, important work with children:

> The process of documentation takes this organic, experiential, fluid curriculum, and groups it into meaningful stories in some way. The stories give you little pieces to hold on to that can represent that time lived. It's partly a sense of relief that this moment is at least captured to some degree, so it's not lost…it's in the history. Partly it's the sense of, 'I've something to show for what we've been doing.' That's still a huge reassurance, for me, and my biggest defence against anybody who might say, 'What do you do here all day? You don't do anything; you don't have a lesson plan.' And I can say, 'Well, no, but I can show you what we did every day this week, and how rich it was.' So that feels like money in the bank, knowing that those stories are there.

Laurie: the phenomenological connection

There seems to be a strong parallel between phenomenology, particularly Max van Manen's description of human science research, and the experience of Ann and Sarah as documentors. The way in which each stands in pedagogical relation to the world, and their abilities to write reflectively on the meanings of phenomena of daily life lived in this community, are reflected in these words of van Manen's (1990, p 2):

> Pedagogy requires a phenomenological sensitivity to lived experience (children's realities and life-worlds). Pedagogy requires a hermeneutic ability to make interpretive sense of the phenomena of the life-world in order to see the pedagogic significance of situations and relations of living with children. And pedagogy requires a way with language in order to allow the research process of textual reflection to one's pedagogic thoughtfulness and tact.

What these particular teachers are doing in their everyday practice appears to be, indeed, un-named phenomenological research of the lived experience of these teachers and children.

Laurie, Ann and Sarah: the disposition to document

Ann and Sarah have each had a remarkable, intuitive response to the work of educators in Reggio Emilia, a response that resonates with a vision of great possibilities. Keen observational skills, delight in and curiosity about children, the ability to articulate and put into text their reflections, a commitment to nurturing relationships, and intellectual engagement that is fostered by the active role of researcher are all dispositions that these teachers bring to their work. This list is also the description of the phenomenological researcher. It may be that it is a relationship of reciprocity—that perhaps initially Ann and Sarah were drawn to the ideas from Reggio Emilia because they resonated within each of them in an intuitive way, and that their subsequent work with pedagogical documentation has fostered dispositions that each already had. Van Manen (1990, p 1) writes, 'when we raise questions, gather data, describe a phenomenon, we do so as researchers who stand in the world in a pedagogic way'. This way of standing in the world is reflected in the way that Ann and Sarah speak of their experience as both teachers and as documentors.

Teaching is excruciatingly complex, idiosyncratic, back-breaking, mind-boggling, exhausting, wrenching. Teaching at its best requires heart and mind, passion and intellect, insight and intuition, spirit, understanding, and judgment. As Ayers (2002, pp 39–40) says:

> Teaching can be an act of hope and love—love for persons, love for life, and hope for a world that could be, but is not yet. Teaching can be, must be if it is to maintain its moral balance, a gesture toward justice.

References

Ayers W (2002) Creating the teacher and changing the world. In E Mirochnik & D Sherman (Eds) *Passion and pedagogy: Relation, creation, and transformation in teaching*. New York: Peter Lang.

Beneke S, Harris-Helm J & Steinheimer K (1998) *Windows on learning: Documenting young children's work*. New York: Teacher's College Press.

Burrington B & Sortino S (2004) In our real world: An anatomy of documentation. In J Hendrick (Ed) *Next steps to teaching the Reggio way: Accepting the challenge to change* (pp 224–37). New Jersey: Pearson.

Cadwell L (1997) *Bringing Reggio Emilia home: An innovative approach to early childhood education*. New York: Teachers College Press.

Cadwell L (2003) *Bringing learning to life: The Reggio approach to early childhood education*. New York: Teachers College Press.

Commune di Reggio Emilia (1987) *To make a portrait of a lion*. [Video]. Reggio Emilia: Centro Documentazione Ricerca Educativa Nidi e Scuole dell'Infanzia.

Dahlberg G, Moss P & Pence A (1999) *Beyond quality in early childhood education and care: Postmodern perspectives*. London: Falmer Press.

Gandini L & Goldhaber J (2001) Two reflections about documentation. In L Gandini & CP Edwards (Eds) *Bambini: The Italian approach to infant/toddler care*. (pp 124–35). New York: Teachers College Press.

Giudici C, Krechevsky M & Rinaldi C (Eds) (2001) *Making learning visible: Children as individual and group learners*. Reggio Emilia, Italy: Reggio Children.

Kocher L (1999) *Butterfly transformations: Using the documentation process modelled in the schools of Reggio Emilia, Italy*. Unpublished Master's thesis. Victoria, BC: University of Victoria.

Krechevsky M and Mardell B (2001) Four features of learning in groups. In C Giudici, M Krechevsky and C Rinaldi (Eds) *Making learning visible: Children as individual and group learners*. (pp 284–94). Reggio Emilia, Italy: Reggio Children.

Readings B (1996) *The university in ruins*. Cambridge MA: Harvard University Press.

Richardson L (2000) Writing: A method of inquiry. In NK Denzin & YA Lincoln (Eds) *Handbook of qualitative research* (pp 923–48). Newbury Park, CA: Sage Publications.

Rinaldi C (1998) Projected curriculum constructed through documentation— *Progettazione*. In C Edwards, L Gandini & G Forman (Eds) *The hundred languages of children: The Reggio Emilia approach—Advanced reflections*. (2nd Ed) (pp 113–25). Greenwich, CT: Ablex.

Seidel S (2001) Understanding documentation starts at home. In C Giudici, M Krechevsky & C Rinaldi (Eds) *Making learning visible: Children as individual and group learners*. (pp 304–11). Reggio Emilia, Italy: Reggio Children.

Shafer A (2002) Ordinary moments: Extraordinary possibilities. In V Fu, A Stremmel & L Hill (Eds) *Teaching and learning: Collaborative exploration of the Reggio Emilia approach.* (pp 183–95) New Jersey: Merrill Prentice Hall.

van Manen M (1990) *Researching lived experience: Human science for an action sensitive pedagogy.* New York: SUNY Press.

van Manen M (1991) *The tact of teaching: The meaning of pedagogical thoughtfulness.* Albany, NY: SUNY Press.

Wheatley M (1999) *Leadership and the new science: Discovering order in a chaotic world.* San Francisco: Berrett-Koeheler Publishers.

Zeichner K (1999) Research on teacher thinking and different views of reflective practice in teaching and teacher education. In I Carlgren, G Handal & S Vaage (Eds) *Teachers' minds and actions: Research on teachers' thinking and practice* (pp 9–27). London: Falmer Press.

Chapter Five

Stories from *Aotearoa*/New Zealand

Kiri Gould
Lesley Pohio

The examples from practice used in this chapter come from Akarana Avenue Kindergarten located in Auckland, Aotearoa/New Zealand.[1] Akarana is one of 107 not-for-profit, sessional kindergartens managed by the Auckland Kindergarten Association. The kindergarten employs three trained teachers and has 90 children. It offers eight sessions a week with 45 children attending each session. The children range in age from three to five years.

---

[1] *Aotearoa* is the Māori name for New Zealand.

There is a well known Whakatauki (proverb) in Aotearoa which says:

Tuia te rangi e Tū iho nei
Tuia te papa e takoto nei

Whakatauki

Join sky above to earth below
Just as people join together

Māori proverb

Introduction

In this chapter we use several examples from practice to examine the themes of social justice, pedagogical documentation and *Te Whāriki*[2] (the early childhood curriculum for Aotearoa/New Zealand). We suggest that the principles outlined in *Te Whāriki* have the potential to be emancipatory if early childhood teachers are willing to engage with these ideas in their practice. We show that the use of pedagogical documentation can create a public space where teachers, children and families contribute to the planning and interpretation of learning experiences for children. Involvement in this process can be empowering for children and their families as they begin to see their 'real lives' reflected in the kindergarten curriculum. Our final point is that documentation alone does not ensure that curriculum is empowering for families. This practice must sit alongside efforts to build reciprocal relationships with families so that they feel they are able to participate safely.

This chapter shows how documentation has been used to invite families to participate in creating meaningful educational experiences for the children at the centre. The teachers at the kindergarten work closely with the families, who actively participate in a range of ways to support the kindergarten program. The kindergarten reflects the mixed socioeconomic and culturally diverse local community. Many of the families have a long established history with the community and it is also a settling place for many new immigrants. The kindergarten's philosophy both reflects and is underpinned by the early childhood curriculum, *Te Whāriki* (Ministry of Education, 1996, p 10), which is founded on the following aspirations for children:

---

2 *Te Whāriki*: The New Zealand National Early Childhood Curriculum. The name literally means a mat because it is envisaged that the curriculum is woven from the principles, strands and goals that make up the document. Each distinct early childhood service in New Zealand will weave their own *whāriki* depending on their own philosophy and structure. These differences make up the different patterns of the *whāriki*.

To grow up as competent and confident learners and communicators, healthy in mind, body, and spirit, secure in their sense of belonging and in the knowledge that they make a valued contribution to society.

Finding out what happens here—sharing teaching and learning experiences

When parents first visit an early childhood centre, they look around to see what happens at that centre. They are looking to see whether their children will be happy there; whether they will 'fit in'. They are also asking themselves, 'Do we fit?' or, 'How will I fit?' As they look around they are searching for clues that might help them to answer these questions. A parent looking around Akarana Avenue Kindergarten for the first time would find many clues that would help them answer the question: 'What happens here?'. High quality visual documentation of the children's experiences at the kindergarten are everywhere. Photos, children's work, and descriptions of learning interpreted by teachers, children and families provide a picture of the past, present and future learning opportunities for children at the centre.

A parent walking around Akarana Avenue Kindergarten today might stop at the photographic display of a recent multicultural festival held at a local park. The cultures of many of the children at the kindergarten were represented at the festival. These photos are positioned alongside pictures of children re-creating their home experiences in their play at the kindergarten. In one photo, for example, the children are making roti at the play dough table. Added to this display, our new parent can read the voice of another parent sharing a similar story about their child's play at home. As she continues reading, she sees how these simple shared experiences have unfolded into a series of events run by families who also wanted to share cooking experiences from their own cultures. She reads how a group of Sri Lankan families, encouraged by the displays, organised a session where they introduced a range of Sri Lankan foods, music and crafts. Around the photos of this day are stories written by other centre families sharing their experiences of the event. A video of the day and a recipe book are also positioned nearby. Through a conversation with a teacher, she learns how a copy of the video was sent to an extended family in Sri Lanka as a way of sharing information about life in New Zealand. Our new parent thinks about family recipes she might be able to share and wonders if she will have the courage to participate in this way.

Nearby, a group of children and parents are gathered around a laptop computer. The computer is placed on a low table for the children to access. Today it is running through a slide show of recent events at the centre. The children are enjoying seeing themselves involved in a range of learning experiences. The adults are provided with a window into the kinds of work their children are involved with at the centre. Our new parent joins the group to watch the slide show and together they talk about 'what happens here' as well as 'what might happen here next'.

She notices a beautiful mosaic table. As the new parent admires the work, she also reads a display which outlines the centre community's growing interest in mosaic. The display tells the story of how this interest has unfolded into a long-term project involving children, teachers and parents learning together. She reads how this project grew from one family's interest and passion for mosaic that was willingly shared with the kindergarten community. She reads about the various mosaic projects occurring around the centre. Other stories tell how children's and parents' interest in mosaic grew and about how they developed skills in mosaic together, through a workshop organised for the local community. She is surprised and excited. She wonders what her child will become involved in and whether she will become involved too.

Sharing curriculum—hearing the voices of family and community

The sharing of the teaching and learning experiences through documentation shows the new parent that there is a culture of openness at the kindergarten. She can see that the relationships between children, families and teachers at the centre are collaborative. She comes to realise that shared experience is central to the kindergarten's program. The documentation describes how interests and experiences have developed at this kindergarten and provides for her an inter-active picture of past, present and future possibilities. The accessibility of the displays, alongside the relationships fostered by the teachers at the centre, creates opportunities for teachers and families to reflect, review and evaluate the work that they create together.

At the heart of this practice is the desire to develop environments that are relevant to the lives of the children and the families who use the kindergarten. They are attempting to create a program that empowers children and families to be active participants in the teaching and learning processes at the centre. The displays about both the mosaic and cooking experiences show how families were able to develop, participate in and interpret learning experiences for their own children.

Canella (1997, p 2) proposes that many of the beliefs and practices that guide the field of early childhood education 'support the status quo, reinforce prejudice and stereotypes, and ignore the real lives of children (and other human beings such as parents and teachers)'. She warns that our views of early childhood education are too narrow, and are positioned within a particular cultural and historical knowledge base (white, patriarchal, middle class and Euro-American) that not only ignores but also silences other perspectives. Canella (1997) asks early childhood teachers to find ways to hear the voices that have previously been silenced and to construct with children, their families and communities collective visions of education that accept multiple perspectives, values, and truths. The teachers at this kindergarten are using pedagogical documentation to access and invite the 'real lives' of the children in their community into the curriculum.

Te Whāriki—promoting the child in context

These kinds of practices are supported by *Te Whāriki* (Ministry of Education, 1996), Aotearoa/New Zealand's national early childhood curriculum. *Te Whāriki* also challenges teachers to acknowledge the 'real lives' of children. This challenge is most evident in the four principles which have been developed around principles of *Māori* pedagogy: empowerment (*whakamana*); holistic development (*kotahitanga*); family and community (*whānau tangata*) and relationships (*ngā hononga*). Key statements from each of these principles are:

Empowerment/Whakamana
The early childhood curriculum empowers children to learn and grow. Early childhood care and education services assist children and their families to develop independence and to access the resources necessary to enable them to direct their own lives (p 40).

Holistic development/Kotahitanga
The early childhood curriculum takes up a model of learning that weaves together intricate patterns of linked experience and meaning rather than emphasising the acquisition of discrete skills (p 41).

Family and community/Whānau tangata
The wider world of family and community is an integral part of the early childhood curriculum… The wellbeing of children is interdependent with the wellbeing and culture of: adults in the early childhood setting; whānau/families; local communities and neighbourhoods (p 42).

Relationships/Ngā hononga
Children learn through responsive and reciprocal relationships with people, places and things (p 43).

These statements illustrate that *Te Whāriki* places its focus on the child in the context of family and community. It emphasises the 'critical role of socially and culturally mediated learning' (p 9).

Careful consideration of the principles in *Te Whāriki* can enable early childhood teachers to respond to some of the criticisms of traditional early childhood practice such as those put forward by Canella (1997). Just as Canella (1997) challenges early childhood educators to find ways to hear the voices of the children we teach, so does *Te Whāriki* require teachers to consider and engage with the wider contexts of each child's life and to develop curriculum that is empowering not only for the child, but also for the family. Keesing-Styles (2002, p 10) points out that *Te Whāriki* 'promotes an educational approach with the potential for the implementation of programmes that are inclusive and emancipatory'. Other writers have also identified the parallels between *Te Whāriki* and the principles of critical pedagogy which aims at the empowerment of students by hearing and responding to their voices and the voices of their communities (Ritchie, 1996). This requires teachers to investigate and implement ways of inviting children, their *whānau* and the community to negotiate and participate in the curriculum. It challenges teachers to seek other perspectives about children's learning (including the perspectives of the child) and to accept diverse interpretations of learning and possibilities for teaching.

In addition, *Te Whāriki* contains a curriculum in *te reo Māori* (Māori language) specifically for *Ngā Kohanga Reo* (Māori language-immersion early childhood centres) that is a parallel document rather than a direct translation of the English language version. It recognises the principle of partnership inherent in *Te Tiriti o Waitangi* (The Treaty of Waitangi). In addition, the bicultural nature of the curriculum is reflected throughout the entire document in its careful consideration of the social, cultural and political contexts of Aotearoa/New Zealand. (Te One, 2003). Therefore, it is a curriculum that 'interweaves educational theory, political ideology, and a profound knowledge of the importance of culture' (p 42).

The extent to which the emancipatory potential of *Te Whāriki* is realised, however, depends on the degree to which early childhood teachers in Aotearoa/New Zealand are willing and able to meet the challenges of the principles in their own teaching practice. *Te Whāriki* avoids prescribing one educational approach. Instead, each early childhood service is expected to weave its own *whāriki* (mat) from the principles, goals and strands set out in the document. There is evidence that some early childhood teachers in Aotearoa/New Zealand struggle with how to use *Te Whāriki* as a guide to practice. Cullen (2003, p 272), for example, states:

> …it could still be argued that the ideals of *Te Whāriki* have barely been touched in many of our early childhood centres, and that many of the programmes today look remarkably like those of the 1980's and 1990's when the terms 'free play' and 'developmental' dominated the discourse of early childhood education.

Using documentation—making practice public

The teachers at Akarana Avenue Kindergarten use pedagogical documentation to respond to the principles of *Te Whāriki* in their work with children and families.

The documentation at the kindergarten serves several purposes. It makes public the work of the children and their teachers. It can reify the importance of the work that occurs there as well as the practices and values of the kindergarten. By making this work public it invites reflection on the purpose, value and direction of the work of children and teachers.

The documentation of shared cooking experiences, for example, reinforces the notion that real experiences are valuable learning opportunities for children. It also sends a clear message that contributions from the diverse range of families are valuable and central to curriculum for all children. Readers of this documentation would also come to know that the interests of children and the skills and strengths of their families and teachers shape the kindergarten's program. All of these groups are able to contribute to the way this program unfolds. Rinaldi (2001, p 83) emphasises this aspect of documentation when she writes:

> Documentation, therefore, is seen as visible listening as the constructions of traces, (through slide shows, notes, videos and so on) that not only testify to the children's learning paths and processes, but also make them possible because they are visible. For us this means making visible, and thus possible, the relationships that are the building blocks of knowledge.

Pedagogical documentation allows teachers to examine their own practices. Teachers, children and families are able to interpret, reflect and contribute to the happenings of the kindergarten because documentation invites a dialogue among them. This dialogue creates multiple perspectives and interpretations. Rinaldi (2001, p 84) points out that the 'result is knowledge that is bountiful and enriched by the contributions of many'.

'Learning stories' as documentation

'Learning stories' (Carr, Cowie, Gerrity, Jones, Lee, and Pohio, 2001) are one form of pedagogical documentation that can be used to create sites of shared dialogue. The use of learning stories is rapidly being picked up by early childhood teachers in Aotearoa/New Zealand as a form of pedagogical documentation that contributes to assessment procedures in New Zealand centres. Carr *et al.* (2001, p 29) define learning stories as:

> ...a particular form of documented and structured observations that take a storied approach and a non-deficit (credit) approach, and an underlying agenda of protecting and developing children's identities as learners in accordance with the national early childhood curriculum, *Te Whāriki*.

They are often supplemented with photos and copies of children's work, and can be written from the perspective of the teacher, the child, or the *whānau* (extended family). The teachers at Akarana encourage families to write learning stories in their own voices and from their own perspectives. Often these stories are written in the family's home language and translated later on. Children are also encouraged to contribute to the writing of their own learning stories. Therefore, one learning experience has the potential to be recorded and interpreted in several different ways. Each interpretation is considered valuable. The multiple interpretations of learning experiences contribute to the construction of a shared picture of the learning that occurs at the kindergarten, as well as possibilities for future learning.

One mother contributed the following learning story about her son, Hikurangi, after the kindergarten (including many families) visited a local *marae* (a traditional meeting place). The *marae* visit was part of a much wider centre interest that began with exploring *kowhaiwhai* patterns and unfolded into a range of experiences around *tikanga Māori*. As *manuhiri* (visitors) to the *marae*, the kindergarten community was welcomed with a *powhiri* (traditional welcome ceremony). Stories of the carvings and panels inside the *marae* were shared as part of this experience. The visit ended with a shared meal in the *wharekai* (dining hall) next to the *marae*. Frances (Hikurangi's mother) writes:

> Hikurangi and Joel held hands and were very quiet and focused during the *karanga* as we were called onto the *Marae*—as were the other children. Hikurangi liked the *waiata* in the *wharenui*, especially 'Whakaaria Mai' which both the *Tangata Whānau* and *manuhiri* sang together, before the *whaikorero* began. After the *powhiri*, Hikurangi drew a picture of a tarantula, which he said would live in Tane's forest. At home, he talked about M's dad speaking in the *wharenui* and remembered seeing his *Koro* (Granddad, my father) doing the same on our *marae*. He loved the *wharekai* too because 'we all ate together'. It was a wonderful, warm, positive experience—*Kia Ora*.

Other families wrote of how some aspects of the marae experience were similar to their own cultures. The experience was interpreted in multiple ways, each valued and valuable for future experiences.

It should also be noted here that the kind of assessment promoted in learning stories is formative. Carr *et al.* (2001) use the following definition of assessment from Drummond (1993, p 13) who states that assessment is the 'ways in which, in our everyday practice, we observe children's learning, strive to understand it, and then put our understanding to good use'. Therefore, assessment through learning stories is not about checking to see what children can and can not do against a list of predetermined skills and competencies but is about creating a shared picture of each child in order to be able to plan for further learning experiences. Carr *et al.* (2001, p 29) have pointed out the potential of the learning stories for enabling teachers, children and communities to engage in dialogue together about learning and teaching and that learning stories (and similar kinds of formative, narrative and credit-based assessment models) can contribute to forming 'democratic communities of learning and teaching'.

Pedagogical documentation, including the use of learning stories as a form of assessment, can be one way that early childhood teachers in New Zealand address the principles in *Te Whāriki*, and begin to address issues of empowerment and social justice in their own practice. However, pedagogical documentation alone cannot achieve this. Documentation can invite participation from centre families, but real participation will only be achieved when it sits within a context that has strong, positive and reciprocal relationships with families. The responsibility for this lies with teachers who must find ways to build these relationships. Pedagogical documentation can then be used to affirm the importance of these relationships and to hear the voices that tell us about the 'real lives' of children.

karanga	call of welcome onto a marae
Kia Ora	greetings/hello
Koro	Grandfather
kowhaiwhai	traditional *Māori* art form based on a spiral shape, often seen on the rafters of a marae
marae	traditional meeting place
powhiri	traditional welcome ceremony
Tane	God of forests and birds
Tangata Whānau	community/family
waiata	song
whaikorero	formal speech
whānau	extended family
wharekai	dining hall
wharenui	meeting house

References

Canella GS (1997) *Deconstructing early childhood education: Social justice and revolution.* New York: Peter Lang.

Carr M, Cowie B, Gerrity R, Jones C, Lee W & Pohio L (2001) *Democratic learning and teaching communities in early childhood: Can assessment play a role?* Paper presented to the Early Childhood Education for a Democratic Society Conference. Wellington: Council for Educational Research.

Cullen J (2003) The challenge of *Te Whāriki*: Catalyst for change? In J Nuttall (Ed) *Weaving Te Whāriki: Aotearoa/New Zealand's early childhood curriculum document in theory and practice.* (pp 269–90). Wellington: New Zealand Council for Early Childhood Research.

Drummond MJ (1993) *Assessing children's learning.* London: David Fulton.

Keesing-Styles L (2002) A critical pedagogy of early childhood education: The Aotearoa/New Zealand context. *New Zealand Research in Early Childhood Education.* 5, 109–22.

Ministry of Education (1996) *Te Whāriki: He whāriki mātauranga mō ngā mokopuna o Aotearoa. Early Childhood Curriculum.* Wellington: Learning Media.

Rinaldi C (2001). Documentation and assessment: What is the relationship? In C Giudici, M Krechevsky & C Rinaldi (Eds) *Making learning visible: Children as individual and group learners.* (pp 78–90). Reggio Emilia, Italy: Reggio Children.

Ritchie J (1996) Early childhood education as critical pedagogy. In H May & M Carr (Eds). *Implementing Te Whāriki: Te Whāriki Papers 2.* (pp 113–25). Wellington and Hamilton: Institute for Early Childhood Studies, Victoria University of Wellington and Department of Early Childhood Studies, University of Waikato.

Te One S (2003) The Context for *Te Whāriki*: Contemporary issues of influence. In J Nuttall (Ed) *Weaving Te Whāriki: Aotearoa/New Zealand's Early Childhood Curriculum Document in Theory and Practice.* (pp 17–43). Wellington: New Zealand Council for Early Childhood Research.

Response to Part One

First Principles

Commentators

Jan Millikan
Margie Carter and John Nimmo

Jan's response

In responding to this cluster of chapters, my reference point for the term 'pedagogical documentation' is from both Dahlberg, Moss & Pence (1999) and a personal communication in 2002 with Vea Vechi, a former *Atelierista* in Reggio Emilia. Dahlberg's coining of the phrase came from the intention of differentiating the way the Reggio Emilia educators were working with documentation as opposed to its common use in education in many countries of the world. The educators in Reggio Emilia, as well as many other educators, have also now adopted Dahlberg's term in discussing the process and content of their work. However, as with many other influences on their work, the Reggio Emilia educators have made it their 'own'.

The key concept I am borrowing as my reference for this response is: 'The Pedagogy of Listening' (Rinaldi, 2003), which emphasises listening with curiosity to the many possible forms of communication by children, colleagues, and parents using all the senses and possible literacies available to us. This involves a desire to understand and find meaning through putting aside certainties and being open to the possibility of changing our minds. The processes involve documenting, theorising, revisiting, reflecting, and collaborating in the constructing and co-constructing of understanding within a context of democracy. Does this also create a context for social justice?

Each of the writers in this cluster of chapters has also made pedagogical documentation their own by relating it to both their cultural context and their vision. They explain how they have created living spaces for children and adults that heighten awareness of the other. This provides the opportunity for creating, and rejoicing in, reciprocal relationships where differences are valued and where no one is anonymous.

Each of the writers invites us to share a provocation in their own particular setting and they identify their particular concerns regarding issues of social justice. They also demonstrate the use of very different possibilities in their ways of working with their identified provocation and their own form of pedagogical documentation.

Janet Robertson in her work with very young children explores the idea of the socially and personally constructed child and challenges our preconceived ideas about the potentials of very young children. Her pedagogical documentation describing the interactions of the children is powerful in advocating for the rights of the child. We are offered the opportunity to reflect on our limited expectations, and perhaps failure, in realising children's potentials in both senses of the word. She also challenges us in asking 'who is responsible for advocating for the rights of children' and illustrates that pedagogical documentation can provide a powerful medium in giving the children a voice that can in turn allow children to be heard.

Janet also refers to the role of the adult in determining appropriate behaviours and consequences, to ensure a sense of wellbeing and belonging for very young children. This raises an interesting question: When does the adult relinquish control in determining what comprises a socially just classroom? When does democracy begin?

The chapter written by Kiri Gould and Lesley Pohio sharing their stories from Aotearoa/New Zealand explores another role that pedagogical documentation can take. This documentation makes visible and accessible the lives of children within their families and the community, as well as in their centre. This intentional openness creates a space for dialogue and provides the opportunity to reverse the traditional role of 'parent as listener' to 'teachers as listeners' in the Rinaldi (1998) sense of the word. The point is strongly made that pedagogical documentation in and of itself will not ensure that social justice is attained for all, but in this instance it provides the possibility for a whole community to listen to each other, which in turn opens the door for meaningful dialogue. The further documentation detailing the response by the families to the visibility of everyday lives can result in revisiting and reflecting, and for developing strategies in the process of this evolving project.

The chapters contributed by Jill McLachlan and the authors from Hilltop Children's Center, Sarah Felstiner and Ann Pelo with Laurie Kocher, address the issue of children's relationships with each other. One of their shared provocations is how to appropriately provide a process for enculturating social values within a particular community of learners.

Jill McLachlan illustrates that the role of the teacher can be powerful, both in determining what acceptable behaviour is and in instigating a process to heighten awareness of those behaviours. Pedagogical documentation is a wonderful tool enabling us as educators to be researchers in the classroom. Jill's experience opens up many questions in relation to children's choices based on gender:

• When do children begin to show a preference for being with others of their own gender?

• Why does this happen?

• Could this be more than discriminatory behaviour, and perhaps an important part of human development?

These are difficult and complicated issues.

This takes us back to the powerful competent child that Janet describes. When are children ready to be part of the decision-making process in determining what is socially just? As adults we have a responsibility in ensuring social justice for all children, but how long do we keep making the decisions? The writers from the Hilltop Center demonstrate both the joy, but also the strength when documentation makes children's lives visible and allows educators the opportunity to reflect together. Their documentation also allows the reader to be involved in the meaning making. As reciprocal learners, these authors refer to the importance of looking deeply at what is occurring and what is underlying children's play, asking the all-important question of not only 'what?' but also 'why?'. This collaborative aspect of interpreting documentation is a crucial factor in the work of educators in the programs for young children in the city of Reggio Emilia. Unfortunately, this collaborative process is extremely difficult in some Australian settings when there is only one teacher in a classroom. If collaboration is viewed as a key factor in pedagogical documentation then the issue of organisation becomes critical.

The involvement of parents in discussing the anti-bias curriculum acknowledges that social justice is not just something that is in the classroom, but needs to be a way of living and believing, the essence of life itself. The authors identify three dispositions that are a key in their classrooms that involve acting and speaking for peace, tolerance and justice.

I believe that this raises an issue for us about universal values. Can we translate values across cultures? Is the word 'tolerance' always appropriate or should some cultural practices not be tolerated? Who decides? A colleague shared a story with me of a conversation with her five-year-old, discussing the death of an aged relative and why she had died. His final comment, after some reflection, was 'who is actually in charge of the world?'

In the democratic classroom, is it the adults who decide what is fair? Do we have the curiosity to ask the children their thoughts about social issues? Who decides what is socially just? Is it possible, that in being socially just to one child or a group of children, we inadvertently are unjust to others?

The writers of these chapters are to be commended for their demonstrated concerns for the recognition of the rights of all children and their awareness, in differing situations, of how insidiously rights may be jeopardised and rejection experienced. Through making their stories visible they provide the opportunity for us to reflect on their theories and compare them with our own, and hopefully have the opportunity to debate them with others.

I believe that social justice is inextricably entwined in a 'pedagogy of relationships', enabled by a 'pedagogy of listening' made visible through documentation. In an impossibly difficult world we must all have the courage to keep hope alive for a desired world that we strive for and build together, communities where everybody has a sense of peace, fulfilment, wellbeing, and belonging.

References

Dahlberg G, Moss P & Pence A (1999) *Beyond quality in early childhood education and care: Postmodern perspectives*. London: Falmer Press.

Rinaldi C (1998) Projected curriculum constructed through documentation—
Progettazione: An interview with Lella Gandini. In C Edwards, L Gandini &
G Forman (Eds) *The hundred languages of children: the Reggio Emilia approach*—
Advanced reflections. (2nd Ed). (pp 113–125). Greenwich, CT: Ablex.

Rinaldi C (2003) The pedagogy of listening: The listening perspective from
Reggio Emilia. *Innovations in early education: the international Reggio exchange.*
Merrill-Palmer Institute, Wayne State University.

About Jan Millikan

Jan Millikan was requested by the City of Reggio Emilia in 1994, to be their
reference person for Australia and New Zealand. Jan established the Reggio
Emilia Information Exchange (REIE) in 1995 to provide a structure for
disseminating information and providing a forum for discussion and debate
related to the principles of Reggio Emilia, and the possible implications for
Australian Education. REIE (Australia) is now an incorporated body with an
elected committee and Jan is employed by the committee as the Director of the
organisation. She is also an Associate of the Education Faculty at Monash
University, a member of the Research Committee and a Primary Years Program
educator for the International Baccalaureate Organisation. She is Chairperson
of the Victorian Education panel for the Churchill Fellowship Organisation
of Australia.

Margie and John's Response

Reading these chapters provoked a lively discussion between the two of us and
led us to think further about our own teacher education work in the United
States. Because we each straddle the worlds of academia and long day child care
programs, we particularly appreciate that each of the writers is a practising
teacher of children who is diligently engaged in what Brazilian educator, Paulo
Freire (1921–1997) calls 'praxis'. Here, they are reflecting on the teaching and
learning process as it relates to some of the central considerations for educators
today:

• the quality of relationships among children, families, teachers, and the community;

• the significance of the culture and context of those engaged in the process; and

• the depth and complexity of curriculum explorations.

Each of the writers is speaking from varied teaching experiences which shape
their reflections on ideas that are important to them and these ideas, in turn,
shape their teaching practices—the cyclical process of praxis which Freire asserts

leads to critical thinking and education as empowerment. As we discussed these chapters, we found ourselves nodding and rejoicing at the implied connections among some of the important ideas these teachers considered—the desire to share power; to be intentional in interactions; to cultivate meaningful curriculum; to see learning as lives being lived; and to use documentation as a tool for ever-deepening reflection. We found ourselves wanting to tease out the possible tensions among their ideas and practices as well, believing that discovering these will prod us to think more deeply about the intersection of pedagogical documentation and social justice. We share here the sparks that flew out for us, the things we wonder about, and the challenging questions we are eager to see explored further.

The quality of relationships

We begin with Jill's resolution in Chapter Two to 'walk beside' children, rather than lead them, and hear resonance with the Hilltop teachers' assertion in Chapter Four that they are building a life (not simply a curriculum) with the children. There is something here that goes beyond the typical focus on the social world in early education. What are the implications of Sarah and Ann's deeply intimate view of documentation as 'love letters' to the children and how does this envelope reach out to include families, even those who don't think and act like us, as active participants in the classroom? Kiri and Lesley call for a democratic community of learning in which documentation reveals the real lives of the children as members of families and communities. What is the role of conflict in the process of such relationship building?

In Chapter Three, Janet warns us about the assumptions and biases that invade our images of the child (and children) and asks us to use documentation as a mirror for self-examination. In this sense, relationships are never really as simple as a transaction between two people. What are the challenges for early childhood teachers in rejoicing in the intricacy and individuality of each relationship while also being open to the multiple connections and perspectives that intersect with each child's identity and history?

The significance of culture and context

In Chapter Two, we see that Jill clearly created a classroom culture of acceptance and collaboration. So when the children began 'the tactics of avoidance' based on gender, she felt like they were being 'robbed of "our culture", that which made us "us"'. This is poignant and leads us directly to Janet's discussion of individual versus collective rights in Chapter Three, so we wonder how a more explicit culture of 'we' might have re-shaped Jill's initial ambivalence to act. If we subscribe to Janet's assertion that the notion of rights is culturally bound, how does a teacher go about forming a classroom culture that seeks to continually widen the circle and include multiple perspectives?

From Kiri and Lesley in Chapter Five, we hear so clearly the experience of families encountering a classroom culture and looking for clues as to whether they and their children will 'fit in'. Visual documentation offers both the potential to widen the lens of how the classroom culture is understood, and simultaneously offers the power to shape that culture. This is particularly true when documentation reflects the experiences of children's homes, as well as the insights of parents on the children's experiences—as happens in Akarana Avenue Kindergarten. We wonder how the 'culture of research' at Hilltop Children's Center that Laurie, Ann and Sarah describe in Chapter Four, might look different if the reflection of parents were as prominent as they are in Akarana Avenue. Would they uncover any significant diversity in their perspectives? With the Hilltop population strongly reflective of the dominant culture of the United States (middle-class European American), will more visibility of their views just further marginalise the views of those not part of the dominant culture of the US? Do children have a right to have their own families dominate the visual images of a centre or is it equally important that their right to experience multiple perspectives prevail?

The depth and complexity of curriculum explorations

All of these teachers seek a meaningful curriculum for children, one that goes beyond the banal and ever pressing emphasis on outcomes and assessments. We hear wonderful examples of seeing children—the way Janet implores us to see them—as 'greedy for knowledge and meaning'. Jill's journey with Year 1 learners leads her to seek out their real concerns and questions, while in Seattle the teachers analyse their documentation to identify the children's underlying developmental themes. All this talk pushes us to ask, 'What do children have the right to know about?' Are we willing to say that all curriculum options should be available to children, or are there some developmental concerns that should always be considered? On the one hand, it is a privileged position to want to protect children from difficult issues, particularly when we see how engaged they are with the deeper issues of fairness, power, life and death. On the other hand, we must consider the kind of meaning they will make of complex issues with which they have little experience. Is it our responsibility to carefully design provocations that will lead the children to explore issues of social justice?

In Chapter Four, Ann argues that a social justice approach requires that teachers engage in close observation of the questions and ideas of children. We agree that transformative education must be grounded in the lives of the learners, but we also notice that child-centred approaches do not always address inequity. To be meaningful, curriculum has to be tied to the wider context of children's lives. Yet so many of the teachers we coach and educate see curriculum in narrow ways —as the pursuit of formal academic knowledge, or as 'interests' contained in an individual child or brewing among a group of children. Kiri and Lesley tell us that the *Te Whāriki* curriculum draws on the connectedness of children to family, community and culture. What dispositions and skills do early childhood teachers need in order to cast a wide net in their thinking about the roots of curriculum?

To conclude, we return to the reflective stance to which each of these educators is so clearly committed. Pedagogical documentation requires teachers to see themselves, the children and their families as researchers, and to engage in collaborative reflection to make meaning together. The 'reflective text', that seems so personal and intimate in nature, must at the same time be a public record in which multiple interpretations become part of the story (see Chapter Five). Collectively, these chapters tell us stories about how pedagogical documentation can be a dynamic encounter between the journey of each teacher, the forging of relationships, and the defining power of history and community.

About Margie Carter

Margie Carter is an adjunct faculty member in the Human Development Department of Pacific Oaks College and also with a local, two-year, community college Child and Family Studies program. She is the co-author of numerous early childhood books and staff development videos, inspired by the values and principles of the Reggio Emilia approach and what is referred to in the US as culturally relevant, anti-bias practices. Margie travels widely to speak, consult and conduct seminars. She is passionate about the role of play in childhood and constructivist learning for children and teachers. For several years, Margie and John Nimmo taught a course collaboratively on Emergent Curriculum at Pacific Oaks.

About John Nimmo

John Nimmo is Executive Director of the Child Study and Development Center and Associate Professor in Family Studies at the University of New Hampshire. Previously he was on the faculty at Pacific Oaks College in Seattle where he began collaborating with Margie Carter. John holds a doctorate in ECE from the University of Massachusetts and was a preschool and kindergarten teacher in his home country of Australia for over a decade. His publications include the popular NAEYC book *Emergent Curriculum* (with Betty Jones) and contributions to both editions of *The Hundred Languages of Children*. John was a Keynote speaker at the first conference on the Reggio Emilia experience in Australia in 1994 and was a Visiting Scholar at Macquarie University in 2002. John is currently exploring the connections between young children in child care and the broader adult community

Part Two

Beginnings

Chapter Six

Growing into Documenting: Stories of War and Secret Places

Belinda Connerton
Catherine Patterson

This chapter is based on an interview between Belinda, a teacher, and Catherine, a university colleague. When the interview was taking place, Belinda was in the process of a career transition. She was preparing to move from a culturally diverse, community-based, urban child care centre in metropolitan Sydney to a new position as teacher of a long day care centre in a small country town in New South Wales. She saw the interview as an opportunity to reflect on her experiences in the child care centre, while at the same time, to consider her new role and its implications for her commitment to pedagogical documentation. At the Sydney child care centre, Belinda was one of a team of three staff with 25 three to five-year-olds. Most children attended on a full-time basis with all children attending at least three days per week. Catherine asked the questions in this interview.

Introduction

This chapter provides insights into Belinda's reflections on her journeys into pedagogical documentation and highlights the importance of a reflective network of colleagues and friends to support the process. Examples are included of several explorations of events that evolved into pieces of pedagogical documentation. These include a tower building experience related to September 11, an exchange with an inner city centre that became *Who are the Koori[1] kids?* and conversations with an individual child: *Life, death and the universe: William reflects.* Issues related to social justice and world events are threaded through the children's experiences and Belinda's approach to pedagogical documentation. The authors identify a number of key points for consideration by others who are thinking through their progress along their own documenting journey.

Let's talk about your experiences with pedagogical documentation. Can you tell us how you got started with this way of working?

Yes, I'd heard of the ideas from Reggio Emilia before I graduated from university. I completed my last student teaching experience as an external student and I remember seeing a video of ideas from Reggio Emilia and talking about it during the on-campus session. I remember sitting there and saying 'How am I supposed to do that while I'm on my student placement?' The tutor said 'It's okay, most centres are not working this way yet, so you're not expected to do this as a student teacher', but the video and the ideas really interested me.

My work with these ideas began with Betty (a local senior adviser for the district). When I began teaching, Betty was talking about emergent curriculum and ideas from Reggio Emilia. Then Kylie began as Director at the centre and she was interested in these ideas too. At the same time, the centre was being renovated and extended. We were inspired by the emphasis on environment in the Reggio Emilia schools and the renovation process provided us with a blank canvas with which to explore ideas about learning environments and their potential impact on children's learning. In this context, we were able to focus on aesthetics It was a very collaborative project and all members of staff were involved.

Then, I can't remember why, but I picked up the book *The Hundred Languages of Children* (1998) and the photographs of Laura with the watch just stayed in my mind. I could really see the learning occurring in that series of pictures. They resonated with me—being proactive about early childhood experiences. Needs-based programming was frustrating me. I felt that it was limiting the potential of children, and my own development as a teacher.

---

[1] Koori: Term derived from Indigenous Aboriginal languages of south-eastern Australia. Meaning 'person' or 'people', it is used as a means of identification by Indigenous Australians of this region. Other terms are used in other parts of the continent.

I think that early childhood is very under-valued and, to me, pedagogical documentation means that children's and teachers' thinking and learning is made visible. I saw it as a way to promote the value of what we are doing and to create a more meaningful and contextualised program.

So originally you were trying to make visible children's learning and teachers' thinking?

Mmmm, and the traditional needs-based, developmental-theory approach, as I said, never actually made sense to me. It never, ever made sense to me because having my own gifted and talented child, I saw a mismatch between developmental theory and reality. There were things that he was doing at a certain age that he wasn't 'supposed' to do until much later, and then things that he was 'supposed' to be doing, he wasn't doing at all. So it made me think that developmental theory wasn't very helpful. Having said that, I think it still has potential for analysis of some behaviour. It's always in the back of my mind and I still use it sometimes as a framework or a guide, particularly when there are little alarm bells going off about a child. I think student teachers still have to know developmental theory because they have to know it before they can let it go.

Do you remember completing your first example of pedagogical documentation?

Yes, I remember where we started. It was based on a story about a child growing sunflowers. I decided to use children's literature as the entry point because I've always been interested in children's literature. The book was called *Tilda's Seeds* (1999) by Melanie Eclare. The children loved the project. We actually harvested sunflower seeds! It was magnificent.

It took a while for the staff to begin documenting children's learning. We had started by looking at our approach to programming, and reconsidering our images of children, and then we focused on improving the environment. Those kinds of changes probably went on for a couple of years.

Now, when I look at the first example of our documentation that we called *Tilda's Sunflowers*, it's obvious that there is hardly any analysis. I remember talking it over with Kylie and she joked, 'I think there needs to be more. Maybe more analysis?' We thought the analysis could go beyond developmental theory.

I remember going to the local RE-Search[2] group clutching my sunflowers and feeling that the work was inadequate when compared to that of other educators at the meeting. In hindsight, of course, I was just starting the journey and others were much further along the path. Attending the RE-Search group was a vital component in my professional development; I was given support, encouragement, constructive criticism and validation of my work as a teacher and documentor of children's work.

---

[2] RE-Search group: Groups of early childhood educators formed to consider implications of Reggio Emilian pedagogy for Australian contexts.

So when you think about some of the topics you've explored, what kinds of investigations (or topics) have you documented?

I remember *Pokémons*. It was a bit 'out there' because it was exploring children's responses to, and play about, popular culture—in this case *Pokémons*. This was some time ago, but I think my attitude was that it wasn't going away, so it might be interesting to listen to the children and find out what it was about. At the time I thought that the children were being very open, discussing shared knowledge and theories about *Pokémons* which seemed to be about power relations, and very violent solutions to conflict. After we talked, *Pokémons* seemed to disappear from the children's play. I mused at the time that their disappearance might have been related to the fact that I had listened and validated their interest in *Pokémons*. What was I thinking? With the benefit of hindsight, I suspect that *Pokémons*. actually went underground, instead of disappearing as I thought. The children seemed to be sharing their interest and theories about the issue, but I now wonder if they would have preferred that I minded my own business and left the world of *Pokémons* alone.

Another investigation I've explored is *Secret places for those who know*. It was an investigation of children's need to create secret places, who owned those places, and who was or was not able to gain entry into those secret places. I remembered that I loved to be away from the sight of adults when I was a child. The children's apparent need to create these places seemed to me to be particularly important in the context of long day care. They were constantly being supervised and observed, and I felt that they had a right to privacy. Upon reflection, I wonder that I may have invaded the very privacy I was advocating for them, even though the children gave me permission to observe and photograph the two events. As I look back at these examples, I find that my thinking constantly changes as I learn and reflect.

Did your examples tend to be long and involved, or were they shorter and more focused?

They used to be big and they usually focused on a huge topic like dinosaurs. They could go on for months and months. It really opened my eyes to how children's abilities are underestimated. I had a child who worked his way through the entire CD-Rom of *Walking with Dinosaurs* and he could use the pictures to change the 'wallpaper' on the screen of the computer. I said to him, 'How did you do that Damien?' He was just phenomenal. He kept changing it. I'd turn on the computer and find another dinosaur on the screen. I remember I was also amazed with four-year-olds using an index to find their favourite dinosaur in a reference book. They could find 'T' for Tyrannosaurus Rex.

Over time, I think I found the long examples became too predictable. Too many topics came up every year because there are lots of similarities in the interests of four and five-year-olds. I got to the point where I was looking for the deeper stories. I mean, how many ways are there for children to explore boxes or to investigate snails? These are good topics and useful places to begin to develop documenting skills, but I wanted more. I know that children love these topics and I know the investigations will 'work' for documentation. Of course, I'd follow those interests and I'd always provide choices, but these may not be the most meaningful ideas to follow for documentation. I still record these conversations in the children's journals, but I wouldn't necessarily follow them up with a major piece of pedagogical documentation.

At one stage you worked with an art specialist. Tell us about those experiences.

I remember we did *Fireworks* for the Sydney Olympics. It had a real focus on art because we had the art specialist working with us. She helped the children explore different ways to represent their ideas. We had three-dimensional work and the children created a great sculpture from long lengths of coloured cane to represent the explosion of fireworks. We made two-dimensional representations with the drawings, using different colours; then one time they drew fireworks using white on black paper. The whole topic started when there were celebrations for the announcement of Sydney winning the Olympics and then one of the children had seen New Year fireworks in Shanghai. So the children were very excited by these ideas of celebration and all the emotions involved. They were able to relate to fireworks as a symbol for celebration.

Did you find that the artist helped your work?

Yes, there's no doubt she had skills in art-making that I didn't have. She was working in a couple of local centres at the time and she was a great help in assisting the children develop visual arts skills. I don't believe documentors need to have access to a trained artist though. I mean, you can do pedagogical documentation without a trained artist, but I'd be the first to say that it does help. She gave me ideas about ways of representing and visual art techniques and approaches that I wouldn't necessarily have thought about. Since then, I've gone on and completed other examples without an artist. In fact, most of my documentation hasn't been with a trained artist.

What would be your favourite example of pedagogical documentation?

September 11th comes to mind immediately. I can remember arriving at work and the radio in my car wasn't working. I arrived at work at the same time as Kylie. As she got out of her car, her face looked white and shocked. She asked me if I'd heard what had happened, realised I had no idea and told me about the horror that had occurred. Then one of the children arrived early and his mother was hysterical because her mother-in-law was in New York and she couldn't get through on the phone to find out if she was safe. Kylie and I sat the children down and we talked about it and invited the children to come to one of us if they wanted to talk about what had happened. We wanted it to be out in the open and not underground in terms of their feelings and their fears.

Later that day, I noticed that particular child and two other boys building the Twin Towers and I just watched and wrote down their dialogue. Over the next few days they just kept building and re-building these towers. They designed a defence system for the towers that had emergency phones for the trapped people and flashing lights on top of the building. They had messages attached to the towers in different languages so everyone could read the signs in their own language. They'd cut them out from newspapers.

What absolutely amazed me was the dedication the boys put into building those Twin Towers every day. I offered to leave their buildings up overnight, but they were happy to pack them up and recreate them the next day. It was fascinating that no other child ever disturbed the buildings. There was a sense of unspoken respect that this was really important. Every day for a week, the rebuilding of the Twin Towers became a solemn ritual when the boys arrived in the morning. I think they'd been responding to family anxiety as well as the media coverage. The child whose grandmother was in New York was one of the key players. His grandmother was fine, but it seemed important for him to build the towers.

What did you do to document this situation?

I sat there very quietly writing and listening to their conversations. I acted as an observer and I wasn't involved in their work at all. They were totally engaged in reconstructing events, in retelling the story.

I don't tape conversations because I find that transcribing them takes too much time and drives me insane! So I've developed the skill of being able to note key phrases as a memory prompt. I can write very quickly and take photographs and I can work from that. I can usually recreate a conversation from the key phrases.

I also asked the boys to draw their buildings. The images of the planes heading towards the buildings were soul destroying—so evocative of the endless media replaying of the planes hitting the towers.

So when you say that you noted their conversations, can you remember the kinds of things they were talking about?

Actually, it's really interesting revisiting it now. I think it's always fascinating to revisit the interpretation of conversations. I've just realised that there wasn't much conversation at all about hijacking the planes or the people in the planes. It was more about the building. There was more focus on the people in the towers. So they said things like: 'Here's a phone for the people inside the building.' Or 'If we put this here, the planes can't fly into the building.' They were thinking about the defences and their conversations were mostly about defending the buildings.

There wasn't a lot of blame or talk about 'bad people'. I'd tended to talk about 'angry' people and there didn't seem to be a sense of blame. I think, *I think* they were trying to change the scenario for these people. It's as though they were trying to fix it and change the event. They seemed to be solutions-oriented. Their constructions didn't seem to be about personal fear. It was more about trying to find solutions to protect the buildings so the destruction wouldn't happen again.

On reflection, I think these events helped to crystallise my thinking about what I, as an educator, should be looking at with the children. It became a social justice issue and I felt compelled to work it through with the children, particularly as some came from Muslim families and were targeted in the community simply because they were Muslims. There has always been a notion that children are unaware of what is happening in the world and should not be exposed to such events. In this situation, there was no escaping the horrifying images of the planes crashing into the Twin Towers. The issues needed to be discussed, and Muslim families needed support. Of course, we advised families to try to minimise what the children were exposed to in terms of media coverage, but it would be naïve to think that the children had not seen the images in the media. The front cover of the documentation was presented as the front page of

Engaging with September 11

a newspaper because the media were so omnipresent, but it was all about the children's responses—some of the statements they made, the ritual of rebuilding the towers and their graphic drawings of what had happened.

Do you usually take on the role of observer?

It depends. Most of the time I am involved with the experience because I believe that educators should be visible in the documentation. I've talked about it with Kylie and we agree that the educator should be there. The adults should be visible to show that they have an important role in the investigation. Sometimes it doesn't seem very respectful to intervene and join in the children's work. It would have been too intrusive if I had asked questions of the children building the Twin Towers. I just have to make a decision at the time about intervening or challenging their thinking.

Sometimes I stand back and watch, sometimes I join in the discussion, and sometimes I offer the opportunity to represent learning in other ways. Other times the investigation affects my planning, but none of those things happen all the time. They are all different. It's important for children's services to be safe places where children can explore these issues, and I respond differently depending on the situation.

I know you have a passion for exploring social justice issues with children. Could you tell us about another example which reflects this commitment?

Well, *Who are the Koori kids?* comes to mind. I always knew that I had to address Aboriginal issues with the children and I didn't feel equipped to do it sensitively. I was worried about being a non-Aboriginal teacher discussing Aboriginal issues with non-Aboriginal children. I was worried that I would do something inappropriate and I wasn't confident about the whole thing. I went to a workshop by a member of the Stolen Generation[3] and she explained the situation at an emotional rather than intellectual level. At the workshop, we had to create an island and make it as beautiful as we could. I remember feeling quite emotionally engaged in my creation. Then she came around with a black pen and began to destroy our work. We were just speechless and watched her pick up our work and literally rip it to pieces. Most of us were pretty tearful. We felt totally rejected. I didn't see it coming, but we were meant to be emotionally engaged with it because intellectually we already knew about it, but this was the emotional understanding. Then I thought 'Okay, I have to do something with the children. What can I do?'

---

[3] Stolen Generation: A term describing the Aboriginal and Torres Strait Islander children forcibly removed from their families and communities and sent to institutions or adopted into non-Indigenous families as a result of government policies of the early 1900s through to the 1970s. A national inquiry into these policies and their effects was conducted in the mid-1990s by the Human Rights and Equal Opportunity Commission (HREOC) which produced *Bringing them home: Report of the National Inquiry into the separation of Aboriginal and Torres Strait Islander children from their families* (1997).

I thought the idea of emotional understanding was really important. It seemed to me that the children needed to feel the story at some level, as well as hear it. So I drew a map of Australia and the children decorated it. I desecrated it with a black marker pen to make the point, but I didn't tear it up because that would be too confronting for them. I had Kylie in the room scribing for me. I asked the children: 'Do you like what I did?' And they said 'Yep'. Kylie and I looked at one another for a moment and then I realised that I was their teacher and they thought that what I chose to do was okay. It took a moment for me to recognise the power of adults and I felt uncomfortable about it. So I said to them: 'It's okay, you don't have to like what I do. Tell me how you really felt?' Then they expressed their feelings of anxiety to me.

When I began to explore their understanding of Aboriginal people, I found that there were many misunderstandings to be clarified. I taught them (and it really was direct teaching), I taught them about the first people of Australia and how the white people (well, really, English people) came here. *Who are the Koori kids?* really evolved from that experience. It developed from their discussions and their drawings. I remember one child who drew the Aboriginal images and she had a white person holding hands with an Aboriginal person. Everything we had talked about was in this drawing. We discussed the notion of 'Sorry Day'[4], the significance of Aboriginal 'Dreaming', the symbolic nature of the Aboriginal flag, and its role in uniting Aboriginal groups with different cultures.

Then I began to wonder about their understanding of Aboriginal people in our community today. It seemed as though they didn't understand that Aboriginal people were real people. It was all a bit too abstract and they didn't know any Aboriginal people. So I tried to find a contact and as a result of my inquiries we went to visit an Aboriginal preschool. The visits were really worthwhile and the kids realised that Koori kids were just kids like them—they all had different families or different beliefs, but there were lots of things in common as well. We visited the preschool for a couple of years and they came and visited us, but when my contact left the centre, the visits didn't continue. *Who are the Koori kids?* is one of my favourite examples of pedagogical documentation. It was very powerful and a huge challenge for me. I knew I was taking a risk at a personal and professional level, but I thought it was really important to explore it with the children. For me, Aboriginal history is one of the most important social justice issues I feel compelled to work through with the children I teach.

---

[4] Sorry Day: First held in 1998, following a recommendation of the HREOC Inquiry into the 'Stolen Generation' and its report *Bringing them home*. It is a day of local events where individuals and communities acknowledge the impact of the historical mistreatment of Aboriginal and Torres Strait Islander peoples—including policies of forced removal of children from their families—and express their hopes for reconciliation between Indigenous and non-Indigenous Australians. Sorry Day events are now held under the banner 'Journey of Healing'.

Then, in contrast to these larger pieces, there was a wonderful smaller piece that I called *Life, death and the universe: William reflects*. It was very powerful in terms of seeing William as a theory-maker. William found a dead ant in the sandpit. This discovery led him to seize the moment to discuss his theories about death. He explained to me what happened when things die. So it was just a conversation between William and me. He said:

> When people die they go to another earth…You have to go in the basket into the space ship. You're still in the basket to go to the moon…The astronaut wears a helmet, the dead people got no astronaut's helmet. He's dead already, he can't breathe. You dig a hole in the moon, the astronaut put the dead people in the hole. Cover him with rocks and sand, and then put flowers on the hole…'

The Bali bombing had just happened when William shared his theories on death. I went back to him and he talked some more about it and how the people died. Then he related it back to his theories about death and explained how the people were now on the moon. I asked him 'How did you feel when you heard about the bombing?' I'll never forget his response. Remember, this was a four-year-old. He said:

> I feel very upset. I still like the good guys. I'm upset with the bad guys. Must be sometimes good guys kill bad guys. The sun eat, eat, eat, so the earth goes 'POW'. Then there's no more earth any more. So the good guys and bad guys die. The earth will stop turning around.
>
> I feel like I was dying. I wish I could be a Superman, so that when the sun does that, I could fly. The earth doesn't really stop moving does it? It's just going around very slow so you can't feel it?

William and I both had tears in our eyes.

Then, in a third discussion, we got into the 'good guys and bad guys'. He went inside and brought out the flag of Australia and he said, 'These are the good guys'. I thought this was about him finding a place where he felt safe. He said the Chinese were the baddies. I didn't really explore that with him. I said that there were good and bad people in all countries. I wanted to get beyond cultural stereotyping. It's very difficult not to lead children, but it was important not to label cultures as good or bad. I said there were bad people in China and good people in China, there are bad people in Indonesia and good people in Indonesia and there are bad people in Australia and good people in Australia, and then I emphasised that most people are good.

The power of William's abilities to express his emotions, and his empathy for the victims of Bali highlights a social justice issue—that of the community perception or attitude that young children are incapable of deep emotion, of expressing these emotions and empathy in regard to major world events. They have a right to a voice. It seems to me that their voices are either not heard or they are ignored. I feel that it is my role to provide for that voice of the children I teach.

Do you write up these small examples or do you use them for reflection?

Oh, these are written up examples, although I don't necessarily write up every example. There is one story that is not actually documented as a written piece, but it is documented in my head. It raises issues about what children should talk about. Children don't live in a vacuum and they should have the right to talk about stuff that concerns them. At the markets one Saturday, we had bought the children a Siamese Fighting Fish and it died over the weekend before they had actually seen it. Our immediate reaction on Monday morning was to get rid of it before the children arrived. Then a staff member said that children need to deal with death and they should have a chance to talk about this.

I agreed and I got the dead fish out of the bin and put in on a paper towel and put in the middle of the floor. I called a room meeting. This kind of discussion was a regular event, as the children were involved in issues regarding the program, and I invited staff to talk about their ideas of death and what happens after death. There was a Muslim casual staff member, a Buddhist staff member, a Christian staff member. I set it up so the children could listen to us talking about our beliefs. Of course, they were more interested in the dead fish! I was asking questions of the staff and the children saw my interest, gradually the dead fish became a little less appealing and they became interested in the conversation. I was modelling respect and interest in the conversation. It's the subtlety of the teacher's role that is hard to explain.

I said to the children, 'I've listened to ideas from the Buddhist religion and the Christian and the Muslim faiths and I think there are lots of similar ideas about what happens after death. Why are people fighting about God?' Hayley turned to me and said, 'They're not fighting about Gods, Belinda. They are fighting about their countries.' Her family is from Palestine, and her comment summed up a particular political perspective about current world events. So that little snippet has stayed with me.

The children decided that we should bury the fish according to Muslim ritual. I wasn't sure that it was appropriate to bury a dead fish in this way, so I checked and I was advised that it would be fine. The children found the best place to bury the fish and they dug the hole and put the fish in. I asked 'What do you do now?' They decided to sprinkle the fish with glitter. I think this was suggested because fairies and magic dust were happening with other children in the room at the time. Then they covered it up and thought it was important to sing to the fish. They decided that *You are my sunshine* would be the best choice because they believed the fish had died of the cold. Although their choice was amusing, at the same time it was incredibly powerful to see them so caring about a fish that they had never met. It was the idea of death that they were trying to deal with, trying to be respectful about the process. It's a bit like role-playing appropriate behaviour for a burial.

As you have continued to explore this way of working, how has your understanding changed?

I guess now I understand that little snapshots can tell us a whole lot about children's knowledge and beliefs. It's not necessarily the large-scale projects that give me that insight. I also think I've developed an instinct about what might be interesting, what might go somewhere. This has refined over time and I think I've become better at it. I've also come to understand the importance of the story underneath the first impressions. That is generally what draws me in. For example, remember that I said the commentary on *Tilda's Sunflowers* was a bit thin? Well, now I know I want the meaty bits underneath. What is really going on? What does that drawing mean? I also find with hindsight, with the benefit of time to reflect, read and research, that my thinking has changed and I often see the stories differently, as I did with *Secret Places* and *Pokémons*.

Recently, it's been great to see colleagues develop their skills and I've enjoyed working with them. We've had a new garden bench installed, and it has become a special place for children to sit and talk. It was interesting to see one of the staff, Marie, notice the attraction of the new garden bench as a 'talking place'. Sitting together on the bench seems to encourage the children to talk and talk. Their ideas and thoughts just spill out into the discussion. The children talk about amazing things; they talk about social justice issues among themselves. Marie had the insight to realise that something special was happening and it would be worthwhile to keep a record of the conversations. This became the documentation of *Stories from a Garden Bench*. It's a good example of a collaborative approach to pedagogical documentation that has been developed by staff working together.

Tell us about how the children influence your decision-making.

I know that anything is possible with the children and I'm open to it. I expect them to be interesting, rich and challenging because that's the way they've been educated. Most children have been at the centre since they were babies or toddlers. I always think I can see the difference in the children who have been at the centre for some time because they know we have a genuine interest and they respond to that.

The best example of that influence is probably *Dreaming with Miró*. The children were really interested in some of the symbolism used in Aboriginal art work. So the idea that circles represented campfires[5] really fascinated them. The art teacher was visiting the centre at about that time and I explained the

---

[5] Circles in Aboriginal art can also represent waterholes (Stokes 1993).

children's interest to her and I suggested that she might be able to extend their learning. When she began to work with the children, they were able to sit with their eyes closed and describe how their brains were working. They looked at all kinds of symbols and their artwork in the documentation was just phenomenal especially where it related to the work of Jean Miró.

I remember the impact it had on one particular child who was very grounded in stereotypical, child-like art such as a square house with a triangle roof and circular figures and lines for arms and legs. The art teacher asked her to close her eyes and make a dreamy painting. It just set her free to be so expressive and so creative. It made a change in her artwork. A little while later, John Nimmo visited the centre and when he arrived she insisted that he was Jean Miró because the two names sounded so similar. She told him that she had been dreaming of him. I tried to explain the confusion to John Nimmo. After he had seen around the centre, I invited the child to show John the documentation about Jean Miró. There is a photograph of Jean Miró in the documentation and I said to her 'Look at the photograph and look at John Nimmo. Do you think they are the same person?' She looked at me, she looked at John and insisted he was the person in the photograph. Yet the two could hardly be less alike in physical appearance. So far as the child was concerned, he had been in her dream and she wasn't going to let go of it. A couple of weeks later she came up to me and said 'I knew it wasn't really Jean Miró—but I wanted it to be.' So it's a good example of seeing the possibility in a situation and documenting it and following it along. This child was so involved in the ideas that she created a link with a visitor that didn't really exist, and I was happy to give her time to think it through. For me, *Dreaming with Miró* came from our exploration of a social justice context—Aboriginal issues—inspired by the symbolism of Aboriginal art.

What have been some of the problems and pleasures of working in this way?

It's a lot more work. It takes more time and it's harder work. But it is so much more interesting, and because it is interesting I really don't mind putting the time into it. It really makes me feel that my job is worthwhile.

The collaborative approach to the exploration of ideas has been really great. I'd show examples to the Director to get her extra insight into the situation. I wasn't looking for her approval. I was seeking another point of view. I worked in a similar way with the staff in my room. I saw myself as empowering staff to be open to new possibilities. I was pleased that the relationship developed and there was no sense of 'You have the qualifications. You get paid more than me and I don't want to be involved.' It actually strengthened the relationship among all of us, by working together and taking on a collaborative role. It was so inspiring for one staff member that she has enrolled at university to study for a degree.

Finding time for pedagogical documentation is often a challenge. We have time allowed for programming, but writing up the children's journals takes up most of that time. Each child has a journal where we keep a record of meaningful aspects of their life at the centre. I think it's important that the journals are beautiful and kept up to date. Most of my work on pedagogical documentation tends to happen at home. It's also a case of seizing the moment. So if I'm on late shift and there are only three children in the room and it's a quiet time, I excuse myself to work on the documentation for a while. I have the computer in my room and I can type up short records while I'm there.

Having the technology available in the room makes a difference. I think it's very important for the children to see us working and paying attention to their ideas and thoughts. It can make them feel validated because I'm working on their project. Sometimes they watch me typing over my shoulder and they can read their own names and they're just as likely to ask 'What did I say there?' Mind you, sometimes I have to ask them what they said and they can generally remember. They know that I'm respecting their work and following it up straight away.

When you look back on your experiences, do you remember any possibilities that came up that you didn't follow through?

Mmmm…there were times when there was something lacking in the initial interest and it just didn't grab me, or it didn't seem to be going anywhere. There are also times when I just had to let things go. I have learned that there just isn't time to follow all the particular treasures that are discovered in children's thinking. When deciding what to explore further, I think it is essential that the investigation engages my interest and provides me with an intellectual challenge because I'm giving my time to it. I want my involvement to extend my personal skills as a teacher. It keeps the passion alive!

How does your work with pedagogical documentation affect your relationship with parents and families?

The issue I faced was that I was documenting for many parents who didn't speak English as a first language. That was very tricky for me, and I've tended to use shorter pieces and make effective use of photographs. The smaller examples are less arduous for parents who may not find it easy to read English. I used to put up the documentation on the wall as a finished product, whereas now I show the process. It's more a work-in-progress and families are able to see an investigation evolve.

Did you get any comments from parents that gave you extra insight or helped determine the direction of the investigation?

Who are the Koori kids? encouraged discussion among the parents. Most of the parents at the centre were first generation migrants to Australia. They had minimal knowledge about Aboriginal history and were moved by what the children were telling them. So it was new for them and it wasn't in any way confronting. When I move to my new centre in the country, I expect some of these processes to be more threatening—and that will be a challenge for me because it's an area I'd like to explore in more depth.

As you think about moving to a new job, how might you go about introducing or building upon these ideas? Have you had a chance to think about how you might move in that direction?

Yes I have, because I see it as a big challenge. I thought that in implementing change I could expect some resistance from staff and parents because in a way that's just human nature. So I'm expecting it and I won't be surprised or offended by it.

It seemed to me that the least threatening change would be to think about the environment and image of the child. How do you see children? If you see them as needy, how does that influence the program? If you see them as competent, it might shift your approach to programming. That's how I thought I'd go. I won't really know until I get there, but I thought that it would not be too challenging.

Have you had a chance to think about your own journey and ask yourself: 'Is there something useful there in the steps I've taken, that might help me in working with other people who are new to these ideas?'

I have thought about that. There'll be four staff that work together over the week, so that will be a change from the number of staff involved at my current child care centre. So, I've thought about saying to the staff at my new centre: 'Look, I've worked this way in the past. Would it bother you if I started working like that here? There'd be no expectation that you would have to work like that as well.' Then I'd just do some very simple one-off examples of documentation so it wouldn't be overwhelming. Maybe I'd just record everyday conversations that show children making friends, or solving problems. I don't want it to seem too hard.

Is there anything you would like to add about pedagogical documentation? What about your experiences with the RE-Search group?

The RE-Search group has had a huge influence on my development as a teacher and on my documentation as well, because I bring my ideas and the examples and share it with colleagues at the meeting. It was like a 'show and tell' session, and I'd always, always get constructive comments and support for my ideas. It was always helpful and supportive. I remember standing in the car park after a meeting and talking, talking, talking with my Director who had come to the meeting with me. It was wonderful because the people in the group had validated everything we were trying to work towards and at the same time we realised how far we had to go. It was really very important to have a group of people like this to help us along.

Did the RE-Search group lead to other opportunities?

Yes, because of my membership of the group I was invited to contribute to Exhibit-On. (See Chapter Eighteen) This gave me the confidence to participate in a 'Meet the Documentors' session at the conference associated with the exhibition. That's when I talked about the *Pokémons* documentation. So it was having a forum where I could share my ideas with interested and supportive colleagues. It probably doesn't matter how it happens really, but it's important to get together with others so you don't feel too isolated. It was so exciting to be asked to present at a conference. I was involved in a session at AECA[6] and I was so nervous, but it was worthwhile. It gave me incredible validation as a professional to be asked to do that. Although it was stressful, it was worthwhile.

Conclusion

This conversation with Belinda highlights a number of significant issues related to pedagogical documentation. First, there is a sense that expertise increases over time. Belinda notes that she now feels her initial efforts were rather limited, especially in terms of the analysis of the children's learning. Her ability to analyse has been refined with thoughtful reflection on her experiences. When Belinda was recalling some of her past experiences with pedagogical documentation, it was evident that she was also re-thinking some of her initial analysis. Reflecting on past analysis and re-thinking original ideas can deepen understanding of children's learning and increase sensitivity towards the possibilities of multiple meanings.

A second key issue highlights the importance of a reflective network of colleagues and friends to support the process. Belinda rarely seems to be working in isolation. Rather, she actively seeks support from her Director and meets with other early childhood professionals who are working towards documentation. She also takes pleasure in collaborating with staff and colleagues to help them grow in their own abilities. Pedagogical documentation is often a collaborative enterprise with staff and parents engaged along with children.

Another key issue relates to the role of the documentor. Belinda explains that she is usually involved in the experience with the children, although sometimes she steps back and acts as an observer. She identifies the subtleties of the decisions made in these circumstances and acknowledges that it is her personal relationships with the children that enable her to feel relatively comfortable with her chosen role.

Finally, issues related to social justice and world events are threaded through the children's experiences and Belinda's approach to pedagogical documentation. She does not believe that children can be shielded from the realities of contemporary life. Rather, her stories of pedagogical documentation show that she is prepared to take risks in her quest to explore children's theories and their ideas about the world in which they live.

---

[6] AECA: (Now Early Childhood Australia, ECA) Formerly the Australian Early Childhood Association. The national organisation, responsible for publications, advocacy, identifying and promoting best practice in early childhood; also hosts a highly regarded biennial national conference.

Postscript from Belinda

Several months have passed since the interview and I am now settled into my new job. The process of implementing changes to the way in which children are perceived, to the environment and to programming has exceeded all my expectations. The staff members have embraced new ideas and challenges and our program reflects the children and staff. The staff are becoming proactive in promoting the rights of children. One staff member is beginning to discuss Aboriginal issues with the children.

When I first arrived at this centre, I found that we were sponsoring Solomon, a little boy who lives in Chad. I was surprised to find that the children did not know about Solomon. Now they have become passionate about this little boy who is so far away. They write him letters, draw pictures, and always bring Solomon (his photo) and the globe (to find Chad) to group time. I have begun to document the growing relationship between the children and Solomon.

To finish—here is a small glimpse of a new beginning in a conversation with Xavier:

Xavier: Belinda, I'm going to bring some money for Solomon and all the people in Chad.

Belinda: That's lovely, but why?

Xavier: Sudan is happening. People are playing with guns and frightening them, so they're running across the road to Chad. Chad hasn't got enough money for food. Solomon might get hungry.

Belinda: So what's happening in Chad?

Xavier: They 'rethugees', they can't go home because they're shooting guns in Sudan. They make them sad and they make them die.

For Belinda, the journey continues…

References

Eclare M (1999) *Tilda's seeds*. Somerset, UK: Ragged Bears Publishing.

Edwards C, Gandini L & Forman G (1998) (Eds) *The hundred languages of children: The Reggio Emilia approach—Advanced reflections*. (2nd Ed) Greenwich, CT: Ablex.

Haines T (1999) *Walking with dinosaurs*. [CD-Rom]. London: BBC.

National Inquiry into the Separation of Aboriginal and Torres Strait Islander Children from their Families (1997), *Bringing them home: Report of the National Inquiry into the separation of Aboriginal and Torres Strait Islander children from their families*. Sydney: Human Rights and Equal Opportunity Commission.

Stokes D (1993) *Desert dreamings*. Melbourne: Rigby Heinemann.

Chapter Seven

Tertiary Education as a Context for Creating Documentors

Joanne Burr
Danielle Crisafulli

Alma Fleet
Catherine Patterson
Pamela Silversides

Trying to learn to do pedagogical documentation as an assessment task creates particular tensions for student teachers. Being a teacher educator trying to share the potential of working with this tool is also complex. This chapter shares the thinking of Joanne, Danielle and Pamela, three new graduates, and two of the staff, Alma and Catherine, from an Australian early childhood teacher education program. In this specialist, four-year Bachelor of Education degree, pedagogical documentation is introduced in the third year professional experience program and developed further in the fourth year. A process that is fundamentally philosophical and pedagogical has become a component of assessment, constrained by the timelines and artificiality of the practicum situation. The power of this way of working, however, has such potential for generating insight and scaffolding teaching that we have persevered. This material was developed originally as a symposium presentation (Burr, Crisafulli, Fleet, Patterson and Silversides, 2001). Several years later, each of the original graduates reflected on more recent perspectives of their documenting journeys.

An e-mail conversation

Dear Alma,

I am in your tutorial class and, as you would be aware, I am on prac at the moment. However, I seem to have a little dilemma. I am unable to take any sort of photographs in the school I am working at, due to their privacy policies. Therefore I am somewhat concerned about how this will affect my ability to complete the documentation assignment. I was just wondering how you would like me to approach this assignment given the circumstances. The Principal of the school has also said that he would be happy to discuss this further with you if necessary.

Thank you for your time, and I look forward to hearing from you soon.
Nicole

Hi Nicole,

No problem. Although it's frustrating, we do have several places with the same policy. We must remember to tell students in advance next year! Save you the anxiety. There are several possible solutions:

- Sometimes unidentifiable photos are okay (backs of heads, hands only and so on), so you can ask about that.

- We have had some effective assignments which had no photos of children, but were built around work samples, sometimes photos of artefacts or project materials, descriptions, conversations—one person used magazine cut-outs of backs of heads and arms to give the flavour!

- Does any of that seem possible for you? Remember, the intent is to gain insight from something (usually unexpected) which the children are pursuing or wish to pursue or are intrigued by. You are documenting that possibility with glimpses into how the curiosity unfolds into further investigation. Think about the ideas and the photos will seem less important.

All the best
Alma

Conversations such as this, whether electronic or face-to-face, are a regular part of the experience of becoming a thoughtful educator who can use the tool of pedagogical documentation to glean greater understanding of children and improve teaching. The process is rarely straightforward. Learning to become a documentor includes philosophical, pedagogical and pragmatic challenges. This chapter will explore some of these challenges through the eyes of three student teachers who were beginning to work with pedagogical documentation.

First thoughts on attempting documentation in Third Year—Danielle Crisafulli

When first introduced to the educational philosophy of Reggio Emilia, I remember being both impressed and astounded. This was not only with the amazing experiences children enjoyed as part of their daily education, but also because of the high level of respect given to the way children learn and socially construct knowledge.

Similarly, the first examples of documentation which were shown to us invoked awe, and a sense that not only had a wonderful means of representing the investigations of children authentically and meaningfully evolved, but also

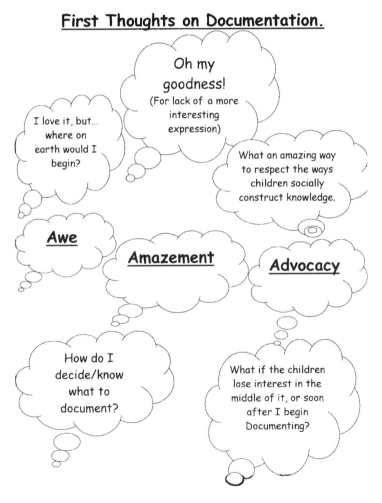

Danielle's first thoughts on documentation

that the value of the work done by professionals in early childhood education had reached a new level of respect in at least one part of the world. I could not help but be amazed when I was first introduced to the educational philosophy of Reggio Emilia and first impressions of documentation inspired similar feelings.

As a student-teacher I remember thinking:

> Oh my goodness, our lecturers expect us to do something like this on prac? Where on earth would I begin? How will I ensure that it is child-led? I love it and want to 'have a go', but how can I do it properly while maintaining other practicum requirements at the same time?

I have heard similar sentiments expressed by professionals within early childhood education who are impressed by documentation but are terrified to attempt it or to even contemplate where to begin. Some ask, 'How on earth will I be able to do this within a school setting?'

I knew that my cooperating teacher was unfamiliar with the philosophy of Reggio Emilia and knew very little about documentation. I worried:

> How can I explain it effectively so that she understands the value in what I want/have to do, and how meaningful it is for the children involved and their families?

Other thoughts at the time were, 'How on earth will I be able to decide *what* to document?' Even today, this is something my colleagues and I ask ourselves all the time; this usually coincides directly with, 'What if I miss something else just as important?' I guess you can never really know if you handle this appropriately.

Another huge issue I was confronted with as a student-teacher was, 'What if the children lose interest in the middle of my documentation, or soon after I begin documenting?'

As a more experienced teacher now, I would answer that with, 'Well, perhaps it's run its course and it's time to let go' or, alternatively, 'How can I find a way to establish whether I can regain the children's interest somehow?'

Then there is presentation and style:

> What will be easy to read, suitable for the intended audience, and most appropriate to respecting and valuing the children's investigations? What kind of style will I use to present it so that it is easy to read and contains all the necessary information and analysis? Do I need parts translated?…

and so on.

Then there were the questions related to:

How on earth can I juggle documentation with all the other work requirements I have to fulfil? Where can I find an extra 24 hours in my day so I can fit it all in? I had better start doing some research, and reading as much information on documentation as I can find.

Finally…advocacy!! I remember thinking what a fantastic way to show the wider community the value of our profession and the work we do with children on a daily basis. Maybe this could be considered the final push for those who are still struggling with the notion of becoming a documentor.

An example from practice teaching: *I wish I had an aeroplane!*

My second piece of documentation at university proved to be an interesting learning experience for me, and although challenging at the time, it very much solidified my respect for the benefits of pedagogical documentation. This investigation was undertaken with a group of three to five-year-olds in a preschool setting.

I wish I had an aeroplane was sparked by a free drawing experience when Michael drew an aeroplane after looking at some pictures I provided. I had brought in cardboard propellers and split pins for the children to use and these became immensely popular. After investing a lot of time, effort, and thought, Michael was so thrilled with the aeroplane he created that he proceeded to fly

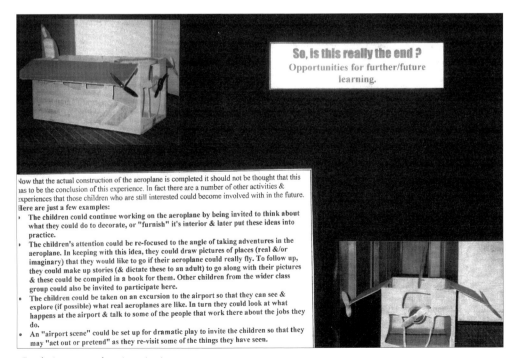

So, is this really the end ?
Opportunities for further/future learning.

Now that the actual construction of the aeroplane is completed it should not be thought that this has to be the conclusion of this experience. In fact there are a number of other activities & experiences that those children who are still interested could become involved with in the future. Here are just a few examples:

- The children could continue working on the aeroplane by being invited to think about what they could do to decorate, or "furnish" it's interior & later put these ideas into practice.
- The children's attention could be re-focused to the angle of taking adventures in the aeroplane. In keeping with this idea, they could draw pictures of places (real &/or imaginary) that they would like to go if their aeroplane could really fly. To follow up, they could make up stories (& dictate these to an adult) to go along with their pictures & these could be compiled in a book for them. Other children from the wider class group could also be invited to participate here.
- The children could be taken on an excursion to the airport so that they can see & explore (if possible) what real aeroplanes are like. In turn they could look at what happens at the airport & talk to some of the people that work there about the jobs they do.
- An "airport scene" could be set up for dramatic play to invite the children so that they may "act out or pretend" as they re-visit some of the things they have seen.

Conclusion to aeroplane investigation

it around the room for the next 20 minutes. When he finally returned it to me he exclaimed, 'I wish I had an aeroplane!' Several of his classmates overheard this sentiment and agreed.

I thought about Michael's comment and wondered if the children could somehow make their own aeroplane. So, after speaking with my cooperating teacher, I met with Michael and four other interested children and we discussed the possibility of really making an aeroplane. We began with a discussion to find out what the children already knew about the characteristics of aeroplanes, then we identified what we would need and which materials we could use.

We found a large air-conditioner box in the preschool storeroom that the children decided would be perfect. Over the next three weeks, the children worked together to build their plane. They decided on everything from the colours, the placement of the wings, the number of windows and the design of the logo on the tail...everything.

As Michael remained a focus of the project and the aeroplane was especially important to him, it was only fair that he would be the first to fly it! The children had a wonderful time being participants in this project; it was the first time they had been offered the opportunity to work on something cooperatively over such an extended period of time. As the documentor, I was constantly amazed with the level of the children's thinking (for example, Bailey coming up with the tail logo, Michael's precision), and their enthusiasm for the project. Although it was very time consuming to put together, it was well worth the effort!

An example from a recent workplace: *So, what is an author anyway?*

When I have caught up with friends from university, I have frequently been asked if I have used pedagogical documentation at work. With their own memories of the time and effort involved, when I say that I have, I am often met with looks of surprise. With this in mind, it is interesting to take the opportunity to reflect back on an investigation that occurred in one of my first years of teaching with a group of three to five-year-old children from a linguistically and culturally diverse community. To me, it revealed many layers of thinking and learning, which the children (and I) experienced throughout the exploration and the documentation process. The final piece of documentation meant that we were able to go back, re-visit, reflect and embrace what we had achieved over and over again.

So, what is an author anyway? came about from daily story sharing sessions early in the year. When I read a story, I would always introduce the book by telling the children the title and the name of the author. I would also usually add, 'An author is someone who writes stories.' After a few weeks of doing this, I realised that when I would mention the author I was met with a series of blank looks. After talking to some of the children, it was apparent that many of them did not understand that authors were real people, or that real people wrote stories.

So, over the next few weeks, I noted the books that children regularly requested to have read to them and embarked on an Internet search for photographs of their favourite authors. These included Mem Fox, Eric Carle, Marcus Pfister and Pamela Allen. As a result, when I read the stories, I could show the relevant author's photo and explain that this was the person who wrote that particular book. Light bulbs began to turn on!

Many of the children really grasped the idea that authors were people, and loved looking at their photos, so to reinforce this interest I set up an 'Author Corner'. This began with a wall display of photos of Mem Fox and Eric Carle surrounded by small scanned copies of the covers of some of the children's favourite books with copies of the books on a shelf nearby. This became a favourite place and discussion area for many children.

Over the next few weeks we continued to contemplate 'authorness'. I suggested to the children that if they wrote their own stories they would be authors too. Two children, Helen and Franca, immediately wanted to write stories. This experience ended up being particularly significant for Helen as, weeks after writing the original version, she decided that she wanted to re-publish it using the computer.

After Helen and Franca's stories were shared with the rest of the class, a story-writing–author frenzy began. This included a small-group, combined effort of a new story featuring Pamela Allen's *Mr McGee*. Eventually, the children's own books were added to the 'Author Corner' and they were treated with a high level of respect that was inspiring to observe. As a result of this investigation, I found that I had created a group of three to five-year-old 'Author Police', who were very put out if the authors and illustrators were not identified in every story as it was read. That included stories at the centre, at home or even elsewhere such as in our local library. In turn, it sparked the addition of several new areas to our room because the children became hungry for more support with writing experimentation (sign-in area) and for a beautiful place to read (quiet area).

The investigation spanned almost seven months and, as a result, I really struggled with what to put in and leave out of the final presentation. This was probably the most difficult component, and it is one that is likely to be faced by many documentors. I challenged as well as trusted myself to include the most meaningful and authentic learning achievements of the children based on what *they* had wanted to learn when the investigation began.

I believe that I have evolved as a documentor with every example of documentation I have collated. I have grown with the children's growth through these investigations. When I listen to children now, I am tuned in to really *listening* and *hearing* what they want to know, and am challenged by the prospect of guiding, watching and documenting their journeys respectfully, appropriately and meaningfully. And, no matter what I think when I reflect back on my earlier efforts, I never regret the fact that I made the effort to try.

My first attempt at documentation as a student teacher—Joanne Burr

Rosa had been showing an interest in drawing maps and I wanted to build on this interest. I made the decision to explore mapping with her and a small group of other children. The children decided to use their school classroom as a model for constructing a three-dimensional Lego representation. They thought that the new Kindergarten children, who would soon be at their school, would need to know their way around the classroom. So, I arranged materials such as Lego shapes and boards on a round table surrounded by a number of small chairs. Initially, four children worked together on the map although other children became involved or left the investigation based on their own interest. While the children worked together on the three-dimensional map, they would often ask each other questions that would lead into new learning directions.

While I found the investigation very worthy of documenting, I now look at it in retrospect and consider ways of enhancing its quality and value. For example, one particular panel highlights an interaction I saw as a turning point of the children's investigation. The children were admiring their completed Lego map when Jennifer looked particularly puzzled and asked, 'But how will the new children know where to go by looking at the map?' Emily suggested they should add arrows and then Jennifer suggested using labels to tell the children *what* the things were on the map.

The panel I made to represent this exchange shows the interaction as well as giving a commentary of the children's conversations. In hindsight, however, it does not clearly demonstrate how or why the children's learning may be unfolding the way it is.

- Why did Emily suggest arrows?

- Has Emily examined Rosa's map?

- Does Emily use arrows to convey movement?

- Why did the children decide to use labels?

- What understandings do Jennifer and Emily hold about mapping right now?

I could have written an interpretation of the girls' solution to the problem they encountered. It would also have been valuable (and possible) to invite other children to provide an interpretation of events as well as asking parents or the teacher's aide. I believe interpretations from a range of people make a valuable contribution. In addition, I could have included some information to contextualise the unfolding investigation. This would influence how the conversations and learning would be interpreted.

For example, consider how the following scene would influence the viewing of the documentation.

> Emily rushed into the classroom on Monday morning with her mum, who said, 'You know Miss Burr, Emily is fascinated with maps at the moment. She was so excited when her aunty drew arrows on the roads in our street directory so that we would know which roads to follow on the way to the family barbecue.'

When documenting, I have found it useful to always ask myself:

- *Why* am I documenting this interaction?

- *What* do the things I have seen and heard mean for each child's learning?

- *How* can I make this learning visible?

My second documentation experience as a student teacher

This particular investigation began during my fourth-year practicum placement when three children showed an interest in dropping items into an outdoor water tray during free play. These four-year-old children made some comments about how different items would sink and others would not. In consultation with the other teachers in my preschool room, we decided to set up an indoor water trough for the children to explore sinking and floating. We arranged a baby's bath full of warm water along with interesting items such as spoons, rolling pins, plastic containers, corks, shells, pegs and blocks from around the room.

Will was one of the first children to explore our new provocation. I sat with him at the table while he explored items that would sink or float. I invited him to sink a simple rectangular plastic container. He found that it did not sink like the spoon and he announced that he wanted to know how to sink it. David and Jack became involved at this stage and they found they could sink an item by using a heavy object in the container or pushing the container down with their hands. The investigation began to unfold as an inquiry into the nature of sinking.

In my approach to recording the investigation, I tried to keep the recording very simple and consistent. I realised it would be valuable to show events in the order in which they occurred, so I used a continuous blue line to represent this and to lead the reader through the events. I also thought it was particularly symbolic of learning that built upon previous knowledge and experiences. I used green backing paper to identify a commentary on experiences, which included my decision-making as well as providing an overview of the learning context. I used photographs to support the contextual information; I thought they were particularly helpful by allowing the reader to step 'into' the investigation and imagine the conversations taking place. Yellow 'thought bubbles' were used for all interpretations made by people observing the children—although I made most of them. I tried to show that my interpretations were not the only answer, but rather, a possibility, so I used words such as 'possible, perhaps, maybe' in all of my interpretations.

At this point of the investigation, David and Will began playing together. Will had discovered yet another way to sink the container—to fill it with water. David had told him that it would not work—but Will showed him. 'Tip the water out and then you put the water in the container and then it tips and sinks.' David commented, 'It does sink, it sinks all the time'.

Within the interpretation bubble, I noted that David appeared to be revisiting his sinking theories. Perhaps he predicted that Will made the container sink by pushing it down with his hand, rather than allowing it to occur naturally. Will explained that it just 'happened' and then began to show David another way. David did not think it would sink, but with Will demonstrating, he reached a new understanding: 'You can sink the container by filling it with water.'

In the commentary, I also used a quote from Rebecca New (1998, p 271–2) who explained that educators in Reggio Emilia 'support children's predisposition to challenge one another's views, all the while providing opportunities for them to revisit, revise and review their theories and hypotheses'. I believe that using quotations from relevant literature helps to ground decision-making in theory and assists others to see what my philosophy looks like in practice.

As a group, the teachers and I decided to read *Who sank the boat?* by Pamela Allen and to provide the children with yet another provocation by introducing the concept of weight and linking it to the concept of sinking. We asked the children if they knew who sank the boat. David came up with the comment 'With so much animals it sinks.' I asked myself if David was beginning to explore the role cumulative weight played in sinking the container.

By the end of the investigation, six children had been actively involved in exploring each other's ideas as well as developing new sinking methods. The investigation ran for nearly a fortnight. When we shared the documentation again at the end of my practicum with the children, they were all able to share their findings with the rest of the group.

I presented the conclusion of the documentation as a reflection of the learning processes that had taken place during the investigation, rather than as an 'ending'. It concluded with possibility rather than suggesting that the children had found out all they needed to know about floating and sinking. Perhaps the commentary could have been improved by using a larger font size to allow for easier reading. It would also have been valuable if others had included their own thoughts about the children's experiences.

This form of documentation was a unique way to follow children's learning and communicate it to those interested in the children's learning processes. It was a great way for me to show how my philosophy of teaching and learning looks in practice. I have found that my role as a teacher was very clear in the examples of my documentation. Probably the most visible roles I have taken on during these experiences have been as an arranger of the physical environment, an active listener of the children during interactions and a hypothesiser.

Student teaching: Summary of final year documentation—Pamela Silversides

In my fourth year as a student teacher, I conducted an investigation with five children (four and five-year-olds) in a school setting: *If you had no bones then you would fall down like the rain and make a puddle: An investigation of the human skeleton.* Overall, I wanted my documentation to be bright and attractive, but not so over-whelming as to distract the reader from the main purpose. I chose to represent the children's words in colour, as that is what drove the investigation; while my analysis, interpretation and ideas were identified in black. I used many photographs and included samples of children's work.

Initial impetus

After Thomas had eaten his lunch, I listened to the children's comments as we discussed the possibility of exploring what happens to our food. This led to discussions about chewing our food, and the role of teeth, and the revelation from Daniel that our teeth are bone. Children say dozens of things each day that could evolve into an experience for documentation and the teacher needs to listen closely and choose comments to follow up when there is potential for a meaningful investigation.

My ears pricked up at their discussion as I saw the possibility for many practical and creative experiences. I discussed my ideas with my co-operating teacher who was keen for me to continue this line of investigation. I found that discussing and collaborating with other adults throughout the experience always led to better ideas.

In general, it was the children's words and endless ideas that drove this inves-tigation, while I was the facilitator who presented experiences to test their hypotheses and confirm their understandings. The investigation continued over two weeks to give the children time to reflect on their thoughts as their work evolved. My decisions to some extent were also guided by the curriculum as I ensured that we covered all Key Learning Areas during this period.

Away we go

I immediately brought in a provocation for our investigation—a cow's shoulder bone. The children engaged in problem solving as they tried to discover which animal it came from and to which part of the body it belonged. The bone was a joint that moved and caused much fascination which then encouraged the children to identify the joints in their own body. We conducted several experiments to demonstrate how hard it is to move without the use of joints.

Throughout the weeks, the children freely explored books and had the opportunity to make their thinking visible through drawings. One fascinating example of their drawing was in response to my question 'What would we look like if we had no bones?' On this occasion, the children and I were truly authentic co-constructors of knowledge, as I did not know the answer to the question I had posed to them. The children were aware of this and knew that their drawing was just as 'right' as my drawing.

Many of the interactions that occurred provided clear examples of the children as co-researchers and co-constructors of knowledge. A perfect example occurred when I provided the children with one piece of black cardboard plus enough chalk for all and suggested that we draw a joint skeleton. I took a step back to watch how they handled this; I was amazed as these four and five-year-old children delegated, negotiated, cooperated and problem solved in order to decide which part of the skeleton to draw. It became clear that these vital skills were just as important a part of the learning process (if not more) as was the content of the investigation.

After more practical experiences, due to the time constraints of practice teaching, it was time to revisit our experience. This session of review was the most vital part of the investigation. The children sat around and explored all the photos and their work samples while I questioned, 'What were you thinking when you were doing that?' 'Can you remember what made you draw that?' and so on. This was very worthwhile as I gained an insight into how much the children had learnt as their new knowledge just poured out. What was salient to them became obvious; for example, when we re-discovered what we would look like with no bones. Joanna came up with the title of the investigation, *If you had no bones, then you would fall down like the rain and make a puddle.* I thought this kind of imaginative comment would only be said in front of early childhood lecturers!

As closure to our investigation, we presented our work to the rest of the class, showing our drawings, photos, skeleton drawing, and bones (we had made bones out of dough and then cooked them to 'make them hard, just like real life bones!'). We then made an interest corner containing all the evidence we had collected. This gave the children true ownership of their investigation.

I sent a letter home informing families of our investigation and inviting them to come to see the children's learning. The parents marvelled at the children's interest and commitment that was highlighted in the photos. This emphasised the role of documentation as an advocacy tool as it clearly demonstrated the amazing knowledge each child had brought to the learning situation.

With the benefit of hindsight

It would have been great to revisit the three-dimensional aspect of the investigation. We made individual bones and skeletons, but there would have been huge potential in making a life-size skeleton out of clay. I should have had more courage to ask questions that challenged the children's and my own thinking—questions for which there is no 'right answer'. These seem to be the best ones to ask, as they allowed me to be an authentic co-researcher alongside the children, thus empowering them.

My current situation and documentation

As a new graduate in a primary school, pedagogical documentation is not a priority for me at present as I am still adapting to the new environment. Although I am not actually documenting children's learning in this way, this does not mean that the important processes of documentation are not taking place. These include active listening, observation and spontaneously facilitating children's ideas. Besides using some of the processes of documentation, I am also trying to integrate the Key Learning Areas to make learning more interesting and meaningful for the children.

Pedagogical documentation is all about engaging children in connected learning. This, however, proved to be a hurdle when I was in school settings as a student teacher. It was evident that the cooperating teachers and parents still primarily saw 'hands-on' experience as a 'fun' thing to do rather than core curriculum. I therefore found that by 're-boxing' the Key Learning Areas through the presentation of a curriculum web, there was concrete evidence of the learning that had occurred. It is interesting that a strategy such as a curriculum web can help justify documentation with principals, teachers and parents. The webs are a valuable tool and I will definitely utilise them when I begin to document in this way again.

Reflections: Catherine and Alma

In order to highlight the unfolding nature of possible documentor journeys, the three novice teachers who reported on their early documenting experiences were invited to reflect on their earlier writing after several more years of teaching experience. In the intervening time, two had taught at the same public school, with one recently getting married and moving communities. The other contributed her reflections from an extended trip to Europe. The third graduate originally taught in child care centres. She has also recently married and now works in a preschool. As their personal lives have evolved in different ways, so has their professional thinking, as offered in the following comments.

Danielle's reflection

It has now been five years since the completion of my tertiary education. In that time, I have been exposed to two very different educational environments, and have had to mould my teaching practices accordingly, even though it has involved working with children of the same age (three to five years).

Looking back, it is interesting to see the different ways pedagogical documentation fits into both settings. Immediately after university, I was fortunate to spend two years at a well-established, community-based child care centre run by a municipal council which embraced the philosophies of Reggio Emilia and held the benefits of pedagogical documentation in especially high esteem. To that end, all staff were encouraged to think carefully about the ways children's learning was not only guided daily to meet individual needs, but also how their interests could be followed on a long-term basis through documentation. Although those more experienced in this way of working were primarily responsible for collating and analysing the documentation and the presentation of individual projects, whenever possible, all staff helped to collect work samples, take photographs, record conversations and find resources relevant to investigations as they unfolded. In turn, those of us with the additional benefit of tertiary experience with pedagogical documentation, acted as resources for anyone seeking further guidance.

In this particular child care centre, access to useful equipment such as a digital camera, scanner, and computers also created a working environment well equipped for supporting children's investigations in this way. In addition, the flexibility of varied contact hours with the children (different shifts each week), and the presence of staff exceeding minimal adult/child ratios, often enabled extra programming time for those involved in research and analysis of pedagogical documentation (although work was also always taken home as well). Less qualified staff were also responsible for helping to maintain required individual records and journals for the children, which was also immensely helpful. This also led to extra time for primary documentors to be with the children, which was always received gratefully.

When the opportunity arose for me to accept a position at a brand new, community-based preschool, I embraced the chance and the challenges that came along with it. The first objective for this new team of people was getting to know one another, and to establish an educational philosophy for the service. In turn, developing a way of programming, planning, and recording information as well as providing an interesting and valuable educational environment—albeit with minimal staff and teaching resources—made for a busy, yet highly productive first year. With only 'trained' staff responsible for record keeping and programming, and being personally responsible for maintaining individual records and journals for 40 children myself, there were limitations. Although the issue of pedagogical documentation was raised and sparked curiosity in those who had not been exposed to it before, amongst a new group of staff with only one member with any prior experience, it was unfortunately inconceivable to attempt it during that first year.

Many of the characteristics paramount to effective documentation and its related philosophies, however, remained a priority. For example, investigating issues and subjects of interest to children on a long-term basis was highly significant. In addition, the role of educators acting as constant guides and facilitators of learning, being active listeners and providing a respectful, flexible, relaxed, unhurried, constantly evolving learning space with equal opportunities for all children to have a voice, opinion and contribution were of primary consideration.

I am provided with a generous amount of programming time each week for the 40 children in the centre (two-day and three-day groups of 20 children each). Nevertheless, time continues to be the most consistent constraint in terms of including pedagogical documentation in my program. I am challenged with the continual responsibility of maintaining individual portfolios, writing, evaluating and maintaining valuable and interesting daily programs, and ensuring that mandatory state organisational regulations are being adhered to. Along with the evolution of the preschool, however, gradually I have been able to incorporate many aspects associated with pedagogical documentation back into my classroom, although not in the depth that I have done in the past. While the ways I record and analyse the children's explorations today are considerably briefer than before, perhaps this refined form of documenting children's learning will challenge me to make my observations and conclusions more succinct and valuable. In turn, although it continues to be inevitable that, as with many other early childhood educators, I spend hours working in my own time at home, perhaps as I become a more experienced documentor, this will be reduced as well.

In early childhood education, children should have access to the same learning opportunities regardless of their level of learning, cultural background, gender, socioeconomic status or any other definable characteristic. There are authentic provisions in the art of pedagogical documentation which give young children an equal opportunity to have a voice in what and how they are learning. In addition, children are involved in decision-making about the way their learning is recorded and displayed for their families and (privacy policies permitting), the communities they live and interact in as well. With this in mind, not only are we conveying the clear message to children that we believe that what they say, think and want to learn as individuals is extremely valuable, but also, hopefully, they will be encouraged by our example to respect and value the opinions and beliefs of one another as well.

Children are often involved in cooperative experiences when they are encouraged to have an individual voice and to embrace their unique strengths, as well as to share their thoughts and skills with those around them. As a result, they may teach each other new things that they may not have discovered as meaningfully on their own, or with an adult. For educators of young children, documenting children's investigations not only makes for an ever-evolving educational program, but it keeps the classroom dynamic and meaningful for everyone in it. Supporting ongoing explorations often provokes challenges of finding relevant resources through family members, or by scouring resource centres, libraries, books and toy shops. It also entices us to take risks, reflect, and wait for possibilities to reveal themselves.

I believe that the value of pedagogical documentation in early childhood educational environments cannot be underestimated. It is difficult to think of a more visual, comprehensive and meaningful way to communicate and validate the complexity behind the way children learn and discover what is important to them. The fact that many adults consistently overlook or underestimate the depth of children's thinking and the contribution they can make—not only to what and how they learn in the educational environment, but also how they view wider society and the world around them—is something that needs to be addressed more widely, both in our classrooms and in our communities.

Joanne's reflection

I am currently in my fourth year of teaching. After completing my degree, I received a placement in a state public school and taught in a relatively affluent middle-class suburban area for three years. This geographical placement came as quite a surprise for me, as we had been told that we would most likely be placed in a 'hard to staff' area where teaching could prove very challenging, particularly for the first few years of a teacher's career. Even though I had initially wanted to work with disadvantaged students, I thoroughly enjoyed a valuable three years teaching in Sydney's north, which presented its own unique opportunities and challenges.

Around nine months ago, my husband and I relocated to a small town in western New South Wales. The town of around 9000 people has a somewhat transient population, with families moving to and from the town according to the availability of work at the nearby mines. The town has a number of well-established and respected primary schools. These include public schools, a catholic and an independent school.

I have been fortunate to work at an excellent public school in our town, which has a student population of around 300. Our school is quite unique in that we have a full time Emotional Disturbance Teacher who assists a number of our children to function in the everyday classroom. This year, due to the exceptionally low socioeconomic circumstances of a large number of our families, our school has also applied for additional funding.

Over the past nine months, I have found myself teaching a number of students whose family circumstances are very difficult. Issues that these students have to live with include child abuse and neglect, physical violence, parent suicide, child-attempted suicide, mental illness, bullying, severe behavioural disorders and the use of weapons. While these issues are faced almost everywhere, the occurrence and severity of the cases I have seen here is alarming.

Our school is equipped with a strong student welfare policy encompassing a range of positive strategies and programs to assist students and families affected by these circumstances. Nevertheless, due to the somewhat 'remote' locality of the town, there is extremely limited professional support available in the form of child psychologists, counsellors and paediatricians. When they are available, families do not always have the money to access these services. Therefore, they are forced to cope the best that they can with what is often a very restricted social support network. This makes the role of the school and teachers pivotal in providing much needed support in a direction toward social change.

In a classroom situation, this has far reaching implications for the teacher. My main aim with my class of Year Three and Four students has been to attempt to create learning contexts in which students are empowered, where I can facilitate the handover of power to people who do not ordinarily have access to it in their daily life (MacNaughton and Williams, 1998). The social and economic diversity the children bring to the classroom presents an unequal balance of access to power, which I want the children not simply to recognise, but to actively challenge. I think it is important for them to realise they can make choices that influence the direction of their own lives and of those around them (MacNaughton and Williams, 1998). Documenting the work of children provides an opportunity for students' voices to be heard and to show that choices made during an investigation determine one's 'path'.

The documentation of children's investigations at university taught me a valuable way to view and support children's learning as well as to stimulate their desire to continue asking questions and seeking answers. While I am not creating documentation at the moment, I recognise that I endeavour to include the main teaching strategies that I used during the small group investigations at university. For example, I encourage students to actively use their voice to share views about problems. They listen to each other's ideas, are learning how to show respect for those perspectives that are different from their own and, importantly, ask questions to find out why things appear to be the way they are.

I often use these discussions as an opportunity to really listen to what the children are saying to each other and how they say it. I use the information I collect as a basis for planning experiences to cater for both current interests and understandings and, with no textbook constraints, the lessons are child-centred and appropriate. This has proven to be an extremely valuable teaching strategy for me, particularly when behaviour management can be an issue. I find it is essential to develop meaningful, high interest activities where children are active participants.

I have found that these lessons, together with a strong set of behavioural expectations, create a level of student engagement similar to that seen when conducting small group investigations worthy of documentation.

As a way of linking lessons or stages of a lesson, I share specific anecdotes that I have heard during previous discussions to stimulate the children's thinking. In this way the student's ideas are shown to be valued. On reflection, I can see how I have borrowed this strategy from my documentation experiences. I find that it is also beneficial to share some of my interpretations of student discussions with my class as well. This works very well although I am very mindful of when and how I share my viewpoints with the group, depending on the level of guidance I wish to offer. In addition, I also spend a considerable amount of time discussing the social processes the children have experienced, asking them to reflect critically on any inequalities they experience or witness during their time together. They also share what they feel is fair or unfair in an event, and how they can recognise, or feel, the difference. Together we then plan to apply new understandings, encouraging healthy, positive relationships and self-esteem development.

Knowledge of how to document children's work has given me the strategies to continually reflect on and refine my teaching while also really taking notice of how the children are learning and developing their understandings in a social context. I have developed a deep sense of respect for the thoughts of children. I have been inspired to analyse these thoughts by sorting through the many words spoken during social interactions in an attempt to identify the ideas and challenges that *motivate* the children to want to learn more about the world they live in. It has also provided me with a method of showing children that they are life-long learners who are *powerful and able* to overcome adversity and, as a result, make deliberate choices that positively affect the way they and others around them participate in life.

Pamela's reflection

I am currently in my fourth year of teaching Kindergarten (five and six-year-old children in their first year of school). As I stated three years ago, with the challenge of 'time', while the processes of documentation most definitely take place, the product is not a priority. The children in my class guide our lessons and I manipulate my planned lessons frequently to follow the children's line of interest, while meeting outcomes and the many other imposed requirements. We continue to be co-constructors of knowledge as I pose questions that none of us can answer!

Over the past year, my interest in visual documentation has taken a new turn as I have been very busy with my school's web page and intranet. With these media, I can see many possibilities, not only integrating technology into the curriculum, but also for documenting children's learning. Currently, the web page 'Featured Classes' contains displays of children's learning in the classroom.

These displays contain actual quotations from children, scanned images of work samples and photos of the processes the children went through to reach their final product. There is no prescription as to the set up of these pages. Teachers simply select a part or whole unit of work that a group of children or the class particularly enjoyed. Often these pages demonstrate experiences that involved a wide range of activities to enable individual learners to reach their own understanding about the concepts taught.

By utilising technology in this way, I am able to demonstrate the amazing process of learning on the World Wide Web (with parental permission). This initiative, however, definitely is developing one step at a time. My next step will be to analyse comments made by individual children and encourage the other teachers to do the same. Using technology as our tool, we can show parents and the wider community the value of 'hands on' and holistic learning. We can encourage the school community to share in the excitement of reaching new understandings and achieving a higher level of thinking through thought provoking questions and allowing children to think 'beyond the boxes' (Fleet & Patterson, 1998).

Conclusion: Catherine and Alma

In summary, some challenges to effective early documentation have become clear. At one level there are pragmatics such as selecting appropriate layout and designs that demonstrate respect for children's contributions and avoiding a decorative presentation. At a more challenging level, however, there are pedagogical decisions such as what to include and what should be left out. It is at this point that some practitioners seem to become overwhelmed with the task of giving the children voice in the process. This often results in beginning documentation including decontextualised chunks of children's conversation that lack analysis and are unhelpful.

The most fundamental difficulties for beginners though, are philosophical. These relate to the image of the child that is held by the adult and conceptions of teaching and learning processes. Difficulty conceptualising children as theory –makers contributes to a reliance on a reporting genre or the display function explained by Forman and Fyfe (1998, p 241). Depending on where the novice is positioned in teaching and learning situations with children, this can result in a focus on self, rather than an exploration of the unexpected or insightful. It seems that opportunities to discuss these experiences with others in a collaborative conversation can help the novice. When contextualised as part of a university assignment, this becomes problematic. Nevertheless, the introduction of these ideas in undergraduate teacher education provides opportunities for these conversations to begin and can be the grounding for richly complex, professional development.

References

Allen P (1985) *Who sank the boat?* Melbourne: Nelson.

Allen P (1987) *Mr McGee.* Melbourne: Nelson.

Burr J, Crisafulli D, Fleet A, Patterson C & Silversides P (2001, July) Becoming documentors. In *Unpacking interpretation: Deconstructions from Australia, America and Reggio Emilia. Conference Proceedings.* North Ryde, NSW: Institute of Early Childhood, Macquarie University.

Fleet A & Patterson C (1998) Beyond the boxes: Planning for real knowledge and live children. *Australian Journal of Early Childhood*, 23(4), 31–5.

Forman G & Fyfe B (1998) Negotiated learning through design, documentation and discourse. In C Edwards, L Gandini & G Forman (Eds) *The hundred languages of children: The Reggio Emilia approach—Advanced reflections.* (2nd Ed). (pp 239–60) Greenwich CT: Ablex.

MacNaughton G & Williams G (1998) *Techniques for teaching young children: Choices in theory and practice.* Melbourne: Addison Wesley Longman.

New R (1998) Theory and praxis in Reggio Emilia: They know what they are doing, and why. In C Edwards, L Gandini & G Forman (Eds) *The hundred languages of children: The Reggio Emilia approach—Advanced reflections.* (2nd Ed) Greenwich CT: Ablex.

Chapter Eight

Pedagogical Documentation in the Early Years of School: A Teacher's Journey

Lesley Studans

Lesley Studans works as a classroom teacher within the Catholic Education system of Parramatta in the western suburbs of Sydney, Australia. Most areas of western Sydney are rapidly expanding and new schools are being developed with an emphasis on the youngest children of the school. The diocese of Parramatta has many early childhood initiatives including: conferences for teachers, a well-attended early childhood summer school, a popular support group and website for Kindergarten teachers, and an emphasis on transition to school.

Beginnings

> The traces that children leave us of their lives and thoughts cannot be enclosed in words alone but need something more: images, drawings, writings and above all narratives.
>
> (Spaggiari, 1997, p 10)

I have a collection of photos of all the classes I have taught since the beginning of my teaching career nearly 20 years ago. Looking through these treasures recently I found the photo of my first Kindergarten class. I tried hard to remember some things about each child. Occasionally cheeky faces reminded me of particular children and their learning but, generally, they look so different in their scrubbed up formal personas, that I cannot remember them.

If I look hard enough in my cupboard, I can find my yearly teaching–learning programs where I recorded the content and objective of each lesson. At the end of each week I had dutifully recorded an evaluation of the learning. 'The children enjoyed this lesson', was written with monotonous regularity—but which children? And why? What did they think? What did they learn? This, of course, I didn't record. Not that I didn't care. I cared a lot about the processes of learning and most especially for the children. 'What starts with "i"?'…. 'Ikebana'. I was surprised by their capabilities. I was perhaps beginning to discover the strong, capable child. These children, now grown into adults in western Sydney, have probably left no trace of their time in Kindergarten beyond a photo and a register of lessons that they apparently all enjoyed. Their parents will have the same photo and a school report which again showed little of their wonderful and much loved children.

Nearly five years ago, I had another opportunity to teach Kindergarten in a different school and I was determined to do better. By this time I had taught in a preschool and had begun my difficult, stumbling journey exploring ideas from the Municipal preschools of Reggio Emilia and their implications for my teaching. I share my journey with you so that you can see that stumbling is actually a positive aspect of the experience and you will begin to discover that, 'everyday things hold wonderful secrets for those who know how to listen' (Rodari cited by Spaggiari, 1997, p 12).

Listening was where I began, or tried to begin. I bought play equipment and good quality art-making materials. To make these materials and equipment readily available, I rearranged the classroom space. I made these changes to support the children in their learning endeavours through desk arrangements that allowed them to talk together leaving space for class meetings and movement activities such as dance and drama. I stocked the class library with information books and literature, and I gave the children time to play with all the materials. I then tried to focus my observational skills by standing back and watching.

Almost immediately, the children were attracted to the writing material. A favourite game was what they called the 'baby school'. Using an easel, large paper and Textas they began to teach 'writing' to 'babies'. Some children were the teachers and some were the babies. Their interactions were intense and loud and filled me with anxiety. This was certainly not beautiful to look at or listen to. This was no Italian masterpiece of education!

I began using class meetings to organise the learning with the children and we decided together to have a baby school one afternoon with real baby brothers and sisters. I took photos, but I did not feel that I had something worthy of 'documenting'.

Soon after, many children began to ask each other, 'Do you want to go to my party? Write your name here.' A child, thus invited, would find it irresistible to write her name on the proffered piece of paper. This game was played by many children over a few weeks. What was it about the list-making that made it so engaging? Sharing with my colleagues at the RE-Search group at Macquarie University, I began to ask 'Why?'. It was not easy to find out why. I was not a good listener, so I kept on supporting their birthday list-making. I gave them materials, opportunities to make lists of other kinds, observed that lots of literacy was being learned and that the vertical form of the list was already known. No one was excluded from the birthday lists. I began to relax, but only a little. It didn't seem that anything much exciting was happening, but how wrong I was.

Still trying hard to listen and learn why, I heard Harry ask Devlin, 'Do you want to come to my party?—Write your name here in Chinese.' Harry seemed to be implying that you couldn't come to the party if you couldn't write Chinese. Harry was from a Hong Kong Chinese background and attended a Chinese language school on Sundays. All the children in his friendship group at school were of Asian heritage. Devlin was not Chinese but was sometimes invited into Harry's games at lunchtime. Faced with this dilemma, Devlin tried to write Chinese but couldn't. He decided that he could be American and created 'American' writing. Other children in the class joined in this serious writing business and produced samples of 'Swedish' and 'Lebanese' writing.

Something wonderful was obviously happening. The birthday lists were no longer the only focus; the exchanges had become definitely more complex, including an exploration of written language forms. Harry had asserted the importance of being Chinese and we had listened. *I had listened!* My teaching would never be quite the same again after Harry's wonderful gift. I learned to go beyond the superficial acknowledgement of culture in isolated lessons or multicultural days so that all children would feel included in my class. In addition to this imperative, I had also seen the initiative of children, who—sparked by a challenge—had created new opportunities for expression.

This realisation of the power of ethnicity came to me through discussion with colleagues at the RE-Search group, but even more so because at last

What to do if you can't write Chinese
or the rules inherent in script

Discoveries in a school kindergarten

What comes before?

The children have been making lists since April. These lists have taken many forms but have mostly been about birthday parties. They ask each other, *would you like to come to my party? ... Write your name here.*

I am pleased to discover everyone is included but observe that 'going to the football lists' and 'going to the museum lists' sometimes elicit refusals. The more powerful attraction of the birthday party means refusals are not likely. Birthday lists seem to be about the need to feel part of the group.

With J, the lists begin a new form with a profound effect on the whole class. He asks D - *Do you want to come to my party? Write your name here in Chinese.*

D and the other children are attempting to write Chinese but J tells them their writing is not Chinese. In the charged moment that follows, D gives up trying to write Chinese, saying, *I can write American.* Thus begins a flurry of writing, American, Samoan, Swedish, Lebanese, and Baby Zoe talk.

J seems to have a different agenda to the rest of the birthday list makers. He is from a Hong Kong background and attends Chinese Sunday school. His friendship group at school all have Asian faces. In many ways J is asserting that to him being Chinese is important. Is this what is happening with his interpretation of the birthday list? It is very interesting that he invites D with his blue eyes and freckled face to write Chinese. J had begun inviting D to play a particular game with his friends at lunchtime. Perhaps he was hoping D could write Chinese even if he didn't look Chinese.

Using Chinese in the context of birthday lists show the other children just how important being Chinese is – as important – or more important – as the birthday party itself. So D who is not aware of his ethnicity creates one he thinks he might have – American. Other children, who are aware of their background, create writing to match.

D's American writing

"My name is different ... its not a capital". I forgot to use an American 'a'. This is an American a ...see' shows teacher the 'a' from the cover of the *Very Hungry Caterpillar*. Look this is different') pointing to the upper case 'r'".

Rules of American writing:
Left to right orientation.
Use American 'a's and 'g's.
Use Capitals randomly.
Never use capitals for the first letter of names.

Below: **A's Lebanese writing**
RULES: left to right orientation
Word spaces

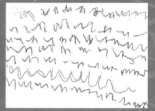

Below: **J's baby writing**
Zoe is screaming (vertical black lines)
Zoe is talking to mummy, daddy and me. (Pink circular script).
Zoe is saying I want my Mummy. (Large black circular script)
RULES:
Left to right orientation.
Noises (not just words) can have writing.

Right: **E's Swedish writing**
RULES:
Left to right orientation.
It has Australian letters but the words are different.

The gift J gave to our class was not so much an opportunity to explore writing. It was an understanding that being Chinese is important. Our ethnicity is important and should be acknowledged in the classroom.

What to do if you can't write Chinese (Exhibit-On panel)

I developed a piece of documentation, *What to do if you can't write Chinese*. The documentation told the story of the learning and, although it felt awkward, I included my reflections and growth. The process of writing helped to sharpen my reflection as I wrestled with finding the words to describe my learning. It felt awkward because it included my voice as a teacher, which I had always thought didn't belong in observations of children's learning. I began to realise then that I actually had a lot to do with the learning. After all, I chose what to observe and record. Acknowledging my role in the learning, showing myself reflecting and growing along with the children rather than removing the personal voice, actually showed the learning more realistically and honestly.

I had discovered the power that documentation had for self-reflection and growth. In later pieces of documentation, I was able to document my learning of many things, such as the power relationships within groups and how groups were able to form agreement. Here is Toby's comment to Steven who was trying to direct Ricardo not to use too many blocks in his robot construction:

Toby: We're all bosses! (to Steven) (Other boys show agreement)
Teacher: You're *all* bosses?
Toby: Because if one person tries to be the boss, the other people get sad
            and then they fight.
Teacher: Does the robot group fight?
Toby: Yes, but not for long because we want to be friends.

Having found my voice and feeling more confident to include it in my documentation I had written: 'Of course Toby's comment to Steven shows that he is trying to lead the group and helping to keep harmony in a sophisticated, wise way.'

Insights gained through this reflective documentation and other investigations—where I watched and guided the children to form groups—have helped me to develop a classroom learning community that authenticates the children's use of their own voices. With this piece of documentation displayed in the classroom, Toby and the robot makers were able to become the group harmony experts and offered advice to the other children when needed. The investigation itself can provide symbols of learning, such as a robot drawing, that give the learning group a sense of identity.

By the end of that first year, each piece of pedagogical documentation I made contained photos, artefacts and recorded dialogue that highlighted the children's thinking. With each piece of documentation, I grew in wonder at the children's ability to work together, pursue big ideas, create theories, and have substantive conversations about issues of great importance to the world. Highlighting the wonderful thinking of children gave them a voice, which I'm sure would not be otherwise heard inside or outside my classroom even within my own small school community. However, for their voices to be heard, I had to take the step to share the learning with parents and teachers, both inside my school community and beyond. It was a seriously scary step as it opened me up to criticism.

It was the children who helped me to do this. Perhaps my muse was Sebastian. His exploration of patterning with coloured plastic chain lengths led to an exciting investigation into the length of a chain. He, along with a small group of children, was able to count 256 links in a chain using mathematical strategies. His mathematical thinking became known in our school community and to himself. This same child, when tested on a well-regarded assessment for mathematics knowledge, had failed to show what the assessment considered to be 'foundation mathematical understanding'. Yet, two years later, he is doing well at mathematics. I like to think that Sebastian was able to start his school learning in mathematics with the emphasis on what he could do. He was able to attempt what he could not yet do with the community of learners in our classroom.

Pedagogical documentation can highlight the learning of children who may not easily succeed in a traditional curriculum and who would otherwise receive little public attention. For example, Michael would often avoid expressing his ideas through writing or drawing but loved to paint. One day after a walking excursion to a local river, I set some watercolours on a table with some prints of paintings of rivers. Michael began exploring how best to depict water through various painting techniques and styles. As he verbalised what he was going to try, other children were learning his techniques: 'I'm going to put white paint on the top to lighten the blue even though it doesn't exactly mix with the blue and it also makes the water sparkle like in the sun.' Seeing his work displayed with a story about his thinking, empowered Michael to see himself as a knowledgeable and clever thinker, an unavailable experience in a classroom where only writing is valued.

My school has many children who do not stay long, but I can look through my copies of the documentation and remember how Amanda knew how to draw cubes, Rhiannon invented Swedish writing, Ahmed found 'church paper' (overhead transparencies) was needed to make our drawn images visible through the overhead projector and Hiro helped to find the bear through poetry and drawing. I can remember them—they have left a trace with me and at my school. I imagine, perhaps pessimistically, that two of these children will leave little traces of their childhood anywhere else, even within their own families. Where children are invisible, then they somehow seem less important.

Confrontations

It has become even more apparent to us that the teacher's practical work is an 'interpretive theory' that integrates stories and micro stories of research with real-life contexts… [The] ennobling of the teacher's work… we have always believed in.

(Rinaldi, 2001, p 154)

After a year of building positive, informative relationships with the parents through meetings, newsletters and informal contacts, I was ready to overcome what I felt was the 'parent bogey' and share the documentation with them. I made A4 sized copies of the documentation and put it in display folders to be sent home. I was surprised by how positively parents received the stories of their children's learning:

Dave: Reading through the portfolio made us feel as if we were in the school with the children, seeing them interact and learning from their disagreements.

Hannah: We found it fascinating to read about what the children's thoughts are and their perspectives.

Mike: We are very impressed by all the work the children did to find out about the overhead projector.

The parents were able to see their children's thinking and keep this as a record. It allowed them to engage with their children's learning beyond the deeply unsatisfactory 'What did you learn at school today?' parent–child dialogue.

One parent, Phil, was a notable exception. He was worried by the invention of 'witch's writing' that his daughter created with some other children. This group of children in the first few weeks of school began playing a witch's game and were creating spells. I gave them an old, bound book and pencils, challenging them to write their spells down. The group of children created a sophisticated writing code together with swirls and zigzags as well as some letters and other symbols such as a witch's hat. The communal witch's writing was compared with the children's emergent conventional writing in the documentation that was shared with the parents. I hoped to highlight for the parents the children's impressive and deep understandings about literacy and how text is constructed.

With such wonderful learning, I wondered why Phil was unhappy. If the children could learn through their disagreements, then perhaps I could too. Unfortunately, I asked the parent to unpack something that was too personal to communicate. I felt embarrassed and the conversation stumbled, but our relationship continued and grew strong again over the next couple of years. When I taught Phil's daughter later, he helped her to download information from the Internet about Halloween for our investigations into celebrations. Witches at school were no longer an issue with him.

By exploring this disagreement, I thought that I would be confronting my fear of parental disapproval, but instead discovered that behind the parents' reactions to teachers there can also be fear. However, the deep level of communication that was made possible through the pedagogical documentation helped expose and shrink fear and created a better relationship. Exploring this disagreement was not always pleasant, but again showed me that the 'parent bogey' is a myth. As a strong teacher with a story of wonderful learning to share with parents, I have discovered there is nothing for teachers to fear.

Sharing such documentation also gave parents insights into the deep levels of thinking that teachers engage in every day. This ennobling of the work of education was to me unintentional but, of course, is logical. How I look at the children affects how I look at myself. The wonderful, capable children, for whom I was advocating through the documentation, do not grow into intellectually and emotionally poor adults. When I say I am a 'strong' teacher, I mean that I am a human teacher. I don't mean at all that I am exceptional. I am like Amanda, Rhiannon, Sebastian, Michael, Toby, Hiro and Harry.

Finding direction

One finds the way using a compass rather than taking a train with its fixed routes and schedules

(Rinaldi, 1998, p 119)

If we limit children, we limit ourselves.

(Malaguzzi, 1998, p 64)

Part of the reason that I was not able to share my documentation with the parents and even many of my colleagues in my first year of documenting children's learning was that I had not sorted out how the learning in my classroom fitted

Representation of drips for 'counting water'

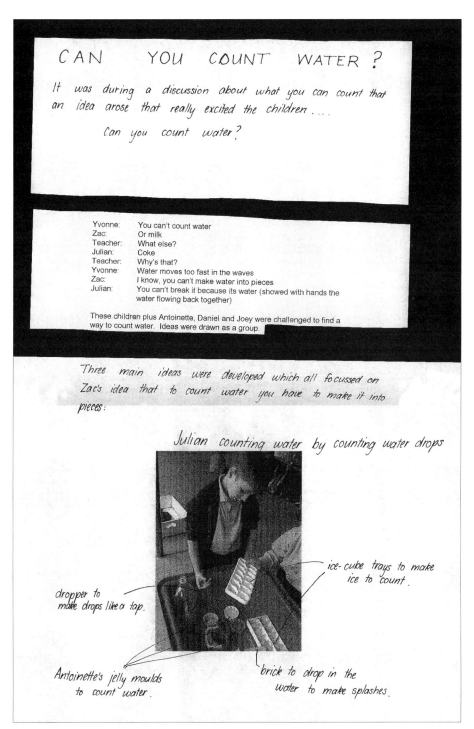

CAN YOU COUNT WATER?

It was during a discussion about what you can count that an idea arose that really excited the children ....

Can you count water?

Yvonne:	You can't count water
Zac:	Or milk
Teacher:	What else?
Julian:	Coke
Teacher:	Why's that?
Yvonne:	Water moves too fast in the waves
Zac:	I know, you can't make water into pieces
Julian:	You can't break it because its water (showed with hands the water flowing back together)

These children plus Antoinette, Daniel and Joey were challenged to find a way to count water. Ideas were drawn as a group.

Three main ideas were developed which all focussed on Zac's idea that to count water you have to make it into pieces:

Julian counting water by counting water drops

ice-cube trays to make ice to count.

dropper to make drops like a tap.

Antoinette's jelly moulds to count water.

brick to drop in the water to make splashes.

Documentation of counting water provocation

with the prescribed New South Wales (NSW) syllabus documents. I felt the learning was substantial and the parents seemed to agree, but without the imprimatur of outcomes and indicators from the syllabus the children's learning would not be seen as significant. Alma Fleet (2004) had suggested that many syllabus outcomes could be achieved through this learning. The challenge for me was to know these outcomes in more detail. For the documentation of a investigation about counting water, which mostly seemed to be about children making theories of counting and measuring, I looked in the Mathematics Syllabus and easily found outcomes in the 'Working Mathematically' section.

I saw that it would be difficult for these outcomes to be achieved except through an investigative focus. So, I now include outcomes with each finished piece of documentation. It has been easy to find outcomes from all syllabus areas. Many times the Kindergarten children were able to achieve outcomes beyond the expected Early Stage One level (in the language of the NSW state documents).

I have been able to experiment with developing investigations through any Key Learning Area, rather than having to have a special time for investigations and/or play on top of an already tight timetable. That schedule includes mandated times for English and Mathematics as well as a tight scope and sequence of content for Human Society and Its Environment, Science and Technology and Personal Development, Health and Physical Education.

So, I discovered that the 'outcomes bogey' was as fictitious as the 'parent bogey'. I now view the outcomes as Carla Rinaldi's compass that I need to take on the journey of learning with the children in my class. I was right to feel anxious that the children in my class achieved the outcomes. I realised that narrowing the focus of education to outcomes only can lead to restrictive educational practices that paradoxically do not achieve the outcomes related to critical thinking, problem solving, co-operation and expression. Children are only expected to achieve the outcomes for the stage that corresponds with their age, when so often they can achieve more. Further, some of my past, traditional practices such as the whole class colouring-in of the same sheet, or creating the same piece of craft, have little or no educational value and actually achieved no outcomes at all!

Moving on

>…we must realise that we need to develop networks to sustain ourselves as learners, so that we can continue to build on our own rich history and present circumstance, as we move into a future that is difficult to visualise or comprehend.
>
> (Millikan, 2003, p 134)

I write as if I have overcome many obstacles and in my first two years I was able to forge ahead. Yet, even though I can see ways around the obstacles of parental expectations, the prescribed curriculum and other obstacles not elaborated on here—such as time, materials and children with special rights—there is still a lot of stumbling to do. After making a start, I now look out the window of my classroom into the outside world.

I work in a diocesan system that has supported me on this journey. I am often asked to share my experiences with other Kindergarten teachers and to do this I work with the diocesan curriculum consultants and the early childhood committee. I also occasionally share my documentation with diocesan administrators to advocate for the potential of children. At the diocesan level there is enthusiasm, support and collegiality.

Yet at the level of the classroom—the level where the children are—there has been very little real change. Kindergarten teachers are certainly aware of the importance of play and creative expression and do incorporate some time for this, but do not yet put much emphasis on the learning resulting from play. Schools are aware of the importance of transition to school, but still make little effort to create a school that is welcoming to the young child, focusing on identifying their deficits rather than maximising their potential.

Within my own school, there is encouragement and dialogue, but the dialogue is not yet substantial. Most colleagues react to the documentation as appealing stories. Ironically, in order to allow the children to socially construct knowledge within a rich, emergent curriculum, I have to work by myself.

I realise that things are changing slowly and there are many hopeful signs. Ideas currently widespread within most schools of my diocese—co-operative learning, multiple intelligences, awareness of different learning styles, whole brain learning, reflective learning—are respectful of the rights of children and create a more inclusive school environment. What is missing is the pedagogy of listening (Rinaldi, 2003) to children, not able to be packaged but much more powerful—empowering to children, parents and teachers.

So, I remain optimistic that more of my colleagues will join me and discover the wonderful secrets in their everyday living with the children in their classrooms. In my efforts to bear witness to the strong, capable child and teacher, pedagogical documentation is my dearest friend:

> …our written reflections…could evoke a number of different sensations…one of those sensations, which may cause a slight irritation, could be the air of optimism that pervades all… After all, education must stand on the side of optimism or else it will melt like an ice-cream in the sun.
>
> (Malaguzzi, 1998, p 96)

References

Fleet A (2004) Imagining the child in school. Keynote address, Catholic Schools and the Religious Development of Kindergarten Children Forum, 1–2 April. Sydney: NSW Catholic Education Commission.

Malaguzzi L (1998) History, ideas and basic philosophy: An interview with Lella Gandini. In C Edwards, L Gandini & G Forman (Eds) *The hundred languages of children: The Reggio Emilia approach—Advanced reflections.* (2nd Ed). Greenwich, CT: Ablex.

Millikan J (2003) *Reflections: Reggio Emilia principles within Australian contexts.* Sydney, NSW: Pademelon Press.

NSW Department of Education and Training (1999) *Starting Kindergarten: Assessing literacy and numeracy using foundation outcomes.* Ryde, NSW: NSW Department of Education and Training.

Rinaldi C (1998) Projected curriculum constructed through documentation— Progettazione: An Interview with Lella Gandini. In C Edwards, L Gandini & G Forman (Eds) *The hundred languages of children: The Reggio Emilia approach— Advanced reflections.* (2nd Ed). Greenwich, CT: Ablex.

Rinaldi C (2001) Dialogues. In C Guidici, M Krechevsky & C Rinaldi (Eds) *Making learning visible: Children as individual and group learners.* Reggio Emilia, Italy: Reggio Children.

Rinaldi C (2003) The pedagogy of listening: The listening perspective from Reggio Emilia. In *Innovations in early education: The international Reggio exchange.* Merrill-Palmer Institute, Wayne State University.

Spaggiari S (1997) The invisibility of the essential. In M Castagnetti, V Vecchi (Eds) *Shoe and Meter.* Reggio Emilia: Reggio Children.

Studans L (2002) How to count water. What to do if you can't write Chinese. In J Robertson & A Fleet (Eds) *Exhibit-on. Provocations: Clarity and Confusion Catalogue.* North Ryde, NSW: Institute of Early Childhood, Macquarie University.

Chapter Nine

Focusing the Lens: Gazing at 'Gaze'

Janet Robertson

The stories told in this chapter arise from Janet's work at Mia-Mia, a not-for-profit child care centre attached to the Institute of Early Childhood, Macquarie University in Sydney, Australia. The gaze and its importance in early childhood, as well as the notion of explaining it in the metaphor of glasses, was first presented at a conference (Robertson, 2001). It was influenced strongly by research she was undertaking at the time exploring the reconceptualisation of education and postmodern theory.

Introduction

As a teacher of young children, interpreting what it is I 'see' when I observe children is central to my role. I use interpretation to chart my teaching course through the moment, the day and onwards through the year. My interpretation of what is happening is constructed by surrounding influences, both covert and overt. These influences create a frame that shapes my 'gaze' and, rather like smoke, the covert influences occlude my gaze without my realising it. I have shaped this chapter around the notion of the gaze and the metaphor of lenses to help us 'see' clearly the influences which shape the three stories I will tell. As always, I am mindful of how complex the endeavour of education is—it is never simple.

> The desire to simplify, to package reality into manageable categories, is a strong human impulse. Dichotomising is a common strategy that flows from this impulse. While dichotomies provide an efficient way to categorize phenomena, they can be misleading in their oversimplification of the world's complexity.
>
> (Mardell, 2001, p 282)

Avoiding oversimplification is one of the primary challenges that we are setting ourselves in reconceptualising our practices. For all of us, whatever life we lead, we construct our notions and our meaning of the world through the 'gaze'. This gaze is the lens through which we construct and in turn are constructed by our peers, environment and context. We filter what we hear and see through this gaze. Professionally speaking, 'the child you see is the child you teach' or, as Glenda MacNaughton (2000, p 74) puts it, 'particular conventions structure how a teacher looks [gazes] at children'. So, it would seem we need to focus on our focus and gaze upon our gaze. I'm now of the opinion that whatever gaze we have, the lens through which we are gazing obscures other possibilities. Oh, how simple it would be to swap one gaze for another and that would be it—the developmental theory gaze for the Reggio Emilia philosophical gaze for instance—or to assume that one gaze at all times is better than another. Unfortunately, life is not simple so education will not be simple either. No single lens through which to gaze, will do. I use the notion of lens to encompass both the larger gaze of the institutions of education, as well as the teacher's more intimate gaze, which occurs whilst in the midst of 'teaching'. I will try the metaphor of lenses or glasses in the hope that it will illustrate the many-layered and multi-faceted sides of the gaze and the interpretations that are shaped by it. So, what lenses do we use?

The personal gaze

Let us begin with the lenses we are all born with. Those readers who do not wear glasses, bear with me. If I take off my glasses, I can see very little, just a blur of colour. Without glasses, colour takes on a primal element. I cannot identify individuals, but overall pattern is evident. I also can't hear very well; it is now I realise how much I rely on sight to hear. I also look different. When I take my glasses off at school the children fall silent, as though I've suddenly become naked.

The historical gaze

When I happen to put on an old pair of glasses, with lenses which no longer suit my eyes, I have to fight nausea and giddiness. Why? My brain expects to be able to see when my arm makes the gesture of putting lens to face. When the vision is blurred, my brain makes heroic attempts to adjust, hence the nausea and unbalance. Is this what we feel when we unearth the origins of our professional gaze—unbalanced? 'There is a need for continual scrutiny of the past, not for the sake of the past, but for the sake of the present' (Hultqvist & Dahlberg, 2001, p 6). So, from the past, what do we need to gaze upon? Perhaps the scientific modernists' slant towards observing young children? (Cannella, 1999; Dahlberg, 1999) This so called 'objective' gaze at children as the research 'subject', has pervaded our everyday work with young children. From this perspective we are supposed to be objective, removing ourselves from a subjective stance. This outdated paradigm should be turned on its head and we should be 'rejoicing in subjectivity' (Millikan, 2001, p 7), gazing *with* the child not *upon* the child, whilst being aware of the influences inherent in our gaze.

What were, and are, the lenses which shaped and are shaping theory? We learn theory at the early childhood academies—university, and other post-secondary institutions—and use these theoretical constructions to support existing practices such as the Quality Improvement and Accreditation System, Key Learning Areas from the NSW Department of Education and Training, or state or national regulations. However, the power base and the assumptions which shape these theories are, and should be, continually questioned, not necessarily to throw them out but to better understand the discourses that shape them. For example, Hultqvist & Dahlberg (2001, p 6) critique developmental theory in the following terms:

> …[there is] a growing body of research which demonstrates that early develop-mental discourse relied on racist thought and excluded all but those children with the right signs: being white, middle class, and living under orderly conditions, preferably in small towns on the US east coast.

Rebecca New's (1994) scholarly critique of Developmentally Appropriate Practice (DAP) inferred a similar thing, although without the power of the term 'racist' as used by Dahlberg and Hultqvist. The continual critique of what was taken as 'a truth' has altered the way developmental discourse is used now, opening opportunities for 'other thinking' to occur. I once wore these scientific modernist glasses and saw clearly then what is now blurred. My understanding then of what was clear, is now unbalanced.

The borrowed gaze

If you were to wear someone else's glasses, for some of you it may be only a slight difference; for others, a canyon of optical challenges. It would seem that you cannot lend your glasses to someone else for them to 'see' what you 'see'. For all of us our gaze is subjective—it is our own, no matter how shaped by past lenses, lives and loves.

Take the example of a teacher witnessing block play, then describing it to another. Both interpret it from their own perspectives. One teacher may consider the children are negotiating and co-operating. The other teacher may interpret the boys' rambunctious gestures and loud voices as monopolising the space, excluding girls who attempted to enter the play. These gendered gazes, both seen through gendered filters, are only made visible when the two begin to discuss what it is each has seen. One gaze is looking through a lens of 'boys co-operating', while the other is through a lens of 'unfairness and exclusion'. It is through rigorous discussion and examination that each borrowed lens becomes useful to the other.

The professional gaze

The truths of the 'institution'—and by that I mean the whole shebang of early childhood education—influence how we work. These 'truths' glaze over our personal gaze. We often wear glasses for different occasions, such as when we put on other lenses for work. We arrive at work one person and pop on another pair of glasses, taking them off when we go home. These lenses, specifically designed for work, alter the reality before us. They create a boundary of gaze through which we see things.

Early childhood has its own institutional boundaries, and it is through these boundaries that we, as the postmodernists say, police and govern education, teachers, children and their families (McNamee, 2000; Cannella, 2001). Essentially this governing is the reinforcing of the 'truths' of how young children should be cared for and educated. Simply put, as a society we won't allow young children under five to roam the streets, or participate in the paid workforce. But beyond the obvious there is governance often only visible when our ideas of early childhood are contrasted with other ideas from other cultures. Perhaps the tourist lens comes into play here, as the camera snaps images across the world. Why are there fences around child care centres in Australia, whereas in other countries there are not? Why does child care equipment look a certain way? In other countries such equipment does not exist and, lo and behold, children manage to grow themselves up, learning whatever it was the equipment was going to teach them. One serious point in unpacking gaze is to really look for the silences, for the hidden or the 'othered' within this governance—to always ask *Why?* or *Where does this idea come from?* In altering our work glasses, or shifting the lens, we may be able to ask these questions.

Global gaze

Is there a Reggio gaze? Well, certainly. The educators who work in Reggio Emilia, however, have their Reggio gaze, as we in Australia have our Reggio gaze (Mardell, 2001). Although linked, they are not and cannot be the same. It seems to me that the underlying thought in both contexts is what counts: this is the image of the child. This image is created from lenses which filter our very understanding of children. For example, the images of the child known from the work context are only partial pieces of the picture of the child.

Is our Australian child the same as the one in Reggio, or America? No and yes. They are all the subject of the gaze, and as subjects they have little power over how we interpret their actions and lives. It is the lens through which we gaze which, in turn, creates what is 'seen'.

Cultural filters

When the word 'Approach' was chosen for the title of the US book, *The hundred languages of children: The Reggio Emilia approach—Advanced reflections* (Edwards, Gandini & Forman, 1998), what other words were discarded? I've always felt the word 'Approach' implies method, and I find it jars, but is this a cross Pacific–Atlantic–Janet translation tangle? I know now it's not, as the educators in Reggio Emilia are exercising more control over the nomenclature of their pedagogy (Millikan, 2001). I know the Swedes had a 20-year affair with the notion that Reggio Emilia was mainly about art and creativity—a notion derived from an original interpretation of sub-titles from a film. This perception has since been recast.

So what interpretation of Reggio Emilia's educational enterprise are we making here in Australia? Perhaps many are taking the practices too literally, rather than thinking about the ideas. Unfortunately our gaze upon Reggio Emilia is often dazzled by the gems which bejewel the outward apparition, the sheer beauty of many of the environmental images that visitors encounter. There are, however, possibilities for localising thinking as noted by Hultqvist and Dahlberg (2001, p 9):

> …in the form of 'indigenous foreigners'…, international heroes such as John Dewey, Michel Foucalt, and Lev Vygotsky…are empty signifiers, homeless figures of thought that circulate freely in the global distributive apparatuses of research and education. When these figures are temporarily arrested in a local context, they take on the characteristic of that context before they move on to other contexts and become the target for further interpretations and reinterpretation.

These authors contest that the local input creates another idea, and this I think is the challenge for our gaze. Mardell (2001, p 280) points out that the 'cultural knots' which become apparent when observing another culture's interpretation of education can serve as a doorway into reconceptualising our own ideas of education. These knots are the untidy complexities that emerge when differing cultural contexts intermingle. Can we make the gaze upon Reggio Emilia's educational experiences a cultural knot, rather than a mere replica?

The observation gaze

With a magnifying lens we can see the minutiae of experiences. We can describe things and events with astonishing detail. However, if using only this lens, the wider picture can be lost. Central to all our work in unpacking the gaze is to unpack our gaze upon the child (Robertson, 1999). The child we gaze upon while at work is different from the child we gaze upon at home.

While looking closely at the text of a transcript of a conversation among three children, we can marvel at their theories and cleverness. We risk, however, forgetting that with every selection there are choices not chosen (Dahlberg, 1999). We must never forget that in choosing bits of transcript for analysis, choices are being made that reflect values cloaked in power. Foucault's oft-quoted phrase, 'everything is dangerous' (MacNaughton, 2000, p 241), is apt here; remember you can burn holes in paper with magnifying glasses.

So, as a practitioner, what lenses do I wear? I hope as many as possible. They also alter as we progress though an experience; lenses and gaze change as events, children and I live our lives together. Often after the event I can put on my reflection lenses and, with the luxury of time and distance, think about what happened. Here are two stories about my life with children which might make these ideas clearer.

What's missing? A story told with multiple lenses

A musician had visited the centre and I had taken photographs of the event. Shortly after his visit, I showed the photographs to four early-bird children at about 7.30 one morning. I admit to having an agenda. I wanted to pop up a quick display in the foyer so families could see the event and the wondrous things children 'got' from it. If you like, I had the display lens on. After the children (aged between three years and four years six months) had a good look, I asked Nerida to 'tell me about it':

> James (the musician) has a, a, a, he has one of the those, they look like dragons (Pointing to drum). And there's Carl and me and Mike and Jane and Anna and Keith and Julie and Vicky and Penny and Geraldine and Ruby and Colin and Caet and Matthew and Kate and Sydney and Alicia and Len.

I interrupt (still with my agenda) 'and what does the drum do?'. Nerida, very polite, turns to me and says gently, 'it shakes', and mimics the movement with her hand. Still not having listened to her, I ask, 'and what did you like best?' She burst into a smile and said:

> I'm thinking of the songs and singing along. And James has lots and lots of instruments, a drum and a guitar, shaker, tambourine, whistle and frog, two frogs that Tom and I used. Colin was using instruments, and James played his guitar.

I bask in this recall, thinking 'this is more like it, I'll be able to make a great display in the foyer to show the parents how clever their children are'. I push the photos towards Tom, who looks briefly at them, then crosses his arms and looks cranky. I move the photos to Carl, who immediately says:

> There is me, and Mike was sitting behind me, and you Nerida and Jon and Mike next to you and Ruby is next to me. He [James] has all these instruments. I like the guitar the best, 'cause I have it at home.

Mike leans over, saying 'look at the red eyes' and all three laugh. Tom still sits back in his chair, looking cross. Then Mike says, 'I'm there, and so are you Carl, there is Oliver and Geraldine and look my brother, Colin.' He scans the group at the table, returns to the photos and says, 'there's you, Nerida and you, Tom'. Tom drops his arms and says 'where Tom?', craning his head forward. It is at this moment I start to refocus my lens. Mike points to Tom's photo and Tom stabs his picture 'Tom!' and then recounts those sitting about him, 'Colin, Vicky and

Kate'. I begin to understand. Tom's reaction to the presence of his image interrupts my agenda. Was his supposed exclusion from the shots so personally distressing he could not participate in a simple discussion?

In a flash, rather like a small movie, I recalled all those other times I have sat with children with photos and patiently sat through the 'this is me; that's you; where are you?' comments, just letting them pass through this stage and waiting for the real thinking to emerge. As I re-viewed this 'movie', I realised that what I had thought was a preface, was in fact central to the entire movie. Children's presence, their notion of group, of needing not only to be present in the photos, but also to recall who else was there and in what position, was central to their even beginning to think about the instruments. When Mike scanned the group at the table, then found them in the photo, he affirmed their joint, virtual and real presence.

As I was in mid-thought, Carl leaned over and said, 'there is me', pointing to a fragment of yellow jumper. Mike and Nerida leaned over and nodded. In a swift change of focus, I laughingly said, 'Well where is your head?' Carl gaily prodded a point above the photo and said 'there!'. I pretended to look puzzled and he launched into a long explanation of why his head was not there, as the camera had cut it off, ending with 'but I was there, yeah'. Out of the mouths of babes. He had spoken the lens word while, metaphorically, I had decapitated him.

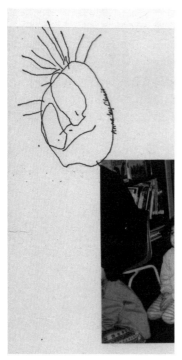

Drawing of staff member's head

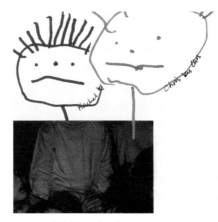

Drawing of children's heads

At last abandoning the notion of a foyer display about musical instruments, I suggested he might like to draw his head. He was out of his chair so fast he nearly fell over. Collecting pen and paper he settled down to a difficult task. Drawing is not really Carl's medium, he's more a builder and talker. While measuring and thinking, he noted Ruby and Anne were missing heads as well and drew them in. His engagement with replacing what was missing attracted others, Mike tackled himself, Geraldine completed Jon's body and legs and Mike drew his entire self and placed it behind Carl's chair.

As you can see, every notion of drawing was 'disturbed' by the need to replace what was missing. Their usual schema for drawing was interrupted and the problem of how to draw seated people strained drawing skills, requiring discussions among all four about how to do it. Intimate sharing, even drawing on each other's paper, characterised these drawings. I certainly had my lens focused on the possibilities for negotiation and problem solving at that moment. I had managed to dispose of my 'art and craft' lens, and use my 'visible thinking' lenses instead to assist me in my gaze upon their drawing.

James the musician

At the end of the table, Chloe had been beavering away on a drawing and she patiently waited till I had time to cut it out. By now, focused on body parts and not actually dismissing her work but leaving it on the back burner, I casually asked her who it was, as she had drawn an entire person. She picked up the photo without the musician, and said, 'It's James [the musician], it goes here', and placed it in the appropriate position aligned to the audience. Oh dear, wide lenses required!

Now I needed the lens of enquiry: Why did Tom feel so put out when, at first, he did not see himself in the photo? Is it that he is so much a member of the group that he can't participate in the group when he is absent from its image? Does he see himself first, and then see the group? Is Nerida's inclusion of everyone, and Carl's inclusion of missing body parts, a symbol of their groupness? Can I surmise that by living together all these years they feel as one, and need to identify the pack before they move on? Or is it that they so appreciate each other's involvement in the lives they lead with us, that it is themselves they note when they note others? Can we track important friendships and significant others by their being mentioned within such a litany? More and more as I think about this, the more I realise I needed a lens of relationship—way beyond the notion of social and emotional development. I needed a relationship lens which places within its focus all of us living at school, boy and girl, present and absent, a lens which is in the Italian, 'Io chi siamo'—'I am who we are', (New, 1998, p 265) or 'we are who I am'.

Beyond the lens of relationships between people, I need a lens of relationships among materials. As Vea Vecchi says (1994), 'all materials have their own ABCs'. Drawing suited the photographs and the ABCs of drawing provided the children with built in problems. I did not need to invent challenges for the children; they emerged as the children tried to fit the missing pieces into the proportions of the photo, challenging the comfortable schema they have for representing people.

Each child's solution to the problems of representation illuminates who they are and how they are shaped by those around them. As Mike wrestled with how to replicate his shirt, he had forgotten he was to draw what was missing, not what existed. Geraldine remonstrated with him, pointing out that his shirt would obscure Jon's face, placing the paper shirt on the photograph to make the point. 'Oh' said Mike, and then sat back perplexed. He made as if to leave. Geraldine leaned across and pointed to the base of the shirt in the photograph, and said, 'you need a bottom, then legs'. Mike, who was then prepared to continue, accepted Geraldine's gift. His need for accuracy was evident when he asked if any one could see his shoes in the other photos as he needed to draw them and could not remember what he was wearing that day. The two of them pored over the shots hunting for the evidence, chatting about shoes. Geraldine and Mike make unlikely colleagues; it is an accident of timing that they have been together each day at this time of the morning. It seems that the lure of the missing parts made for this unusual intellectual alliance between disparate ages and natures.

The children's experiences with these snapshots illustrates that a photograph can be a door to other possibilities. Two readers of the same photo will invariably create two meanings. Therefore the lens (in the human sense) through which the photo is constructed is necessarily important and worthy of critique. Do we edit as we click the shutter? Yes. Consider how many photos we have in our collections of crying children? Probably few, if any. I suppose we worry that pictures of crying children will give the wrong impression, and therefore we silence a vital part of children's lives.

The notion of child as reader of images empowers the child to be an active receptor of text or image (Fuery and Mansfield, 1997). This, no longer passive, reader requires our acknowledgement of the power of a 'writerly' text or image, one 'in which the text is actively constructed by the reader' (p 207). This presupposes that a photograph itself is taken with that intention in mind. So a pre-photograph lens is required: No longer are photographs happy snaps to show parents, but are illustrations of our gaze.

As Gunilla Dahlberg (1999) says, there must be 'an ethics of encounter' when engaging in relationships. And indeed there is a 'choice, a choice among choices, a choice in which pedagogues themselves are participating. Likewise, that which we do not choose is also a choice' (p 33).

Was I in danger of seeking the 'Reggio investigation' and missing a profound moment and insight into the inclusion of children here? It is possible that the 'Reggio moment' can obscure other moments. This 'ethics of an encounter' troubles and delights me. Always as we pursue a path, we choose not to select other paths. My delight is in those other paths that I still glimpse as I pass; my worry is that I don't want orthodoxy to dictate the paths I choose.

Circles: stories told with the relationship gaze

Next I will tell several stories about circles. The first has been told on a previous occasion (Fleet and Robertson, 2004). The toddlers (children aged between two years and two years ten months) had been able to make a standing ring or circle all year. Usually an adult participated in making the circle, sorting out all the odds and ends once the children had partially assembled the circle. The process seemed to fascinate them. They held hands and arranged each other within the circle, giggling, swinging arms and smiling at each other across the space in the middle. This passion for circles has intrigued me. What is it? I decided to put their desire to the test. This time I asked the group if they could make a circle on their own. My role as photographer seemed to help the children realise I was not in a position to help them.

From their starting positions, the children quite easily joined hands, in much the same order that they had been sitting. Very young children such as Poppy, Jeff and Ruby acceded to the 'power' of the group, just standing and having their hands held by more experienced circle makers. Ryan, seemingly excited by the emerging shape, galloped around the edge for a while, initially missing out on finding a gap and joining hands. However, he was drawn to one edge of the circle and held Ruby's hand. Movement now ceased, they appeared satisfied with the shape. Stan shot through the younger children's complacency by announcing. 'It's only a half circle.'

Charley, assessing the situation, seemed to realise that Ryan's position presented the problem. I'm not sure whether he thought by moving himself he could bridge the gap between the edges, or whether he intended to drag the circle around towards Leah, who was on the other edge. Marrisa, realising that if Ryan moved towards Leah the gap would close, left her place and took Ryan's arm and pulled him over to Leah. Unfortunately, Ryan let go of Ruby's hand, thereby making another gap. At this point Poppy, on her sixth day with us, let go both hands and stood off centre, her hands occupied by her bag. Charley and Marrisa unaware of the breaches in the shape, returned to their places. Stan moved around to hold Jeff's hand, stopping that gap. Charley left his place once more, and remonstrated with Poppy, 'hold hands, no bag, hold hands'. Poppy, with little English, considered this for a moment. Charley returned to Ryan, held his hand firmly and dragged the circle around towards Poppy. Marrisa and Louis quickly held hands bridging the gap left by Charley. Then the masterstroke— Charley reached down and held the strap of Poppy's bag, she took one look, turned sideways and held Ruby's hand with her left. The circle was complete.

It took seven minutes for the eleven children to achieve the circle. Those children who remained in place were seminal in the process. By maintaining the shape they allowed Charley, Marrisa and Poppy to make the appropriate corrections. To create the circle each individual had to suppress his or her other desires such as to run, walk away or dance. Charley's and Marrisa's obvious leadership, Stan's complacency puncture, Poppy's courage in allowing Charley to touch her precious talisman from home, Charley's empathy in knowing the bag was precious and his tenderness in allowing her to still keep it, and Ryan's ceasing to gallop, were integral to the circle eventually being formed. It seems that the group utilised the skills each child brought to the group, and thus the circle was not only a joint enterprise but represented joint expertise (New, 1994).

I have repeated this request several times over the years, and it is always different, and the same, with children achieving the standing ring as a joint enterprise utilising joint expertise. In 2002, the group (children aged between two years and three years one month) accommodated with great tolerance a child whose contribution to the circle-making was to always sit in the centre of the emerging shape. Chloe's desire was to be in the prime position for first go at the game, once the circle was complete. Her action of remaining seated (a rather brave resolve as the embryonic circle swayed and gyrated around her), gave the rest of the group a focus around which to circle. One could take the position that Chloe was being self-serving. However, at times during the formation of the ring, the intentions of the others faltered, and she would burst into song giving a lusty rendition of her favourite game, 'Sandy Girl'. Given this audible prompt, the others would once again re-grasp hands and attempt the ring again.

Lured by the sound of singing, Joe, a child with Down syndrome, appeared at the door just as the group managed to encircle Chloe. Joe's preferred mode of communication at the time was signing, so when Anna turned her head and saw Joe at the door, she dropped her hand from the circle and signed 'come', calling his name. He moved towards the group, who all remained still, Anna organised for Joe to hold hands on his left, then grasping his right she completed the ring again and they began to play the game.

Such inclusion and competence on the part of Joe, Anna, Chloe and the group once more affirmed for me that membership of the group is central to life, for all of the group. The lens or gaze upon Chloe by the group could have been censorious, but with amicable tolerance it accepted Chloe's need to be where she was, in return for her singing prompts. At one time I would have felt saddened by Chloe's presumption she would be first, but in taking my cue from the group, I watched and accepted, and then realised how well they know her. As Mardell (2001, p 280) says '…fairness does not have to be sacrificed by such an interpretation of equal opportunity'. Her contribution outweighs her presumption of being first.

As a postscript to this circle work, when Anna saw the photographs accompanying their achievement that day, she became engrossed in the shot of her signing to Joe to 'come'. Serendipity, or poor shutter work, meant the lens had captured her hand up in a 'stop' sign, rather than down in the beckoning movement. Silent for a long time, she turned to me and said, 'No, it Joe come, not stop, see' and pointed to the next photo in the sequence, of Anna clasping her hand to Joe's. To further embellish her recasting of the true events, she drew the circle of children with Joe holding her hand. Such behaviour represents joint ownership as well as a child's expectation that her contribution will be valued through reciprocal action.

My gaze encompasses the idea that a group consists of an individual within the group, not a group of individuals. It is a gaze which believes and celebrates that a group is central to life. It is also a gaze that presumes children are capable, both as group members and as a group.

Conclusion

These simple stories are redolent with personal gaze, and are totally subjective as I am unable to extricate my own thinking from these events. I chose these small stories, rather than perhaps more extended experiences with children, as they illustrate clearly my involvement, my use of lenses, and the influence of gaze upon teaching.

For this chapter, I had many more lens metaphors to play with—goggles you spit on to keep them fog-free; safety glasses for Foucault's 'everything is dangerous' notion; kaleidoscopes to return my gaze back to me in rearranged pieces; the kiddie glasses for perpetually happy children engaged in worthwhile experiences without a sad or bleak thought in their souls; the nice lady glasses for the teacher who never asks the difficult or awful questions (such as 'if someone is not your friend, what are they?', during genial discussions about 'what is a friend?'); or binoculars both forward and backwards; telescopes; contact lenses; can you kiss with glasses on?—the list was long. You will be relieved to know the metaphor can only be strung out so far. Suffice it to say, all gaze is contextual and cultural (Mardell, 2001). Everything we 'see' is through a lens.

The gaze is plural, subjective and powerful, especially when turned on children. Like night vision goggles, it can give the illusion of seeing in the dark and of omnipotence. In the ethics of encounters, we are obliged to be cautious and questioning in our gaze and in our subsequent use of it. We must also be rigorous in our examination of the past, present and future gaze. May the gaze be with you.

References

Cannella G (1999) The scientific discourse of education: Predetermining the lives of others—Foucault, education, and children. *Contemporary Issues in Early Childhood*, 1 (1), 36–44.

Cannella G (2001) Natural born curriculum: Popular culture and the representation of childhood. In J Jipson & R Johnson (Eds) *Resistance and representation: Rethinking childhood education* (pp 15–22). New York: Peter Lang.

Dahlberg G (1999, September) Three different constructions of the child. In *Unpacking observation and documentation: Experiences from Italy, Sweden and Australia. Conference Proceedings*. North Ryde, NSW: Institute of Early Childhood, Macquarie University.

Edwards C, Gandini L & Forman G (1998) (Eds) *The hundred languages of children: The Reggio Emilia approach—advanced reflections*. (2nd Ed). Greenwich, CT: Ablex.

Fleet A & Robertson J (2004) *Overlooked curriculum: Seeing everyday possibilities*. Research in Practice series. Canberra, Australia: Early Childhood Australia.

Fuery P & Mansfield N (1997) *Cultural studies and the new humanities: Concepts and controversies*. Melbourne: Oxford University Press.

Hultqvist K & Dahlberg G (2001) *Governing the child in the new millennium*. New York: Routledge.

MacNaughton G (2000) *Rethinking gender in early childhood education*. Sydney: Allen and Unwin.

McNamee S (2000) Foucault's heterotopia and children's everyday lives. *Childhood*, 7 (4), 479–92.

Mardell B (2001) Moving across the Atlantic. In C Guidici, C Rinaldi & Krechevsky (Eds) *Making learning visible: Children as individual and group learners*. (pp 272–7). Reggio Emilia: Reggio Children.

Millikan J (2001, July) Rejoicing in subjectivity. In *Unpacking interpretation: De-constructions from Australia, America and Reggio Emilia. Conference Proceedings*. North Ryde, NSW: Institute of Early Childhood, Macquarie University.

New R (1994, September) Implications of the Reggio Emilia approach for inclusive early education. In *The challenge of Reggio Emilia: Realising the potential of children. Conference Proceedings* Melbourne: University of Melbourne.

New R (1998) Theory and praxis in Reggio Emilia: They know what they are doing, and why. In C Edwards, L Gandini & G Forman (Eds) *The hundred languages of children: The Reggio Emilia approach—Advanced reflections*. (2nd Ed). Greenwich CT: Ablex.

Robertson J (1999, September) Observation and documentation: Interpreting the journey. In *Unpacking observation and documentation: Experiences from Italy, Sweden and Australia. Conference Proceedings*. North Ryde: Institute of Early Childhood, Macquarie University.

Robertson J (2001, July) Unpacking the gaze: Shifting lenses. In *Unpacking interpretations: De-constructions from Australia, America and Reggio Emilia. Conference proceedings*. North Ryde, NSW: Institute of Early Childhood, Macquarie University.

Vecchi V (1994) Presentation to the Australia and New Zealand study tour. Reggio Emilia.

Response to Part Two

Beginnings

Commentators

Margaret Clyde
Wendy Shepherd

Margaret's response

Chapters Six to Nine contain the stories of both practising and student teachers in their search for the most appropriate ways to work with young children. The focus is on enabling children to have opportunities to explore areas of real concern and/or interest to them, in their own ways, in their own time and in the context of working with peers.

The teachers appear to have been carefully selected to represent a broad spectrum of the teaching field: an experienced teacher from a culturally diverse child care environment who moved to a small rural day care setting, student teachers in their third and fourth year of study, a teacher returning to work in an unfamiliar position in a Kindergarten (the first year of school) in the catholic education system and, finally, a recognised teacher in a responsible position in a university-based child care centre. The group could not have been more diverse, yet their focus is as one—to use the factors of pedagogical documentation in order to 'engage the children' in connected learning (Belinda). As Danielle wrote (Chapter Seven):

> Its value cannot be underestimated; it is difficult to think of a more visual, comprehensive and meaningful way to communicate and validate the complexity behind the ways children learn and discover what is important to them.

None of the interviewees suggested that the process would be an easy one. Danielle reported that the examples of documentation shown to her student group (Chapter Seven):

> …invoked awe, and a sense that not only had a wonderful means of representing the investigations of children authentically and meaningfully evolved, but also that the value of the work done by professionals in early childhood education had reached a new level of respect.

Joanne, a student teacher, reported that 'her role as a teacher was very clear' when she reflected on the kinds of pedagogical documentation she had used. She came to the conclusion that she perceived her professional role as 'an arranger of the physical environment, an active listener of the children during interactions and a hypothesiser' (Chapter Seven). Consideration of teacher role is clearly an important point to consider in light of Lesley's response to working with 'kindergarten-grade children' with special needs. Lesley has recorded her views very strongly (Chapter Eight):

> Pedagogical documentation can highlight the learning of children who may not succeed in a traditional curriculum and who would otherwise receive little public attention.

Lesley reported that she purchased play equipment, 'good quality art making materials' and determined the best way to re-arrange the classroom so that these materials were readily available to all the children. In addition, she obtained books on many subjects but, most importantly, she ensured that the children had the time needed to experiment with the materials.

Pedagogical documentation offers opportunities for teachers to send subtle messages to young children. Firstly, children can be involved in deciding how their learning will be recorded and displayed for families and community members to share. (This depends upon privacy policies permitting the exhibition of children's work). Secondly, this signals to the children that children and their teachers are 'co-constructors of knowledge' (Pamela), that teachers believe that children's thinking and learning is extremely valuable and 'they will be encouraged by our example to respect and value the opinions and beliefs of one another' (Danielle). Thirdly, Danielle has reminded readers that while the teacher and children may be co-constructors of knowledge, children 'may teach each other new things that they may not have discovered as meaningfully on their own or with an adult' (Chapter Seven).

While it is imperative that children share their ideas, skills and knowledge with their peers, it is equally important that parents have the opportunity to share the children's work. It offers parents insights into the complex thinking that children [and teachers] engage in every day. Lesley (Chapter Eight,) suggests this sharing of ideas between children and parents is more satisfactory than the traditionally perfunctory question parents ask children such as, 'What did you do in school today?'. It is also an opportunity for parents whose English is limited to have access to more pictorial and three-dimensional materials than to long written explanations.

While teachers would find digital cameras, scanners and computers useful, many would not have access to such equipment. In this kind of documentation, the more traditional recording methods such as photographs, models, paintings and drawings will serve as 'advocacy tools' (as Pamela describes them). She augments her documentation with examples of children's active listening and observations of children's developing skills in group situations, in areas such as hypothesising, explaining, respecting the views and values of one another—crucial areas in the development of young children's social skills. This documentation clearly demonstrates the kind of conceptual knowledge which each and every child has brought to the process.

A final point upon which we need to reflect is a comment from Pamela relating to the way in which teachers make choices about topics for investigation. (Chapter Seven):

Children say dozens of things each day that could evolve into an experience for [pedagogical] documentation and the teacher has to listen closely and choose comments to follow up when there is potential for a meaningful investigation.

Clearly, documentation can be used for advocacy. This is illustrated in several of Belinda's provocations, for example those related to the 'Koori kids', children from Muslim families, and the Twin Towers, all of which were topics mentioned by the children. She writes (Chapter Six):

> *Who are the Koori kids?* is one of my favourite examples of pedagogical documentation. It was very powerful and a huge challenge for me…I thought it was really important to explore it with the children. For me, Aboriginal history is one of the most important social justice issues I feel compelled to work through with children I teach.

Other areas Belinda reported covering with her group of three to five-year-olds included the death of an ant and a fish, and the Bali bombings. She summed up the reasons for these topics in the following way (Chapter Six):

> The children talk about amazing things: they talk about social justice issues among themselves. Marie had the insight to realise that something special was happening and it would be worthwhile to keep a record of the conversations. This became the documentation of *Stories from a Garden Bench*.

Joanne's summary encapsulates the need for teachers of young children to offer provocative topics to children and, finally, to engage in appropriate documentation of the process (Chapter Seven):

> Children are lifelong learners who are powerful and able to overcome adversity …make deliberate choices that positively affect the way they, and others around them, participate in life.

Finally, it is critical to note Janet Robertson's reminder that our 'gaze' on children, their response to provocation and our interpretation of it, are subjective. Never underestimate the complex ways in which children learn; try to discover what is important to them.

About Margaret Clyde

Previously an Associate Professor in Early Childhood at the University of Melbourne, Margaret is now an early childhood consultant. She has been involved in program development for over 35 years in various tertiary institutions throughout Australia and is recognised nationally as an advocate for young children and their families, and for professional development of early childhood personnel. She has co-authored several books and written chapters in international journals. Glenda MacNaughton calls Margaret the 'matriarch of early childhood in Australia'.

Wendy's response

Each of the authors in this section of the book describe a personal journey of discovery about the complex practice of pedagogical documentation, just one of the many 'gifts' from the schools of Reggio Emilia in Northern Italy. In receiving this gift, practitioners should respect the integrity of the practice and engage in the process with a professional commitment to understanding how best to translate this integrity within different cultural contexts.

On reading the chapters in this section of the book, it is evident that each author has certainly crossed her personal Rubicon as documentation, while appearing to be deceptively simple, is actually extremely challenging. The practitioners' stories reveal the intellectual rigour, engagement and level of collaboration that their experience with documentation required.

Documentation is not just about recording and displaying what it is that children do. Forman & Fyfe (1998) see it as a tool for explanation, understanding and provocation. They add that (p 239):

> ...knowledge is gradually constructed by people becoming each other's student, by taking a reflective stance toward each other's constructs...a negotiated analysis of the communication process itself.

Significantly, each chapter here gives an example of a teacher who has learnt from children and their families and colleagues. Each has reflected on, and benefited from, seeking the perspectives of others and they have provided a rich analysis of their experiences. The social justice issues that Belinda Connerton (Chapter 6) tackled with her children are in a sense a provocation as, often in early childhood programs, practitioners struggle or resist dealing with issues that are viewed as controversial.

On the first reading of each chapter, it became clear to this practitioner that before embarking on the task of documentation, there is the need for a pedagogical positioning of the self. As well, each author declares a commitment to being a thinker, an observer, recorder, collaborator, negotiator, futurist and archivist in order to reflect on children's play, theory building and conversations with authenticity. Being knowledgeable about theory appears to provide the support for taking risks in the process of hypothesising and thinking about children in a very public way. It is clear in each of the discussions that all of these skills required of the professional, committed teacher, are hinged on the ability to see the multiple possibilities and to think deeply and profoundly about what it is that children say, see and do.

Interestingly, developmental theories alone did not guide the thinking of the teachers; they also considered the context of the situation, the child's lived experiences and their community and family contexts. Janet Robertson

(Chapter Nine) suggests that developmental theories be just one of the many ways to view children and to consider the possibilities of their experiences. I agree with Janet that it is important to acknowledge the rich history of developmental theory and the value of theoretical knowledge. Yet, it is necessary to move forward to explore current theories and perspectives about early childhood education and recognise the importance of children's lives that are lived outside our settings.

Drawing on the perspective of others is obviously a critical component of the reflection process, as explained by some of the authors. The opportunity to collaborate with others, however, depends on the management structure and culture of the educational environment. Time to attend to extra curriculum tasks is often limited. Joanne Burr, Danielle Crisafulli and Pamela Silversides (Chapter Seven) have experienced various levels of professional support for engaging in the documentation process. Lesley Studans (Chapter Eight) reflected on the difficulty of working in relative isolation in her school, yet with support at the system level, while Belinda (Chapter Six) had the support of her sponsoring body which promoted the practice in all of the centres within the organisation. Betty Hopson, the manager, with an understanding of the value of the practice, allocated time for staff to engage in documentation projects and for staff to communicate with each other and with families, thereby creating a community of learners with a commitment to recording and documenting the learning process. How inspirational that people persevere without this or any support!

In summary, there are many lessons to be learned from these quite different experiences and stories. The most important, it would seem, is the need for there to be support from management and the need for a collaborative culture. Management must also be aware of the value that documentation can add to educational programs and the relationships that are formed within the school community. The support cannot be tokenistic; it must be within the management structure, complete with funding to enable and motivate staff to engage in the process.

Next is the need for a professional commitment to the task, for becoming critical, and to seek more questions than answers. It is necessary to be both accepting of, and to challenge, the point of view of others and to take professional risks in documenting. We need to avoid resisting the difficult life issues of death, tragedy, power, racism and bias in our programs, embrace the challenges and diversity and finally, have a commitment to on-going professional development.

Documentation has the power to change the world-view of children as 'at risk' or 'in need' to an understanding of the child (as in Reggio Emilia) 'as rich, competent and intelligent, a co-constructor of knowledge, a researcher actively seeking to make meaning of this world' (Abbott & Nutbrown, 2001, p 129). Perhaps this book will provide the inspiration for changing the views of educational departments, institutions and their managers, to encourage them to consider the many possibilities that documentation can offer.

Engaging in pedagogical documentation provides practitioners with a framework for continual discussions with, and about, children. As teachers and documentors, our roles can be enhanced by the experiences and opportunities children provide, thereby enabling us to understand them more profoundly.

About Wendy Shepherd

Wendy Shepherd is the Director of Mia-Mia Child and Family Study Centre, the demonstration long day early childhood program associated with the Institute of Early Childhood, Macquarie University. Wendy has also had experience as a teacher in the early years of school as well as teaching and directing in preschool programs.

References

Abbott L & Nutbrown C (Eds) (2001) *Experiencing Reggio Emilia: Implications for preschool provision*. Buckingham: Open University Press.

Forman G & Fyfe B (1998) Negotiated learning through design, documentation and discourse. In C Edwards, L Gandini & G Forman (Eds) *The hundred languages of children: The Reggio Emilia approach—Advanced reflections*. (2nd Ed). (pp 239–59). Greenwich CT: Ablex.

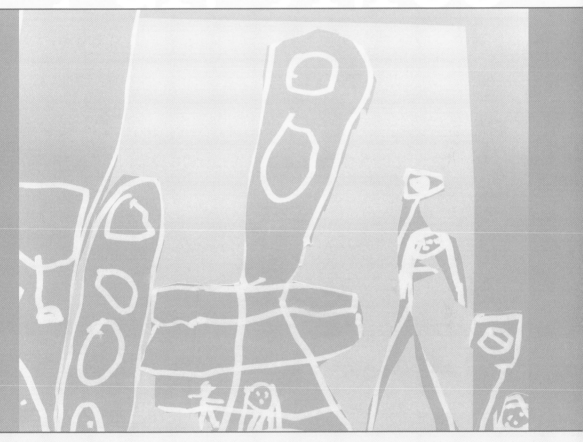

Part Three

Engaging the Hard Questions

Chapter Ten

At the Crossroads: Pedagogical Documentation and Social Justice

Ann Pelo

Ann writes this chapter from the perspective of a mentor to the staff at Hilltop Children's Center, a full-day, urban child care program in the United States. The position of mentor teacher was created at Hilltop in 2003 as a strategy for creating a shared understanding of core pedagogical principles and establishing common teaching practices among the teaching staff. Hilltop had long been influenced by the teaching and learning in Reggio Emilia but, until this position was created, there was little institutional support for centre-wide efforts to weave these influences into daily practice. After 12 years of classroom teaching, which launched Ann on her journey into pedagogical documentation, she became Hilltop's mentor teacher. In this work, she partnered with individual teachers, worked with classroom teaching teams, and facilitated centre-wide professional development gatherings, with a year-long focus on pedagogical documentation. This focused attention on the rhythm of observation, reflection, and planning, shook loose old habits and patterns, opened new possibilities, and sparked new participation by teachers who had long been on the periphery or entrenched in old ruts and routines. The experience described below confirmed for Ann the power of pedagogical documentation as a doorway into teaching that is full of zest, engaged awareness, and playful exploration.

Introduction

Too often in our field, passionate advocates of anti-bias practices and committed practitioners of Reggio-inspired pedagogy live in separate worlds, each with its own focus, vocabulary, and curriculum emphases and practices. These two arenas are perceived as distinct and self-contained, with little exchange or dialogue between them.

But the crossroads where social justice work and child-centred, Reggio-inspired teaching meet is a place of vitality, challenge, and profound engagement with fundamental values and vision. At the crossroads, we are called into a way of being with children and families that demands passionate dialogue and action. At the crossroads, we are challenged to listen closely to children's understandings of their lives—their expression of individual and family identities, their experiences of culture and relationships, their encounters with justice and oppression. At the crossroads, we are asked to weave together the dispositions to pay attention, reflect on children's play and conversations, plan from our reflections, and tell the stories that enrich our community. At the crossroads, we are called to weave together a commitment to responsive pedagogy with a commitment to work for just, non-violent communities.

When social justice work and child-centred, Reggio-inspired teaching come together, we find a shared image of the child as a keen observer, attending to the ways in which people are similar and different, and to the layers of cultural meanings and judgments attached to those similarities and differences. We recognise that the child is at risk for developing biases about others and inaccurate images of herself without guidance and support from caring, aware adults. We understand the child to be passionate about expressing her understandings—eager to communicate what she notices, what she feels, what she believes, what she questions. And we know the child to be capable of deep study and critical thinking, and enthusiastic about taking action that brings her ideas to life.

At the crossroads, we find a shared image of families as embedded in culture which gives rise to ritual and tradition, language and expression. We recognise that all families and individuals experience and participate in the dynamics of bias, oppression, and privilege that characterise our communities. We believe that families are eager for dialogue with each other and with teachers to explore the ways in which these dynamics impact on their children's development and learning, while at the same time they feel vulnerable and protective about taking up issues like racism, classism, heterosexism, ablism, and sexism, particularly in connection with their children's lives.

At the crossroads, we find a shared image of teachers as people learning in relationship with children and families. We understand teachers as facilitators of children's passionate pursuits and as guides and mentors for children's learning, creating a context in which children can take up the issues that matter to them—including issues related to unfairness and inequity. We recognise that teachers are eager to engage with families in authentic dialogue about values and the expression of values in daily life and, too, that they feel vulnerable and unsure about how to begin these dialogues.

Another way in which social justice work and Reggio-inspired teaching come together is the shared image of teachers as agents for social change. One important role of pedagogical documentation is to make visible the lives and experiences of young children, too often sidelined and discounted in our culture which claims to 'leave no child behind' (US Congress, 2001).

Another important aspect of teachers' social justice work is to advocate for more just and equitable communities, including advocacy around issues of compensation and working conditions for early childhood professionals. On the most immediate level, this means participating in efforts addressing the financial crisis in child care in the United States, where the wages of child care teachers are so low that teachers frequently leave the field. These efforts, like the National Worthy Wage Campaign and corresponding local movements, are aimed at creating institutional priorities and structures that provide the tools, resources, and working conditions that allow teachers to engage in the practice of pedagogical documentation. This engagement moves beyond 'keeping children safe' and 'meeting licensing regulations' to deep, collaborative engagement with children and families, while earning a liveable wage which supports their investment in their profession.

With these points of intersection between social justice work and Reggio-inspired pedagogy, we can, I believe, make the bold statement that when we are genuinely engaged in pedagogical documentation we *will* take up issues of social and environmental justice with children and families. The only way we can avoid these issues is by deliberately ignoring them when they arise—ignoring children's observations of differences and the cultural biases that accompany those differences, ignoring children's observations of unfairness, ignoring children's requests for our help in understanding the communities in which they live.

And this would be terrible violence, this denial of children's right to think critically about and engage with their world. Children will call our attention to social justice issues and when we practise pedagogical documentation, we will partner with the children around these issues.

A story to illustrate...

Four boys, seven and eight-years-old, slip into the silky, shimmery, calf-length, pink and purple dresses in the drama area. They accessorise with layers of beaded necklaces, scarves, and fancy hats, laughing and laughing as they transform themselves with their over-the-top outfits. They're calling out to each other, 'You look like a girl!' 'You look really weird!' 'Hey, now I'm a lady, look at me!' Their laughter catches the attention of other children in the after-school program, and they gather around the drama area, laughing and pointing. 'Get chairs! You can be the audience', calls out one of the boys, and a drag fashion show is born.

The boys prance and mince for the gathered audience (which includes five other children, girls and boys, and the two after-school teachers), not saying much but laughing hard. One of the boys, Drew, seems a bit tense, his laughter strained, a bit manic: perhaps a sign of discomfort under the silliness? Another boy, Liam, seems wholly at ease with the flowing silk and satin. The children in the audience mirror this range of responses to boys in 'girls' clothes; there's some shrill, fast laughter, some easy joking, some delighted giggles.

After about 15 minutes, the performers begin to tire and the audience members begin to disperse. One teacher helps the performers put away the costumes, while the other teacher guides the other children towards snack.

The teachers, jackson[1] and Elaine, brought their observation notes and a couple of photos of this 'drag show' to our weekly staff meeting. After reading the notes and studying the photos together, we reflected on individual children's responses to the performance. As we talked, I asked jackson and Elaine to point to specific observations—kids' comments, body language and expressions captured in photos —to anchor their reflections.

'Liam's family has a fluidity and ease around gender. They encourage both Liam and his younger sister to take on a range of roles and ways of being in the world. I think that for Liam, this "drag show" wasn't particularly remarkable, except, maybe, for the wild laughter and antics of the other kids', one teacher commented. 'He didn't say much during the whole thing, and his outfits were the least outrageous, like this wasn't a big deal for him.'

---

[1] jackson prefers to use the lower case for his name.

'Drew seemed sort of tense about the whole thing, under his laughter', Elaine reflected. 'His laughter had an edge to it, and he moved really fast and wild. He was the one who commented again and again about looking like a girl, about being like a girl.'

'While I watched, I wondered if Drew and a couple of the other kids were using this opportunity to see how it feels to be "female". They're old enough now to understand social mores about boys in girls' clothes, so they had to make this into a joke, but maybe it's the best way they know, to try on these other identities', jackson mused.

With jackson's comment, we began to reflect on the meaning of the drag show for the children participating and watching. What were the children curious about, or trying to figure out, with their dressing-up and performing? What understandings or misunderstandings or experiences were they drawing on? What theories were they working from? In our conversation, we drew on other observations of the children's play and informal conversations, as well as on our understandings of these children's particular lives, worldviews, and experiences. After nearly an hour of study and reflection, we generated a hypothesis: These children—the players and the audience members—were curious to explore what it means to be a boy or a girl; What does it feel like to be a boy? A girl? What, fundamentally, *is* a girl? A boy?

We recognised that these children, certainly, have been exploring these questions throughout their childhoods, from various developmental vantage points. We believed that they were ready to take up these questions again from the vantage point of their current developmental perspectives, cognitive abilities, and social understandings.

We considered several possibilities for ways to extend the children's exploration of the meaning of gender and identity, and settled on our next step: Elaine and jackson would read X, a fabulous children's story, by Louis Gould (1982), which describes the early life of a child named 'X', whose gender is kept secret from everyone, including Xself! After reading the story, they'd invite the children to create simple sketches of X, which would both challenge the children to wrestle with how to represent gender and genderlessness and give us more information about the children's understandings.

This initial observation, study and planning, marked the beginning of an exploration of gender identity and social justice that lasted for six months. The exploration grew step by step, observation by observation, as we practised the circling, spiralling study and planning process of pedagogical documentation: observation, giving rise to reflection and study and hypothesising, giving rise to next steps and unfolding possibilities, giving rise to new observations, and so on. We had to be diligent about staying grounded in specific observations of the children's play and conversations as we took up this topic, about which we all have strong beliefs and powerful personal experiences. When we caught ourselves straying into more general conversations about sexism and gender identity and ways to 'teach' kids about these issues, we returned to the specific words and images on the table in front of us: What were the children saying, playing, and representing about their understandings of gender identity? These observations guided our planning day by day, week by week.

As this exploration unfolded, we became more specific and clear in our hypotheses and questions, distilled from our observations about the children's interactions with the provocations we offered:

> How much weight do the children give to biological markers of gender identity, and to external markers like clothes, hair styles, accessories, to mannerisms and language, to activities? What are the children's understandings and values around our culture's gender rules? What are their beliefs about exceptions to those rules: is there a point at which the exceptions disprove the rules?

And our planned next steps, week by week, became increasingly fine-tuned, as we learned more about the children's specific understandings, misunderstandings, and questions.

During the six-month exploration, we invited the children to rewrite classic fairy tales—*Sleeping Beauty, Little Red Riding Hood, Cinderella*—replacing the female protagonists with male heroes. We invited the children to create paper dolls of themselves: large-size, full-body photos with several acetate overlays on which they could draw moustaches, or braids and bows, or skirts or baseball caps or hiking boots—ways to playfully experiment with external, cultural markers of gender identity. We read *The story of X* again, and the children created more elaborate portraits of X. We wrote the next chapter in X's life, with the children as characters in the story. And we explored possibilities for activism: What could you do if a kid gets teased in the playground? How might we respond to advertisements that play on cultural ideas about what girls and boys ought to like? This is pedagogical documentation in action, at the place where it intersects with social justice learning.

How we came to live at the crossroads

I'm the mentor teacher in the full-day child care program at Hilltop Children's Center, a role inspired by the work of the *atelieristi* and *pedagogisti* in Reggio Emilia. I work with teachers individually and in teaching teams and with the staff as a whole to support and facilitate reflective teaching practices anchored in key elements of anti-bias, Reggio-inspired pedagogy. Our collaborations are grounded in the cornerstone elements of pedagogical documentation: observation, reflection and study, planning, and telling the story. And, often, our collaborations involve social justice learning.

As we've become more and more skilful at the practice of pedagogical documentation, social justice issues have risen to the surface and become a focus of our teaching and learning. For many years we wanted anti-bias, social and environmental justice work to be front and centre at Hilltop; for a painfully long time, this happened only sporadically and, then, only in a couple of classrooms with participation from only a handful of teachers. This was the case for Reggio-inspired, 'emergent' project work, as well: a few teachers carried the vision for this work and attempted to realise this vision in their classrooms, struggling with isolation and yearnings for more authentic collaboration. To address the challenge of creating shared understandings of, and practices around, anti-bias and Reggio-inspired teaching, we added the position of mentor teacher to our staff. My first year's work as mentor teacher centred on pedagogical documentation: we practised and practised the cycle of observation, reflection, planning and telling stories, coming at this cycle through many doorways. By the end of that first intensive year, this way of being with children, families, and co-workers had become part of who we were. And in the course of this practice, issues of social justice crept into our discussions and our planning, until, indeed, it fell front and centre, an organic extension of children's pursuits and passions. When we paid close attention to what the children were playing and saying, we heard, again and again, children exploring the ways in which people are the same and different, and the cultural values and biases associated with identity differences. The children were our guides, leading us to the crossroads, as we embraced the practice of documentation as a verb.

Documentation is a verb

We'd used the word 'documentation' at Hilltop as shorthand for the pieces of writing posted on the curriculum boards or slipped into children's journals. The transformation of our understanding began with a change in discourse. We began to use 'documentation' as an active verb rather than an inert noun, embracing it as a vibrant practice—the practice of deep engagement by adults in the lives of children. We replaced the word 'documentation' with more descriptive and specific words in an effort to call attention to the cornerstone elements:

- observing closely and making notes;
- studying our observation notes;
- planning next steps; and
- telling the story.

Observing closely: The foundation of pedagogical documentation

The first cornerstone of documentation is observation. As teachers—people committed to inquiry—we strive to pay attention to the everyday, ordinary moments of each day. These ordinary moments are the fabric of children's lives: they offer glimpses into the children's hearts and minds. When we pay attention to ordinary moments, we begin to know the children deeply. Listening, watching, taking notes—observation is the beginning of documentation.

We collect 'traces' of our observations—taking notes, making audiotapes of children's conversations with each other and with us, taking photographs, making videotapes, collecting children's work. These 'traces' provide the raw material for our sharing, reflecting, and planning. Teachers take time to review their observations, transcribe audiotapes, choose sections of videotape, and organise photos. This work actively engages us—it is done to help us plan ways to sustain, extend, and deepen children's play and learning. It invites us to immerse ourselves deeply in the children's play, paying close attention to their words, their gestures, their expressions, capturing the details of their play that help us know them intimately and well.

In this first step of pedagogical documentation, we're intentionally listening for children's cries of 'That's not fair!' and other cues that children are thinking about issues of difference, justice, and equity. We're alert to children's comments about skin colour, gender, body size and physical ability, family make-up and other issues related to identity and culture. We intervene in the moment, when needed, and we bring our observations of children's play and thinking about social justice issues to our co-teachers so that we can grow explorations and in-depth projects that extend and deepen children's learning.

As we become more skilful listeners and observers, the children's work to understand issues of identity, difference, justice and bias becomes more apparent to us. For example, in our youngest group of children—children just turned three years old, teacher Molly overheard this conversation about identity and power:

Bridget: Heth has a little power. She doesn't have enough, because she's little and so she has only a little power.

Rachel: Bridget, Heth has control of her own body. You are not the truth of her body. Her body does have power! There's little power and big power right in her belly. It's inside you and you can have enough power. Heth can have enough power.

Molly jotted down the children's exchange and brought her notes to our staff meeting, commenting that 'I'm not sure what this means exactly, or what we ought to do next, but the kids are clearly trying to understand power—who has it and where it resides.' Meanwhile, several comments over the course of a week or so in our group of three, four, and five-year-old children, called us to attention.

'You can't play in this game because you have brown skin and that's not a pretty colour', said a light-skinned child to a dark-skinned child.

A teacher intervened at this point with a clear statement that 'It's hurtful and unfair to keep someone out of a game because of the colour of their skin.' She stayed with the children to support them both, as they figured out a way to play together.

> 'Is your skin getting darker while you get older?' a child asked Miriam, a teacher who is Filipino.
> 'Your hair goes with your skin, and you have brown eyes, too', another child commented to Miriam, stroking her dark hair and her dark skin.
> 'When I go to kindergarten, I hope I don't have a dark-skinned teacher. People with dark skin are bullies', a child told her mother.
> 'I'm surprised about that idea!' her mother replied. 'Your teachers Miriam and Liane have dark skin'.
> 'Yeah, I know, but I like them', answered her daughter.

Teachers brought notes about these exchanges to our staff meeting. They were concerned and eager to discuss how to address issues of skin colour difference and its cultural meanings, with the children.

Studying and reflecting: The bridge between observation and action

We bring our notes, photographs, and transcriptions to our co-teachers and to children's families. In collaboration with these colleagues and companions, we review our observations and reflect together about what they tell us about children's understandings, misunderstandings, theories, and questions. When we come together to study our documentation, we take up questions like:

- What are the children curious about? What are they trying to figure out?

- What knowledge and experiences are the children drawing on? What theories are they working from or testing?

- Do we see any inconsistencies in the children's thinking? Are there 'soft spots' or misunderstandings in the children's thinking?

- How are the children building on each other's ideas, perspectives, and contributions?

- What do we want to learn more about, after watching and listening to the children?

- What insights does this observation give us about possible ways that we could deepen our relationships with children's families?

These discussions help us develop hypotheses and questions to pursue with the children.

Exploring power

As we considered the conversation between Rachel and Bridget about power, we reflected on the relationship each of them has with Heth, the smallest child in their group, as well as on the ways each of the three children carry themselves in the world. A teacher shared a brief conversation she'd had with Rachel a few weeks earlier, in which Rachel had declared that her brother has a lot of power, because he's a boy, and that she wanted to be in his classroom group because that group of kids has power and her group doesn't. Intriguing to hold this statement alongside her quick defence of tiny, ultra-feminine Heth!

We named a theory that seemed foundational to their thinking, that power is correlated with size. We wondered what the children meant when they talked about 'enough' power—and, indeed, what they meant by 'power'. And we wondered where the children understood power to reside.

The meaning of skin colour

As we began to sift through the children's comments and questions about skin colour, we acknowledged the extra charge these comments held for each of us: a Filipino woman who had wished for light skin as a child; a native Hawaiian woman proudly championing her culture in the face of racism; two European American women engaged in anti-racist activism as adults and acutely aware of the power and privilege associated with white skin in a racist culture. With these experiences acknowledged by us all, we turned to study of the children's comments. We named several themes and questions that we saw in them:

- Brown is ugly. Is this about skin colour or a preference for all things pink and dainty?

- Does skin colour change? Are babies born light-skinned and their skin darkens as they age? Is colour something added to skin or intrinsic to skin?

- How do skin colour, hair colour, and eye colour come together to create a person's physical identity?

- Unknown people with dark skin are frightening—but relationship transforms fear.

We began to formulate ways to take up a conversation with the children's families about their curiosity and theories about skin colour, recognising that any exploration of skin colour and bias would need to involve children's families.

Planning next steps to extend children's investigations

We end our discussions by planning next steps—the concrete action that we'll take with the children to invite critical thinking, to nudge them to take new perspectives, to encourage them to reconsider their theories, and to facilitate activism. Questions that guide our planning include:

- What changes could we make to the classroom environment?

- What materials or 'provocations' could we add to the classroom?

- How could we participate in the children's play?

- How could we invite the children to use another 'language' to extend or shift their thinking?

- How might we use our notes and photos to help the children revisit their ideas?

- How will we be in dialogue with families about this exploration, inviting their reflections and insights as well as letting them know what we're thinking and wondering?

As we consider extensions of children's social justice explorations, we watch for possibilities for activism. How might the children's concern about and passion for fairness and equity open into action? We recognise that young children's activism looks different from adult activism, certainly, and that it is less about creating systemic change than it is about creating the dispositions of change-makers. We hope that the children in our care come to see themselves as people who notice injustice and bias and who join with others to take action in the face of unfairness. So, as we plan from our observations and reflections, we listen carefully for any ways in which children are identifying that 'we should do something about this problem!'.

Exploring power

We decided to gather more information about the children's understandings—and to invite the children to become more aware of their understandings—by asking Rachel, Bridget, and Heth to sort a collection of photos of people according to whether they had power or not. This initial meeting with the 'power girls' (as we came to call them) sparked a heated and forceful discussion about whether power is an internal quality reflected in a person's eyes or a physical application of strength and might. Molly's notes about this debate launched us into another round of study, reflection, and planning, and an in-depth exploration of power was born.

The undertaking was quickly expanded by an early controversy. The three children affirmed, again and again, that power is active: 'Swinging isn't powerful because you're not doing anything.' They agreed that power is linked with strength, substance, and toughness: 'Clay is powerful because it's tough.' 'You have to be big and fat to be powerful.' They disagreed sharply, though, on the relationship between beauty and power. Heth commented that 'Princesses are powerful, because they're so beautiful.' Rachel's reaction was fierce: 'Princesses kill people who aren't beautiful enough. I don't want to be a princess; they'll kill me because I don't like to wear dresses. That's why I want to be a boy. They have even more power than princesses.' The debate about this was contentious, and led us to an overt focus on the relationship between gender and power which drew on the languages of colour, movement, clay, drama and storytelling, and woodworking.

The meaning of skin colour

We decided to shine the spotlight on skin colour by inviting each child in the group to create a detailed self-portrait, first sketching their face, features, and hair with a black drawing pen, then mixing the colours they needed to capture their skin, hair, lip, and eye colour to fill in their portraits. As they worked on these portraits over several weeks, the children talked with each other and with the teachers about their understandings of the origins of skin colour.

These conversations provided an opportunity for teachers to correct misinformation that skin colour changes over time, or is an overlay on top of light skin (a common misunderstanding among dominant culture children who assume that light-coloured skin is the baseline). These conversations also gave us

Self-portrait 'palettes'

Using mirrors for self-portrait work

opportunities to talk together about the children's families, tracing skin colour and other identifying features in their family lineage. And through our conversations, we learned more about the children's questions and understandings, information that guided our on-going study and planning.

As this work was taking place in the studio, we engaged with the children in an exploration of the meanings of skin colour through a range of experiences. We brought in a persona doll (a detailed description of persona dolls can be found in Trisha Whitney's book, *Kids Like Us*) with dark skin whose stories of exclusion and name-calling sparked passionate discussion and problem-solving by the children. We called attention to books about people who took action in the face of racism. We made a regular practice of taking field trips to a beach in a part of the city with a wide-ranging diversity of people. And we watched for opportunities for individual and group activism, steps as simple as supporting a child who confronted a friend: 'It's not fair to say brown is ugly because that would hurt a brown-skinned person's feelings.' And we wrote to and talked with the children's families along the way, sharing our observation notes and our reflections, and inviting their suggestions for next steps.

Telling the story

Our notes, photographs, transcriptions, and collections of children's work become tools for communication. We use the traces of our observations to create written documentation that tells the story of the children's explorations, our reflections and hypotheses, and our plans about how we'll extend the children's learning.

This written documentation takes many forms, including narratives for bulletin board postings about curriculum, journals for individual children, documentation panels and bulletin board displays, and handmade books.

Particularly when we take up issues of social justice with young children, we need to share with families the stories that ground our exploration. Families, like teachers, have values and beliefs about these potentially controversial issues that they communicate to their children and the children bring those values and beliefs to their work on social justice issues. Families' values play a role in the unfolding of a social justice exploration, just as do teachers' values. When these values are acknowledged and discussed, there is true collaboration between teachers and families. When teachers seek out families' perspectives and invite their participation in reflection and planning, differences can be acknowledged openly, support can be frankly offered and received and relationships can deepen in unexpected and potent ways.

Written documentation creates a foundation for dialogue and collaboration between families and teachers. At Hilltop, we've heard again and again from parents that their children's transcribed conversations and comments are pivotal in their engagement in, and curiosity about, unfolding investigations, explorations and projects. In our written documentation, alongside the children's words, images, and work, we aim to include our reflections, hypotheses and questions; our planning for next steps; and specific questions for families, asking for their feedback and suggestions.

Photo of the artist

Self-portrait: Seeing myself

Exploring power

In the days immediately following the tumult about princesses, beauty, and power, we gave each girl's family a copy of the transcribed conversation, along with our initial questions and musings. We asked families for insights about their children's understandings of princesses. The stories we heard from Rachel's, Bridget's, and Heth's families were pivotal as we planned next steps. We learned about Rachel's determined conviction that she would be a boy one day, and about her absolute rejection of all things 'princessy' like sparkly dresses and tiaras. We learned from Heth's family about her passion for princesses. And we learned from Bridget's family that her princess play often involved princesses healing and helping others. This information guided our planning, as we continued to offer the children opportunities to examine the relationship between power and gender.

The meaning of skin colour

As we began our studio work with self-portraits, we wrote to families sharing the comments that children had made about skin colour, and our thinking about the underlying themes and questions. In addition, we included a brief overview of how children develop understandings of race and its cultural meanings and a synopsis of the anti-bias goals identified by Louise Derman-Sparks and the Anti-Bias Task Force (1989). We offered these in the context of child development research that informs our work. Finally, we asked families to share their reactions, hopes, and concerns with us. We heard from some families individually and from some families during an evening discussion that we planned. Families shared their dis-ease, their vulnerability, their hope:

> 'I didn't expect my child to be thinking about this hard stuff so early in her life.'
> 'I don't feel ready for this. How should I talk with my child about racism? What words, exactly, should I use? Are there books we can read together?'
> 'How exactly do kids think about race and skin colour? It's charged for us as adults, but surely not for them, not yet. How can we talk about it without bringing all our 'stuff' into it?'
> 'I'd like to think there are ways we can talk about these issues with the kids that could heal some of the hurts of our generation, so that we're not talking about racism as a reality that they just have to live with, but as something that can be transformed.'

We took notes during our conversations, and drew on these notes in the same way we draw on our observations of children's play and conversation, as we planned how to proceed with an exploration of skin colour and identity in a racist culture.

Clearly, written documentation is not a final, stale product. It is a lively tool for communication, for new learning, and for relationships. We use written communication in a range of ways (see Gandini and Goldhaber, 2001):

- We share written documentation with children. When children revisit their experiences by looking at written documentation, they often decide to take up an exploration from a new perspective, or to invite other children into an extension of their earlier work. They reconsider their theories and explore new understandings.

- We share written documentation with families. A primary goal for our work is to deepen and strengthen the relationships between families and children during their days apart. One key way that we do that is by telling the stories of children's days in our program, so that families come to know their children more fully in this context. In addition, we hope to involve families in meaningful, intimate ways in the daily life of our classrooms. This can only happen when we create many windows through which they can observe their children's days in our program.

- We use written documentation as a tool for social change. The stories that we tell of children's investigations and play have the potential for changing how people understand and value childhood. We share our stories with other early childhood professionals and with visitors from the community. Our stories call attention to the too-often unheard or disregarded voices of children.

- We use written documentation to create a history for ourselves and for the children and families in our program now and in the future. Participation in an unfolding story is a cornerstone for creating community. Our written documentation tells the stories of our shared experiences which, woven together, become the fabric of community.

Life at the crossroads

Pedagogical documentation leads surely and inescapably to social justice work with young children. When we listen to the children, allowing their passions and pursuits to guide our planning, we will find ourselves at the crossroads with anti-bias, social justice efforts. It is, truly, unavoidable.

Simply listen to the children! Young children pay close attention to what's fair and what's not fair—a common cry in any group of young children is 'That's not fair!'. This acute observation and concerned analysis is part of their developmental work: How am I the same as others? How am I different than others? What is it like to be someone else? (Think of all that drama play!)

We honour children's questions about identity, about the ways in which people are similar and different, and we hold clear hopes for how they'll answer these questions. We want children to know themselves as compassionate, reflective, resourceful, competent, generous people. We want them to know others in the same way, and as deserving of the same joys, delights, and resources that they receive.

We want them to become skilful at taking others' perspectives. We want them to ask hard questions and engage in critical thinking.

And if we pay close attention to the children, giving them the support they deserve as they pursue questions of identity, culture, and community, they will lead us right to the intersection with social justice issues. And that is the moment of truth for us. Will we go to the crossroads with them, affirming our belief that they are resourceful, engaged participants in their communities, or will we turn aside, unwilling to take up the challenging, invigorating work of exploring issues related to race, class, body size and ability, family make-up, and gender?

When we step firmly into that place of intersection, we deepen and draw on children's dispositions to be change-makers, dispositions to:

- notice and accept differences;

- collaborate with others;

- pay attention to other people's ideas, feelings, and needs;

- speak out about fairness and unfairness; and

- take responsibility for solving problems, offering their ideas and action.

Through their participation in social justice explorations:

- Children come to see themselves as change-makers: their dispositions for noticing injustice, caring about the people involved, coming together with other folks to think critically about the injustice, and taking action to confront injustice will be strengthened into life-long habits.

- Children come to new understandings and experiences of connection with people who are different from them, breaking down the boundaries between people and growing relationships where there might otherwise be disconnection and indifference.

- Children who are culturally privileged develop understandings of how to use privilege in the service of justice and equity.

- Children who come from cultures other than the dominant (white, straight, middle/upper class) culture deepen their identities as people who can resist injustice, claim their power, and become activists on their own and others' behalf.

- Relationships between teachers and families become more authentic, as people dive into challenging, value-laden issues in partnership with each other.

Documentation is a verb, a way of being in relationship. So, too, attention to issues of social justice is a way of being in relationship that honours identity and culture and that demands action. Pedagogical documentation, embraced fully, carries us to the crossroads and calls us to live in authentic, vulnerable, transformative relationship with children, their families, and each other.

References

Derman-Sparks L & The Anti-Bias Task Force (1989) *Anti-bias curriculum: Tools for empowering young children.* Washington, DC. National Association for the Education of Young Children.

Gandini L & Goldhaber J (2001) Two reflections about documentation. In *Bambini: The Italian approach to infant/toddler care.* New York: Teachers College Press.

Gould L (1982) Baby X, Oh what a baby it is. In LC Pogrebin (Ed) *Stories for free children.* New York: McGraw Hill Books.

Pelo A & Davidson F (2000) *That's not fair: A teacher's guide to activism with young children.* St Paul: Redleaf Press.

Shafer A (2002). Ordinary moments, extraordinary possibilities. In *Teaching and learning: Collaborative exploration of the Reggio Emilia approach.* Upper Saddle River, NJ: Merrill Prentice Hall.

US Congress (2001) Education Act: No Child Left Behind. Washington DC.

Whitney T (1999) *Kids like us: Using persona dolls in the classroom.* St Paul: Redleaf Press.

Chapter Eleven

Unsure—Private Conversations Publicly Recorded

Sandra Cheeseman
Janet Robertson

At the beginning of these conversations, Sandra was a parent with two children at Mia-Mia, a not-for-profit child care centre attached to the Institute of Early Childhood, Macquarie University in Sydney, Australia, where Janet taught the group of two and three-year-old children. Sandra was also the Staff Development Co-ordinator for SDN Children's Services (a not-for-profit organisation operating a number of children's services throughout New South Wales and the Australian Capital Territory) and had visited the schools in Reggio Emilia. Janet and Sandra, teacher and parent, colleagues and fellow travellers to Reggio Emilia, were ideally placed to have these prickly, troubling and rich exchanges.

Introduction

Issues of ethics in the process of pedagogical documentation have been the topic of many conversations between us since 1999. These conversations form the backbone of this chapter, though we first presented our thoughts to a conference in 2001 (Robertson and Cheeseman, 2001). Our discussions were fuelled by niggling concerns about privacy, individualism and the shared understandings of differing cultural values. We wondered if these values were so culturally embedded that they were not able to cross borders. Is pedagogical documentation à la Reggio Emilia possible in other cultures? Ethical questions asked and answered by the Reggio Emilia community also need to be explored by those embarking upon pedagogical documentation in other places. Aside from the issue of literally copying what another educational community does, there are significant ethical concerns that require careful thought and consideration.

Two dilemmas of children's rights are explored within the chapter. These are:

* consent to participate and children's right to privacy; and

* issues of intellectual property.

We start with a story from Janet and her group of children, which illustrates these points.

Help, help Mummy, help!

Cate, Colin, Luke and Bill were the initial players in this game. It was the beginning of the year and the children were just three years old. In the very beginning, Cate seemed to take a leading role. Her excellent language and group proficiency kept the game located near the fish tank and the tree house near the blocks. Small wooden animals and plastic horses 'galloped' across the shelf, 'talked' to each other, and then returned to either the tree house or the table. Inevitably, one of the animals would fall off the table and the words 'help, help, Mummy, help' would be uttered. A rescue would be enacted and the creatures returned to the house. In this early phase, the game was repeated daily.

Cate left the centre a week after we first noticed this game. She had been a key player, and her presence seemed to make the game very visible to us. The minute she left, the game changed and became even more 'hidden'. If we even moved towards the block area, the boys became silent, still, averted their eyes and shied away from the lens of the camera. We became interested, wanting to know more about the group dynamics and roles. We puzzled over this for a while but respected their reticence. I even wrote up some documentation about private games.

If we watched covertly, it was possible to see some changes to the plot and game. No longer were other animals used; only horses featured in the play. Three key horses were grey, brown and red. The boys dressed for the game in gumboots, magicians capes and gloves. They used the same area each day, moving between the shelf and tree house. Fewer and fewer words were uttered, or that we could hear, but the refrain 'help, help Mummy, help' was used frequently.

We interrupt the story to reflect on the two dilemmas raised earlier. Points arise from discussions about the many interpretations of pedagogical documentation that we have both witnessed in recent years.

Sandra: Teachers inspired by the schools of Reggio Emilia recognise the potential of pedagogical documentation as a teaching and learning tool. As teachers make attempts to define and contextualise their approach to documentation, they make a number of decisions in the process of changing their teaching practice. As with any novice, the focus in the early stages can often be on the self rather than the child or children. In the quest to achieve this perceived holy grail of early childhood expertise, are we always mindful of the voice and thinking of children—their right to privacy and personal moments, their right to ownership of their thoughts and notions, their right to decide what is preserved and what is lost? What is the context of these rights in an Australian setting? In considering the place of documentation in any setting, I believe that we must balance the benefits of documentation against the costs to the child. The benefits may enable the voice of the child to be heard, but this could be at the cost of a loss of privacy and the child's right to a sense of agency.

There is no desire through this dialogue to diminish an enthusiasm for pedagogical documentation, but rather to ask the questions and promote a more critical understanding of the complexities of children's experiences and the context of ethics, values and beliefs that surround our explorations with them. When I first began to consider these questions, they provoked an uncomfortable interruption to my enthusiasm for innovation in early childhood curriculum. I was inspired by the documentation of the schools of Reggio Emilia, but felt strongly that there were significant cultural differences that made some aspects quite irritating. Our underlying values about things like privacy, sense of community and even our countries' histories directly influence our interpretations of pedagogical documentation. When visiting Reggio Emilia, I could easily see the cultural significance of documentation within the community—their shared desire to change their future as a result of their past, their deep desire to work together, their strong identification with the importance of the community over the importance of the self, along with their very communal way of life—so very unlike my suburban, Sydney experience. I felt a strong need to grasp my context and understand my own assumptions. To offer further complexity, I was viewing all of this through multiple lenses—the teacher, the advocate, the mother—and each view was always clouded by the others.

Consent to participate and children's right to privacy

We make a number of assumptions about children's willingness to participate in pedagogical documentation. What drives the creation of documentation? Clearly the teacher must be willing and interested to work collaboratively with children. While many children appear keen to be involved in a project and willingly contribute their thoughts and responses, some will rarely show interest. Some further questions should be asked at this juncture.

Janet: Let's begin with the question: Do children realise that their contributions will be edited, interpreted and made available for public discussion?

Sandra: There is a great enthusiasm for listening to, and watching over children, to capture that rich dialogue so meaningful in documentation. We are tempted to make assumptions that children don't mind this, that it is all a part of being in an early childhood centre. We have always listened into children's conversations and used this material to inform our future planning. The public display of these conversations within documentation may represent an assumption on behalf of the teacher that children consent to this practice.

Janet: In any educational endeavour, the power relationship is such that the adult will edit and interpret children's work. Putting aside the path of pedagogical documentation and returning to more traditional methods of observation, evaluation and assessment, the conjecture could be made that the child is never asked for consent or even offered the possibility to refuse such recording. To compound this, they are not even given the opportunity for the adult's written work to be publicly critiqued (in the spirit of collegiality). Rarely seeing the light of day, and shown only on request to parents, these records have been considered the basis for all planning, programming and goal setting for children by teachers responsible for them. Within the modernist project (Dahlberg, Moss & Pence, 1999) of child development, teachers are supposed to write about children in an objective manner. This scientific pose belies the fact that all 'observation' is subjective (MacNaughton, 2000); in traditional methods, certainty reigned.

Within the scope of pedagogical documentation, the opportunity exists for others to engage in the subjective assumptions the teacher is making about the data being edited as it is visible. This therefore provides an opening for intellectual challenge and engagement in the material. An element of 'I think', enters the assumptions written about children.

There are moments that can be recorded and used within pedagogical documentation, but perhaps not publicly displayed. It is then appropriate to use this material with staff to try and unpack children's understandings about such things as racism, or gender issues. Without the act of documentation, the staff may not have had the opportunity to explore these issues, and the collaboration and connection with those children who are making these constructions would not be possible. We are not excused the job of entering into the role of moral agent simply because something is uncomfortable and we don't want to put it on the wall. We don't have to display everything on the classroom pin board. As time goes by, something may emerge from the experience that is more appropriate to use publicly. We must use our judgment and power about what is made public or remains private, not abdicate from the task itself.

Sandra: What is a child's right and capacity to give consent to participate in pedagogical documentation? When transcripts of children's conversations form a part of documentation, are the children aware that their conversations are being overheard and recorded?

Janet: It is important that children are aware that they are being observed (for whatever purposes) and if electronic recording is utilised, it needs to be obvious. I ask children if I can take photos and respect their negative responses when they happen. The more subtle clues children proffer as a refusal should be sensitively acknowledged. The aversion of eyes, stillness, a head turning, or hands over work are all indicators that this is private to the child. In any circumstances I would hope that this is respected. As in the story of 'Help, help Mummy', the boys clearly did not want us to know what they were doing. Infants and non-verbal children are a particular challenge because an understanding of consent may be difficult to assess. Sensitivity and a profound relationship with the child is the first port of call, in deciding whether to continue to record.

My understanding and use of pedagogical documentation is that as it is embedded within the forecasting process and momentum of the investigation, children and adults are contributing and reflecting on what has been gathered previously so they can move forward. In reflecting on the previous work, more indicators of children's reticence or reluctance to have parts of their thinking, words or work used, will become obvious. The children are given some power in the process simply by asking whether they want it included or not, and by complying with their requests. Older children can be empowered by including them in the decision-making for the final displayed piece of documentation.

Sandra: Why do we not apply the same enthusiasm for pedagogical documentation to our own experiences as we do for the children? I have often thought that it would be quite beneficial to complete a documentation of a staff meeting. I am certain that this would prove a valuable reflective tool. All dialogue, mannerisms, non-verbal eye-rolling and so on, along with photos of critical moments could be captured, edited and interpreted by a different staff member each month. We could learn so much about the way our team makes decisions, who dominates, who has all of the bright ideas, who is lacking in inspiration. If it was displayed in the foyer, wouldn't it be a useful tool for parents to better understand the thinking and development of their staff? Making learning visible—what a great idea! For most of us this possibility would dissuade us from participating. We might even consider it an intrusion and an undermining of our professional status.

Janet: I try to put myself in their shoes. If I was doodling during a meeting and, on returning to the meeting room hours later, found it displayed on the wall, I would be mortified. I can think of many displays of indifferent paintings slathered all over the wall of traditional classrooms, and I wonder if children were asked if they would like their work included in the chaos. As a recent subject of a research project, even with my consent, I felt uncomfortable and treasured the withdrawal power I had as part of the ethics approval.

It is important to consider our role in collaborating with children throughout the process, and at the same time making visible what we have done and said within the investigation. I guess the adage 'do as you would be done by' stands us in good stead.

I cringe when I go into infants rooms in child care centres and there is a large white board with children's names listed down one side and details of their bowel motions listed down the other. Would you like your menstrual cycle written on the staff room wall? Such lack of privacy makes the argument about naming children in pieces of pedagogical documentation spurious. Recent hysteria about privacy within child care centres and preschools in New South Wales has led to the practice of using an initial instead of the child's name when making observations or public reports in program books. With respect, respecting the child's right to a name and not an initial or code, is the point. If all publicly offered information about a child is respectful, well presented and done with the consent of the child, then privacy becomes contextual.

For many reasons, in the process of a piece of documentation, the editor makes decisions about what will be included and what excluded:

- What constitutes appropriate subject matter and what topics do we exclude or silence?

- Does the act of documentation romanticise the child's experience due to our editing of subject matter, findings or behaviour?

Sandra: The complexity of life is lived out in a children's service. When we work with children, we are privy to the rawness of their lives, their celebrations and their agonies, their thinking and creative sides and their mean and miserable sides. As documentors, we have the capacity to highlight or to silence the child. We make numerous decisions about what 'makes it in'. We rarely see the mean and miserable represented in a documentation —and perhaps rightly so. But in playing this editorial role, we run the risk of offering only the romantic view of the child. The exceptional child who demonstrates extraordinary capacities—this always makes great documentation—the child who can label her or his representations, the child with the wild imagination, or the child who loves to be photographed. Is there room for the child who is none of these? Does the teacher see this child? We are not explicit and yet we are very clear in establishing expectations for children, their parents and the broader early childhood sector. Of course we want to recognise the potentials of children and realise their extraordinary capacities, but are we clear in our image of the child? There is a complex tension between promoting the capable and resourceful child and recognising the scope of capability and resourcefulness within an individual child.

Janet: The permanence of a frozen, fleeting moment shapes what we want to say about young children. The tacit knowledge that it is 'forever' and publicly scrutinised shapes what we chose to 'look' at with or about young children. The topic the subjects are considering almost silently dictates the choice. Few of us would make public an argument by two children that displayed openly racist remarks and values. We would seek to shelter the children from public condemnation (even if the 'public' is the other children and parents who frequent the centre). Would we openly display the words of a child who coerces another to kiss them in the guise of a game of Snow White even when the kisser is reluctant? Probably not. What intrigues us is whether the notion of 'pedagogical documentation' has become veneered with niceness. Are choices about what to document predicated on whether it is possible to publicly display and discuss it within the community? Are we in danger, here in Australia, of documenting only the sunny child? And if we do document the dark side of children, to whom do we show it?

Sandra: Are there children who lend themselves more easily to contributing to documentation?

Janet: This may indeed be true for many forms of capturing or recording children's learning and behaviour for whatever purpose. If we talk about the more extended form of pedagogical documentation in which participating children and adults collaborate to give the experience momentum and purpose (from whatever perspective they bring), then it may be a question of whether we can see each child's contribution. Understanding how children operate in groups is not (in our understanding) a prominent part of the way teachers look at young children. A silent child, whose only contribution is silence, may have been the glue that held the group together. Highlighting such peace making and persistence encouraging behaviours, can show how children work together in many different ways. On the other hand, as mentioned before, to select topics the 'documentor' feels comfortable with rather than look at the child's ways of being shows the paucity of the documentor, rather than the possibilities of both the child and the endeavour of pedagogical documentation. I guess it comes down to what you think it is for.

Intellectual property

There are many issues to consider here. In any product of work we construct a sense of ownership. We have laws that indicate ownership rights and as adults we work hard to protect them. Where is the sense of ownership in a piece of pedagogical documentation?

Sandra: We acknowledge that the experience is shared; however, the power of the adult can dominate here as decisions are made about how children's ideas are interpreted, questioned or represented within the documentation. I often wonder whether we steal from children—their ideas, their hypotheses, and their wisdom. We have the power to manipulate, interpret and represent their ideas according to our crude and contained views. Is the child able to clarify, correct or alter our perceptions? Is it truly collaborative?

The focus of ownership then shifts to the natural life of the documentation and who determines what becomes of it. Where and to whom is it shown, where is it stored and how will it be used in the future? Where will it be laid to rest? Of course, staff who document put great time, energy and personal exposure into documentation. In many cases staff members have been instrumental collaborators and have the editorial control both in content, and design layout. Even so, is it fair that they should feel entitled to ownership?

Finally, we might consider whether permanence is always a valuable thing. Our prior experience is relatively limited. In the past, photographic permanence was accessible mostly to the wealthy. With the recent explosion of multi-media we have far more exposure and greater capacity to leave our mark for the future. The use of photography, video and audio recording is now commonplace in early childhood settings. What was once a fleeting, forgettable encounter is now potentially the subject of continual 'unpacking' and 'de-constructing'—evidence to a wide audience that is not easily erased. Of course, we are mostly dealing with happy events that we enjoy treasuring and it is true that this permanence provides us with the opportunity to re-visit and review events, to gain a broader perspective. We have too little experience of widespread permanency to really understand how it will contribute to our future understandings of us. While there is obvious benefit in re-visiting some events, surely there is also benefit in not re-visiting others. We have many dilemmas ahead in deciding where each encounter will fit and according to whose perspective.

Janet: Again I hark back to the traditional methods of recording information about children. Without collaboration between adult and child, the power relationship is skewed and the information collected becomes the subjective property of the adult about the child. Within pedagogical documentation, however, the act of collaboration throughout allows children entry into the decision-making process. In such a climate of collaboration, the joint ownership is obvious, and it is a fallacy to presume ownership by either the children or teacher.

Sandra: Who then determines the life of documentation? How is it stored and used in the future?

Janet: An interesting point. We all change over time, and images and theories we held years ago can come back to haunt us. The question is, does this haunting shape who we are now? In part it does, as all our experiences help create who we are.

It is whether this shaping is positive or negative. I toy with some images that are considered fundamental to our communal understandings of recent history. The photos of John Kennedy Jr saluting his father's coffin and the girl running naked down the track after a napalm attack in Vietnam are seared into our psyche. John Jr and Kim Phoc grew to be adults at the same time, leaving and taking the image of those photos with them. How much did the experience shape them, and how much did the image of the experience shape them? I wonder if they wanted the image retrieved, or if they both felt comfortable with these intensely personal experiences becoming public icons?

The *pedagogisti* in Reggio Emilia have used a series of photographs of a young infant creating a theory with her teacher about watches to illustrate their image of the child as a powerful theory maker. How does Laura feel about ticking watches now as she has grown into adulthood? Were there times when the image haunted her, and possibly other times when it buoyed her? Is she aware that her infant curiosity has become an international resource for advocacy?

Sandra: I wonder if life is meant to be captured for all time?

Janet: Yes and no! In traditional educational forms of recording, it is often a shallow subjective couple of phrases captured for all time under the heading of a 'developmental profile', which says little about who the child is. On the other hand, if in a fragment of conversation the child says something profound, then recognising power, competence and creativity may outweigh some uncomfortable feelings about continuing use of the material.

If one of the purposes of pedagogical documentation is to shine a light on the process of children's learning so that adults may better understand their own part in education and learning, the capturing of life for all time is important. It is how we exhibit these moments, what censoring goes on in the decision-making about what topics and experiences are made public, and what respect is accorded to both adults and children engaged in the process, that remains important and within our power. In the confines of professional development, I have often used an argument between three toddlers that includes one of the children losing control and hitting another on the head with some tongs. How the others reacted, how they regrouped, how play resumed and how the tong-wielder was forgiven within the group is important. It would be easy to misread this piece. However, the inclusion of intellectual rigour, discussion, and interpretation, make the group dynamics visible to the reader and invite other viewpoints.

Sandra: I'm not convinced. I don't think that we know the answer to this because we have limited prior experience of electronic media and the global possibilities for images and text. Now there are more opportunities to capture and retain images and it is tempting to see the potentials rather than the risks. Assumptions are made on behalf of children. Are we assuming that children can give informed consent? Really, we have no idea.

We will return now, to end Janet's story presented at the beginning of this chapter.

As you will remember, the boys' hidden game was gnawing at my thoughts. What was going on? Over the months, other elements were used. The horses began to fly, at first unaided, then on owls and later on small coloured window blocks, which seemed to transport the horses, and there were 'help, help buildings' in which the horses spent some time. We began to notice noises which sounded suspiciously like gunfire. The horses no longer seemed to be rescuing each other, instead it looked as though they were fighting. Gestures became larger, and the boys eventually colonised the space by the large movements and sounds they made.

But they never overstepped the bounds, or 'rules' of the room. At no time did they tell other children they could not play there. They just kept on playing around them, until the newcomer left. They never made the gun sounds close to staff, and immediately stopped if one of us went and sat in the blocks area to support other children in their play. They did not knock buildings down, or push other children. They tidied up as they went. When it was time to come inside they made a bee-line for the gumboots (to complete their costumes), but if they missed out they waited patiently until they could have them, using sophisticated bargaining language to get them without overbearing tactics. And they continued to keep it a secret, censoring their play whenever an adult came close.

As you can imagine, I was busting to know what was going on and, as this play evolved over five months, we gleaned more and more information over time (see, for example, Paley, 2004). The penny dropped for me one day when I saw the game being played outside without the horses as props. Bill stood with one arm forward and the other akimbo on his hip then 'flew' towards Luke shouting 'help, Mummy help' and Luke joined him and they flew about the playground. They had transposed themselves as the horses.

'Help, help Mummy' was a superhero game. We now believe that the horses were a strong meld of Power Rangers, Superman, Batman, Ultraman and Spider-man. Indoors, the horse substitutes acted like super horse heroes, coming together at the call, 'help, help mummy', defeating the baddies and returning home victorious.

The boys had played in code for months, keeping the real intention of the game hidden from our censorious eyes and ears. 'Very young children learn what is valued, tolerated, and expected as they observe and analyse the tacit as well as explicit messages for peers and adults in the early childhood setting' (New, 1998, p 251). To place this clandestine game in context at Mia-Mia, staff disapprove of the shooting of guns or 'dead games' (the term the children coined). Earlier in the year, we'd had an epidemic of toddlers and preschoolers shooting each other. The older children soon engaged in the dialogue about appropriate ways to solve disputes for both adults and children. With the toddlers, however, it was a different situation. No matter how often we discussed the hurt, fear and power of weaponry and death and nicely explained that it was not appropriate, eventually we had to ban it. Families had been expressing concern about 'shooting' and nothing seemed to put a dint in it. The toddlers' excitement over shooting was reinforced by superhero figurines brought to school by several children. We had tried to make superheroes into ordinary folk, going to the toilet, cooking and getting into trouble with their mum and dad and so on—to no avail. The toddlers continued to shoot everyone in sight. So eventually we said 'no more' and banned them. We know that in doing so, we locked ourselves out of any further dialogue with children about moral landscapes of violence and social justice. But frankly, we had had enough. I hoped that over time, maybe when the two-year-olds were four, we could talk about it.

Once I interpreted the play with horses as superhero play, it was possible to look at it with more critical eyes. It was wonderful to see the power of the boys to keep their intention hidden from us for so long. Their coded play was ingenious. The horses as super horse heroes, the triangle blocks as rockets, the danger, fall and consequent rescue, all codes for fighting and winning.

Eventually the boys became so confident of their right to play the game, I was allowed to take photographs. I used the photographs to ask them about specific moments in the play. I had noticed that when the horses plunged into the basket of film canisters the fighting noises and gun sounds were masked by the sounds of the canisters rattling about. When asked what was happening with the film canisters, Luke and Colin looked at each other and were silent until Luke said 'swimming' and Colin said with emphasis, 'yes'. The grey and brown horses die, but when asked what had happened to them, again there was that moment of collusion until the boys said they were 'sleeping'. Bill was not so sure about this 'outing' of the game and was silent, eyes averted the entire time he looked (glanced) through the photos. It was only with the support of his mates that he embarked on clay representations of the game.

Once again, I asked the children to draw and then work in clay about the game. Bill declined, but the drawings by Colin and Luke show the game in action. They represent a map and a sequence of where things happen. In clay, at last able to talk openly, problems of plot and detail could be sorted out. How the horses (alias superheroes) flew the rocket, had to be nutted out—all the while remaining in code. Inevitably as the game became more exposed, the game itself changed. The boys seemed to delight in the problems these horse heroes had in steering the craft and ended up agreeing that they hold on with both hands (hooves?) and teeth.

In interpreting this vignette of play, and our part as adults in it, it is clear the boys created a code, another example of the hundred languages. They did it to make sense of power and a motif—might is right—whilst avoiding censure. They had clearly understood our position and its presumed consequences if they were found out.

In discussion with the boys' families, it became clear that they had no superhero in common. One knew about Power Rangers, one had seen Batman and Ultraman and another Superman. All three had seen snippets of other superhero shows and promotional material and played with figurines brought in by other children or siblings. Their co-construction of a metaphoric superhero with powerful attributes was a testament to their desire to make some sense from disjointed experiences and understandings. To achieve this common understanding when talking and playing in code was phenomenal.

This rich learning, as their ideas collided and metamorphosed into the horse hero, was possible because they were in a small group and they were given, albeit unknowingly, repeated opportunities to engage in the game for long periods. They clearly made headway as their desire to continue overcame all the obstacles in their way. The need to remain cryptic added complexity. We had also respected their right to privacy; remember I had been unable to take photographs for five months. We rightly interpreted their stillness and averted eyes as a request not to pry. Providing such opacity (Rinaldi, 2002) and respect is one way to avoid the 'panopticon' (Rabinow, 1984) or surveillance models in our ideas and practice about teaching.

Sandra: To say that documentation brings with it some controversy is not to say that all things that went before were right and proper. In my view, it is possibly that the emergence of documentation and the complexity that it brings enables us to encounter the controversies. The issues have probably always been there—we were simply never sufficiently provoked to consider them closely. In this story, Janet presents us with these complexities and uncovers many of the dilemmas and choices that documenting teachers have before them. Janet's decisions about and responses to the children's unrecognised actions posed a frustration that could easily have been 'solved' by a premature assumption that it was her situation to control. So much more was understood and gleaned from the patience and respectful approach that she preferred.

Conclusion

We believe it is true—ideas from Reggio Emilia can't cross borders in their entirety. They can, however, influence what happens on the other side of a border. Our borders of culture, individualism and educational truths influence what and whom we look upon, and how we look. The idea of pedagogical documentation gives us a chance to reconsider our own dearly or unknowingly held beliefs about observation, privacy, teaching and education. With respect, care and collegiality, documentation is possible within our educational culture. It will, and should, look and feel different to that seen in Reggio Emilia. If used in the spirit of a research tool for children and adults, it is possible to create a way of thinking out loud about children, providing necessary opacity and respect.

References

Dahlberg G, Moss P & Pence A (1999) *Beyond quality in early childhood education and care: Postmodern perspectives*. London: Falmer Press.

MacNaughton G (2000) *Rethinking gender in early childhood education*. Sydney: Allen & Unwin.

New R (1998) Diversity and early education: Making room for everyone. In C Seefeldt & A Galper (Eds) *Continuing issues in early childhood education*. (pp 238–67). Columbus, Ohio: Merrill.

Paley VG (2004) *A child's work: The importance of fantasy play*. Chicago: University of Chicago Press.

Rabinow P (1984) *The Foucault reader*. London: Penguin Books.

Rinaldi C (2002) Research and learning. *Childcare Information Exchange*, 5, Issue 145, 16–20.

Robertson J & Cheeseman S (2001, July) *Voices in documentation: A private conversation publicly documented*. Paper presented at the biennial Australian Early Childhood Association Conference. Sydney, Australia.

Chapter Twelve

The Power and the Passion: Popular Culture and Pedagogy

Miriam Giugni

Miriam Giugni has worked in the field of early childhood education for the past 12 years in both rural and urban contexts, including Australian Aboriginal communities. She is passionate about social justice. This passion is reflected in her research interests, which include media and cultural studies, feminist studies, 'race' relations and identity politics that are critical for the production of democratic early childhood praxis. This chapter draws on research Miriam completed for her Honours thesis.

Introduction

> A [popular] media culture has emerged in which images, sounds, and spectacles help produce the fabric of everyday life, dominating leisure time, shaping political views and social behaviour and providing the materials out of which people forge their very identities.
>
> (Kellner, 1995, p 1).

In this chapter, I will argue that popular culture is a contested context for young children, families and early childhood educators. How we choose to document and reflect on this is a crucial question for early childhood educators. Using a cultural studies framework, I will present some opposing perceptions about the relationships among four domains: popular cultural products, childhood innocence, quality education, and identity work. Firstly, I will review a selection of the literature that features current debate about children and popular culture, introducing the concept of 'moral panic' (Thompson, 1998). Secondly, I show the ways in which childhood innocence and 'moral panic' are interlinked. Finally, I will present a discussion and examples of some of the ways young children use popular cultural products in the rituals of their everyday identity work. I use the term 'haggling' to illustrate the complexity of children's identity negotiations. Here, I will introduce the ways in which children use the body as a site to negotiate and produce their identities. Throughout, I will pose questions in order to create possibilities for early childhood practice and pedagogies of documentation.

Currently, there is much debate regarding the use of popular cultural products in early childhood education. It seems educators are grappling with pedagogical approaches such as banning popular culture in educational contexts, allowing it with adult imposed rules, investigating popular culture to pacify play, allowing popular culture in the classroom without critique, and not knowing what to do when 'it gets out of hand'. Additionally, it seems that children are playing with toys, like Barbie and Batman, and 'not learning'. There are many sociological issues bound up in each of these pedagogical approaches that I will address in order to present some alternative views about what children do with popular culture, how it produces their 'identity work' and how this can become part of the everyday and the early childhood curriculum. Identity work, then, is the basis of an alternative curriculum.

This chapter aims to demonstrate what children are doing with media products in their 'everyday' living, in order to show the ways children constitute their identities through daily rituals. Additionally, it elaborates on the media and cultural studies genre in early childhood education, by showing that identity formation through media products is not limited to isolated interactions with media products, but includes reference to them in daily discourses of play (I use the term discourse to mean the ways in which people speak, act, think and feel).

Further, this chapter shows how pedagogical and theoretical strategies can be practical and effective in both research and early childhood praxis. Therefore, it contributes to the creation of new vocabularies—different from those offered in conventional early childhood discourse—through which both children and adults can reconceptualise 'identity' and uses of media products. Finally, and importantly, this chapter participates in, and contributes to, the interdisciplinary movement in which early childhood education is currently located. Throughout, I will demonstrate the ways in which I chose to document particular stories with young children along with the uses of these stories as a tool for critically reflective practice.

Media research: A popular culture

In the past 20 years, popular media products and narratives have not only become easily accessible to young children, but products such as Barbie and superheroes have been specifically marketed to preschool aged children (MacNaughton, 1996). As a result, it is possible for children's 'everyday' living to be totally consumed by a range of media products (Luke, 1997; Kenway & Bullen, 2001; Arthur, 2001). Therefore, media products are integral to the processes of identity formation and the production of subjectivities (Hall, 1990; Blackman & Walkerdine, 2001; MacNaughton & Hughes, 2001). Specifically, media products are significant in early childhood education. This significance is a challenge for many early childhood educators owing to the ways children and popular media culture are perceived and the ways the relationship between children and media intersects with early childhood education (Seiter, 1999).

The importance of theory: Passionate positions on popular culture

Generally, adults have regarded children's use of popular media products as socially unacceptable. At its most extreme, this response manifests itself in the form of a 'moral panic' that is a response to the disruption of children's perceived appropriate, moral and social development (Thompson, 1998; Luke, 1997). This 'moral panic' has two significant results: it acts as a scare tactic which works to maintain the status quo, and it creates a fear that children will be 'dirtied' from their pure and innocent state through engagement with cultural products (Walkerdine, 2000). Children's response to this 'moral panic' is to operate 'in secret' and go 'underground'. The invention of this 'secret underground' is largely due to the ways in which adults construct childhood through narrow systemic regulation as an innocent, predetermined, social category, (Steinberg & Kincheloe, 1997; Cannella & Kincheloe, 2002). The regulation, disapproval and control of children's experiences with media products are, therefore, precisely the causes of children's resistance and subsequent practice in the 'underground'. Moreover, this regulation has become a focus in early childhood education during a time where philosophical ideas concerning children, media, identity and society are shifting (Silin, 1995). So, debates have emerged concerning children's consumption of, and interactions with, media products.

The focus of these debates is the 'moral panic' that often accompanies children's interactions with popular media products (Thompson, 1998; Jones Díaz, Beecher & Arthur, 2002). These debates represent both 'conventional' and 'contemporary' ideas about childhood. By 'conventional' I refer to perceptions of the child as innocent, unthinking and predetermined (Cannella, 1997; Dahlberg, 1999). By 'contemporary' I mean perceptions of the child as a thinking active agent. These two approaches, 'conventional' and 'contemporary', are characterised by disparate theoretical frameworks that define identity. It is important for educators to understand the theoretical underpinnings of both frameworks to enable possibilities for change in everyday practice.

Firstly, conventional ideas of early childhood, like the early 'media effects' paradigm, have been established in a framework constructed predominantly in developmental psychology, the very familiar framework which underpins Developmentally Appropriate Practice (Bredekamp & Copple, 1997) and some cognitive and social constructivist approaches to education. Here, scientific 'cause and effect' processes underpin the relationship between children and media. As a result, the child is perceived as predetermined, following a linear progression of 'development' (Tobin, 2000). In this framework, children unthinkingly and passively 'soak up' messages from their environments which, in effect, produce their identities. This model of learning and identity formation, referred to as the 'sponge model' (MacNaughton & Hughes, 2001), frames the ways that children are perceived and therefore constituted. Consequently, the methods used to interact with and educate children are governed by these perceptions, particularly in the ways children are compelled to learn normative social behaviours (Foucault, 1977). Therefore, the introduction of media culture into educational programs is seen to influence and affect children in 'negative ways', due to their perceived inability to critically consider the messages, meanings and ideology, media culture presents.

However, this 'sponge model' as a way of viewing children's identity formation through manifestations of media culture is problematic and thus has been critiqued by educationalists (Davies, 1989; MacNaughton, 1996; Hughes & MacNaughton, 2000; MacNaughton & Hughes, 2001). Their conceptions of children, media culture and identity are theorised through feminist poststructuralist, critical theories and cultural studies. By deploying these theories, educators may perceive children as active, critically thinking, decision-making agents in their learning processes and identity formation (Davies, 1989; Walkerdine, 1990).

Further, these educationalists argue that the body is central to the ways in which children negotiate, critically think and produce their identities.

From this contemporary perspective, then, children actively participate in the processes of their learning and identity formation including their frequent interactions with media culture. Although children are perceived as having the agency to make decisions, this does not imply that they have an unlimited choice of subject positions to deploy. Rather, they are constrained by both their subjectivities constituted by gender, 'race', sexuality, class, geographical location and language, and by the limited selection of social discourses available to (re)constitute and deploy these subjectivities (Hughes & MacNaughton, 2000). Such theories demonstrate the ways in which the limited range of choices mediate and constrain children's identity formation. These theories illustrate the perceived contentions implicit in media products, which in turn contribute to the various ways children receive and resist media messages. This reception and resistance is integral to the manner by which children learn and constitute cultural identities.

Understanding theory: magnificent metaphors

In order to reflect and analyse the children's interactions, I use theories which are articulated through metaphor. Firstly, I use a theatrical metaphor to theorise (make sense of) the ways identities are 'performed' and 'staged'. This theoretical framework draws on the work of two main theorists: Erving Goffman (1952) and Judith Butler (1991). This theoretical paradigm is referred to as 'performativity'. Secondly, I use the work of Pierre Bourdieu (1977) who uses an economic metaphor to explain and demonstrate the ways in which people exchange knowledge—people place value on knowledge, things and places and the ways in which having access to knowledge, things and places that are perceived as valuable, constitutes identity. Some terms which will become familiar throughout the chapter include cultural capital and currency which are exchanged in a cultural market. (In the pages that follow, cultural capital, for example, might be having possession of a Barbie doll; simultaneously, it could simply mean having knowledge of Barbie products.) So, to illustrate the children's identity work in the context of popular culture, these two metaphors are interwoven. Together I use them to argue that children's identity performances, produced in and through discourses of popular culture such as Barbie, gain cultural capital which, in turn, enables participation in desirable friendship groups.

Secret children's business

In a recent research study which created my Honours thesis, I investigated the ways in which children constitute their identities in the context of popular culture.

I called their identity work 'secret children's business' (Giugni, 2003a) because much of their play with cultural products occurred in the 'secret underground' context I described earlier. This study was undertaken in a long day care centre in the inner west region of Sydney, Australia. Eight three and four-year-old children participated in the study and acted as active researcher partners (see: Giugni 2003b). The children who participated in this study are identified by pseudonyms. Apart from the participation of an Indigenous Australian child, the children represent a sample of post-war multicultural Australia in terms of ancestral ethnicity and geographical region: Greek, Italian, English and Irish descent.

General findings from the study revealed how children used their bodies as the means by which they shaped, fashioned and produced desirable ways of 'being' and 'becoming'. Contexts of popular culture framed many of the discourses these children mobilised in their identity work. Thus, these identities were ascribed to the body within children's friendship networks. Therefore, 'the body' in all its manifestations, was the primary site for the negotiations of identities which enabled participation in friendship groups. 'The body' was the central site for the inscription, resistance and production of three recurrent domains that I called:

- *colouring in the body*—which showed the ways in which children signified subjectivities such as gender or 'race' with colour;

- *augmenting the body*—where the children used cultural products, artefacts, speaking positions and embodiment to physically enhance their bodies in order to perform or wear: whiteness, emphasised femininity, hegemonic masculinity and heterosexuality; and

- *(re)producing the body*—here the children used the context of the family to reproduce heteronormative constructions of gender and age. Consumerist identities were deployed as part of their performances (Giugni, 2003a).

These domains articulated the context of children's daily interactions in the child care centre and consequently defined friendship groups. Subsequently, the ways the children participated in their friendship groups created their contexts for participation, belonging and the creation of their early childhood curriculum (Giugni, 2003a).

These findings are not intended to act as a universal claim or generalisations for all children or other educators. Rather, as Ryan & Campbell (2001) suggest, they are the result of a study which was undertaken at a particular time and place for a particular purpose. What they may offer is a sense of the complexity popular culture plays in children's lives, along with the way children take up, receive and resist cultural discourses in the context of an early childhood curriculum.

In what follows, I will draw on the first and second themes, 'colouring in' and 'augmenting' the body, to illustrate the ways children interacted with cultural products and the ways they created their own curriculum. I demonstrate here choices I make about documenting and interpreting children's identity work. These choices include the selection of stories, the ways in which these stories are used to critically reflect on early childhood education and the purpose of documenting such events.

In addition, the stories presented in this chapter are part of a data base the children and I put together during and after the research process. Sharing this responsibility with the children made the process very complex but ethically enhanced in terms of what was recorded and who maintained intellectual and cultural property. The analysis and theorisation are my contribution to a collaborative observation and documentation process. My continued 'grapplisation' with the ethical issues that arise from documentation as a research tool and an early childhood pedagogy, compel me to constantly critically reflect and theorise in order to seek the most equitable and democratic methods available.

'Colouring in' and 'augmenting' the body

The children's use of cultural products was gender specific. So, this discussion will account for the 'gendered' uses of specific cultural products. I will begin with an introduction to the children's uses of cultural commodities followed by their stories. These stories will be told in three sections titled: *Sparkly, A-cute little* and *Suits that suit: Boys in black*.

By using Barbie and Batman accessories, products and secret disguises, the children orchestrated negotiating processes whereby they enhanced the representations of their bodies by using the images of Barbie and Batman. These enhanced images were presented through augmentation of the children's bodies with cultural products supported by their reiterative (repeated) discourses. I define the children's negotiating process as 'haggling' to illustrate the dynamic process of exchanging cultural capital (Bourdieu, 1977). These exchanges are made with reference to the children's constitution of their augmented bodies.

The body images of Barbie and Batman were ubiquitous throughout the children's interactions. Within these interactions, the child's body was augmented through reference to, and use of, the cultural accessories and products associated with these colour defined identities. The children's discussions revealed the importance they placed on the creation of their own identities. The children's performed identities were intimately linked with their knowledge of specific cultural commodities and the uses to which they were to be put in negotiating an individual's cultural capital. Moreover, the children also used these products to create their own performance scripts by associating particular kinds of products with particular identities. This use of products was subject to the cultural endorsement of the children's performances and agreement on particular properties that constituted identity. For example, the girls established that anything 'sparkly' was associated with Barbie which, in turn, represented their preferred performance of femininity. Similarly, the boys constructed identity through wearing a 'superhero suit' and identified the 'suit' as an image of power.

The presence and absence of particular cultural products were the key signifiers of power, knowledge and authenticity. The children scrutinised clothes, accessories and make-up to identify themselves and others through their desired cultural images. By wearing or using these cultural products, the children accumulated 'cultural currency' which they used in their local 'cultural market' (Bourdieu, 1977). The negotiations of cultural products, the attribution of meaning and their subjective use, occurred on a daily basis and often constituted the initial greeting between children. This greeting became a strategy, an 'identification ritual', which the children used to initiate their interactions within their friendship groups. These interactions were gender specific.

Sparkly

I will begin with the girls' use of cultural products in their 'identification ritual' to show the ways they negotiated their identities as curriculum using cultural products. The girls looked for embodied inscriptions that represented their gendered discourses of femininity: Barbie clothes, 'sparkliness' and make-up. The following interaction is an example of their morning greeting. My choice to document and critically reflect on this story allows me to begin to see the importance of something as simple as a morning greeting (identification ritual) in an early childhood setting. In this scene, Laura is seated beside the entrance to the garden on a lounge draped with a piece of shiny fabric dusted with gold stars. Eleanor arrives, wearing pink stockings laced with silver thread. They make eye contact and smile. Eleanor sits beside Laura on the lounge where the inspection begins (Giugni, 2003a, pp 67–8):

Laura: Are they Barbie stockings?
Eleanor: *Yes* because they are sparkly! Barbie has sparkly stuff.
Eleanor caresses her stockings. Laura points to the piece of fabric on the lounge which is blue with gold stars and asks:
Laura: Is this Barbie?
Eleanor: Yes of course, it's sparkly!

Here, the association of 'Barbie' with 'sparkly' indicates the girls' ability to label clothes that may not carry 'the brand name'. This labelling is a specific technique for the augmentation of the body which is an important part of the morning greeting. It appears that this labelling is imperative in order to perform femininity correctly (Davies, 1989; 1998). As a result, this labelling creates possibilities for the bargaining and measuring of cultural currency. This cultural currency takes the form of knowledge which is discursively (regarding the practices of speaking, thinking, acting and feeling) constituted through the girls' agreement that sparkles equal Barbie. This discourse constitutes 'sparkly' as a product of the marketable Barbie style femininity these children 'perform'. In this example, both children conflate the word 'sparkly' with the Barbie brand and, therefore, 'sparkly' inscriptions have cultural currency in this cultural market.

The 'sparkly' inscription becomes a valuable point of identification in daily scrutiny. The dichotomy of 'to have Barbie' or 'not to have Barbie' is calculated through this specific 'sparkle' discourse where authenticity is measured by 'sparkle value'. This discourse is, however, not limited to the glittery appearance of clothing and make-up. The inscription of the 'sparkle' also marks the 'fun' personality where the subject's outward appearance presents the complete female image, an important part of the relationships among this group of girls. In the following scenario, Daisy and Laura are sitting in the cubby house talking. The melodramatic vocal expression the girls use in their interactions suggests that the words, with their connotations, are pleasurable to speak. Moreover, the pleasure these words ascribed to their bodies appears in their movement and facial expressions (Giugni, 2003a, p 68–9):

Laura: Barbie's so beautiful and fun…
Daisy: and she wears pink.
Laura: Yeah she's just sparkly and beautiful and sooo fun!
Daisy: …and Barbie's got pink and sparkly stuff.
Laura: ….yeah she is so fun and beautiful and sparkly.

This example illustrates the girls' image of Barbie as sparkly, fun and pink. It illustrates the augmentation of 'sparkly', 'fun' Barbie from her usual state of 'pinkness'. The girls' discourse about Barbie's pink 'sparkliness' suggests a link between her fixed image of beauty and her 'fun' public performance; an example of Erving Goffman's (1952) credited 'front stage' performance. The 'prescribed' identity offers a means for 'performing' successful and pleasurable femininity. 'Wearing pink', 'being pink' and being 'fun' equate to an image of beauty the girls recognised through Barbie's fabricated 'corporeal performance' (Butler, 1991). Put simply, this means the way children use their bodies to physically perform identities. In addition, this performance (re)produces an identity that allows exterior textual readings of femininity that 'hyperinfantalise' (make child-like or infant-like) the image of woman/girl (Thornham, 2000). This construction of femininity represents a conventional, stereotyped image constituted on a macro level and omnipresent in popular cultural products.

The consumerist discourse reiterates the power associated with this image of femininity on both macro and micro levels (Seiter, 1993). For example, the contradictory positions regarding Barbie's body image are argued by Mattel, on one hand, to be aspirational and by a range of researchers, on the other, to be a site for problematisation (MacNaughton, 1996; Mitchell and Reid-Walsh, 1995;

Rand, 1995; McDonough, 1999; Hughes and MacNaughton, 2000; MacNaughton & Hughes, 2001; Norton, Olds, Olive & Dank, 1996). As a result, they connote the power of desire associated with the image of Barbie, her fixed, adorned, accessorised identity. Desire impacts on the reception of and resistance to prescribed cultural texts. This desire includes the aspiration to culturally and materially augment one's self in order to achieve the appearance required for successful, feminine performativity in a cultural field. Hence Barbie's image, created in conventional and easily accessible discourses, perpetuates a hegemonic (expected dominant) performance of femininity (Rand, 1995; Hughes & MacNaughton, 2000) which these children decide to take up. In this study, there were many instances where the girls' reception of Barbie's desirable dominant image was expressed through the property of hair. The following interaction between Daisy, Laura and Lucinda dramatises their reception of a desired cultural image (Giugni, 2003a, p 70):

Daisy: My Barbie has long hair.
Laura: My Barbie has long hair too…[holding a Barbie doll] and she [Barbie] has long hair.
Lucinda: She's [Barbie] got hair all they way down here [points to her ankles]. She never cuts her hair.
Laura: I like Barbie with long hair because I like wearing ponytails like this Barbie.

Laura's final comment appears to be a 'direct deposit' from the product into her augmented hair performance! It appears that Laura chooses this image based on her desire to '[wear] ponytails like this Barbie'. This interaction is an example of the girls' conventional use of their Barbie currency in their cultural market. The girls' use of the product appears to be limited by the static image of long hair that Barbie 'never cuts'. Thus, hegemonic femininity is active between the local and global cultural fields. Although the girls appear to have a preferred image of correct hair performances, there is, however, a counter response to Barbie's long-haired image (Giugni, 2003, p 70–1):

Eleanor: I cut my Barbie's hair. I didn't like her long hair so I cut it. My mum has short hair and I have short hair and I said to my mum can I cut Barbie's hair to make her beautiful like us and she said I can…my mum said it is like when they burn their bra. Barbie can look like me.

This counter response foregrounds a contradictory position to both of those argued by Norton et al. (1996) and Mattel. Eleanor's 'inverse augmentation' illustrates her use of agency to shape the cultural product: Barbie is made to 'fit' Eleanor's image of femininity, herself. Here, the role of desire appears to subvert the dominant image received by Daisy, Laura and Lucinda creating a counter-hegemony (resistance to expected dominant ways of being). Moreover, Eleanor contextualises the subversion of cutting Barbie's hair by likening her mother's parallel reference to the 'bra burning' feminist movement of the late 1960s and early 1970s. Eleanor articulates an apparent liberation through her rejection of Mattel's intended reception of Barbie's long haired image of femininity. It appears that Eleanor's desire is to experience radical resistance to the perceived anti-feminist image Barbie espouses. Simultaneously, perhaps Eleanor's conception of self is produced through her deliberate augmentation of Barbie's hair to meet a desired image of femininity for both herself and her mother. Here she deploys the concept of 'sameness' to culturally endorse the reverse augmentation.

The girls' interactions regarding their own and Barbie's hair demonstrate that their choices are inspired by desire. The desire for an augmented physical performance appears to be motivated by opposing aspirational images. This example demonstrates the complexity and range of possible responses to the reception/ resistance debate concerning Barbie's intended message. By using this story as a site for critical reflection, I begin to see the ways in which popular culture is imperative to the ways in which this group of girls make sense of themselves and each other. This method of documentation and reflection allows me to consider the ways I can use popular culture in the early childhood program. Importantly, I can also see the ways very young children can produce their identities in and through dominant discourses, which compels me to begin searching for ways to include critique as part of the children's identity work and daily curriculum.

The next story offers an alternative way of viewing children's interactions with cultural products by examining their conversations and actions in negotiating identities and power. This approach to viewing the way children practice relationships enables educators to look beyond their curriculum, to see that children negotiate power as their curriculum.

A-Cute Little

This story will show how the children negotiated power by identifying specific characteristics of Barbie products. This specificity and detail in defining and refining the methods they used to talk about Barbie products illustrate the constraints of the girls' desired image. The following discussion demonstrates how the girls' discourse is further (re)constituted in, and through, their use of language which, subsequently, becomes the context for their cultural practices. Additionally, this story shows the ways in which children include and exclude each other from play, based on possession and knowledge of cultural products.

The girls' identification with Barbie products (by brand and by association) characterises their desire to maintain the value of their pink, sparkly embodiment of femininity. The presence of these commodities 'on the body' was a measure of the girls' desired cultural image, which was illustrated in the first story. Their measurement of value occurred through interactions and language where the cultural image was defined and negotiated through what the girls were, or were not, wearing. Frequently, the negotiating process shifted from the material clothing items to the ownership of a range of cultural products that were allegedly 'at home'. Hence, the augmentation process is linguistic and discursive as well as material (Ochsner, 2000; Phillips, 2002; Hughes & MacNaughton, 2000). In the following exchange, the girls are sitting together in the cubby house, conversing (Giugni, 2003, p 72):

Eleanor: You don't have Barbie stockings.
Laura: I got a Barbie pool at my home…
Lucinda: I got a Barbie doll, a little doll
Eleanor: …and I got a Barbie swimming costume and I…
Daisy: …and I got a little Barbie Bus…
Laura: …and I got a Barbie bag with cute little things in it.

Knowledge of these products, what they were and their operational discourse, became a powerful means by which the children negotiated 'cultural capital' (Bourdieu, 1977). Material possession of the products was no longer the most important form of cultural currency. Rather, power was exercised through the girls' ability to label a Barbie product convincingly. This example demonstrates the reiterative details of the girls' 'identification ritual' illustrated earlier in the chapter. Additionally, this interaction illustrates how their knowledge, and use of cultural products is augmented through language—from direct body contact to an inventory of cultural accessories.

The link between the girls and Barbie appears to be the central focus of this interaction. Their 'haggling' over their cultural Barbie currency suggests an inscription of consumerism, which is of course an integral part of contemporary capitalist society. So, the narrowly defined Barbie discourse was refined through the emphasis on the possession of cultural products. Eleanor begins the 'haggling' by articulating that none of the other girls have Barbie stockings. As a response to this provocation, each of the following five statements were spoken through the first person singular, perhaps indicating the individualist disposition of ownership which manifests competition. This individualism also represents the capitalistic relationship between the 'self' and 'success' (Goffman, 1952). The successful participation in this interaction was linked to the thematic product association of the Barbie brand. The girls' hierarchical haggling universalises the power associated with Barbie products through negotiating specific details as finer, more valuable currency.

The display of knowledge of Barbie products gave rise to a specific discourse of femininity where 'littleness' equalled power: the 'littler' the better. This discourse appeared to be the pinnacle of power for these girls. The use of the word 'little' became a tool for the acute focus of power as Lucinda specifies, 'a little doll'. Laura, in response, sharpens the power of 'little' by using a double adjective 'cute, little things', to define little in a context, a type of little, 'a-cute little'. Discursively, ways of performing a particular kind of corporeal femininity are being established; 'a-cute little' was the measure of desire that these girls used to perform and practise dominant feminine discourses by constituting smallness as powerful. The girls' discursive performance capitalised on the opportunity to use language as a means of negotiating and refining their augmented images of femininity which they used as cultural capital in their Barbie mini market. Numerous studies have drawn attention to the 'unreality' of Barbie's body dimensions, perhaps due to their rarity and the difficulty of achieving them (Norton et al, 1996; Margo, 1997; Dubin, 1999; Jones, 1999). Likewise, the conception of 'smallness' is significant to the success of marketing a desirable idea. 'A-cute little', female body image is exemplified by the children in this study as desirable and powerful, demonstrating the dialectic between local and global images paralleled by those presented to children and adults. This 'little' disposition may also represent the conception of childhood both materially and discursively. Here the discourses that produce children's worlds collude to perpetuate the 'infantilised nature' of childhood discussed earlier in the chapter.

The girls' 'haggling' over these Barbie products increased the cultural capital of Barbie (and financial capital of Mattel). The layering of cultural products in negotiating image and identity through cultural knowledge presented an opportunity for the children to compose an extensive inventory of Barbie products. The items on the inventory became part of the vocabulary for interchanges through which relationships were built. The girls used their knowledge of products and their associated use as a way of getting to know each other. Consequently, their friendships were made through cultural practices constituted in dominant discursive feminine identity. The discussion of performative feminine identity appears to be an increasingly recognisable, cultural practice. Their vocabulary included reference to products which assisted in their discourse of cultural and physical augmentation. 'A-cute little sparkle discourse' enabled the girls to move up the 'corporeal ladder' within their 'enhanced image' exchange rate. Subsequently, this image exchange constituted the girls' daily cultural practices—'haggling' and 'looking good'. These findings parallel those of Hughes and MacNaughton (2000, p 60) which demonstrated the hegemony of children's identity work constituted in popular media culture. So, from this perspective, children's relationships are created on the basis of consumerism as well as interests and gender. This collection of contexts offers a challenge for early childhood educators to consider the implications of an analysis of power and fairness in the creation of equitable and socially just pedagogies.

The augmentation process of gender performativity was not limited to the girls. The boys' deployment of a desired image of masculinity in and through cultural products was evident throughout their interactions. The following story will investigate how the boys set up their investment profile through a performance of augmented masculinity.

Suits that suit: boys in black

The following episode is an example of the boys' daily interactions. Their interactions featured detailed discussions about the 'suit' they wore. The 'suit' signified a particular, desirable identity, for example, the 'black suit' deployed a Batman identity. There is also evidence of other superhero identities and characteristics; however, they are not specifically 'named' by the boys. Nonetheless, these characteristics did attain the desired cultural attestation as they suited the discourse of 'super-masculinity'. In the context of this story, the term 'super-masculinity' is used to demonstrate a particular form of masculinity enhanced through the 'super' genre! In the following vignette, Colm has arrived at the child care centre and makes an entrance which initiates an 'identification ritual', a daily practice for these boys. Colm runs into the garden and announces 'I'm wearing my Batman suit and you can call me Batman'. Nicolo, Tonio and Mardi, already in a group, move together to the entrance to greet Colm. Talking, they walk toward the 'back stage' at the rear of the garden (Giugni, 2003, p 75–6):

Nicolo: That's cool!
Colm: Yeah I'm cool and powerful in this suit. Everyone thinks I'm cool in it too. *Power!* [he runs to the 'back stage']
Tonio, also dressed in a Batman suit, speaks to Nicolo and Mardi:
Tonio: …and I'm in my cool suit that's why I'm so strong and these black suit are for boys…
Mardi: …and I've got a webber shooter in my suit…
Nicolo: …and I've got Batman t-shirt!
Nicolo grins as he exposes his Batman t-shirt from underneath his jumper.
Tonio: …but it's not a suit.
Nicolo's grin quickly slips away. His facial expression suggests a feeling of disappointment. He slowly lowers his jumper.

In this exchange, the boys' 'haggling' over their augmented bodies approximates that of the girls. The 'haggling' by the boys occurs in two ways: first, through the use of cultural products as currency; and second, through the signified identity represented by the cultural products—in the boys' case, Batman.

Despite the similarity, there is a significant difference between the boys' and girls' use of cultural products in the constitution of their gendered identities. The girls' discourse concerns Barbie and Barbie products, while the boys' discourse is constituted through the transformation into Batman. Additionally, the hierarchical power of the augmented body was measured. There were stratified levels of augmentation which became the cultural currency of the 'secret superhero business'. The difference is apparent when Colm assumes the identity of Batman by stating: 'I'm wearing my Batman suit and you can call me Batman'. This transformation from boy to superhero is also the transition from masculinity to super-masculinity!

The performance of 'super' successful masculinity is achieved through wearing a 'suit' where a disposition of power is assumed through the image of the augmented body. The Batman logo which accompanies the 'suit' becomes the extended augmented identity through which power is signified and claimed. This is evident in Nicolo's response to Colm's self-stamped Batman identity. When Nicolo expresses 'that's cool', he provides Colm with a cultural endorsement. So, Colm's claim to this powerful Batman identity is reiterated and extended. Additionally, the 'suit' becomes a cultural ascription that, throughout the interactions, increases the currency invested in this identity.

The boys' positioning of themselves indicates that a particular kind of masculine, heterosexual identity is marketed to young boys (Seiter, 1993; MacNaughton, 1996). Conceivably, this marketing strategy contributes to the boys' construction of a public/private world divided between 'boy' [or normal man] and 'superhero'. The boys assume a public position throughout their interactions which involves their chosen 'super-masculine' performance. The success of this performance depends on two factors: firstly, the augmentation of the body with the black suit and/or Batman brand clothing items to heighten the physical image of masculinity; and secondly, the culturally affirming audience where the discourse is (re)constituted. In a similar fashion, the 'black suit' connotes the public world of 'work'. This connotation reiterates the public performance of masculinity constituted in the Batman identity work these boys undertake on a daily basis. Their work is funded by the masculine performance economy. French (1999, p 148) indicates that:

> ...boys will make their own decisions about the construction of their gender identity and will make choices...based on the available [cultural] resources which they consider most appropriate and effective in a given social/[cultural] environment.

In addition, this assertion reiterates that the discourses these boys choose in their cultural market are those that represent successful hegemonic masculinity. The boys in this study demonstrate this successful masculine performativity through the power webbing dispersed throughout their cultural negotiation. This cultural negotiation represents Goffman's (1952) notion of the public performing audience 'crediting' a cultural actor with a specific identity performance.

This successful public performance of masculinity is defined by Colm's declaration that 'I'm cool and powerful in this suit' and because 'everyone thinks I'm cool in it too'. The second sentence is indicative of the way Colm uses the concept of 'cultural negotiation' as a determinant of the position of power he claims through stating clearly, and convincingly, that 'everyone thinks I'm cool'. The other boys do not challenge this claim. Rather, they too perform this kind of masculinity. It appears that Colm has set up a stage for a 'super-masculine' show. Each of the boys contributes to Colm's powerful performance by sharing their knowledge of super 'suits'. This is achieved through discursively accessorising the 'super' image by declaring a specific performance scripted for the Batman image. For example, Tonio appends that the suit provides him with 'coolness' and strength. Through this verbal contribution, Tonio adds the physical attribute of strength to the already 'cool' super identity. He expresses further that 'these black suit are for boys' thus highlighting the gender specification of 'black suits' and the public 'masculine' form of power associated with wearing one. Although the 'black suit' attributed to Batman was the focus of identification, Mardi continued the cultural accessorising of the 'suit' with the addition of a 'webber shooter' which, even though it is a Spiderman accessory, was nevertheless convertible currency in the interaction.

In this scenario, colour, costume and 'coolness' represent masculinity. However, there is a strata hierarchy of augmentation items ranked by transformative value. Nicolo's Batman t-shirt, marked by the Batman logo, appears to be a problematic form of cultural currency. It is a clothing item which has the required Batman (superhero) logo, but, conversely, does not act as a valuable superhero artefact. This is made apparent when Tonio reminds Nicolo that his t-shirt is 'not a suit'. Conceivably this is because the t-shirt is street wear rather than the super 'suit' required for identity work and, therefore, fails to signify 'coolness', strength and power. A brand name t-shirt merely shows one is a Batman supporter, while the magnitude of the 'suit' transforms the body and represents a replica of Batman enabling a specific performance of masculinity: super-masculinity. This super identity enables the dual performance of the child's and the superhero's identity. The apparent transformation undertaken while wearing the suit gives these boys the power to 'play out' desired super-masculine scripts. Davies (1990) argues that clothes give access to, and act as the signifier of, gendered identities. She states further that 'lived narratives take the form they do because we can imagine ourselves being a certain kind of person' (Davies, 1990, p 328). This 'imagined kind of person' becomes or is transformed through participation in the desired discourse. The boys' use of the 'black suit' to represent their discourse of masculinity constitutes the language of their lived narrative, their narrative of the 'good guise'. Their performance is simultaneously enabled and limited by the costume. This limit subjects Nicolo dressed in his t-shirt to a position where he can merely admire and be impressed by the surrounding 'suited' superheroes. The level of augmentation, then, is the measure of cultural capital in this 'super-market'.

Conclusion

These stories show the ways in which children use cultural products in their physical and discursive augmentation processes. The complexity of this augmentation process exhibits the children's desire to perform particular gendered identities. The implications of these complex processes are the context through which educators can begin to imagine the importance of cultural products in some children's lives. Further, we are faced with the challenges of working with children's constructions of desirable discourses through which they think and act. More importantly, our response in the forms of documentation of these desirable discourses is fraught with political and ethical challenges. Some of these challenges include seeking ways to negotiate with children in equitable ways in observation and research processes, such as giving children sovereignty over the educators' use of their stories, dialogue and perhaps photographs. Additionally, we must question the purpose of our use of children's identity work. Here it is used to seek the ways in which children receive and resist ways of being a (heterosexual) girl or boy, hence the deployment of rigorous theoretical foundations. In this way, documentation and analysis can become a method for seeking cultural change in our work with children.

So, following are some questions for further thought:

• How do we use popular culture as a curriculum context?

• How do children use popular culture to create curriculum?

• What are the ways in which we document children's use of popular culture? Should we?

• What is our documentation of children's use of cultural products used for?

• How can we use the concept of 'haggling' as a pedagogical tool for understanding the ways in which children negotiate identities, cultural products, and power in their friendship groups?

• How can we begin to 'haggle' with children's uptake of dominant discourses and constructions of identity?

• How can 'haggling' enable educators to work toward transformative pedagogies that seek and work for equity?

• How can transformative pedagogies be developed where 'identity work' is central?

• How can documentation enable critical reflection for educators to work for multiple ways of producing identity?

This chapter has argued that the use of popular cultural products in early childhood education is complex, contested and contradictory. Nonetheless, it has offered possible ways forward by asking questions about what children are doing with cultural products on a daily basis. It has shown that documentation can be used to examine power relations in a critical and reflective way. In addition, this chapter has demonstrated that the ideas we choose to analyse in our work with children can move beyond the cognitive successes of children's learning. Rather, we can begin to examine the ways in which children's thinking, speaking and acting in everyday life produces and reproduces dominant and limiting ways of performing gendered and heterosexual identities. Thoughts for consideration include the ways in which cultural products are used to include and exclude children from friendship groups and the ways in which children construct themselves in and through consumerist and commodified identities. By developing a pedagogy of questioning, educators may enable alternative and transformative ways of working with children and their experiences with popular cultural products.

References

Arthur L (2001) Popular culture and early literacy learning. *Contemporary Issues in Early Childhood*, 2 (3), 295–308.

Blackman L & Walkerdine V (2001) *Mass hysteria: Critical psychology and media studies*. New York: Palgrave.

Bourdieu P (1977) *Outline of a theory of practice*. Cambridge: Cambridge University Press.

Bredekamp S & Copple C (Eds) (1997). *Developmentally appropriate practice in early childhood programmes*. (Rev Ed) Washington DC: National Association for the Education of Young Children.

Butler J (1991) *Gender trouble: Feminism and the subversion of identity*. Routledge: New York.

Cannella GS (1997) *Deconstructing early childhood education: Social justice and revolution*. New York: Peter Lang.

Cannella G & Kincheloe J (Eds) (2002) *Kidworld: Childhood studies, global perspectives and education*. New York: Peter Lang Publishing.

Dahlberg G (1999, September) Three different constructions of the child—the childhood landscapes. In *Unpacking observation and documentation: Experiences from Italy, Sweden and Australia. Conference Proceedings*. (pp 19–37) North Ryde NSW: Institute of Early Childhood, Macquarie University.

Davies B (1989) *Frogs and snails and feminist tales: Preschool children and gender*. Sydney: Allen & Unwin.

Davies B (1990) Lived and imaginary narratives and their place in taking oneself up as a gendered being. *Australian Psychologist*, 25 (3), 318–32.

Davies B (1998) The politics of category membership in early childhood settings. In N Yelland (Ed) *Gender in early childhood.* (pp 131–48). London: Routledge.

Dubin S (1999) Who's that girl? In YZ McDonough (Ed) *The Barbie chronicles: A living doll turns 40* (pp 19–40). Australia and New Zealand: Bantam.

Foucault M (1977) *Discipline and punish: The birth of the prison.* London: Penguin.

French S (1999) Masculinity and violence in the playground. In K Biber, T Sear & D Trudinger (Eds) *Playing the man: New approaches to masculinity* (pp 137–49). Annandale: Pluto Press.

Giugni M (2003a) *Secret Children's Business: The black market for identity work.* Unpublished Honours thesis. University of Western Sydney, May 2003.

Giugni M (2003b) 'Adults Only': Secret children's business. *International Journal of Innovation and Equity in Early Childhood,* 1 (1), 47–58.

Goffman E (1952) *The presentation of the self in everyday life.* London & New York: Penguin.

Hall S (1990) *Popular culture* [Video recording] Deakin University, Open Campus Programme: Victoria.

Hughes P & MacNaughton G (2000) Identity formation and popular culture: Learning lessons from Barbie. *Journal of Curriculum Theorizing*, 16 (3), Fall, 57–68.

Jones WS (1999) Barbie's body project. In YZ McDonough (Ed) *The Barbie chronicles: A living doll turns 40* (pp 91–110). Australia and New Zealand: Bantam.

Jones-Díaz C, Beecher B & Arthur L (2002) Children's worlds and critical literacy. In L Makin & C Jones-Díaz (Eds) *Literacies in early childhood: Changing views challenging practice* (pp 305–22). Sydney: MacLennan & Petty.

Kellner D (1995) *Media culture: Cultural studies identity and politics between the modern and the postmodern.* London: Routledge.

Kenway J & Bullen E (2001) *Consuming children: Education-entertainment-advertising.* Buckingham: Open University Press.

Luke C (1997) Media literacy and cultural studies. In A Musprat, A Luke, A & P Freebody (Eds) *Constructing critical literacies: Teaching and learning textual practice* (pp 19–49). Sydney: Allen & Unwin.

McDonough YZ (Ed) (1999) *The Barbie chronicles: A living doll turns 40.* Australia and New Zealand: Bantam.

MacNaughton G (1996) Is Barbie to blame?: Reconsidering how children learn gender. *Australian Journal of Early Childhood*, 21 (4), 18–24.

MacNaughton G & Hughes P (2001) Fractured or manufactured: Gendered identities and culture in the early years. In S Grieshaber & GS Cannella (Eds) *Embracing identities in early childhood education: Diversity and possibilities* (pp 114–30). New York: Teachers College Press.

Margo A (1997) Why Barbie is perceived as beautiful. *Perceptual and Motor Skills*, 85, 363–74.

Mitchell C & Reid-Walsh (1995) And I want to thank you Barbie: Barbie as a site for cultural interrogation. *The Review of Education/Pedagogy/Cultural Studies*, 17 (2), 143–55.

Norton K, Olds T, Olive S & Dank S (1996) Ken and Barbie at life size. *Sex Roles*, 34 (3/4), 287–94.

Ochsner MB (2000) Gendered make-up. *Contemporary Issues in Early Childhood*, 1 (2), 209–13.

Phillips K (2002) Textual strategies, plastic tactics: Reading Batman and Barbie. *Journal of Material Culture*, 7 (2), 123–36.

Rand E (1995) *Barbie's queer accessories*. London: Duke University Press.

Ryan S & Campbell S (2001) Doing research for the first time. In G MacNaughton, S Rolfe & I Siraj-Blatchford (Eds) *Doing early childhood research: International perspectives* on theory and practice (pp 56–63). Sydney: Allen and Unwin.

Seiter E (1993) *Sold separately: Children and parents in consumer culture*. New Brunswick, NJ: Rutgers University Press.

Seiter E (1999) *Television and new media audiences*. Oxford: Clarendon Press.

Silin J (1995) *Sex, death, and the education of children: Our passion for ignorance in the age of AIDS*. New York: Teachers College Press.

Steinberg S & Kincheloe J (1997) Introduction: No more secrets—kinderculture, information saturation, and the postmodern childhood. In S Steinberg & J Kincheloe (Eds) *Kinderculture: The corporate construction of childhood* (pp 1–30). Boulder, Colorado: Westview Press.

Thompson K (1998) *Moral panics*. London & New York: Routledge.

Thornham J (2000) *Feminist theory and cultural studies: Stories of unsettled relations*. London: Arnold.

Tobin J (2000) *Good guys don't wear hats*. Teachers College Press: New York.

Walkerdine V (1990) *School girl fictions*. London & New York: Verso.

Walkerdine V (2000) Violent boys and precocious girls: Regulating childhood at the end of the millennium. *Contemporary Issues in Early Childhood*, 1 (1), 3–22.

Chapter Thirteen

Interrogating Diversity

Alma Fleet

In a book embedded in social justice, the need to name a chapter on 'diversity' may seem redundant. Nevertheless, the need for a named chapter seemed essential. Parts of this chapter were developed originally as a keynote presentation for the conference entitled *Unpacking interpretation: Deconstructions from Australia, America and Reggio Emilia*, in Sydney in 2001. The thinking has been revisited and recent stories have been added, including those from fourth-year student teachers in their final year of a university B Ed (ECE) teacher education program.

Introduction

Definitions of diversity evolve in complex ways. This chapter approaches the concept through stories which help generate rich narratives that move beyond earlier narrow definitions. It listens for the voices of those who have been silenced and considers the relationship between the notions of celebrating and honouring diversity, as well as considering problematic topics in the context of pedagogical decision-making and documentation.

During a study tour to Reggio Emilia in 1996, Carlina Rinaldi mused with members of a visiting delegation about possible impacts of migration on their small community. Increasingly, migrants were coming from North Africa and elsewhere to establish themselves in this wealthy region. Having visited Melbourne in 1993, the senior pedagogista from Reggio Emilia knew that Australia was a more visibly diverse society than theirs, and wondered if we might help them with their journey, as they were helping us with ours in other ways. Perhaps Carlina was thinking of challenging children's thinking. Certainly this was the perspective in one piece of documentation that we saw in a centre in Reggio Emilia. This was an investigation of skin colour—of what children thought it meant to be 'black' or 'white', and the relationship of skin colour to the colour of blood or to a heart or soul.

Subsequently, in 1997, in the elegant flag-bedecked Town Hall in Reggio Emilia, representatives from different countries in an international delegation stood to thank the people of Reggio Emilia and to share their impetus for joining the delegation or vision for their local future. Near the end of the queue of passionate people, there was a single speaker, a woman travelling on her own who worked in a refugee camp near a Palestinian/Israeli disputed border. She spoke briefly and quietly about the richness of ideas that were being offered to the rest of the world by the Reggiani. She concluded by saying that she now had a challenge of interpretation herself—that she wanted to find a way to celebrate children's thinking in a site where sadness and crisis were entrenched, where there were no attractive centres, no resources, where all that her children had was their own name.

Most of us, thankfully, are not in such stark circumstances. We may, however, need to revisit some of our basic assumptions to accommodate the richness of possibilities around us without thinking only, for example, in terms of physical resources.

Careful words

What about celebrating diversity? What is lurking in this vocabulary? The word 'celebrating' has had a brief but full life in the Australian educational lexicon. It's a word that has brought vibrancy to some otherwise mechanical aspects of curriculum.

'Celebrating diversity' is a more positive slogan than struggling with superficial interpretations of 'multiculturalism' and less narrow than work associated with people described as having 'special needs'. Nevertheless, it has begun to have a rather hollow ring. When words take on more responsibility than their previous existence might have prepared them for, they often become shallow and tokenistic. This seems to be happening to 'celebrating'. Celebrating diversity in schools and other childhood sites seems to be reduced to a 'multicultural dance day' or cooking fest, the tourist curriculum which has been critiqued by Derman-Sparks (1989, p 7).

Caution about this line of thinking led to the construct of 'honouring' rather than celebrating diversity in the New South Wales Curriculum Framework guidelines for prior-to-school settings (2002). Probably we have to make do with the word 'celebrating' for what we do at birthday parties and so on, but it is only a placeholder when talking about the complexity of diversity. There are so many elements to be included in the diversity party: differences in race; in languages and cultures; lifestyles and beliefs; physical and mental conditions, characteristics, gender and abilities; personalities and inclinations; geography and economic circumstances.

There certainly is a need to move beyond a multicultural curriculum to the broader conception of an anti-bias curriculum (Dau, 2001), and onto advocacy (MacNaughton, 2004), not only to extend awareness beyond regional versions of culture to other aspects of difference, but to generate a proactive stance towards societal inequity. It is interesting that, to some extent, 'multiculturalists' in the United States are seen to be engaged in transforming or redistributing cultural capital (Olneck, 2000). Some Australians seem to have left the debate at the level of acknowledging stereotypical cultural characteristics associated with food, clothing or holidays, without reshaping the discourse to at least recognise the mini-cultures of each home and work place. The complexity must be extended into the fabric of our policies and practices. They must be embedded in underlying philosophies as well as being considered in every day decision-making. This has been the intention in *Te Whāriki* (1996) in New Zealand (explored by Pohio and Gould in Chapter Five and by Bayes in Chapter Sixteen).

How do we get such diversity into any conversation? In an attempt to give voice to those who are silenced, who do we ask to tell their stories? An Australian Aboriginal staff member? A male early childhood teacher? A single mother living in low income housing? A gay children's services worker? A Korean parent? A partially sighted student teacher? Children who have been born in the third world? The list becomes a nonsense and introduces more pitfalls of tokenism. The diversity literature is only marginally helpful. Rebecca New (2000, p 8) may give us a starting point. She writes about:

…several principles which might well support more effective and equitable processes for determining what adults hope and plan for young children in the United States.

Her list includes the goal to 'foster diversity in quality and respect the quality in diversity'. This moves us beyond celebration. It gives us permission to define excellence through multiple perspectives, situations and ways of being.

We don't have to seek diversity—it surrounds and includes us. A few examples from professional experiences may extend the discussion. Each is available for our interest and consideration because it has been recorded though the eyes of a pedagogical documentor. So, let's consider the content of several investigations through the lens of diversity. There are two aspects of the role of content selection to be emphasised. One focuses on the participation of children who are marginalised and the other highlights less visible aspects of sensitive curriculum.

Decisions that encourage engagement

Pedagogical decision-making includes selection of content that invites engagement and helps to overcome marginalisation. Engaging content might be seen as that which enables a range of children to become involved in genuinely interesting, personally relevant opportunities. One student teacher described a situation in which she was able to be proactive (Pavia, 2001, p 2):

> Some of the children did not enjoy participating in social/group activities (may have been a result of their language difficulties or frustrations). These children were often overlooked by teachers and peers. Implementing a child-initiated project which had an active social group focus could develop and extend the children's verbal and non-verbal language, participation in social learning situations, sharing and negotiation skills, team work, collaboration, cooperation, self esteem, confidence, self help skills, and primarily the co-construction of knowledge.

Having reflected on her observations, she was able to extend a child-initiated project in order to include 'overlooked' children. Such decision-making requires focused attention on the nature of involvement as well as identifying who is participating in an experience.

The potential for building on individual perspectives in the context of a small group was demonstrated when another student teacher, Maria, built on the children's enthusiasm for cake building in her three-year-olds' sandpit. Her observation of their consistent fascination provided an opportunity to include one child who had not been settling at the centre and another whose limited English had caused him to hang back from daily activities, until the cake baking became so irresistible that he joined in the play. Insight is not often credited with preventing marginalisation of children but, in this case, a philosophy of inclusion was grounded in an awareness of children's interests. By the end of her practicum period, Maria was rewarded with the previously reluctant child enthusiastically racing into the centre with a photo of him happily baking a cake at home.

In discussing effective programs for linguistically and culturally diverse children and families, Tabors (1998, p 24) notes a range of important strategies for teachers. She writes that 'social isolation and linguistic constraints are frequently a feature of second-language learners' early experience in a setting where their home language is not available to them' and suggests forms of classroom organisational and linguistic patterning to assist. She overlooks, however, the point that choice of content and thoughtful observation by the teacher can create an engaging context which invites second-language learners into inclusive encounters based on peer-mediated social interaction. In this case, both the supportive environment and the magnetism of cake baking as curriculum enabled two previously marginalised children to become integrated into the life of a centre and gain access to the social construction of knowledge inherent in that context. The process of documenting the encounters provided Maria with a springboard for her planning that enabled an entry point for two families and rich growth experiences for their children.

Connecting with ignored curriculum

People are automatically diverse because each of us is an individual with a basket of regional and personal characteristics—but the existence of variety does not guarantee valuing of family traditions or individual perspectives. There is the imperative of moving past the acceptance of invisibility. In engaging with diversity, there is a need to confront less comfortable topics and build on children's natural curiosity rather than silencing it. Two stories will help to illustrate these possibilities.

During a practice teaching block, Despina Kakakios (2004) was teaching Year One children in a public school populated by families from various geographic regions. During the practicum she developed a piece of pedagogical documentation entitled, *Exploring Diversity within our Classroom: I'm Bangla because I speak Bangla...* (Bangla is a local name used by the children in this school to refer to a major language of Bangladesh and Bengal, also known in English as Bengali). Excerpts from Despina's rationale and the experiences that developed reveal a powerful set of experiences (Kakakios, 2004):

> Numa had had an interesting conversation with the class room teacher. Numa said, 'I'm Bangla because I can speak Bangla'. The teacher asked her if she knew where the teacher was from. Numa said, 'You're English because you speak English'. But the teacher said 'But you also speak English'. The teacher asked

Numa if Asli, Boio and Kenneth were from Bangladesh. Numa said, 'No because they do not speak Bangla and do not go to Bangla school'. The classroom teacher informed me that they have had this conversation before.

Numa had recognised that her cultural background is different from the other people in her class. She understands that she is able to speak a language that her teacher and peers cannot. There is great cultural diversity within the classroom and in the school. The classroom's physical environment does not reflect the cultures of the children:

> Teachers should work towards creating an environment where children develop a sense of themselves and of those from different cultural backgrounds as vital, worthwhile people, each with uniqueness and value (Briggs & Potter, 1999, p 288).

I decided to investigate with the children the diversity…in the classroom so children could develop an awareness of their classmates' cultures, how they are the same and how they are different. It is important for children to understand and be aware of cultural diversity in order to develop acceptance (Arthur, Beecher, Dockett, Farmer & Death 2001).

I asked the same question again to see if Numa's thoughts had changed. 'How do you know you're Bangla?'

Numa   (five years, eleven months, born in Japan, Bangladeshi background): Uh, I don't know.

Asli   (six years, four months, born in Australia, Turkish background): I'm Turkish. My mum and dad taught me Turkish.

Numa: I know now. I go to Bangla class and Mrs Sia taught me.

Kenneth   (five years, ten months, born in Australia, Chinese background): I'm Sydney. I was born in Australia.

Asli: So was I.

Ms Despina: I was born in Sydney but my parents were born in Greece. My family is Greek Australian. Where were you born Boio?

Boio   (six years, six months, born in Papua New Guinea, Papuan background): I don't want to tell you. I'm shy.

Asli understands that 'we acquire our culture from our family members' (Arthur *et al.*, 2001, p 27). Asli knows she was born in Australia and she also understands her cultural background is Turkish. Asli helped Numa realise since she attends Bangla class, her culture must be related to this language. Kenneth knows that the country you are born in gives you your national identity.

After having further conversations with Boio, it appeared that she did not have a positive image of her culture. The role of the teacher is to help children develop a positive attitude towards their cultural identity, to feel proud of their background and support their self-esteem (Arthur *et al.*, 2001). Helping Boio develop a positive attitude towards her cultural background includes providing an environment that allows the children to talk freely about their own culture and differences (Briggs and Potter, 1999). I decided to explore further with the children our similarities and differences so that the children learned to accept and appreciate differences in themselves and in other people. Together we brainstormed how we know we are the same and how we know we are different.

The children began noting the physical differences between themselves.

Asli: We have different hair styles. I have my hair in ponytails. Numa and Kenneth's hair is short. Boio's hair is very curly. We speak different languages at home. I speak Turkish.

Numa: I speak Bangla.

Kenneth: My Grandmother and my parents talk in Chinese. My skin and Asli's skin is a little bit brown. Boio's and Numa's skin is brown. We have different eyes. Some have round ones, little bit small and different colours.

Through this conversation the children realised that their physical appearances were both similar and different.

Day Two: We reflected back on what we had said the day before…The children noted that some children had a great deal of confidence in themselves while others did not.

Day Three:…the children wanted to discuss their abilities and talents…

Asli: I'm good at drawing, writing, telling scary stories, thinking, being a show off, spelling and singing in Turkish…

…Asli and Numa each sang a song in their own language. They showed great pride in their heritage and culture…

Over the next few days, children talked about their families.

Day Five:…The children asked me about my family. 'Do you have a daughter?' 'Who is your mum?' I brought in a photo to show the children my family. They were interested to see who my family members were and what they did. This encouraged the children to bring in family photos from home…

On the sixth day, discussion centred on the characteristics of being part of a school community. On Day Seven, the children thought about their previous discussions.

The children noticed that Boio had not shared with the children her cultural identity. I asked Boio if she was ready to share it with us. Boio wanted to share with me and whispered in my ear 'Papua New Guinea', Boio asked me not to tell the other children, she wasn't ready to do that, I kept my promise.

The following day included this conversation:

Asli: I'm Turkish

Numa: I'm Bangla. I was born in Japan. My brother was born in Bangladesh, my friend Nadia is Australia.

Kenneth: I'm Australian and Chinese.

Asli: Boio where are you from? We won't laugh

Numa: Tell us Boio; we won't laugh

Boio: Okay, I will whisper it to you.

Boio went around to all the children and whispered in their ear 'Papua New Guinea'. The children responded supportively towards her.

Asli: Papua New Guinea is a great country. I want to go there.

Numa: So do I. I haven't been.

Ms Despina: I would like to visit too. What can you tell us about your country?

Boio: When I go back to visit my country with my mum and aunty you can come with us.

    Talking about our differences and similarities allowed Boio to develop confidence in her own culture. She was able to share with the children where she was from when previously she didn't want to share it with anyone...

Despina's investigation enabled the valuing of culture as a component of self, part of valuing 'the whole person' as well as contributing to the elaboration of identity. These conversations built on a foundation of trusting relationships to privilege the discussion of diversity, moving past the acceptance of invisibility and the myth of the 'melting pot'.

Let's consider another 'standard' topic—the senses. In this case, Lucy Bradstreet, a student teacher, captured a conversation that unfolded in a Year Two class (mostly seven-year-olds). She reported in her interpretation that:

This conversation shows that the girls are intrigued with the components of the ear. They possibly did not know that there are so many parts. After this conversation occurred, Lori came and approached me, posing her question. The girls were intrigued with the meaning behind why I wore hearing aids. Were they interested because they had not met anyone with hearing aids before? Did they understand how sound travels through the air to be received by the brain?

Lucy decided to bring in a large ear replica from the university library for the children to explore and to help her to find out what the girls understood about hearing.

Posing the question back to the three girls, they replied:

Zara: Sounds go into this part and travels through the tube. Then the sound goes into the brain.

Belinda: But when I have a blocked ear, I can't hear properly!

Zara: Yeah, you have to go to the doctor and (s)he looks inside it with that torch.

Belinda: Then you get eardrops that make the blocked part go away.

Zara: Ms Bradstreet, is your hearing like a blocked ear?

Were Belinda, Zara and Lori socially constructing knowledge of myself as a hearing impaired person in their classroom?

Lucy explained that she had a hearing loss because she was born early and her hearing didn't develop fully. The girls had the opportunity for scientific learning, for empathy, for genuine engagement with a meaningful topic. Ally wanted to know how Lucy could learn to talk, if she couldn't hear. Lori asked, 'As you grow and your ears get bigger, do you have to get new hearing aids?' Lucy's interpretation in her piece of pedagogical documentation continued (Bradstreet, 2001):

> The girls displayed curiosity and very interesting questioning. The students' level of thinking displayed areas of new knowledge unfolding as they were posing further hypotheses to be investigated. Their understanding of why people have to wear hearing aids or to use sign language became the focus of conversation…

Adults who have not had the opportunity to specialise in early childhood studies often have difficulties reconciling these stories of learning with mandated curriculum requirements in formal schooling. It is worth noting Lambert's (2000) paper on problem-solving in the first years of school. This author constructs the argument in terms of curriculum opportunities—such as Lucy's hearing aids—being seen as opportunities for *inter-domainal problem-solving*. Due to the integration of a number of cognitive processes and decision-making frameworks, problem-solving is highly regarded as a goal of schooling. When the problems are pre-determined with closed narrow outcomes, they are, however, so distinct from life encounters that the problem is a *little p* word rather than a conceptually engaging challenge. Lucy's work extended opportunities for conceptual engagement.

Making uniqueness visible in teacher education

In addition to exploring the potentials of pedagogical documentation, how do we help student teachers deeply understand the philosophies underlying their teaching? As staff working in this area, Catherine Patterson and I sought an entrance point, an opportunity to share the processes and potential of recording an investigation through analytical eyes, something which accommodated different learning styles and perspectives. We needed an authentic provocation which could resonate for the group. As is often the way, a difficult situation provided the unexpected possibility.

We had been assigned an uninspiring teaching space, a traditional, rather dark tiered lecture theatre. Catherine and I created a new aesthetic by draping the lectern and whiteboards with fabric and adding interesting and attractive objects to counter the dry ambience. We noted Tarr's (2001, p 38) comments on the contrast between early childhood environments in Reggio Emilia with most programs for four and five-year-olds in America and Canada:

> These two spaces reflect distinct cultural values for children: the typical North American classroom reflects notions of preparation for the future world of work, of an environment that isolates particular aspects of a culture that simplifies visual forms, and protects children from the outside world. Its visual aesthetic reflects mass marketing and craft-store culture. It does not challenge children aesthetically to respond deeply to the natural world, their cultural heritage, or to their inner world.

In the context of our university teaching, the first week's result was striking, with an Arabian coffee pot and large brass tray countering the usual lecture theatre sobriety. For the second week, a colleague, George Lewis, brought in the old toy chest which he kept in his office as a reminder of family times.

After the lecture, a student offered to help us carry back our books and the toy chest. She and George began to talk about the history of toy boxes in their respective families. As we were carrying the load past bemused university students, George told how he had painted this sea chest which his father had brought back from India and the student began to reminisce about the toy box she had acquired from her brother overseas.

The rich links with diverse family experiences and personal memories became very enticing. My chest of Chinese camphor wood had been storage for a doll collection that had never been played with, gifts from a travelling aunt with thoughts of a little girl she'd never had herself. Images of dreams and memories cascaded through the stories we were telling. We then talked about how we might share this emerging investigation with other students, remembering the challenges of assessment and limited time, where we could offer only personal interest and enticing ideas, but no marks. We offered the possibility of the investigation to each of our tutorial groups and followed where the journey led.

George's sea chest of family memories

These are pieces from the documentation of one tutorial group's thinking.

Remembering toy boxes

We began by drawing something related to a toy box—one remembered from home or imagined. The following week, we wrote about our toy boxes or the idea of a toy box. Ken remembered the flying sawdust as his Grandad sawed and then taught him to sand the wood, his mum bringing out a drink and some cakes on the warm day, and then painting the pieces together. Photographs were added to the collection and discussion took us in different ways. What other containers are used to hold toys? One [self-chosen] group was interested in the socio-political aspects of toy boxes—Who has them? What about the people who can't afford toys? Another group became intrigued by the question of Treasure chests— What do adults have instead of toy boxes?...which spilled over into private memories of shoe boxes and jewellery cases...

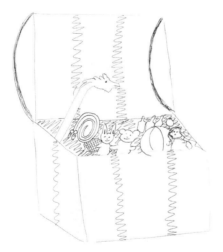

Lisa's remembered toy box

The casket contains the things that are unforgettable, unforgettable for us, but also unforgettable for those who we are going to give our treasures. Here the past, present and a future are condensed. Thus the casket is memory of what is immemorial...(Bachelard, 1994).

Lisa wrote:

> The toy box that I had as a child was gotten rid of a long time ago.
> However, I have never given away any of my toys and soft bears that I had
> as a child. My toys have come with me from each of my childhood
> houses, to the one I'm in right now…The toys I have kept now take pride
> of place in a walk-in wardrobe…scattered on the top shelf of the
> cupboard specifically placed so I can see each and every one…

A bed of toys

and Amanda:

> a toy box…what's a toy box? Growing up I always remember my most
> treasured toys carefully arranged around the perimeter of my bed, with a
> small, thin stripe down the centre for my body…I absolutely adored the
> feeling of being enclosed by these toys!

and Sharmeeta:

> I remember the first time I was presented with my special toy box. I was
> five years old…this toy box as I remember vividly was not only significant

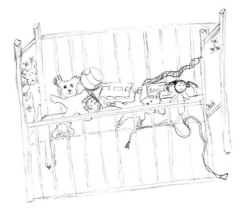

Drawing of a cot of toys

to me in relation to its aesthetic appeal; the detail and work that went into its intricately and precisely woven rattan in the unique shape of a basket. In fact the basket was traditionally used in the harvesting of paddy in the fields of the outskirts of Malaysia…

and Melissa:

I don't have any strong memories of toy boxes but I do remember the very few toys we had. They were all stored in the old cot…we mostly had teddy bears and dolls so it was fun to jump or lie among the musty smelling teddies…The 'toy cot' was located in my parents' bedroom and it was always dimly lit as the light struggled to get through the blind. This created a sense of mystery and secrecy to the whole toy seeking event…

The stories spilled out around the group; these memories encapsulate much that matters about diversity and engaging links with families.

When diversity-respecting curriculum is confronting

In recognising diversity, the consideration of differences must move beyond the obvious. For example, Backshall (2001, p 11) challenges us to think about the dissonance between our timetables and the view of time held by different children. In her conclusion about time orientation, she reminds us that:

…rules vary between cultures and sometimes societies. A good example is that for some it is rude to arrive on time, for some it is rude to arrive late and for a third group of people, the time is not set but the task of coming together is of the utmost importance.

How do we manage different perceptions of time? What about other diversities: Are we listening to those who speak different languages or value different things than we do? Can we just make sure that we talk to more people, visit communities other than our own, listen to people's stories and try to understand their perspectives? We may need to remind ourselves to listen more thoughtfully. Do we look at our planning and recording to see if the variety around us is reflected in the daily experiences of the children?

Do we establish relationships with families that help all of us respond comfortably in unfamiliar situations? How do we resolve our dilemmas when diversity becomes conflict, when different versions of child-rearing or different cultural groups collide in our centres? What happens when family values challenge philosophies of some staff members or when philosophies of staff challenge beliefs of parents? What happens when diversity becomes political? This possibility is reflected in the following story of Natalia that was shared by her teacher, Catherine Lee, when she was leading a workshop about possible approaches to pedagogical documentation. While the specifics of this story relate to the political scene in Australia, the issues are recognisable elsewhere. The first voice that we hear in this story is Diana, Natalia's mother

Natalia's story through her mother's eyes:

Following the Tampa debacle [a complex naval incident in Australian waters in which refugee families were deemed by some politicians to be 'throwing their children overboard'] we were worried about the Australia that we would be passing on to our children and the fact that it had become 'Australian' to be xenophobic and mean-spirited. We decided that we should expose the children to the fact that there were ways to go against this trend and to include them in events such as the Reconciliation Walk [amongst all Australians, especially those Indigenous to the land], the Sea of Hands [a people's initiative to show support for reconciliation with Indigenous Australians] and so on.

Having read a letter to the editor of *Sydney Child* [a community newspaper], I was reduced to tears by the plight of asylum-seeking children and started attending ChilOut (Children out of Detention) meetings. I related the stories told at such meetings back to the children in language they would understand…I drew on storytelling and fables to try not to make these stories too chilling—I was still dealing with a four-year-old child. Basically Natalia became aware that these kids and their families had had to flee their homelands because they were no longer safe and that they had knocked on the door of Australia to let them in.

However, the…men in charge of Australia…made all the good people of Australia believe that if we let them in they would be dangerous. Instead, we locked these families up in 'jail-like' places and would only give them yucky food…And then when the kids were hungry they weren't allowed to eat because it wasn't the right time of day. The kids were not allowed to go to schools and sometimes a whole place full of children would have one soccer ball to share between them.

I informed Natalia that we were going to go to a rally the next day to tell the old men that they shouldn't keep these children in jail. She asked what a rally was and I explained it to her. She said if that was the case she had better make a poster to take with her. When I questioned how she knew that she said that she had seen a cartoon…where the kids had gone on strike about a book being banned and they had all picketed with posters. When I asked her what her poster would look like she said that it would look like a no-smoking poster. The next day at pre-school she made this poster which was a red circle with a picture of children behind jail bars and a big red cross through it.

We attended the rally [SAD = Suits against detention] and on our way home we discussed her impressions. Her biggest impression had been of the mother who had been talking on the microphone and had been comparing the treatment of asylum seeking children to those of the assembled crowd. Natalia had thought that the mother had a child in detention and was worried about her kids. She regaled the train commuters with slogans she had learnt there…

Her other impressions on the events of the day we learnt from reading her pre-school journal. Natalia remains an empathetic child who hates to see anyone upset (indeed she caught me crying the other week and started crying at the sight)…

Natalia's story through the eyes of her preschool experience

One morning, Natalia came to preschool with a large piece of cardboard. This is not unusual for the children as they are encouraged to follow up ideas from home. Natalia announced she was going to make a poster that she could take to a rally. She said she was going to protest about the children who are in detention centres that are like 'jails'. Natalia is a very empathic and socially aware child and so her passionate declaration did not surprise us.

Natalia painted children behind bars and then painted a big red cross through her poster. While she painted, other children watched, some just walked by and others asked questions. Natalia told the other children about the rally and the need to tell the Prime Minister that children should not be in detention centres. Some children listened and then said 'oh' and others challenged her and said that there were no children in jail. Natalia assured them that there were children in jail and that she was going to do something about it.

Later in the day, a staff member who was concerned that Natalia was to be involved in a political rally asked me to speak to Natalia about what might happen at the rally. I had not attended a protest rally and so had no first-hand experience to draw on. I spoke to Natalia about what she thought might happen at the rally and how she may feel. I drew an analogy between the rally and the Easter show. Natalia had been to the Easter show and we discussed crowds of people, noise levels and the possibility of losing sight of her mum in the crowd. After our discussion, Natalia looked thoughtfully at me and then placed her hand on my arm and said, 'I won't be scared Catherine'. I had not mentioned that she may be scared, however, Natalia obviously picked up that I may have been concerned for her.

Natalia and I talked about documenting the rally in her journal and she was very excited about this idea. Natalia drew a picture about her idea of what may happen at the rally. She drew a picture of herself and her mum holding up their posters and she also drew the detention centre with the bars on the windows. She said:

> They're doing what we're going to do today in the afternoon. They're marching around putting their signs up like I made yesterday, telling people that we don't like what John Howard (the Australian Prime Minister) is doing. He's the person putting the kids in the centres and only feeding them rice and not very healthy stuff. One kid comes from Fiji, one from Africa, one from Greece and one from Noosa [a northern holiday town]. We're going to try to stop John Howard from doing that, making them sad. I'm going to the rally with Aunty Tina, that's mum's sister, and my mummy.

Later in the afternoon, Natalia held her poster and demonstrated how she would march around at the rally, calling out, 'Children out of detention centres, children out of detention centres!' Natalia proudly showed her mum her poster when she arrived at the preschool to take her to the rally.

The next day, when Natalia arrived at the preschool she was not as excited as the day before. Tired from the previous night's events she also sadly said that the rally was a 'little bit boring'. Natalia represented the previous night's events in her journal, drawing pictures of herself, her mum and aunty holding up their posters. She said:

> That's me holding up the sign. My mum was there and holding up a sign too. There's my aunty, she's holding up a sign too. My aunty is a little bit bigger than my mum. At the rally, first it was really early. We brang toys in case we got lonely cause we were the first ones there. We were at the very front. Then lots of people came along and then they were doing lots of speeches about the children in the centres. And then one of the mothers of the kids from the centre said, 'We want our children to grow up and be strong and eat the proper stuff and to drink and to play.' We're going

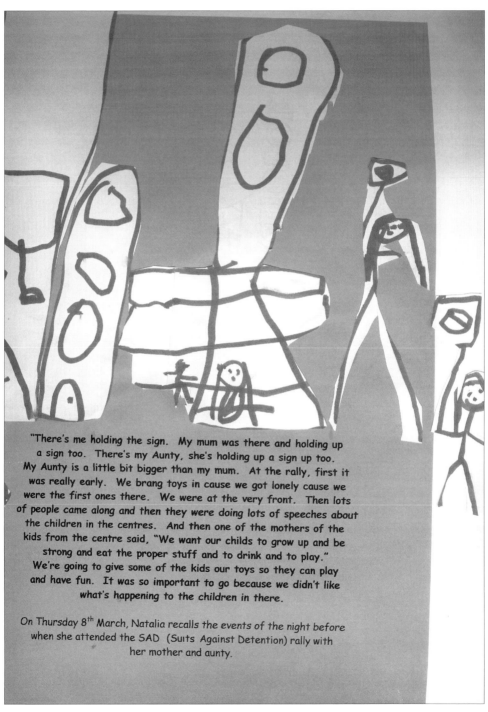

"There's me holding the sign. My mum was there and holding up
a sign too. There's my Aunty, she's holding up a sign up too.
My Aunty is a little bit bigger than my mum. At the rally, first it
was really early. We brang toys in cause we got lonely cause we
were the first ones there. We were at the very front. Then lots
of people came along and then they were doing lots of speeches about
the children in the centres. And then one of the mothers of the
kids from the centre said, "We want our childs to grow up and be
strong and eat the proper stuff and to drink and to play."
We're going to give some of the kids our toys so they can play
and have fun. It was so important to go because we didn't like
what's happening to the children in there.

On Thursday 8th March, Natalia recalls the events of the night before
when she attended the SAD (Suits Against Detention) rally with
her mother and aunty.

Excerpt from Natalia's preschool journal

to give some of the kids our toys so they can play and have fun. It was so important to go because we didn't like what's happening to the children there.

Natalia then asked me, 'Did John Howard's mum read the same books to him when he was little, like you read to me?' I said I didn't think so as John Howard was much older and some of the books had not been written when he was little. I asked Natalia why she had asked this and she replied, 'If she had read the same books then John Howard would know that when you get cut we all bleed the same colour even if your skin is a different colour'.

I was amazed and yet not surprised by Natalia's depth of empathy and logical thinking. Natalia had always displayed an insight into other children's behaviour that seemed beyond her years. She had been very interested in the book *Whoever you are* by Mem Fox and saddened when she saw the page with a child with dark skin, crying, cradling a bleeding knee. The text read 'pain is the same and blood is the same'…she decided that she may write a letter to the Prime Minister and tell him about the books.

Natalia conveyed such compassion, empathy, passion, understanding and empowerment in her discussions about the children in the detention centres. She brought her voice to preschool and we listened as she shared her concern and thoughts. As staff, our view of children being capable and resourceful was reaffirmed. The subject matter alarmed one staff member who questioned whether this was a suitable topic and the rally, a suitable activity for a four-year-old. We discussed the importance of supporting children in being advocates, like ourselves, for children, and supporting the open discussion of social justice issues and strengthening partnerships with families. We agreed that this issue and event was important in the lives of Natalia and her family and came to the conclusion that this is what was meant when we had advocated an approach that included listening to the child's voice and incorporating the child's voice in our curriculum. We were challenged by Natalia's knowledge and her ability to explain her cause to others, both to adults and peers.

A four-year-old child challenged some staff and parents to examine their views and to gain more knowledge. Some parents requested that articles about children in detention centres be available for parents to read and some became proactive by joining groups to voice their concern. A four-year-old made an issue about children, become real.

Natalia's experience is a powerful one. Olneck (2000, p 324) reminds us that:

The incorporation of students' cultural repertoires…can have the effect of redefining as 'relevant' rather than 'tangential' or 'off the point', the perspectives that students bring to the classroom.

This recognition of perspectives and values is critical to the ownership of knowledge and the locus of power in deciding what is valued in the group or classroom. Presumably we are all trying to extend the blinkered visions of teaching and learning shaped by our experiences, and to make visible those who have been made invisible because of normalising educational frameworks.

As this story was more evident in journal exchanges and shared storying than in wall panels or centre-bound booklets, some might not understand the link with pedagogical documentation. The philosophy associated with analysis and reflection is key, the intention to look behind behaviour to explore the puzzlement or underlying ideas. The journals themselves (or portfolios) can contribute to pieces which help illuminate pursuits by the group and unexpected aspects of children's engagement. The teaching associated with insightful pedagogical documentation attempts to recognise the integrity of each experience rather than imposing a predetermined way of being or set of outcomes.

How do we translate these grand intentions to daily life? Does the recognition of difference mean that all points of view are equally valid; that, for example, children can choose whether or not to wear hats in the sun? No. Does it mean that individuals can choose to be hurtful because that's the currency of the streets? Probably not. But somewhere between the sweeping generalisations and the frustrating particulars, there is a 'thirdspace' (Soja, 1996) of opportunity, something which is bigger than our current conceptions of what is meant by individuality or diversity, something richly complex, multi-layered, fluid and hesitant of categorisation or labelling.

We are looking beyond culture in this discussion of diversity, even beyond the everydayness of the cultures we each inhabit. There is the important element of mindset to be addressed, of thoughtfulness in constrained situations. For example, there was a case in which a student teacher was required to teach 'pirates' as a unit in the school's local Human Society and Its Environment (HSIE formerly Social Studies) curriculum. From a social justice perspective, students at the Institute of Early Childhood have been taught to question 'doing pirates' because of the reality of the pirate experience for many recent Asian migrants. For them, a pirate is not someone with a funny patch over one eye and a parrot on his shoulder, yelling, 'heave ho, me hearties' with Disney enthusiasm. This new millennium pirate is part of a mercenary gang that has attacked your family or tried to sink your boat as you were trying to escape atrocities in another country. This is a topic of survival, not of entertainment. Given the context, this student teacher noticed that children were particularly interested in the idea of treasure, hiding it and making maps to find it. She was able to avoid the 'pirate entertainment curriculum' and instead explored with them what treasure might be.

Thinking back to the Toy Box investigation, this school topic can be an equally valuable opportunity for each family to contribute a story of treasure—perhaps a button that a grandmother brought with her when she escaped from a war zone, or a collar once worn by a favourite pet, or a program brochure as a reminder of a once in a lifetime presence at a major event. The offerings will not be bags of jewels, but rather treasure steeped in personal experience. This is a curriculum choice that embeds diversity, simultaneously meeting fundamental mandated objectives (and early childhood goals), as well as the principles of making parents partners in schooling (rather than just minding the snack shop), and valuing what knowledge each child brings to school (rather than a narrow skill focus on knowledge of colour, shape and number). It also promotes deep rather than surface learning, and demonstrates that outcomes can still be met while personalising learning.

In the current fragmented world, interrogation of the concept of diversity is as important as all our well-intentioned efforts to honour, engage with and trouble the idea. The progress is in knowing that the matter is not straightforward. Whatever we mean by diversity is not only demonstrated in the ways we teach, but illustrated in the ways we live our lives.

References

Arthur L, Beecher B, Dockett S, Farmer S & Death E (2001) *Programming and planning in early childhood settings.* (2nd Ed) Sydney: Nelson Thomson.

Bachelard G (1994) *The poetics of space: the classic look at how we experience intimate places.* (M Jolas, trans) Boston: Beacon Press.

Backshall B (2001) *The culture of time: Implications for early childhood practice.* Paper presented at the Australian Research in Early Childhood Education conference (ARECE), Canberra.

Bradstreet L (2001) *Why do some people have to wear hearing aids?* Unpublished major assignment; ECHP422. North Ryde, NSW: Institute of Early Childhood, Macquarie University.

Briggs F & Potter G (1999) *The early years of school: Teaching and learning.* (3rd Ed). Sydney: Longman.

Dau E (2001) *The anti-bias approach in early childhood.* (2nd Ed). Sydney: Pearson Education Australia.

Derman-Sparks L (1989) *Anti-bias curriculum: Tools for empowering young children.* Washington DC: NAEYC.

Fox M (1998) *Whoever you are.* Sydney: Hodder Australia.

Kakakios D (2004) *'I'm Bangla because I speak Bangla': Exploring diversity within our classroom.* Unpublished major assignment; ECHP422. North Ryde, NSW: Institute of Early Childhood Macquarie University.

Lambert EB (2000) Problem-solving in the first years of school. *Australian Journal of Early Childhood.* 25 (3), 32–8.

MacNaughton G (2004) *Shaping early childhood: Learners, curriculum and contexts.* England: Open University Press.

New R (2000) What should children learn? Making choices and taking chances. *Early childhood research and practice.* 1 (2), 1–13 (online) <http://www.ecrp.uiuc.edu/v1n2/print/new/html>.

New South Wales Department of Community Services, Office of Child Care (2002) *NSW curriculum framework for children's services: The practice of relationships —Essential provisions for children's services.* Sydney: Office of Child Care. New Zealand Ministry of Education (1996) *Te Whāriki: He Whāriki Mātauranga mō ngā Mokopuna o Aotearoa: Early childhood curriculum.* Wellington: Learning Media.

Olneck M (2000) Can multicultural education change what counts as cultural capital? *American Educational Research Journal*, 37 (2), 317–48.

Pavia N (2001) *Discover the path that leads to the golden treasure.* Unpublished major assignment ECHP422. North Ryde, NSW: Institute of Early Childhood, Macquarie University.

Soja EW (1996) *Thirdspace: Journeys to Los Angeles and other real-and-imagined places.* Massachusetts: Blackwell Publishers.

Tarr P (2001) Aesthetic codes in early childhood classrooms: What art educators can learn from Reggio Emilia. *Art Education*, 54 (3), 33–9.

Tabors PO (1998) What early childhood educators need to know: Developing effective programs for linguistically and culturally diverse children and families. *Young Children*, 53 (6), 20–30.

Response to Part Three

Engaging the Hard Questions

Commentators

Anthony Semann
Anne Stonehouse

Anthony's response

The history of ideas, pedagogies and documentation arising from the schools of Reggio Emilia have had a profound influence on educators globally. Such ideas have influenced many classrooms and played a vital role in ensuring that curriculum content remains the focus of quality educational practices. Surprisingly though, limited reference to the intersection of Reggio-inspired teaching and the practice of social justice have been made in scholarly works. It is therefore timely to have a body of work engaging in dialogue specific to the trials, successes and lessons learnt from ensuring that principles of social justice are embedded into early childhood teaching and curriculum.

Principles of social justice demand that society afford equity and systemic fairness to all people regardless of sexuality, age, ability, ethnicity, gender, religious and political positions. The world is rich in diversity and difference; and the reflection of this diversity is vital to the delivery of quality early childhood programs. As a practitioner committed to ensuring that equity underpins classroom pedagogies, it became evident that the preceding authors have taken an important step in sharing a number of valuable personal narratives, which highlight the vital role critical reflection plays within early childhood services.

Ann Pelo's personal narrative of children exploring gender through dramatised storylines demonstrates how children's identity formation can be used as a point of extension by adults to challenge children's understanding of themselves and others, and to broaden issues of equity within curriculum. Similarly, Miriam Giugni took to analysing children's 'identity work' through an extended analysis of discourse and play in the context of popular culture. Both authors, therefore, urge educators to engage in a reflective reading of children's play and dialogue and explore possibilities of troubling existing knowledge relating to human diversity and difference. The contributions made by both Ann and Miriam raise the following questions for educators to consider:

- How can educators critically reflect on children's narratives and storylines?

- How can educators pursue a path of critical reflection?

- How can a variety of theoretical frameworks be engaged in analysing the diverse range of documentation being utilised within educational settings?

The increased popularity of documentation internationally has seen its application in a variety of educational settings. Refreshingly, as a collective, the authors have raised the opportunities documentation can provide in strengthening teaching practices with young children. Documentation as an anchor for reflection has been raised on numerous occasions as a catalyst for creating a more reflective teaching community. Alma Fleet's reference to pre-service students using documentation as a tool of reflection, and Ann and Miriam's use of personal reflection within curriculum development, brings into light the diversity of reflective opportunities which may be created through the process of teacher documentation.

Discussion relating to children's rights and documentation as a tool for teaching has been well and truly overdue. Sandra Cheeseman and Janet Robertson's chapter is therefore timely as questions are raised regarding invasion, privacy and consent. These authors raise important questions that will undoubtedly niggle away at many educators who announce children's rights as part of their personal teaching philosophy, and who may have never considered the tension that can arise between the use of documentation and the rights of students. Such questions extend on the importance of educators using collaborative approaches within the practice of documentation, as they argue for an increased dialogue between adults as observers and documentors, and children as the observed. Relating to this complex discussion, Miriam also illustrates the risks and troubles associated with 'haggling' with children in order to break down discourses that perpetuate heterosexism, gender inequity, and ageism.

Documentation serves as a useful tool on many fronts as the authors have clearly demonstrated. Importantly, Sandra and Janet have raised the issues of documentation as a tool to make visible to educators, children and families, the teaching and learning which has occurred throughout the day while, critically, Miriam uses documentation as a tool for troubling dominant discourses operating within the broarder society. Ann's use of documentation is primarily as a tool for personal reflection, whilst Alma highlights the important role of documentation for students to explore diversity issues whilst on a pre-service practicum. The importance of such diverse contributions demonstrates the multiple roles documentation may have in early childhood education. Whilst diverse and broad, all come with a clear set of complexities which require further analysis by educators willing to use pedagogical documentation as a tool for teaching. Within such frameworks, complexity should be embraced as a tool for growth rather than the traditional halting of thinking that may arise when faced with uncertainty.

For education to become a site of democracy and social justice, Alma and Ann call for an increased dialogue and a move from tokenism within curriculum to a more substantial dialogue regarding diversity and difference. Experience tells us that bringing social justice issues to the forefront of our work comes with risks. A belief in equity, however, requires a commitment to making equitable practices visible as part of classroom pedagogies. Together, the authors have clearly argued that the use of documentation allows for a diverse range of social justice issues to take centre stage within the early childhood and pre-service teacher classroom.

About Anthony Semann

Anthony Semann has worked in early childhood education for over 13 years as a classroom teacher, policy developer, program manager, university lecturer, centre director and consultant. He has published widely in the diversity field specific to issues of sexuality, children's rights, anti-racist education and curriculum. He has been politically active within early childhood for a number of years and has contributed his skills to a number of boards within and external to early childhood education. Currently Anthony Semann is the Director of Semann and Slattery Training Consultants, an educational training and consultancy firm based in Sydney.

Anne's response

Reminders of the real world

These chapters require us to contemplate how to deal with the unorthodox in terms of children's interests. Sexuality, violence, racism, detention of asylum seekers, gender stereotypes, sexual preference, the nature of femininity and masculinity—all are at times high on children's agendas and very powerful in the lives of many children, and none appear on lists of common topics dealt with in early childhood programs. Protest rallies, drag fashion shows, shooting horses, and becoming Barbies, are not generally thought of as the stuff of early childhood curriculum! In this way, all four chapters push the thinking of practitioners about what is reasonable, appropriate and important to deal with in curriculum and, more complexly, how to deal with it.

Traditionally, the stereotype of early childhood professionals as 'nice ladies' carried with it, accurately or not, the image of early childhood services as 'nice places', where people use words and don't fight, where effort is always rewarded, where people are generally caring and kind. The reminders in these chapters of what is really on children's minds, pushes readers to think about the relevance and authenticity of the curriculum, and consider appropriate links between what is going on in children's lives and what is happening inside the program. If there is little congruence, we run the risk of the experience in the early childhood program being written off as pleasant and comfortable, but as having little relevance for how a child might live life. All four chapters are a call to deal with what really matters rather than what is comfortable.

Respect and the image of the child

Each of the chapters implicitly or explicitly adopts a perspective on the child. Sandra and Janet's chapter places right at the centre, the question: 'What does it mean to truly respect the child as a partner and collaborator?'

This question leads to many others that practitioners face every day:

- What is our duty of care?

- When do we intervene?

- How much do we exercise control over children—both their behaviour and their experience?

- How do we balance children's need for safety and guidance with their right to privacy?

- How can we sensibly, authentically, genuinely and respectfully involve them in making decisions about their own experience?

- To what extent can the young child appropriately be a collaborator in the provision of her or his own experience?

- To what extent does the answer to this question necessarily depend on the child's ability to communicate and to comprehend the communications of others?

Sandra and Janet raise legitimate questions about the extent to which we can get into the heads and hearts of children, and the extent to which we unknowingly and perhaps unhelpfully ascribe our own feelings and responses to their behaviour (the comparison of displaying records of babies' bowel movements and adults' menstrual cycles, is perhaps an example of this).

It seems to me that by virtue of children needing our care, our guidance, our protection and our teaching, we cannot get away completely from the fact that we have more power than they do. In the end, the best we can do is to use that power wisely, in their best interests. In doing so, we can do our best to empathise and see things from their perspective. We can also share power with them appropriately and do so by taking their agenda into account. Ann Pelo makes the point that it is easy to lose sight of the children's agenda and impose your own, out of a sometimes unacknowledged belief that we know best.

Honouring diversity and borrowing sensibly

It occurred to me as I read the chapters, that the way Reggio Emilia has been adopted and mimicked in some places is rather like a tourist curriculum. Appropriation of the obvious is what the tourist curriculum is about. Having a light box, displaying documentation all over the walls, re-labelling themes as projects, and/or claiming that you are 'doing Reggio' has much in common with claiming that you are 'doing multiculturalism' because you play a Greek CD occasionally, have a wok in the home corner and saris with the dress-ups, and invite a didgeridoo player once a year!

It does seem at times that documentation has become a kind of fad and, as is usually the case with fads, sometimes it has been adopted uncritically and without questioning why. Alma Fleet's 'point about the point' of documentation is an apt one to keep in mind. She writes that:

> The philosophy associated with analysis and reflection is key…The teaching associated with insightful pedagogical documentation attempts to recognise the integrity of each experience rather than imposing a predetermined way of being…

That is the essence of good teaching. As Alma says, 'The progress is in knowing that the matter is not straightforward.'

Ann reminds us that documentation is dynamic, and what matters is not that you do it, or even how you do it, but rather what you do with it and where it leads you.

The need to think deeply, to collaborate, to take risks, and to disagree

Finally, these chapters provide powerful evidence that working well with children, or working in any role that supports the development, learning and wellbeing of children, requires continuous reflection, courage to take reasonable risks, willingness to collaborate, and comfort with conflict and disagreement. All of this is a powerful reminder of the complexity of being an early childhood professional. There are so few easy or universal answers. There are so many times that it is essential to exercise professional judgment. This is evident in the authors' perspectives as well as in their approaches to practice with children.

One of the most complex issues is the extent to which the teacher leaves values at the door. Clearly early childhood teaching is not value free, but putting values into practice is more complex than naming them. The line between professional values and personal values is often not clear. Environmental issues, policies about refugees and asylum seekers, attitudes towards guns and other weapons, treatment of Indigenous people, and many others are those where the teacher's attitudes may conflict with the majority views in the community.

The dispositions and skills of documentation must be built in to teacher education. Alma writes about using a 'learnable moment' (interest in the toy chest in the lecture theatre) to generate a powerful collection of learning experiences for student teachers. As a result of the investigation into toy chests, no doubt student teachers understood concepts about found possibilities, using the unorthodox, exploring both similarities and differences—making meaning from what is there—and, very importantly, taking risks. This is a powerful example of practising what you preach and, in doing so, providing no doubt a very convincing lesson to students.

Alma asks 'How do we help student teachers deeply understand the philosophies underlying practices we recommend?' Just as relevant is the converse:

How do we help student teachers take the philosophies we teach and match them with their practices? Or understand the philosophies sufficiently that they engage in practices that are compatible with them? In all our research, theorising, problematising, and hypothesising, we need to keep firmly in mind that what really matters in the end is children's experience.

About Anne Stonehouse

Anne Stonehouse has worked in Melbourne, Australia, as a consultant and as an acquisitions editor for an early childhood teacher resource publisher. She has worked as an author, academic, conference speaker, presenter of professional development, and consultant in Australia and overseas for over 30 years. She has published widely. In the past few years, Anne has undertaken several significant consultancies. For example, with the Office of Childcare in the New South Wales Department of Community Services, she produced a curriculum framework for all services for children from birth to school age and was involved in a Training Consortium promoting the Framework throughout the state.

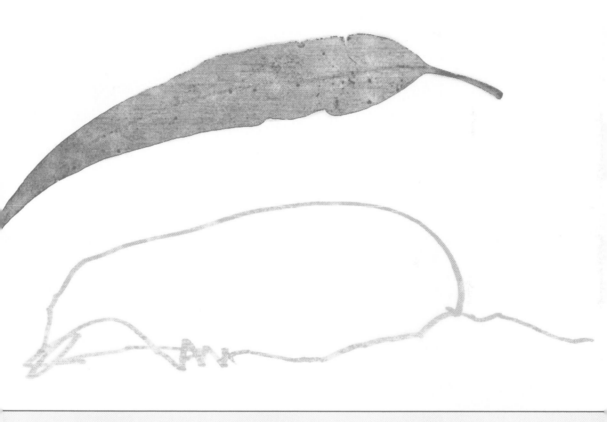

Part Four

Chapter Fourteen

Three Narratives:
The Sun, the Boat and the Flag

Janet Robertson

These stories take place in the playground at Mia-Mia, a not-for-profit child care centre attached to the Institute of Early Childhood at Macquarie University in NSW, Australia. Much attention has been paid to the aesthetic environment, both indoor and outdoor, to reflect the centre philosophy of education based on relationships. The playground is a garden with both intimate hideaway spaces and larger open ones, shady trees and a wide verandah. The space is used by 38, two to six-year-old children. One day a week, Janet, who is normally the two and three-year-olds' teacher, takes the role of the outdoor teacher.

Introduction

Using the strategy of teacher storytelling, this chapter will examine the importance of pedagogical documentation in highlighting teacher decisions with and about children. Making visible what we do with children, opening it up to others so they may engage in the discourse in which we either knowingly or unknowingly situate our teaching, allows for multiple perspectives to be created. Hopefully this creates a context in which we become researchers in our own practice and theory. Making our thinking visible can be scary, a bit like baring one's soul. The act of teaching in Australia is such an individual and private experience. So, the notion of intellectual critique and collaboration being an intrinsic part of the day is one which, perhaps, suffuses us with both fear and envy—fear, because we might be insecure about our skills and theoretical position and the expectations that collaboration and critique might bring; and envy, because we might want to share the load of thinking with others and be able to celebrate or commiserate in the ebb tide of the day. Taking the stance that no one way of thinking is right and letting go of certainties (Dahlberg, 1999; Millikan, 2001), I grab hold of the opportunity in pedagogical documentation to create ideas beyond my own, to share how I teach, and thereby learn more about children and my teaching from others. A short story will introduce the issues being raised here.

She and he suns

Watching, supporting, and researching with children the ways in which they make sense of a gendered world, gives us an insight into the scripts they (and we) might be 'reading'. I like to explore the discourses the children are using as they construct their multiple understandings of male and female. Sometimes this evidences itself in their understandings of nature. One morning four children, aged from four to five, and I were sitting on the verandah. Gen commented on the sun, 'Oh, she's gone behind a cloud.' A gentle discussion began about whether the sun was a boy or a girl. Adding paper so they could make their ideas visible, it became apparent that not only did they hold views about the sun's gender, but also that colour itself was strongly gendered.

The children all believed that there were multiple suns, a new one each day. Half of them held the view that the suns were the same gender, either male or female, while others believed that suns were male and female and alternated depending on factors such as the weather. Children's own gender did not always predict their gender choice. However, the moon that appeared later in the discussion was a male, as there is a man in the moon.

Such an exploration can be dismissed as fanciful, but in many cultures the sun is gendered and given such attributes as beneficence and cruelty. The gender to

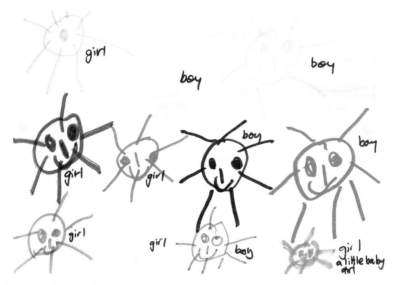

Drawings of he and she suns

which this attribute is given—either male as cruel or beneficent, or female as cruel or beneficent—sheds light on the culture's discourses about gender. When five-year-old Gen surmises, 'The sun is a girl because she tries to get up whenever she can', she is perhaps reflecting the discourse of the selfless mother.

Gender, or male-ness and female-ness, is a part of our make-up. At birth we are immersed in a milieu crackling and creaking with histories, fizzing with expectations and ways of being, laden with power and its attendant apparatus of privilege and repression. Gender and the status it gives us is present in our every moment. This, of course is both a positive and a negative. How we as teachers and theorists engage in pedagogy that includes understandings of gender and its role in the framework of who we are and who children might be, is culturally bound.

Always mindful of problematic adoptions of what is wrongly called the 'Reggio Approach' in places far removed from Northern Italy (Dahlberg, 1999), we still might consider how the Italians can challenge our thinking about gender and education of youngsters elsewhere. The Reggio Emilian educators have an understanding of difference, including gender, as a factor in learning— to be harnessed, cherished, and questioned. They contemplate the notion of equality (Rinaldi, 2001, p 41):

> What concept of equality are we developing?…In order to educate ourselves [educationalists], we must try to understand the differences rather than have any pretensions to eliminate them.

They bring to the educational table the possibility that to educate within a paradigm inclusive of difference, creates more complexity, understanding and fairness (Rinaldi, 2001, p 41):

> Is the aim to make everybody equal, or to give everyone opportunities to develop his or her own subjectivity (and thus difference) by interacting with others, where this incudes elements in common as well as elements that are different?

This position has been critiqued by Browne (2004, p 59), who sees the Reggio Emilia endeavour coloured by:

> The[ir] unwillingness to engage in critical analysis of gender issues with the children [which] simply serves to support the existing social status quo and gender power relations within society as a whole.

I believe that both the Reggio Emilian educators' position, and the position of Browne, should influence our theory and practice. Both points of view assist us to think about our understandings of fairness, and of difference. To consider gender equity only, or Reggio Emilia's educational experience only, as the tools in our shed of educational thinking is a false dichotomy (Mardell, 2001). Just as the Reggio Emilia educational experience is in danger of becoming a 'truth', the discourse of gender is endangered by those who wish to 'exclude alternative ways of understanding and interpreting the world' (Dahlberg, 1999, p 13). It is good that we are troubled, accepting that difference is not the issue, but how it is perceived and its consequences. As a teacher I can interrogate both the difference and the consequence simultaneously.

The belief that Reggio Emilia's educational experience is somehow a 'recipe' or a 'model', which can be transferred holus–bolus across borders and seas, needs critiquing. Many times have I heard the folk in Reggio Emilia say words to the effect 'we are Reggio Emilia and you are you; do not copy us, create your own dialogue and experiences'. I am not Italian and have no grasp on where their discourse on gender equity stands. If gender identity is a cultural construct, how could I? In the spirit of not copying but creating, can we accept the challenge to work towards social justice, including gender equity, through the lens of pedagogical documentation? I believe so.

The role of gender in early education, how it ripples through everything we do as teachers (gendered) and children (also gendered), bears close examination. Being able to enter the dialogue about gender, its fairness, its unfairness and its opportunities, is an essential part of a teacher and child's gaze. These following stories, snapshots of gender constructions taken from much larger experiences, can be viewed from multiple points. The gaze of feminism, or of gender equity, needs to be examined as we work within the challenges of Reggio Emilia. I like the many differences between boys and girls, as I like the many similarities. I am mindful of the problem of lumping all boys or all girls under some homogenous label, as with women or men, Christians or Muslims and so on. The problem of creating a binary of boys or girls as though they are in competition with each other (Browne, 2004) is as silly as a binary of adults or children. The many diverse masculinities and femininities are what I delight in. Within a group of boys there are as many ways of being a boy as there are boys. The same can be said for a group of girls, or a group of children. I often use these diversities and similarities to highlight, challenge or enhance the ways children are thinking. This does not, however, allow me to perpetuate unfairness nor to condone without scrutiny, experiences or conventions which are shaping my pedagogy.

It is important to examine and become a knowing participant, or a 'moral agent' (Dahlberg, Moss & Pence, 1999, p 38) about the ways in which children construct their notions of gender. As a knowing participant, I must use these constructions to assist children to become group learners and, of course, to interrupt unfairness and exclusion through teaching. One of the gifts from Reggio Emilia is to 'allow' us to celebrate gender differences, to harness them and make them work for us (and children), whilst at the same time making sure that we are offering multiple versions of femininity and masculinity.

The next story, 'A fishing expedition: five narratives', illuminates the choices which are not chosen, as well as the potential of an observation to be 'read' from many perspectives. It is followed by a final story that looks at the creation of a flag by two groups of children.

A fishing expedition: five narratives

Four boys are pretending to fish from a small white dinghy moored on the grass in the playground. It is an engaging moment for all of them. From my perspective, there is one boy playing for whom such collaborative and successful play with his peers is not common, so it was particularly rewarding to see him included. This partial transcript of their 30-minute play shows rich and rewarding experiences. The boys have two buckets, two rods and a rope. They are all four-year-olds.

Doug:	I nearly fell out.
Mark:	I'm standing.
Max:	I got two buckets.
Connor:	When you have finished can I have it?
Doug:	When you have finished with that rod can I have it?
Mark:	Yes, I got one so fast! I got a fast fish!
Max:	I caught a fast shark.
Connor:	I caught a huge fish.

Mark: This is how it goes.
Max: You have to put the fish in the bucket here.
Doug: Do you want more fishing rope and the bucket? Oh, it's gone
            (floated away), help save the bucket and get it back. I found it!
Max: I'll get it.
Doug: I'll get another .
Connor: I don't like eating cold fish.

This plot is rich with drama, rescue, success, negotiation and humour. They construct shared meanings of the sea; the boys are totally caught in the moment, the grass rippling and alive with abundant watery life and danger. As the teacher who set up the boat, and is 'in charge' of the playground that morning, I could feel satisfied that I had done my job well. A challenging child has had a marvellous morning without arguments or tears and used words of negotiation, such as 'when you have finished', without prompting and succeeded in a co-construction of understandings about fishing.

However, as the storyteller, I have taken a liberty with the sequence of events. Just preceding this game, two children were playing in the boat, Jean and Max. They speak Cantonese and it seems this is one of the links in their friendship. Max is a child who makes friends across gender and ages, often showing care for much younger children. Jean is a child strongly influenced by her family's traditional notions of gender and it is rare to see her play with boys. She is often quite disparaging about some boys, disliking their overt physical play. At home she is expected to be quiet and gentle. As the two sit fishing, they chat animatedly, in a mix of English and Cantonese, about the fish they are catching. They sit side-by-side, bodies touching, with the still stance of serious fisher folk, watching the 'water' for fish. Every now and then they point to one, voices hushed. There is a feeling of serenity, and it really seems the grass is glistening with fish scales.

About ten minutes pass, and the three boys approach the boat. They leap on board, rocking the boat both figuratively and literally. The fishing idyll is shattered, as the intruders clamber about, gathering rods and buckets. Jean turns her head, and Max leaves her side to join the boys. Jean remains playing alone in the prow of the boat for about two minutes, as the boys crash around, yelling wildly about sharks. She then steps out of the boat. It seems to me she is deliberately shattering the pretence of water as she walks across the grass to me and, as she passes me, she comments, 'I think I've finished now.' The sudden incursion of the boys made Jean and her rights invisible.

I was interested in the boys' unheeding exclusion of Jean. Had they any idea what had happened? Would Jean have been able to stop it? The ethical choices of stopping the play and trying to include Jean once again in the game, or asking the intruders to play somewhere else and return when Jean and Max had finished, or to allow the boys to continue and address the exclusion afterwards once play had ceased, presented themselves. Weighing it up, and knowing it would be unlikely Jean would like to play with the intruder boys, I chose the latter. As with any decision there are always choices unchosen (Dahlberg, 1999). Nevertheless, the sequence of events made me uncomfortable.

The next day I sat with each of the players separately and showed them ten photos of the play in sequence, writing down what they said. I found that I needed to ask the three intruder boys where and why Jean had gone. Max acknowledged her right away, but seemed to have no idea why or when she left. In his transcript, the richness of his game with Jean is evident in the long lists of fish that they caught or saw. Jean's transcript corroborates this. Jean ends hers by saying, 'I miss everybody, but not boys.' In all the transcripts it is possible to see different constructions of the events. Mark appears to be oblivious of Jean's existence until prompted and then to please me, adds something about her. Doug gives an explanation, 'She went to get something for us', while Connor dismissed her, making her leaving premised on a choice to 'play with something else'. My interest in Jean and her whereabouts clues the boys into my agenda.

I asked each of the participants to draw their memory of the game. Mark and Doug drew images of the boat and the fishing rods, with long explanatory rambles about the game. Neither drew people nor mentioned Jean. Max drew the grass but told a tale of 'I and Jean and catching big shark and some fish, and some crocodile fish and some green fish, and rainbow fish, ring fish—lots of fish.' It seems very evocative of his time spent prior to the change in plot. Jean drew the boat and two figures, Max and herself, both with rods and fish in rippling water.

Connor drew four figures fishing, and then added as a very small afterthought a miniature Jean in the bottom corner of the page.

Jean's boat drawing

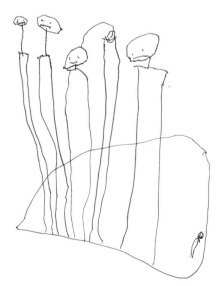

Connor's boat drawing

By using the five narratives, it became possible to glimpse how each child interpreted the event, and for us to glimpse some of the multiple discourses each child brought to the interpretation. The boys each had their understandings of masculinity; however, as a group on this occasion they adopted a rambunctious, very physical script (MacNaughton, 2000) and image of masculinity.

In this story we cannot just look at the exclusion and dismiss the other co-constructions which occur. An image of children as seekers, creators, re-creators and participants in the construction of their gender and its experiences, and that of their companions, must also make room for the success of the group in assisting its members to create a 'third space' (Soja, 1996) in which the fishing fantasy occurs. Within this third space, they created common understandings culled from popular culture and personal experience. Only one child had actually been fishing; the others seemed possibly to be making meaning from information garnered from television, books and stories. What happened to Jean was unfair, and needed to be addressed, but it is also unfair to gloss over the achievements of the intruders in the creation of the fishing game.

These five narratives were written up in a form of pedagogical documentation to make visible to other adults aside from myself the ethical issues that 'taking sides' and unchosen choices could engender. It gave us as a staff the impetus to look and listen to children's daily gender storylines (MacNaughton, 2000). It also gave us an opportunity to support multiple gender scripts, and to ask about the fairness of some experiences. We began to explore the many male and female ways of being that were manifested in our beliefs and those that the children were constructing. As a group of teachers, we became very interested in how to interrupt masculine and feminine discourses when they were evidenced in unfairness. Without the moment caught in time, we would not have been able to collectively engage in thinking about our notions of fairness, of choices unchosen and of moving forward our debate. As one staff member, I might have continued the investigation, but the existence of pedagogical documentation enabled the staff community to join in the discussion.

The flag

It had long been an aspiration of mine to work with a group of children to design a flag for Mia-Mia. The possibilities for examining children's understandings of icons as representative of place, as well as the necessary negotiation to achieve design consensus seemed to me to be immense. In 2003, the opportunity arose and a long-term investigation began. I wanted to work with the oldest children, as the completed flag would be their farewell present to the school. By happenstance, the ten eldest were two groups of five-year-olds, five girls and five boys. These were also close friendship groups, who knew each other well. I decided to work with the two groups separately for design and concept, bringing them together whenever the design process required a decision. I hypothesised their familiarity and therefore 'shorthand' in thinking together would enhance their work. I believed that they would approach the task of design differently, but was unsure of how. Two design journeys began.

Drawings of a Korean and an Australian flag

The boy group readily identified national flags, poring over charts of flags and countries, showing competent knowledge about which was which. They readily shared this with others in their group. On finding out about the story behind some flags, in particular the Aboriginal flag of Australia (the black people walking on the red earth under the yellow sun), they started to compose verbal stories for imaginary flags. A Scary flag was proposed in hushed tones with terrifying creatures, ghosts and venomous insects. A more animated tone was used for a Naughty flag, which was to be covered in acts of malicious or mischievous behaviour such as pinching and verbal unkindness for the former, or practical jokes for the latter. One of the purposes of critical reflection became evident to me as I revisited these two flags long after the project was completed. It occurred to me how important it might have been to ask at the time whether the Naughty flag, when flown, would condone those acts, or warn of them. I could berate myself about the 'missed opportunity'; instead I see it as a learning moment for myself. Next time I will listen more closely as children make meaning about complex topics. The purpose of pedagogical documentation is not to look endlessly for mistakes, but to see moments when you become the learner.

This group's contribution to the icons proposed as representative of Mia-Mia, were the rabbit, rabbit poo, the building, a rocket, stars and people. They quickly delegated the drawing of these icons to those they considered would be able to do it 'great' and so three sat and watched Max and Ron draw, adding comments about deficiencies in the drawing, which were accordingly 'corrected'.

The group of girls took a different direction. From the beginning they were impressed with the task and took particular care to make sure their flag was 'beautiful'. Uninterested in books of real flags, they seemed to use the medium of drawing together as a way of reaching consensus about what would go on the flag. Every time we met, they drew flags whilst we chatted. The conversation would be speckled with, 'pass me the green pen, please' and 'can you draw me a heart?', and with pauses while they looked at each other before committing to a decision.

They made the following offerings as icons for the flag: the rabbit, ducks, rainbows, hearts, and friends. When told of the boy's ideas they eagerly accepted the idea of the star, said the people could be friends, giggled at the mention of rabbit poo, dismissed the idea of the building as too big and admired the coincidence of the choice of rabbit and ducks. Kath then gave reasons as to why the icons were there, 'The star to watch over Mia-Mia; the rabbit because we love her; the hearts because we love and are loved; friends as you have more than one friend and the ducks because it is their home.'

As there was only one flag, both groups had to agree on the icons. I expected more discussion about this, but both liked each other's ideas. I was unable to pinpoint when or why the rabbit poo, rocket, and rainbows were disbanded, but they were not mentioned when they were drafting the drawings for the motifs. Together they agreed on the placement of the icons, using the overhead projector. Both girls and boys were vociferous when barracking for their ideas, giving reasoned explanations, which were eventually negotiated into the completed design.

I asked the boys to vote for the colours for the completed design. All five sat with me and I asked each boy what colour they were voting for and wrote it down. The six choices were made with much discussion. Wallace said at the beginning that 'one colour could lose and the rest would win', so in each voting round four of them would choose the same colour and the fifth would select an outsider. They alternated the fifth person, so all five had a turn at being the loser and each hammed up their distress at 'losing' amid great hilarity. In choosing the colours for the completed design they took a realistic approach, brown for the rabbit and ducks, yellow for the star, red for the hearts and green for the grass. Once they had established the protocol, it was all done and dusted in five minutes.

Wallace and Max laboured for about three minutes colouring the final design with Textas, before suggesting using the computer paint program. The others agreed with alacrity, and spent a jovial afternoon teaching each other how to navigate through the steps in the software. They became so competent with the program that they deliberately made mistakes to provide themselves with extra challenge. They made strict verbal rules for turn-taking, and reiterated these constantly.

Voting by the girls was vastly different from the boys. At no point did they speak about their decision until they were sure that their choice was everyone else's. When voting on their final colour choice, they sat around a table. Scattered in front of them on the table was a swathe of colour pens. As I asked the question of each girl, 'Which colour would you like for the rabbit?' they would look down, then eyes to the left and right making furtive contact with the others. At first I thought I was intimidating them, and retreated from the circle, looking away. They knew all along this choice would have to be made, so it was not a lack of understanding which had created what I first assumed was unease. As I waited and watched, Joyce slowly leaned forward and tapped a pen with her finger. There was no response from the others, but I noticed a joint focus on her act. She tapped another pen, barely moving her wrist, the finger just stretching to the next pen. Again there was no response. The third tap, on a bright pink pen, elicited a response. One girl nodded slightly, another looked at the tapping finger and smiled, and a third reached over and tapped the same pen, while the fourth looked directly at Joyce. At this point Joyce announced her decision, 'pink'. This silent process was repeated for each choice. At times the solemnity was broken by gales of laughter about each final decision, or pens dropping on the floor, or jokes from passing friends. Nevertheless, the tension prior to consensus was palpable. It was as though they were collectively holding their breath until the star was really going to be 'red'. It seemed to me the girls wanted absolute certainty that their choice was the approved choice of the others. The consensus was reached without dispute or dissent within the group and without words. They took 40 minutes to make the six decisions.

The boys' flag

The girls' colour choices were not at all pragmatic, and featured pinks, reds and purples. When they used the computer to make the final copy, they found that they had to change their background choice of pink, as three of the icons were already pink and immediately vanished in a dazzle of pinkness. The on-the-spot change in colour choice was made quickly by clicking on a variety of choices, all of which erased one or more icons. The first time they moved away from the spectrum of colours in the pinks, and thereby kept all the icons, they agreed it was the one.

Turn-taking at the computer was subtle, and predicated on ability rather than length of time or completion of elements within the design. Victoria was adept at navigating through the program and able to rescue them when things went awry. Joanna was good with the mouse, Kath worked out how to shade the colours and Mallory knew how to get the program to print. Each girl looked comfortable in her role and spontaneously clapped when the final copy popped out of the printer, 'We did it!'

All the children in their class (23) made the final colour choice between the two groups' proposals. The vote was with raised hands. The completed choices were on an overhead projector, the images thrown up on the wall. The boys, when 'their' colour was proposed, called loudly to each other, encouraging hands up, often voting with both hands. There was some cajoling of other children, 'Yeah, you like this colour.' Conversely, when it was not their colour, they volubly reminded each other to keep their hands down. The girls on the other

The completed flag

hand continued their silence, but used physical means to remind each other of what to do. When it was not 'their' colour they held each other's hands down, and if they were too far away to reach, touched each other with toes. Joyce partly lay on Mallory, worrying perhaps she might get a rush of blood to the head and vote for anything. Equally, when it was 'theirs' they thrust each other's arms up, including the arms of other children who had not been in the design group. The final product is a meld of the two, partly pragmatic and partly decorative.

The children show immense pride in their work and can all reiterate what each motif means. Obviously the way the groups worked would have been different whatever combination of participants had been chosen. The mere fact that the flag was my idea influenced what eventuated, as I'm sure they were mindful of pleasing me. As a wielder of power as their teacher, I am under no illusions that my presence is anything but silent. The erasure of the 'poo', silently agreed by children, is a sure sign that they are aware of my presence and the ultimate purpose of the flag as a present to the school. I see this as a positive— they know what is appropriate—not as a negative censuring of children's expression.

The keystone of each group—that they were close friends—assisted them in their work. They knew each other's strengths, did not need to embroil themselves in turf wars about who would be first and were able to support each other within the group. When the two groups met, it was as designers, rather than as opposing sides, reaching compromise and solutions. Joyce and Wallace were unofficial leaders of each group and were respectful of the decision-making process. The overall result is a melange of the culture of the school, personal styles within the groups, adult scaffolding and a joint desire to make the flag as magnificent as possible. I don't credit the element of gender with exclusive shaping of how and what was achieved; that claim would be specious. The need of the group of girls for silent consensus surprised me, having thought they would be very verbal about choices. My surprise stemmed from unconscious stereotyping of girls' linguistic ability. Now I am alert to the modus operandi of finger tapping, I would like to watch for this in the future when working with children.

These two particular groups worked in this way. I know other combinations would work differently, even if the gender combination was the same. For me, watching how these two groups worked gave me the compass for how the project would unfold. At the end of each session, I would consider what had been achieved, what directions had been taken, what ideas had been proposed, rejected and accepted and how best to move forward with the children. More often than not, the children suggested tasks for next time either directly, or through a problem they encountered. At one point, I realised that Kath could not visualise the full-scale flag as we had been constantly working on A4 sized paper. I asked the others if they would think about this until we met again. It was apparent they had puzzled over it in the interim, but could not find a solution. When I offered them the overhead projector, they were then able to transfer small images to large sheets projected onto the wall by tracing the lines. I expected they would all need to undertake this task, but there was an 'ah ha' moment for most of them and the painstaking chore was undertaken by only three. Grasping the tool, they then utilised it to make overhead copies of all the icons and arrange the flag designs in many combinations in real size without transposing them by hand. Kath's original mystification actually accelerated the process of design for both groups.

The ballot for rabbit motif

Certainly the gender of each participant is important, as one is inextricable from the other. But I don't believe gender alone determined the end result. Happenstance made this a group divided by gender. Each group had equal rights and opportunities throughout the design and voting process and the flag is a joint endeavour. Learning to acquiesce, to follow, to pick the best person for the job, to vote, to accept critique, to offer advice, to lead, to get over disappointment, to proffer ideas, to sustain enthusiasm over months, to negotiate between individuals and groups were all important here. The point of the project, to make one flag, negated the issue of a flag each, or one for each group.

Furthermore, it is possible that we as a profession hold dear the notion that children's 'real' learning is confined to the classroom. One glaring example of the belief that 'real' learning only occurs inside, is the marginalisation of outdoor spaces as sites for valued learning. Children are allowed outside for a good run and free play, but return inside to learn. An image of children as learners *wherever they are* is not one we treasure, nor do we seem to value learning if it is not indoors in a classroom. This outdoor flag-designing investigation lasted months and was cloaked in a mantle of the teaching of democracy. The motifs (such as which version of centre rabbit to include), colours and drawings on the flag were voted for, within the group.

Learning how to vote, learning that some votes did not 'win', learning how to lobby for your candidate (be it a drawing or colour) and accepting the results of the ballot, far outweighed the magnificent end product, which flutters atop the playground flagpole.

Conclusion

These three stories are examples of baring one's soul. I hope that every reader will take a different perspective when thinking about what they would have done in similar circumstances. The point of telling the stories is that you are able, in part, to enter the learning world I inhabited with children on three separate occasions. Pedagogical documentation has enabled some of the ethical issues, choices, strategies, mistakes and reflections I experienced to be partially evident to you. This coming out of the educational closet takes courage, is not a 'truth' and is cloaked in my subjectivity. As Gunilla says, 'there is never a single true story' (Dahlberg, 1999, p 33). The power to make significant change in early childhood education, or not, resides in part in our hands. Current debates about social justice and how we may disturb traditional modernist 'truths' about gender, can be made visible through pedagogical documentation. If we are not prepared to show others what we are thinking and the choices we are making, then we do both them and our selves a great disservice. We perpetuate the un-critical, un-collegial, isolated teacher paradigm, confining pedagogy to the dark—and risk becoming technicians, not educators.

References

Browne N (2004) *Gender in the early years.* Berkshire, England: Open University Press.

Dahlberg G (1999) Early childhood in a changing world—a practice-oriented research project troubling dominant discourses within the field of early childhood education. In *Unpacking observation and documentation: Experiences from Italy, Sweden and Australia. Conference Proceedings.* (pp 3–14). North Ryde, NSW: Institute of Early Childhood, Macquarie University.

Dahlberg G, Moss P & Pence A (1999) *Beyond quality in early childhood education and care: Postmodern perspectives.* London: Falmer Press.

Mardell B (2001) Moving across the Atlantic. In C Guidici, C Rinaldi & M Krechevsky (Eds). *Making learning visible: Children as individual and group learners.* (pp 278–83). Reggio Emilia, Italy: Reggio Children.

MacNaughton G (2000) *Rethinking gender in early childhood education.* Sydney: Allen and Unwin.

Millikan J (2001) Rejoicing in subjectivity: An overview based on a personal interpretation of the schools for young children in the city of Reggio Emilia. In *Unpacking interpretation: De-constructions from Australia, America and Reggio Emilia. Conference Proceedings.* (pp 5–23). North Ryde, NSW: Institute of Early Childhood, Macquarie University.

Rinaldi C (2001) Infant–toddler centres and pre-schools as places of culture. In C Guidici, C Rinaldi & M Krechevsky (Ed.). *Making learning visible: children as individual and group learners.* (pp 38-46). Reggio Emilia, Italy: Reggio Children.

Soja E (1996) *Thirdspace: Journeys to Los Angeles and other real-and-imagined places.* Oxford: Blackwell.

Chapter Fifteen

The Power of the Listened Word

Alexandra Harper

The children in this chapter are seven and eight-year-olds in a public school in suburban Sydney, Australia. Most children in the school speak English as a first language. Their teacher, Alex, is now in an executive position in the school, having worked previously in teacher education and in a family-grouped, alternative school.

Introduction

It amazes me that simple exchanges can lead to complex journeys. In one such situation, a seemingly inconsequential conversation took place between me and another teacher. Over a cup of tea in the staffroom, she said, 'I've been meaning to tell you about something that happened the other day and I know you won't be offended.' I was intrigued by her comment. She began to share a story of an incident that occurred when she was on playground duty. During lunchtime, a boy from an upper primary grade had initiated the following conversation with her:

> Child: Mrs Harper's a bit unusual, isn't she?
> Teacher: What makes you say that?
> Child: She teaches differently.
> Teacher: In what way?
> Child: I don't think she teaches from the curriculum.

The teacher was correct in assuming I wouldn't be offended by the conversation. Moreover, I was flattered that this child had taken the time to think about me, especially given that he had never been in my class. I was also interested in why this teacher had chosen to share this moment with me. I am eternally grateful that she did, as she sent me on an unplanned journey. My trip commenced with the consideration of two questions:

- How did this upper primary boy see 'the curriculum'?

- What observations may have led this child to perceive that I did things differently?

This chapter will endeavour to explore these two questions and the personal journeys that helped me begin to uncover their answers.

How did this upper primary boy see 'the curriculum'?

Curriculum is a complex subject and one that cannot be explored in depth within this chapter. It is important, however, to describe the context where my learning journeys took place. In New South Wales (NSW), the school curriculum is divided into six mandatory Key Learning Areas each with their own syllabus and support documents. Each individual syllabus document is segmented into stage units that cover primary school levels, from the first year of school through to Year Six. From this starting point, many schools develop their own operational scaffolding—often in the form of scope and sequence documents to support ease of implementation. In some cases, the result is subject-based programming designed in advance for the whole term or entire year. A future curriculum (as described by Arthur, Beecher, Dockett, Farmer and Death, 1996) thus becomes culturally embedded practice within the school.

Providing all NSW teachers with mandatory documents will not result in uniform interpretation and implementation. One could argue that this isn't warranted or even wanted. However, given an educational environment with a focus on consistency of judgment and equitable education for all children, the intention behind such government directives can be understood. As educators, we appreciate the subjective nature of our profession and how this affords individual interpretation of government documents. One educator's under-standing and implementation of the syllabus will be different from another's. This is a direct result of the interplay between a teacher's educational philosophy and pedagogy. One might espouse a future, an emergent or an accelerated curriculum, or a combination of these and/or others. A single aspect of a syllabus document can lead to extensive variations within classroom practice. When considered in this light, the complexities of curriculum are wide ranging. Putting all of these elements in the context of the boy's observations, I was intrigued by how he developed his definition of 'curriculum'. I wondered what school experiences, and maybe family discussions, had generated his understanding. I would have loved to have an insight into what he meant by the word 'curriculum'. Could he have been referring to curriculum as simply 'what happens' (Jones and Nimmo, 1994, p 12). Or was he considering it on another level? I was left with these unanswered questions. Furthermore, I pondered how his observations of my pedagogy differed from his definition of curriculum.

For me, the syllabus documents are a contract between my employer and myself. These documents are in place to create consistency and equity in a subjective workplace. My challenge is to work from, and within, the requirements of these documents whilst respecting my context, philosophy and the people I engage with in dialogue every day at school. Given this perspective, I am in a unique position of power. I make the choices in creating the bridges between the syllabus documents and the children. The ways in which I work with children creates their experience of the syllabus documents and in turn their developing understanding of curriculum. James, Jenks & Prout (1998, p 41–2) put it this way:

> Curricula, we would argue therefore, are more than the description of content. They are spatial theories of cognitive and bodily development and, as such, they contain world views (Young, 1971) which are never accidental and certainly not arbitrary. They involve selections, choices, rules and conventions, all of which relate to questions of power, issues of personal identity and philosophies of human nature and potential, and all of which are specifically focused on the child.

The following descriptions of classroom events characterise a sense of the curriculum as experienced by the children in my class. The comment, 'I don't think she teaches from the curriculum', can be understood by revealing my ways of working within the expectations of State-wide syllabus documents.

What observations may have led this child to perceive that I did things 'differently'?

As part of my pedagogy, I value the relationship between the curriculum and listening. It is the achievement of a balance between responding to the children and the syllabus requirements that provides me with invigorating challenges.

The last 18 months have seen a shift in how I listen to children's conversations. Previously, I would focus on observations that gave me access into a child's cognition, their developing factual (and predominately scientific) theories about the world. These were concepts that I could hold onto and reflect upon. I could also, more often than not, obtain extensive support material in order to extend the children's investigations. I perceived these journeys to have a definite starting point, a progression and development of ideas and a move towards closure as negotiated by the children, myself and often parents. I was listening to and reading the children's intent (Oken-Wright & Gravett, 2002) and developing their ideas into a fluid and inclusive curriculum. I felt confident that I knew where they were coming from and I could foresee possibilities to scaffold their learning.

The resultant pedagogical documentation was easy to record in a range of narrative formats, beautiful posters and annotated photographs. In addition, the examples of documentation provided a new way of sharing the children's learning with their parents and the wider community. The children enjoyed the increased value and attention that was placed on their work by our educational community. In meeting State department requirements, such investigations provided assessable data that could be related to the many outcomes and indicators included in syllabus documents.

Just after this period, I began to question the selective nature of what I listened to and acted upon. I had to reflect upon my use of power as the teacher. My pedagogy incorporated negotiating the curriculum with the children and, consequently, social construction and democratic decision-making were at the forefront. However, an uneasy feeling began to build about my role in overseeing and ultimately controlling the investigative decision-making in the classroom. I began to reassess my role in selecting which conversations were 'worthy' of exploring. Why did I follow up on some conversations and not others? I started to acknowledge that I saw some topics as too hard and therefore overlooked and discarded them. Naively I thought I could hold onto them 'until another time'. Unfortunately, often that time never came. The choices I made must have communicated certain messages to the children. At first I thought it was a matter of confusion in reading children's intent. I soon realised, however, that it was much deeper than that. In fact, as the following discussion will highlight, it led to a reconsideration of my image of children.

Initial changes

My first step, in order to address this, was the decision to be more active in trying to give all my 32, third-graders the chance to express their views. I continued with the established weekly routine of classroom chats and introduced a 'Thought Book'. This book was made readily accessible to the children so they could write or draw in it at anytime. The children respected the negotiated rule and agreed not to read another's contribution unless invited to do so. The 'Thought Book' led to a range of investigations—the human body, relationships between people, fear, bullying and the general day-to-day things that the children wanted to share. These were all manageable journeys to undertake—sometimes confronting, but accessible and easily accounted for, in terms of the curriculum. After two school terms of working in this way, a shift started to occur in the discussions the children were having. The following conversation occurred in response to media reports of English boys being found playing on railway tracks.

Huang:	Those boys have no family so they do bad things.
Scott:	They should go to gaol for one year. A nine-year-old should be more thoughtful and responsible.
Sophie:	The boys could have been killed.
Alison:	Maybe they didn't know how dangerous it was.
Andrew:	The six and four-year-olds were doing it and the nine-year-old just came along.
Emma:	They should not go to gaol because the nine-year-old wasn't thinking straight. He was being stupid. We don't know why they did it.
William:	I disagree with Scott. What if I did it?
Claudia:	Are you a boy? Is this England?
William:	I didn't mean to do it. The parents mustn't care about him at four [years of age] to be out alone.
Claudia:	Maybe they were angry.
Toby:	Two boys escaped from the detention centre you know and when they went back to the detention centre they were put on wires and whipped by the guards.
Mrs Harper:	How do you know this Toby?
Alison:	You see it on the news. Putting kids in detention centres for months. It's not right.

Bruce:	Only parents should go.
Huang:	A person was murdered in a bar. Two Korean people died in a river. Why did that happen?
Nelson:	It's illegal to whip people.
Claudia:	I don't think counsellors would whip them. They are helpers.
Sophie:	They illegally entered the country.

This was a passionately felt discussion and I was out of my depth. I was surprised at how the children were communicating in an adult way about society. They continued to explore these issues by dividing into a series of smaller groups, joining and separating in various combinations in a natural ebb and flow. This style of interaction continued for nearly two hours whereupon the children went out to morning tea. I was left exhausted and pondering—where to next?

While considering this, I was faced with the realisation that even though I thought my pedagogy was grounded in social constructivism, there were still components of my thinking that were at odds with it. In contemplating the exploration of these social justice issues, I was worried that I may corrupt the children's understanding of the world. It seemed easier to present a sanitised version of world events. The notion that there is a separation between the world that adults and children experience was embedded in this thinking. I was marginalising children as decision-makers and not acknowledging their opinions of contemporary social and political issues. In doing so, was I reinforcing a Western truth. James *et al.* (1998, p 62) state:

> …western childhood has become a period in the life course characterized [sic] by social dependency, asexuality and the obligation to be happy, with children having the right to protection and training but not to social or personal autonomy.

The simplistic nature of this thinking was nostalgic as well as disempowering. It was reminiscent of an age-levelled and staged curriculum where children sequentially moved through content. It limited thinking to a child/adult dichotomy based only on the passage of time and a maturity of the body. Childhood was seen as a process of preparing children for adulthood complete with adult responsibilities and an ability to deal with an adult world.

I began to ponder whether I would offend parents and staff in exploring these sensitive issues. I wondered if it was my role to foster an introduction into the 'real' world for these children; whether I was accountable to discuss these issues as they were raised within our class forum and, if so, was I capable of doing so. My mind was awash with these thoughts as well as the beginning of an uneasy self-examination in relation to exploring these questions. Unfortunately, while doing all of this thinking several weeks went by and when I finally embraced the idea of going ahead, the moment had passed and the children told me that they were not interested in discussing this topic anymore. They wanted to make a documentary on the human body. I felt depressed in that I had lost an opportunity —a journey missed.

Reflection on experiences

On further reflection, however, I realised that I had undertaken a journey. Listening to children in this instance fostered an expedition of reviewing, re-addressing and re-developing my personal beliefs and values. I needed to reconsider my image of the child. I saw children as social constructors of their knowledge and I acted from this principle. The children in my class were actively engaged in negotiating programs and were supported in voicing their concerns, views and evaluations of whatever occurred in our room. In an investigation of the human body (a topic instigated by the children through the 'Thought Book'), the notion of joint planning was foregrounded. The children decided that they wanted their parents involved, so a note was sent home advising of a joint planning session one afternoon—one grandfather even came! For those parents and carers unable to attend the planning session, a note was sent home to ensure that they had the opportunity to share their ideas, questions and concerns as well. The children researched their chosen system of the human body. They wrote information reports that met departmental outcome requirements and consistency in grade assessment tasks. Furthermore, they devised interactive PowerPoint presentations, which they saved onto disc to share with their families at home. They also loved to share these presentations with visitors to the school. To extend their skills in using the PowerPoint program, the children asked to document a morning they spent dissecting various animal organs with a visiting nurse. The investigation culminated in a human body documentary scripted, acted, directed and set designed by the children.

I saw children as competent beings, not as passive recipients of a syllabus. I acknowledged their ability to work autonomously and become authors of their own learning. Consequently, one of my roles in the classroom was to be an active listener and attentive observer, supporting each child. I saw children as inquisitive and striving to actively engage with the wondrous world around them. I valued the right of each child to be supported in developing meaningful relationships with other humans, objects, thoughts and the environment. As shown in the work on the human body, I aimed to work in a truly collaborative way in valuable and real relationships with the children and their families.

However, despite holding these images of children, I had used my 'power' as the teacher to reinforce a distinction between children and the perceived adult world. I had created a barrier that sanitised global issues. I wished to protect children from the 'realities' of the adult world and, in doing so, prevent access into what I consider the harsh and 'uglier' side of humanity. I wanted each child to feel secure and safe. It was a heart-felt gesture, but what was underlying my intentions? I realised it was my acceptance of Rousseau's image of children as innocent. Did I really believe this?

No, it was more complex than that. I appeared to hold varying images of children. These came into play depending on the context in which I was considering them. I appeared to hold one set of images for children as learners and another for children as social beings with the ability to discuss social justice issues. I valued their developing perceptions, but I felt certain areas shouldn't be explored without parental involvement or school support. I had to acknowledge that children experience the same world events as adults (Dahlberg, Moss & Pence, 1999, p 51):

> He or she is not an innocent apart from the world, to be sheltered in some nostalgic representation of the past produced by adults. Rather the young child is in the world as it is today, embodies that world, is acted upon by that world—but also acts upon it and makes meaning of it.

It is perhaps idealistic, some may consider naïve, to think that children are unaware of the happenings around our globe, particularly over the last few years. If I believe that children are co-constructors of their environment and they actively seek to make meaning of the world around them, I have to acknowledge that they may need time to reflect upon, discuss, analyse and postulate their own theories of why people act the way they do. I began to consider that it might be a right of children to have this time. In addition, I believed they should be supported in developing a critical eye in considering how they were receiving information, why they were receiving the information and the nature of the information they were receiving.

Advances in technology have generated highly visible channels for the communication of information. From a very early age, children are embedded within these media and, in turn, within the realities of the world. When they enter school, they come with a range of experiences and a developing sense of socio-history, both on a personal and a more far-reaching level. They are already constructing their role(s) in society and considering their social responsibilities. To respect the thought processes of the children, I had to accept that they were developing socio-political belief systems along with concepts and skills. This certainly added a new dimension to the consideration of understandings as outlined in the syllabus documents!

To empower the children I was working with, I needed to appreciate that they were living and interacting in a complex world and rapidly moving into an unknown future. Beare (2001) predicts that this future will include a total reconstruction of the workplace as we know it. There will be internationalised workplaces with inequalities in distribution of the world's resources and perhaps enforced international environmental responsibilities (p 15):

> In a world like this, it is important for me to know what I stand for. I will look to my school to help me form my values and decide on my system of beliefs. I have to be careful about what I believe and what I take for granted without thinking.

If I was truly committed to empowering children in engaging in this future world, I had to honour it in my current philosophy and pedagogy. There was no longer scope to ignore social justice issues. From this point on, I decided to support children in exploring multiple truths present in the world today and help them to consider numerous viewpoints in developing their own theories. I decided I would not miss another journey.

Further changes

Another year and another class of 31 third-graders. During a handwriting lesson, one student casually started chatting with me about recent world events. She shared her wondrous ambitions for the world and I am glad I made the time to listen:

Rachel:	Why can't we just ask to meet them and say we want peace?
Peter:	As if. They would just shoot us.
Rachel:	We have to do something. What can we do Mrs Harper?
Mrs Harper:	I don't know Rachel.
Rachel:	How could you not know?
Mrs Harper:	I don't have any answers for this. I don't think many adults do.
Rachel:	But I want to know what we can do now. Tell me. Tell Me. TELL ME.
Mrs Harper:	I can't, Rachel. I don't have the answers for these questions.
Rachel:	How can that be?
Mrs Harper:	Maybe if we work together we can think of something?
Rachel:	Okay.

To support Rachel's understanding, I had to carefully consider the actual intent behind this interaction. At first I believed it was Rachel's search for world peace and how it could be achieved. Reconsidering the transcript at home later that evening, I became aware of Rachel's belief that adults hold the answers. I could recognise the cognitive conflict that arose for her because I didn't provide them. In fact, when looking at the transcript it became clear that Rachel thought I was withholding solutions to her quandary. This was a powerful insight for me, given the journey I had taken in my own exploration of the duality of the world adults and children inhabit and their roles in it. Did Rachel perceive a distinction between adult and child roles in society? Did her belief system separate the world children and adults experience? She certainly had an expectation that children ask questions and adults answer them. Did I have to explore this further to find out whether she was referring to adults per se or solely to me as an adult teacher? I would love to share this transcript with her to revisit and discuss these questions.

At the time, to respect the power of Rachel's thinking, with her permission, I shared the conversation with the rest of the class. It led to a fascinating discussion on beliefs and how the beliefs people hold affect their actions. It also highlighted how the sharing of one powerful thinker's thoughts can encourage the involvement of many:

Lydia:	They must believe in something.
Ryan:	There was a lady on TV who helped poor people called Mother Teresa. She has had two miracles. She needs three to become a saint.
Chris:	If someone believes in something strongly they will help someone.
Alice:	Nelson Mandela had strong beliefs. He thought white people were taking over Africa and teasing blacks and he stood up for them and went to gaol for forty years.
Elouise:	I think it was thirty.
John:	Some people believe in something so strongly they think they can do something about it.
Jacob:	I saw this movie and he wants world peace and he believes in it so strongly, so he does it.
Mrs Harper:	Do you mean Gandhi?
Jacob:	Yes.
Wendy:	A long time ago in London a female dressed up as a male and went to war and looked after the soldiers and became the best surgeon known as Dr James Barry I think.
Antonia:	My daddy told me a story about a sailor who saw the rubbish in the water and made Clean up Australia Day.
Pablo:	My dad told me a story about Martin Luther King and he was a black and blacks weren't allowed wherever whites were. He tried to make black and whites equal in the USA. He got killed because the whites didn't like him standing up.
Elouise:	That's not fair. Nelson Mandela did this too. He saw some things weren't fair and did something about it. He saw that there were cups for blacks that were old and rusty and white china cups for the whites. Nelson Mandela took a china cup because he thought it was stupid and he got punished.

Rachel: Has anyone read the story of Helen Keller? She had determination. She was blind and deaf. Anne Sullivan came and was determined to teach her to see and hear in her own special way.

Time after time listening to children's conversations affirms my image of them as powerful thinkers and this conversation illustrates their strengths. The depth of knowledge that the children brought to the discussion was amazing. They used narratives to make sense of their present world. These children were actively engaged with their society and approached it with both contemporary and historic orientations. Moreover, they used narratives to make meaning of human socio-history in order to facilitate the development of their own belief systems. The children were searching for meaning and I was determined to support and not directly influence the formation of their thoughts. I saw this as crucial, as I wanted their belief system to be facilitated in an environment that was as judgement-free as I could manage. I wanted their values and beliefs to be their own and not simply what they felt they were expected to believe.

In order to honour this as well as explore the social justice issues raised, I thought it was necessary to empower each child to work within the bounds of their own definition of childhood. Did they see childhood as a period of innocence or rather see themselves as active members of society both being acted on and acting upon it? I encouraged each child to consider the presence or absence of boundaries between the adult/child world. Individually the children decided if they felt comfortable and/or interested to pursue any or all of the social issues raised any further.

Some children decided that they would like to study famous people to understand how their beliefs influenced their actions. As the school year was drawing to a close we did not have the luxury of time, so we decided to share the work between home and school. The children began reading about various individuals and it soon became obvious that they had strong interests. These ranged from Gandhi to Steve Irwin; from Dian Fossey to Rowan Atkinson; from Valerie Taylor to Fred Hollows and from Julius Caesar to Leonardo Da Vinci.[1] A morning was set aside for the children to share with parents and other classes what they had discovered. Many children came in character as their selected person and all engaged in conversations that highlighted the link between a person's beliefs and their actions. Many children were as passionate in their presentations as the person they were portraying.

---

[1] Steve Irwin (Australia's Crocodile Man); Dian Fossey (primate scientist); Valerie Taylor (Australian shark rights advocate); Fred Hollows (Australian eye surgeon); Rowan Atkinson (British comedian).

Coinciding with this investigation, the class was fortunate to be visited by a group of older students from the local secondary school. These students were sharing an assignment with our class. My understanding of their assignment brief was that they were required to design and make a picture book for eight-year-olds that subtly portrayed socio-political messages. Some promoted awareness of stranger danger, others marine conservation, but it was a book regarding racism and the children's responses that astounded one student-author and myself:

Student: So can you tell me anything about this book? A message?

Harry: Yes, you talk about spots and stripes. That is a bit like black and whites in America. Martin Luther King fought hard to help the blacks live better.

Elouise: It was the same in Africa with Nelson Mandela. He saw that blacks and whites were treated differently and tried to do something about it. That is similar to your book about spots and stripes.

Pablo: Yes. It shows we can all be friends. It doesn't matter if you are black or white, or have spots or stripes. If you look for more than that we are all the same. We are people and maybe can be friends.

Student: Wow!

The children were indeed exploring complex issues and doing so in a sophisticated, thoughtful and relevant manner. Furthermore, they were using aspects of history to guide and inform their thoughts about the present. Unfortunately, we ran out of time and we were not able to consider how we could develop world peace, and in doing so support Rachel in answering her question. The children seemed satisfied, however, with our progress in exploring several of the issues that may affect peace and justice in our world.

Paralleling these children was a small group of girls who decided school was a sexist environment and they wanted to do something about it. One of these girls had been carrying this cause for a period of time. In term three we had visited Elizabeth Farm (a historical farm maintained for educational purposes) and the children had undertaken some historical research about the farm and life in Sydney. This included a study of the lives of the people living at Elizabeth Farm. One girl was outraged about the treatment of Elizabeth Macarthur, 'She did all the work and John took all the credit. It is only right that he went mad!' Inspired by Elizabeth Macarthur's story, the student began to negotiate additional time to read up on other 'famous' women. She uncovered some fascinating stories.

As time progressed, she gained a following among some of the girls. Soon this group decided that girls are treated differently to boys in our contemporary society. The girls had many animated conversations about the injustices of being female. It was during one of these discussions that one of the boys in the class informed them:

This is just your thinking. This is how you think boys think about girls. It is not how I think, and some of the other boys and I are not happy that you say all boys think this way about girls.

The girls thought about this and decided that they wanted to know what other people think. They sat down and developed a plan:

Anna: Let's survey everyone in the school.
Madison: Yeah. That's a great idea.
Wendy: It's too many people. How can we do that and anyway, how can we force everyone to do it?
Rachel: I think we should survey some classes and all the teachers.
Madison: The teachers. That's funny. I wonder if they'd do it?
Anna: We can ask Mrs Harper if we can put it in their pigeon holes and see who does it.
Rachel: That's great. I think we also need to survey parents. They might have some good ideas.
Abigail: Adults have different ideas to kids. We might need different surveys.
Rachel: That's true. Adults know nothing about wall ball.
Madison: Yeah, we could only ask kids about that.
Wendy: Let's do two surveys then.
Anna: Great, but what if people lie on the survey? Write what they think we want?
Madison: That could be a problem.
Rachel: I know, let's video kids playing.
Anna: Yeah, in the playground. We'll spy and get to know how boys are different to girls.

The girls developed their surveys including questions such as:

- Do you think boys are stronger than girls? Why?

- Do you think girls are there just to stand and look pretty? Why?

- Do you think boys gang up on girls to impress them? Why?

- Do you think girls are smarter than boys? Why?

They collected the answers from our class, a Year Six class ('They would have great things to say as they're nearly teenagers'), some teachers and some parents. When analysing their data, the girls started sorting the answers into categories of 'good' and 'bad'. The same boy from the earlier conversation came and asked them, 'What makes you decide it is a good or bad answer? You just say it's good because it is what you think.' The girls took this to heart and re-defined a good answer as one in which a person clearly states why they think the way they do. 'Yes', 'no' and 'I don't know', simply were not good enough. Unfortunately, this took them longer than expected and, by the end of the term, they decided there was no time to video children in the playground. Their conclusion to their survey was that everyone thinks differently. 'Just because you are a girl or a boy doesn't mean that you have to think in a particular way or think about boys and girls in a particular way.' The young boy who came to see their results stated, 'I told you that. People just think what they think. It doesn't matter if you are a boy or girl.'

The actual conclusions reached by the girls were not the most pivotal point of this investigation. Rather, it was their exploration of how beliefs are formed and the processes they went through in exploring and evaluating their own beliefs. Beare (2001) argues that education must concern itself with belief formation and provide students with the methodologies to research and make judgments as well as 'showing students how they come to believe what they believe, and how those beliefs impregnate their own daily living' (p 19). I feel these girls were working towards this and they felt empowered by the process. Their reflection and research hopefully will generate thoughtful and meaningful, but no less passionate, explorations of gender issues in the future.

Final thoughts

Both these investigations were complex, subjective and emotional explorations of social justice issues. In turn, some children's belief systems were developed further. I have only included a few of the conversations that were shared and transcribed. I have not included any of the 'famous people' presentations. I felt the value of these investigations was in listening to each other and the value attributed to what was being said. It was in the listening that the issues and each child's beliefs were given life and made real. Their thinking existed and was visible through conversation. At times the children were seeking meaning beyond their everyday vocabulary and therefore struggled to find the right words to express themselves.

I decided to be an active member of these conversations rather than a documentor. As a result, there are no posters, photos or other tangible evidence of these investigations. I do not see this as unfortunate, as sometimes it is more important to live the investigation rather than document it. I had to weigh up the value of creating a product that shared the process or engage in the process fully. I feel these investigations benefitted from my decision. After stating this, however, I must acknowledge that on previous occasions, pedagogical documentation has provoked and stimulated the undertaking of investigations. Put simply, it is all a process of personal development, an evolution of my philosophy and pedagogy.

The choices I make are a result of the journeys I have taken and consequently are constantly being reviewed, questioned and changed. I hope they always continue to be so.

I'd like to conclude this chapter by revisiting the exchange that started it all.

Child: Mrs Harper's a bit unusual isn't she?
Teacher: What makes you say that?
Child: She teaches differently.
Teacher: In what way?
Child: I don't think she teaches from the curriculum.

I do not have the answers to the questions raised by the young boy. All I can say is that I don't see myself as doing anything unusual or different and certainly do not set out to do so. I do know, however, that by listening to children and reflecting on what they are saying, I learn more about myself. Furthermore, I realise that children are not only co-constructing knowledge in terms of content and understanding, but they are also trying to create opportunities to make sense of their world, a world that is more visible to children than ever before. One could argue that it is not possible to assume that we can protect children from the less desirable aspects of human nature and I question the delusional fact that we were ever able to so. My experiences have led me to conclude that children are grappling with social justice issues. We need to acknowledge and empower them by supporting the development of their understandings and beliefs. This requires a personal shift in each teacher's interpretation of the curriculum. The scope is there and supported by the outcomes. It is the willingness of educators to take the initiative and delve into areas that have no clear content, no clear start and finish and no set answers, that is crucial.

References

Arthur L, Beecher B, Dockett S, Farmer S & Death E (1996) *Programming and planning in early childhood settings* (2nd Ed). Sydney: Harcourt Brace.

Beare H (2001) *Creating the future school.* London: Routledge Falmer.

Dahlberg G, Moss P & Pence A (1999) *Beyond quality in early childhood education and care. Postmodern perspectives.* London: Falmer Press.

James A, Jenks C & Prout A (1998) *Theorizing childhood.* Cambridge: Polity Press.

Jones E & Nimmo J (1994). *Emergent curriculum.* Washington: NAEYC.

Oken-Wright P & Gravett M (2002) Big ideas and the essence of intent. In V Fu, A Stremmel & L Hill (Eds). *Teaching and learning: Collaborative exploration of the Reggio Emilia approach.* (pp 197–220). New Jersey: Merrill Prentice Hall.

Chapter Sixteen

Provocations of *Te Whāriki* and Reggio Emilia

Chris Bayes

At the time of writing, Chris was a professional development facilitator working with early childhood centres in Auckland, Aotearoa/New Zealand. Chris continues to have an interest in creating curriculum with teachers, children and parents that engages them intellectually, emotionally and spiritually. She was granted a Winston Churchill Fellowship in 1999 and this took her to Reggio Emilia, Melbourne, Germany and London, to study the implementation of the theory and practice of Reggio Emilia in different cultural settings. Since then, she has been working alongside a number of teachers to provoke their thinking about teaching and learning and curriculum implementation.

Introduction

In 2002, the Ministry of Education funded a professional development program entitled 'Provocations of *Te Whāriki* and Reggio Emilia', to support educators in four, full-day, early childhood centres in Auckland, Aotearoa/New Zealand. The intention was to use the theory and practice of Reggio Emilia alongside *Te Whāriki* (the New Zealand Early Childhood Curriculum) to provoke teachers' thinking about curriculum implementation. At the completion of this innovative initiative, a research study was conducted that examined the educators' perceptions about changes to their beliefs, attitudes and practices around teaching and learning. This chapter reflects the growing understandings that have developed over a number of years for this group—teachers, a professional development facilitator and several academics—as we have worked together to make new meanings. This growth has also been influenced by colleagues from across the Tasman. As this 'community of learners' worked together, a collaborative approach developed which has meant we have gained from each other's generosity, spirit and energy. A well known *Māori* proverb reminds us that it is people who make the difference in our lives.

> *He Tangata, He Tangata, He Tangata.*
> *It is people, It is people, It is people.*

Te Whāriki, the Aotearoa/New Zealand early childhood curriculum, has been influencing teaching and learning in early childhood centres for nearly ten years. Teachers in New Zealand who have been provoked by the theory and practice of Reggio Emilia have found numerous connections between this philosophy and that espoused in *Te Whāriki*. The way in which the curriculum document has been written allows for multiple interpretations. The lens through which teachers view the document determines the way in which they interpret it and thus implement curriculum. Joy Cullen (cited in Hamer & Adams, 2003), discusses the sociocultural nature of *Te Whāriki* and suggests that because teachers don't have a good understanding of the teaching suggested by this curriculum, they may fall back on an 'individual construction of knowledge and a more passive teaching role' (p 7) rather than engage in teaching practices that promote group learning within a cultural setting which would be conducive to the teaching philosophy promoted in the document. The way in which *Te Whāriki* is viewed affects the way teachers engage in investigation and research with children, initiate parent partnerships and undertake pedagogical documentation.

Pedagogical documentation makes learning and teaching within the community of learners visible to children, teachers and parents. This form of documentation can help us 'see' and 'hear' the learning that is happening around us and increases the opportunities we have to share information with children and parents.

It enhances ways for teachers to engage children in learning that centres on life experiences. Malaguzzi (cited in Edwards, Gandini & Forman, 1998, p 83) wrote that:

> Learning and teaching should not stand on opposite banks and just watch the river flow by; instead they should embark together on a journey down the water.

Pedagogical documentation differs from other forms of documentation by bringing teaching and learning closer together. It helps us get off the banks of the river, idly watching the curriculum flow past, and allows us to embark on a journey together down the river.

Pedagogical documentation is more than teachers showing pictures and describing what children are doing. Effective documentation of children's and adults' investigations and research is like an ongoing Learning Story (Carr, 2001), which is made up of discrete, smaller Learning Stories that develop over time. When skilfully used, documentation links learning from day-to-day, week-to-week, and is created over many months. This way of documenting children's learning includes teacher reflection, conversations and questions, and also evaluates the learning process over time (Dahlberg, Moss & Pence, 1999). Just as there is no right way to implement curriculum, there is no 'one size fits all' when it comes to documentation. The fact that curriculum is created by the people and the community that come together, means that documentation looks different in each setting. Just as curriculum is created, so is documentation.

The evolution of ideas

As teachers in the professional development program have become more familiar with the theory and practice from Reggio Emilia and the theoretical knowledge that supports a sociocultural approach to teaching, they have developed new ways in which to make children's and teachers' learning visible to the community. Their assessment practices are changing to reflect these new understandings, bringing stronger and closer connections between assessment and documentation.

The Learning Stories framework developed in Aotearoa/New Zealand by Carr (2001) supports teachers to identify five dispositions for learning. These dispositions include children 'taking an interest, being involved, persisting with difficulty or uncertainty, communicating with others and taking responsibility' (Carr, p 23), and are embedded within the strands of *Te Whāriki*—wellbeing, belonging, contribution, communication, and exploration (Ministry of Education, 1996a). Teachers are also using Learning Stories to make other aspects of children's learning visible including their skills, knowledge and growing under-standing of the wider world around them.

Learning Stories have been adapted in the four centres in the program to reflect more of a sociocultural emphasis on assessment, by capturing children's learning experiences in group situations, as opposed to only using them to reflect on individual learning. This way of 'listening' to children's learning, in turn supports teachers to 'see' children within a sociocultural lens which, in turn, changes the way they understand the learning process and respond to it (Cullen as cited in Hamer & Adams, 2003). *Pedagogisti* from Reggio Emilia underpin their pedagogy on the values and beliefs that they deem important for children's learning. In Aotearoa/New Zealand, the Learning Stories framework is providing teachers with useful and meaningful ways in which they can assess whether their teaching is supporting children to 'grow up as competent and confident learners and communicators' (Ministry of Education 1996a, p 9). Teachers need to be 'listening' closely to children (both verbally and non-verbally), when they engage in capturing Learning Stories. By bringing children's voices to the fore, they can go some way to ensuring social justice is taken into consideration, whereby both the privileged and the silenced become active protagonists of curriculum implementation. By connecting deeply to what is being said and not being said, teachers can skilfully engage in strategies that develop all children's learning potential within the learning community.

Teachers in Aotearoa/New Zealand have struggled for many years to make their assessment, planning and evaluation practices manageable, relevant and useful in informing their practice. It is essential that planning has a direct impact on what happens for children's, teachers' and parents' learning, as opposed to teachers spending many hours on planning that distances itself from children. If teachers can put time into engaging in curriculum implementation, as opposed to planning the curriculum, partnerships with children and parents will begin to make stronger connections to learners and learning (Hill, 2003).

Te Whāriki defines curriculum as (Ministry of Education, 1996a, p 10):

> … the sum total of the experiences, activities, and events, whether direct or indirect, which occur within an environment designed to foster children's learning and development.

Learning Stories allow for assessment of children's learning to capture this wider view of curriculum. *Te Whāriki* was developed in partnership with *Tangata Whenua* (Aotearoa/New Zealand's indigenous people) and has been heavily influenced by Māori ways of seeing the world (May, 2003; Reedy, 2003). Within sociocultural theory, Māori pedagogy sees children's learning as integral to *whānau* (family) and community (Hemara, 2000). The principles from *Te Whāriki* (empowerment—*whakamana*; holistic development—*kotahitanga*; family and community—*whānau tangata*; and relationships—*ngā hononga*) are at the very heart of Māori pedagogy and these principles give rise to the five strands: wellbeing—*mana atua*; belonging—*mana whenua*; contribution—*mana tangata*; communication—*mana reo*; and exploration—*mana aotūroa* (Ministry of Education, 1996a).

In my experience as a professional development facilitator, *Pakeha* (non-Māori) teachers' understanding of Māori pedagogy is still in its infancy. An increased understanding of Maori pedagogy could assist teachers to implement and document curriculum in ways that reflect the dual pedagogy (Māori and western education) that underpins *Te Whāriki*. By gaining an understanding of Māori pedagogy, teachers could enrich teaching and learning experiences for all children. The current political climate in *Aotearoa*/New Zealand, however, could see an erosion of the gains made by many teachers who have shown a willingness to develop their knowledge and skills in this area. The outcome of the debate around the relevance of the Treaty of Waitangi for New Zealanders today, will shape the way in which our society sees their obligations towards bi-cultural education for tomorrow and beyond.

There are theoretical tensions within *Te Whāriki* (Cullen, 1996) and also within the *Revised Statement of Desirable Objectives and Practices* (Ministry of Education, 1996b) which sets out the requirements that educators and management must meet in undertaking their obligations for Education funding (Ministry of Education, 1996a; Ministry of Education, 1996b). These documents put an emphasis on individual performance and outcomes. *Quality in Action* (1998, p 30) states that:

> … educators should demonstrate knowledge and understanding of the learning and development of each child, identify learning goals for individual children…

as well as promoting learning occurring as a result of 'people, places and things'. *Te Whāriki* states that learning is expected to occur holistically and within reciprocal, responsive relationships (p 14). It also speaks of the child being at the centre of teaching and learning whereas Loris Malaguzzi writes of children, families and teachers being central to the education of children (Edwards, Gandini & Forman, 1998). Maori pedagogy, like the pedagogy of Reggio Emilia, places the *whānau* (family) and community at the heart of the educational process (Edwards *et al.*, 1998; Durie, 2003).

The concept of a 'community of learners' is having a growing influence on how teachers are viewing learning and teaching processes. With thoughtful consideration, Learning Stories and documentation can give teachers the opportunity to reflect sociocultural theory as promoted by the theory and practice of Reggio Emilia, *Te Whāriki* and Māori pedagogy. For this to be successful, teachers need to consider ways in which they present children's and adults' learning occurring within the group context, as opposed to learning that occurs in individualistic ways. Giudici, Rinaldi & Kreschevsky (2001), in their research on children as individual and group learners, bring to our attention the belief that both children and teachers engage in learning and teaching as a cognitive, aesthetic and emotional act, and that assessment and documentation are not separate entities but are one and the same. Seeing children's learning as part of a group learning process which is revealed through documentation could assist teachers to work in ways that are more relevant, meaningful and useful.

Teachers need to be cautious of a 'how to' approach to documentation and curriculum. Unless they begin to weave their own *whāriki* (mat), they are in danger of 'doing' *Te Whāriki*. Weaving curriculum is complex and requires reflection, time and constant dialogue with the people at the very heart of the teaching and learning process. Margaret Carr's processes within the Learning Stories assessment framework of 'describing, discussing, documenting and deciding' help us to work from a credit model whereby teachers focus in on what children can do. This process helps give structure to assessment and the dialogue occurring between teachers, children and their parents and encourages us to see children 'being ready, being willing and being able' (Carr, 2001, p 107).

The teachers from the centres in the professional development program have been developing their knowledge of Reggio Emilia in relationship to *Te Whāriki* in order to consider the values and beliefs that are creating and re-creating the philosophy that underpins their curriculum delivery. When the educational philosophy from Reggio Emilia is understood by teachers, investigations, research and documentation look, and are, different. This philosophy includes such things as a pedagogy of listening; a revisiting of the image of the child, teachers and parents and the role each of these protagonists play in learning; the importance of reciprocal, responsive relationships; the environment as the third teacher; and the role of a community of learners. Each of these aspects of Reggio Emilian philosophy interconnects with, and affects, the others. No philosophical point stands alone.

In early childhood education, there are many aspects to quality curriculum delivery that come together and have an effect on each other. These 'elements' of curriculum implementation or documentation, like philosophical beliefs, are not isolated from each other. Deleuze and Guattari's (1987) rhizome theory presents teachers with a useful way in which to reflect on the inter-connectedness of philosophy, curriculum and documentation. A rhizome doesn't have a beginning or end but is always in the middle connecting to other things. This idea of connectedness relates to the principle in *Te Whāriki* of 'holistic' education and is supported by Pere's (1991, p 58) image of *Te Wheke* (ancient symbol of the Octopus) which 'illustrates the interdependence of all things across the universe'.

Documentation can be seen as the tip of the 'Reggio' iceberg. It is often the element of Reggio Emilian pedagogy that educators wish to emulate, often without having an understanding of the other elements which make up the 'whole'. For pedagogical documentation to be effective, it must connect and reconnect with the other aspects of curriculum implementation. Underpinning the tip of the Reggio iceberg, where documentation sits, are such things as the philosophical beliefs around teaching and learning as espoused by *pedagogisti* in

Reggio Emilia; the professional leadership in the centres; the time given for staff to reflect, debate and discuss; the knowledge and experience that they have developed; and the learning culture that has been developed within the 'community of learners'.

Changing styles of curriculum implementation: an example

Over the last ten years or so, teachers in New Zealand have been challenged by sociocultural ways of teaching and learning and implementing assessment practices that reflect this orientation. There appears to have been a move away from theme teaching to project work. However, it seems that the teaching and learning process remains fundamentally the same. Documentation might show photos and a description about what has taken place but the learning occurring has not been captured. The reflection, questions, and discussion that teachers engage in, is not captured. It has been shown in the professional development program that when teachers learn new ways of thinking about teaching and learning, they begin to 'see' children differently and change occurs in the teaching and learning process. As a result of this change in understanding around 'projects', the terms 'investigation and research' help describe the process of pedagogical documentation. When teachers learn new ways to listen and interact with children; when they begin to see learning as a central motive for being together; change the way they think about children and parents as learners; and create ways to research and reflect on their teaching; they not only change the vehicle of teaching and learning, but the journey and the destination of learning changes. Changing our ways of working with children and parents influences the way in which we document the learning taking place.

Teachers in New Zealand are challenged by government requirements to provide documentation to demonstrate their knowledge and understanding of each child and to set individual learning outcomes in place (Ministry of Education, 1996b). At times, teachers report a tension between these requirements and the desire to develop effective and meaningful methods to incorporate documentation into their centres that reflect children as group learners. A useful model aligned with action research is provided in *Quality in Action* (1998). This model assists teachers to see assessment, evaluation and planning as a cycle that spirals upwards and onwards, feeding on what has gone before. It is critical, however, for us to remember that just as learning doesn't occur in 'tidy' boxes, neither should documentation. Interactions with children at any one time incorporate all aspects of the cycle—from gathering information, analysing and reflecting, through questions and dialogue with colleagues and children, deciding the next step, implementing teaching and learning strategies, and on to evaluation.

These occur as interconnected parts of the whole, linking assessment and documentation together. Our reflection and planning must always bring us closer to children and learning, as opposed to planning that isolates teachers and teaching from learners and learning. A story that helped me develop my understanding of this comes to mind.

The scenario

An educator had captured a superb photo of a child blowing a 'fairy' (seed pod with wings) in the air. He was working hard over quite a long time at making sure it didn't reach the ground. The photo captured a child intent on what he was doing. The educator knew something special was happening, but was not sure how to proceed with this moment. We then speculated on what the consequences for teaching could be.

Focusing on teaching strategies

The teacher might get into discussion with another teacher about how they could lead this on to other things. They would brainstorm and come up with many ideas. For example, over the next few days they could get out the bubble blowing, straws, the vacuum cleaner, wind socks, pin wheels and so on. These are ideas based around 'activities' which seem at first glance to relate to the child's observed interest, but which serve to place the teacher and teaching at the centre of curriculum implementation.

The second way forward focuses in on the learner and learning

On the other hand, we might invite the child and one or two others who are interested, to print off the photo together. We hang it on the wall at children's level, put a tape recorder or video camera nearby, and move in to record and listen as the children respond to the photo. Once the conversations are flowing freely, other avenues to pursue the interests that develop will bubble up. Ideas to move forward are created together. The teachers would take a few minutes to reflect together on this experience, adding new thinking to their growing understanding about the learning taking place. This becomes the first Learning Story. Tomorrow gives an opportunity to revisit this experience, share the conversations children were having and to link this into the ongoing Learning Stories that could develop over many weeks (Clemens, 2004).

The staff in centres who have been participating in the professional development program *Provocations of Reggio Emilia*, have begun to create interesting ways to meet their obligations to record individual learning, while creating useful and meaningful documentation practices which connect them more than previously, to implementing curriculum reflecting sociocultural theory. Although the centres have developed quite different ways to make children's learning visible, they have been working towards creating interconnected documentation. This includes documentation that is presented in the centre on the walls and re-presented in children's portfolios, weekly centre diaries and collated in folders.

The documentation displayed in the centres from both short-term and long-term investigations is created with children as curriculum is developing, and focuses on children's and teachers' investigations. It is loosely connected to the action research cycle (Tripp, 1990) and is made up of group and individual Learning Stories, photos, questions, conversations and children's work. It includes parent input, teacher reflection, evaluative comments and proposals for where the work may be heading. At points during a long-term investigation, the documentation is summarised so that more space is made available. The work taken down is collated in large clear files and the centre documentation continues to develop and grow. This file acts both as a memory for the children, giving them opportunities to revisit and reflect on their experience for many months and years to come, and as a method of 'accountability' to show that teachers are basing curriculum planning on their knowledge and understanding of the children in the centre.

The Learning Stories that are written within the investigation are included in the portfolios of the children involved. These stories are individualised to reflect the learning that is occurring for each child within the context of the learning group. It also gives feedback to the child and his or her parents regarding the significant learning that is occurring for the child and where that learning might be going. At the end of the investigation, the overall investigation is summarised into a Learning Story and included in each of the children's portfolios. This Learning Story identifies some of the significant learning that occurred during the investigation.

Each week teachers create a centre diary that summarises some of the teaching and learning that has occurred in the centre using a number of incidental learning experiences as well as any investigations that may be underway. This diary includes some of the same aspects of documentation that are included in the centre's and in children's portfolios. The reflective and evaluative comments in the weekly diaries appear to be particularly well received by parents. Feedback from parents has meant that teachers take care to include something about each child during each month. It is encouraging to report that the body that is charged with undertaking quality assurance audits in New Zealand early childhood centres, the Education Review Office, has included complimentary comments in regard to the documentation of children's learning in recent reviews from two of these centres. These reviews have recognised the way in which documentation is intrinsically linked to the assessment, evaluation and planning of curriculum.

Recently, the teachers involved in the professional development program have begun to talk about the ways in which the theory and practice of Reggio Emilia can inform teacher appraisal. Can we use the pedagogical documentation that is being created to support teacher development? Appraisal that is underpinned by respectful, reciprocal relationships, images of teachers as being strong and capable learners, where listening is central and the community of learners is an important part of reflecting on each other's development and growth, will look substantively different to what occurs currently for some teachers in early childhood centres. Once again, there is an opportunity to use the Learning Stories framework within the context of teacher appraisal. Teaching Stories put the lens onto what the teacher does and says to support the learning that is taking place. Effective pedagogical documentation in teacher portfolios could be at the heart of appraisal and could begin to link teacher development to what is happening for the community of learners in centres. It could enhance the quality of reflective dialogue between teachers that should underpin appraisal.

Conclusion

Pedagogical documentation that gets at the heart of the teaching and learning process must take into consideration the interconnectedness of curriculum implementation. Effective documentation is supported by a number of critical elements that need to be understood and acknowledged if teachers are to make children's and their own learning visible to the community of learners that come together in early childhood centres and schools. When values-based education creates philosophy, and this in turn creates curriculum and determines what learning we value and how we will make that learning visible, we can then engage all children, teachers and parents in curriculum that celebrates learning and ensures children are growing up in places where their learning is truly valued. It is not until all children's voices are heard by teachers, that both the silenced and the privileged will become active protagonists of their own and others' learning.

References

Carr M (2001) *Assessment in early childhood settings. Learning stories*. London: Paul Chapman Publishing.

Clemens G (2004) personal communication.

Cullen J (1996) The challenge of *Te Whāriki* for future development in early childhood education. *Delta, 48* (1), 114–25.

Dahlberg G, Moss P & Pence A (1999) *Beyond quality in early childhood education and care: Postmodern perspectives*. London: Falmer Press.

Deleuze G & Guattari F (1987) *A thousand plateaus: Capitalism and schizophrenia*. Minneapolis: University of Minnesota Press.

Durie M (2003) *Te pae mahutonga: A navigational guide for the promotion of secure identity and best outcomes for Māori children*. Paper presented at the Eighth early childhood convention: Making changes for children now: Shaping early childhood today, 22–25 September, Palmerston North, New Zealand.

Edwards C, Gandini L, & Forman G (Eds) (1998) *The hundred languages of children: The Reggio Emilia approach—Advanced reflections*. (2nd Ed). Greenwich, CT: Ablex.

Giudici C, Rinaldi C & Krechevsky M (2001) *Making learning visible: Children as individual and group learners*. Reggio Emilia: Reggio Children.

Hamer J & Adams P (2003) *The New Zealand early childhood literacy handbook: Practical literacy ideas for early childhood*. Palmerston North: Dunmore Press.

Hemara W (2000) *Māori Pedagogies. A view from the literature*. Wellington: New Zealand Council for Educational Research.

Hill D (2003) *Curriculum: context and complexity in early childhood settings*. Paper presented at the Eighth early childhood convention. Palmerston North, New Zealand.

May H (2003) *Te Whāriki—TRCC Course*. Orakei Marae: Auckland, New Zealand.

Ministry of Education (1996a) *Te Whāriki: He Whāriki Mātauranga mō ngā Mokopuna o Aotearoa: Early childhood curriculum*. Wellington: Learning Media.

Ministry of Education (1996b) Revised statement of desirable objectives and practices (DOPs) for chartered early childhood services in New Zealand. Wellington.

Ministry of Education (1998) *Quality in action: Te Mahi Whai Hua*. Wellington: Learning Media.

Pere R (1991) Te Wheke: *A celebration of infinite wisdom*. Gisborne: Ao Ako Global Learning.

Reedy T (2003) *Te Whāriki—TRCC Course*. Orakei Marae: Auckland, New Zealand.

Tripp D (1990) Socially critical action research. *Theory into Practice*, 29 (3), 158–66.

Response to Part Four

Looking Deeper, Seeing More

Commentators

Diti Hill
Jenny Porter

Diti's response

Many early childhood practitioners work within a tradition that demands they abandon their own knowledge and experience in favour of the institutional and organisational life of the particular settings within which they educate young children. This tradition, which is deeply rooted in the discipline of psychology, sees teaching as a narrow, and often technical, one-way response to predetermined and 'known' assumptions about learning and learners. Practitioners learn that their own knowledge and experience, and the way in which they constitute this to themselves and others, is less important than loyalty and conformity to the set values and accepted pedagogical practices of the educational setting within which they work. They learn to address their doubts and answer their own questions privately, in silence. Curriculum implementation, assessment and evaluation become predictable and regular aspects of practice and any self-doubt gives way to a sense of normality and security.

These three chapters challenge such a tradition, across two nations and across the early childhood sector, birth to eight years. They focus instead on the vital role that practitioners can play in living out their lives with children. Janet Robertson talks about 'coming out of the educational closet' and giving others permission to 'enter the learning world' she shares with children. Alexandra Harper talks of working actively and uniquely, 'from and within' the requirements of curriculum documents, and then journeying responsibly and responsively through the learning/teaching process. Chris Bayes talks about practitioners who are striving to bring what they do, 'closer to children and learning'. In each narrative, the authors grapple with conveying to others the complex interface between what they 'see' has happened and the conflicting and varied frameworks within which this 'seeing' can be made familiar.

Janet has chosen 'teacher storytelling' as pedagogical documentation with other, more particular narratives (for example, the fishing expedition) embedded within it. Through Alexandra's documented narrative flows a strong pedagogical thread, yet she chose 'to be an active member of (the) conversations rather than a documentor', with 'no posters, photos or other tangible evidence'. Chris tells the professional development story of the practitioners with whom she worked closely and discusses the relationship between the curriculum-related New Zealand Learning Story and a pedagogical responsibility that has grown from exploring the Reggio Emilia experience. A narrative or 'storying' approach legitimates the subjectivity of 'seeing', of identifying the 'seen' and of documenting the 'seeing'. It allows practitioners to resist accepted but often limited ways of documenting and to contemplate the learning/teaching process in ways that can be as unique and meaningful as the experiences they reflect.

Pedagogical documentation challenges practitioners to consider the many choices that they make throughout their time with children and to think reflectively about the inevitably moral and ethical nature of those choices. When documentation is knowingly pedagogical, practitioners not only make choices in the moment, but they are also compelled to revisit those choices, knowing that they must mull over the issues of social justice that lie beneath every social interaction. Such issues mostly remain invisible to those who see their teaching role as being limited to an externally-defined demonstration of outcome-oriented learning gains for children.

Practitioners who document broadly and pedagogically, whether the documentation is identified as a 'learning story', a 'teaching story' or a 'learning/ teaching story', are constituting themselves and their relationships and interactions with children in particular and committed ways. Representing and problematising documented decisions and choices, enables new decisions and choices to be considered in an open-ended and on-going process that resists conforming to a national agenda yet exists within it. Alexandra sees herself as being uniquely positioned in her commitment to teach within a curriculum but from which she is perceived by a child not to be teaching!

Dahlberg, Moss and Pence (1999) talk of the importance of taking in multiple perspectives, inviting other constructions and perspectives and ensuring that documentation does not itself become a practice for exercising power. From this point of view, it is essential to be open to new ways of configuring old knowledge. For example, the sociocultural approach to learning and teaching is mentioned by Chris and very much promoted as 'current theory' worldwide. However, if this approach is understood and applied to practice only within a familiar psychological agenda and the discourse of 'learning and development', documentation will be limited to the assessment of children's learning and the sociocultural view will disappear into interpretations about who and what adults think children are. Such a narrow perspective may prevent practitioners from seeing and documenting the real and shared issues of democracy and social justice in an early childhood setting. A broader, more tentative and necessarily more complex understanding of the term 'socio-cultural' opens up the possibilities for pedagogical documentation and equalises the power.

When documentation is pedagogical, teachers articulate the vital role they play in continually reflecting and acting upon the way in which institutional directives and policies impact upon the flow of children's lives in early childhood centres and classrooms. Chris talks about teachers who have come to grapple with their own pedagogical practice and their understanding of a national curriculum, through the documenting of Learning Stories. When sharing the story of *She and he suns*, Janet includes the perspectives of both teacher and child in her discussion. In her accounts of exploring race and gender, Alexandra emphasises the importance of listening to children and trusting in the ongoing development of their own belief systems.

All three narratives support the case for dialogue through pedagogical documentation in an effort to increase democratic participation and advance principles of social justice. It is important that those wishing to share the world with children rather than define it for them, resist the psychological tradition that focuses on the learner as recipient and the teacher as a weak wielder of knowledge and power through institutional directives. Pedagogical documentation is challenging and intellectually demanding, but it can also form a deep, satisfying and meaningful part of practitioners' professional development.

Reference

Dahlberg G, Moss P and Pence A (1999) *Beyond quality in early childhood education and care: Postmodern perspectives*. London: Falmer Press.

About Diti Hill

Diti Hill is a senior lecturer in the Faculty of Education, University of Auckland. While pursuing a Master of Arts in anthropology and linguistics, she became interested in the area of early childhood and subsequently has spent the past 30 years practising, lecturing, and researching across a range of New Zealand early childhood settings, including 20 years in the New Zealand Playcentre movement as a parent. Her passion is challenging pre-service student teachers and practitioners in the field, to consider their interpretation and representation of theory and research in practice.

Jenny's response

At MLC School, we have been on a *Transforming Learning* journey for the past eight years. Initially, this strategy arose from the whole school community engaging in some 'crystal ball gazing' to determine how to best prepare the girls for the challenges of the then, fast approaching twenty-first century. Our school believed that in this future scenario the rate of social and technological change in society would demand:

- more flexible learning systems within the school, using technologies;

- skills for emotional literacy; and

- curricula tailored to meet the needs of individual students.

The philosophy of teaching and learning to emerge from Reggio Emilia seemed to us to be an ideal vehicle to explore what *Transforming Learning* might look like in practice—albeit in a very different place and context. The junior school's (K–5) staff was convinced this philosophy should be examined across the whole department, not just within the early childhood section.

Our initial discussions with consultants Alma Fleet and Catherine Patterson, centred on the transactional nature of good teaching and learning. For learning to be meaningful for children we believed they must be allowed the opportunity to express their current knowledge and understandings, and indicate what they wanted to learn and know in the future. We also started to look at the very compartmentalised nature of our curriculum and think about how learning in and about our world is usually not so conveniently segregated. We started planning integrated units of work and specialist staff in the areas of art, drama, music, and research were included along with the class teachers in this planning. Implementation of these units centred on the areas of study known as Human Society and Its Environment (HSIE) and Science and Technology.

This was a major step for us. As Janet Robertson says (Chapter Fourteen).

> The act of teaching is, in Australia, such an individual and private experience that the notion of intellectual critique and collaboration as an intrinsic part of the day is one which perhaps suffuses us with both fear and envy.

Whilst this movement into a more cohesive and collaborative presentation of curriculum would seem to have been very successful, it also raised many more questions for the staff. Listening to the girls and finding out where they were at was all well and good, but we had a New South Wales Board of Studies curriculum and the requirements of school registration hanging over us. How could we achieve the flexibility talked about in Reggio and still mould it to suit the girls' needs?

Our next step on the journey was to investigate documentation. Our initial attempts identified just how hard it is to really listen with open ears, eyes, hearts and minds. We have been most fortunate to have another learner on the journey with us, consultant Christine Stevenson, who has been helping us in our attempts to make learning visible. Chris Bayes comments that (Chapter Sixteen):

> ...pedagogical documentation is more than teachers showing pictures and describing what children are doing…Just as there is no right way to implement curriculum, there is no 'one size fits all' when it comes to documentation.

This has certainly been an important understanding for us.

What we have learnt from examining the documentation of conversations with and between children and other records of learning is just how little we really know—about the world, how we learn, the way children go about making sense of things, what they are really saying or questioning. I come away from some of these discussions acutely aware of the limitations of my own knowledge. Our co-learner, Christine, will so often add another dimension to where we might go with further learning explorations or a possible explanation of what a child might be intending. Documentation has provided us with some wonderful provocations as teachers!

Frustrations have emerged, but we have learnt to listen to each other and try and understand where we, as individual teachers, are coming from. Just as our students are all at different stages on their learning continua, we too are at very different stages in our learning and understandings about pedagogy. Whilst the notion that Italian staff meetings are conducted around a table over a bottle of wine accompanied by the passionate banging of fists might appeal to my more romantic ideal of professional learning, our Australian equivalent is by cultural necessity a little different.

Pedagogical documentation is helping us to focus on what the children are saying rather than us clinging to an 'individual construction of knowledge and a more passive teaching role' (Chapter Sixteen), as stated by Chris. I think the point Janet (Chapter Fourteen) makes, sums up what we are discovering:

> If we are not prepared to show others what we are thinking, the choices we are making, then we do both them and ourselves a great disservice. We perpetuate the un-critical, un-collegial, isolated teacher paradigm, confining pedagogy to the dark, and risk becoming technicians, not educators.

The next challenge in our school is to act on the documentation. In my discussions with staff members, they acknowledge as Alex Harper (Chapter Fifteen) does:

> ...I began to question my selective nature of what I listened to and acted upon. I had to reflect upon my use of power as the teacher. My pedagogy incorporated negotiating the curriculum with the children and consequently forefronted social construction and democratic decision-making. However, an uneasy feeling began to build about my role in overseeing and ultimately controlling the investigative decision-making in the classroom.

Our current provocations include: going where the children want to go and not where we think they should, being willing to unravel their thinking when it is not always entirely clear to us, following trails of knowledge previously outside our experience, and giving all children a voice.

It is exciting to be helping create a culture that is moving from a competitive to a collaborative environment—where it's okay to say 'I don't know', and to realise colleagues may have some of the answers, where we realise children contribute much to the shared interactions of daily learning in our classrooms, and where we see the joy of engaged learners. *Transforming Learning* is for us a fabulous professional journey—certainly not just a destination.

About Jenny Porter

Jenny Porter was a teacher, consultant and principal with the NSW Department of School Education for 20 years. She worked in rural areas in the north and north-west of the state as well as outer western Sydney. She has also enjoyed 12 months teacher exchange in Northern Ireland. Jenny has worked at MLC, an independent girls' school, for seven years as Head of the Junior School, and as part of the whole school management team. Teacher professional development, leadership development, and early childhood education are areas of great interest for her. She is currently Vice President of the Australian Primary Principal's Association.

Part Five

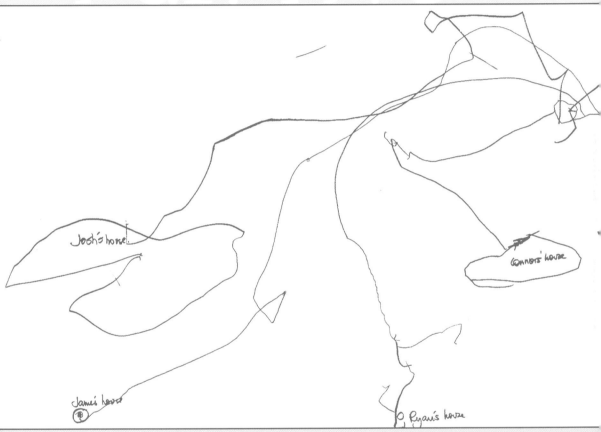

Pulling Together, Reaching Out

Chapter Seventeen

Five Voices:
Interrupting the Dominant Discourse

Alma Fleet   Catherine Patterson
Margaret Hammersley   Lisa Schillert
Edith Stanke

This chapter is based on conversations that were held to plan a presentation at a national conference. The power of the conversations inspired the authors to present them to conference participants as a Readers' Theatre. At the time of the conference, Margaret, Lisa and Edith were working together in a child care centre when Alma and Catherine (colleagues from Macquarie University) invited them to share their experiences of pedagogical documentation. The centre was a community-based long day care centre for children from birth to five, located in a predominantly white, middle-class suburb of a regional area in New South Wales. The centre was well-known for exploring ideas emerging from Reggio Emilia.

Introduction

The experience of pedagogical documentation in some Australian settings is being used as a provocation for interrupting early childhood planning discourse. While some of the ideas being explored have originated in discussions between Italy and Sweden, they have continued to unfold in Australia in ways which further the discussion about the narratives of childhood (Hultqvist and Dahlberg, 2001). In particular, co-constructivist frameworks provide an opportunity to challenge ways that adults and children inhabit their shared pedagogical spaces.

The use of pedagogical documentation as a core component of interaction in early childhood settings provides potential for postmodern approaches to meaning making. Further, in current sociopolitical contexts, there is a need to challenge modernist approaches to accountability. Five people who have worked with and analysed documentation as a vehicle for reconceptualisation will offer insights to extend conversations around these issues.

What is implied by the term 'pedagogical documentation'?

Briefly, for this purpose, the idea of pedagogical documentation relates to work that has been inspired by thinking in Reggio Emilia, Italy, and in Sweden. The complex ideas provide opportunities for people to revisit their beliefs and approaches to work with young children and their families. Distanced from a transmission view of teaching, the ideas value children's perceptions, integrity and tenacity. Grounded in meaning making, the panels, posters, portfolios or videos created include artefacts which are collected, discussed, revisited and analysed. These serve as sites for conversations with families, children and staff, to help further extend planning conversations and to gain insight into children's thinking and ways of being. From this perspective, children are seen as being hypothesis makers, as having theories about the world, as being scientists, artists and insightful decision-makers. As Dahlberg, Moss and Pence (1999, p 153) stated, 'It is, above all, a question of getting insight into the possibility of seeing, talking and acting in a different way, and hence cross boundaries…'.

In addition, from an Australian perspective, Robertson (1997, p 15) wrote that:

> Documentation of children's abilities and potential can change our images, thereby creating a different culture…Our documentation can create another culture about what toddlers can do. Our documentation can create another culture of what preschoolers can do, and our documentation can create another image of what teachers can do, because it makes children and learning and knowledge visible…documentation can create and support children's culture in the centre.

Those working as documentors with children tend to see a more powerful child contributing to the shaping of the environment, than has historically been evident. These staff members move beyond interactions that are controlled by ritual or routine. They seek ways of working together which privilege children's voices in the shaping of interactions within early childhood settings. They enable the interruption of the discourse of deficit planning—the concept of adult-driven planning based on what children don't know and can't do. Traditional ways of observing children may be reframed as evidence of the inequity between adult and child, as surveillance (Tobin, 1995), or as reflecting an accountability driven medical model of practice. (See Chapter Eleven.)

Opportunities to challenge orthodoxies

The interest in pedagogical documentation in Australia has become an opportunity to trouble existing pedagogies and practice. These ways of interacting, recording and thinking about practices in early childhood centres impact on all aspects of centre life. Those who are engaging with the possibilities are confronted with colleagues who are not.

Edith: The possibility of this conference paper led me to consider the challenges I have personally encountered when attempting to introduce change. In my work with children I sometimes feel that my journey with the children is the easy part. It's the journey with parents and colleagues that I find the most challenging and which is arguably the most critical. After all, change starts with convincing the decision-makers in society that this particular change is necessary and valuable.

I think that parents have a right to make choices about the type of educational experiences their children will encounter. They have a right to know that there are different ways of teaching and that one may be more suitable for their child than another. In my everyday work I am continually challenged when attempting to engage parents in re-evaluating educational processes or engage them in a project their child is involved in. At times I have found it helpful to pose the following questions to myself. What is of interest to them? What will provoke them? What provocation, invitation, or investigation will be impossible for them to resist? And so I have found that the idea of engaging children's minds by starting with something that is of interest to them holds true when working with parents.

…I started wondering whether the same applies in relation to colleagues. If I want somebody to come on a journey with me then that journey would need to be of interest to them. What interests my colleagues?

I guess it's different for everyone. For one this might be environment, for another, it might be meaningful relationships.

Perhaps irresistible provocations could open new doors in the change process?

Edith's comments promote reflection. Johnson (2001, p 307) has written about the possibilities of 'excavation work' in association with the 'transgressive movement' of ideas, suggesting that in seeking to challenge existing practice, it is necessary to 'excavate' or unpack or sift through current ideas and practices. He uses personal story and field critique to encourage us to pursue a 'variety of trajectories' (p 308) in reconceptualising the landscapes in which we think and work.

For those of us working from within the academy, it is a challenge to become part of the lived experience of those working with children on a daily basis. Given the challenge of not 'othering' colleagues with whom we are seeking new knowledge, the valuing of collaborative conversations becomes essential to research activity. There is a tendency by some in the academy to minimise the thinking of colleagues who are not yet reading and writing within any of the 'post' mystiques. The ideas projected may confront the dominant discourses, but the language used may be framed as every day conversation. The position taken here is intentionally inclusive of a range of voices, all of which contribute to theory-based practice and practical theorising.

A conversation (Readers' Theatre)

The perspectives offered in this conversation come from the field as well as the academy. The people who speak have all taught young children, but some now spend more time working with adults while others spend more time with young children and their families. Some have urban backgrounds and others are suburban and rural. They are all Australian residents now, originally from three different countries. Edith, Margaret and Lisa worked for several years at the same child care centre and are all now at different centres. The professional qualifications of these women range from a child care diploma to a PhD, demonstrating participants' commitment to life-long learning. The group has predominantly Anglo roots, is female and reflects a thirty-year age span.

Catherine (to the audience/reader): We would like to invite you to a hypothetical situation. While these people will be sharing real experiences from a range of places and other discussions, this is purely a constructed situation.

We are observing a meeting at Blue Gum Children's Centre. Alma is the local Children's Services Adviser, Margaret is the Director of the centre, and Edith and Lisa are room leaders. All three staff members are fascinated by the ideas associated with pedagogical documentation and have been working hard to encourage other staff to share their enthusiasm.

Alma: You've been sharing some great stories. They help us think about what it is that's hard for people to get their heads around; there's the interpretation of observations, there's the lay-out, there's the actual choice of what goes on the wall for public viewing. What about you, Lisa? What difficulties are you finding?

Lisa: I think the hard thing is: what do you document? What bits, what do you choose? (others agree) Like I know the bit that I want to document, but the rest of the staff in the room want to document things developmentally, not from 'the child's uniqueness' idea. It's the process that's interesting, not only the product. Like a child painted an A; he didn't mean to really, it's just that the strokes went like that. Someone said, 'Hey, it looks like an A'. I agreed and I got really excited about it, but they just wanted to document which hand he had the brush in! Not that he actually connected that shape with the letter A and the literacy aspects; they were more concerned that he was swapping hands and all that, and I began to worry, am I looking at the right thing?

Edith: But that's what we were discussing at our last regional meeting, weren't we? We all went around the circle and talked about what we were all documenting in our centres, because we were wondering what people found worthy of documenting.

Lisa: And is it only the good times? Only the good times, only the good things? And because the year is so new, the collaborative groups of children haven't really formed yet. They're all still so individual; they're not joining up, so as far as a project of group work, it's not there. I'm thinking about doing 'myself and others', because if I put a lunchbox on the table, every single child in my room knows who owns it, without me saying 'This is Jo's lunchbox'. They all know each other's things! The parents bring the lunch box in, but the children have just picked it up naturally that every time we sit down at the table, Jo has *that* lunch box and that Ben has *that* lunch box. I found it really amazing that they are picking up all those things, and I thought, how can I document this? This is really unique. These kids recognise things; they pay attention to what is going on. Like I thought that was more important, in this time of the year than actually doing block towers, you know, like I thought 'Wow', but I don't really know how to document it. I'm still thinking about it and seeing what they're saying. I need somebody to talk about it with…

Edith: It's like you're seeing something amazing, something amazing about these children. Like at the moment, in my room, we're doing something that's turning into something that's bigger than Ben Hur… because Naomi's so excited because she's seen something amazing about the children. She's over the moon she's so excited, she'll go home and work till midnight to type up everything. And she'll come back with two pages with tiny 12 font typing on A4 paper that she's going to put up on the wall. It's a description of what's happened, it's a running record. It's that same issue that you're talking about. It's so hard to say, 'but if you saw something amazing, how can you just take that and describe it'; and I can't do it either. If I could, I would say, 'the amazing thing that I saw was…'. That's really hard because you feel the parents need to know the background and they have to know what was said. It's hard to describe the actual learning or the amazing thing that happened…that interpretation is hard.

Alma: That is tricky. I wonder what you'd most like to discuss with her? Would you want to talk about the difficulties of reading dense text (pages of 12 font writing) up on the board and explore other layouts? Or would you want to pursue something about the difficulties of analysing the exchanges that Naomi saw? Or would you be trying to find ways to save her from doing this thinking at midnight!

Lisa   (to Edith): I think you have, *you've* changed your writing; I haven't changed what I write, I still write it developmentally. You now add 'you', I don't know how to explain it, but I know what I feel when I read your documentation to what I've read in the past. I feel you've really grown and you're willing to throw out ideas and expressions.

Edith: But I feel really terrible doing that because I think I'm passing my judgment on this and I could be completely wrong.

Lisa: No, no no! It's not completely your opinion. You've still questioned the child; you've still reflected on what's happened. You get around it by asking questions like, 'Is this what is happening? Or maybe it's this.'

Margaret: But isn't that your prerogative as a teacher? Isn't that where your role is?

Edith: Yeah, yeah, and I do it, but I still sometimes worry. You know that documentation I did about the boy who was painting? He was painting on his own and I was painting with some kids at the easel next to him. He was painting a square, and I said, 'Oh, you're doing a house are you?' and he said, 'Nope'. And he just kept painting; he wasn't into talking. So I said, 'Are you drawing a square?' and he said 'Nope' and just kept drawing and he wasn't talking to me. Then the other kids got into it, with 'No, he's not drawing a square, he's drawing this or that' and they all had their own opinions. In the end of course he just keeps going 'nah' and keeps painting. So I decided that he didn't want to talk, and we left him to it. Half an hour later he came up, really proud of his painting, and said, 'It's a picture frame'!

Alma: That's wonderful! (Laughter)

Edith: And he probably knew all along, because he had this 'nope' expression, 'you guys are not going to get this!' (All laughing) But then I thought, if I just found that painting on the drying rack at the end of the day or something, and I might have put my interpretation on it…

Lisa: But that's what I mean that's different. Your interpretation is never that.

Edith: To some degree we do that though. To some degree we sit there and wonder about it and have opinions about it and that's all based on your own background and experiences.

Alma: When you write it up though, don't you say: 'Perhaps this is ……' or 'I was wondering about whatever'. Instead of saying 'Johnny painted a house'. You'd write in an exploratory, interpretivist way, so that you're showing yourself as a thinking being. That's what's so lovely about it, because it is professional behaviour.

Edith: It's so hard for some people—unless you are a person who is that way inclined anyway, who will lie in the grass and watch the trees sway and hypothesise. If you're not that kind of a person, if you don't think in that way, if you want 'a' plus 'b' plus 'c', this is how it goes and follow this formula—it's really hard to try to wonder.

Alma: There may be something about different thinking styles, personality types that are not sympathetic to this way of working. It's certainly hard for people who don't understand the underlying philosophy and opportunities. Maybe it's related to temperament or learning orientation?

Lisa: Some staff are trapped by their training. I said to them that what they were writing is fine, but it might be better to write it down, then step back from it and keep looking. Can you make a web from that observation? 'What else did he say? What else did he do?' Trying to grow in that way and think about the image of the child. And I still get trapped because of my training. I write that very formal kind of observation that I was trained to do. When I was a student, I used to sit there in class and watch that video and I had to get my observations right. I was racing to write about all the details. I know you need those observation skills—but you also need the insight into other ways, and insight into your own inner child and being creative.

Alma: Maybe it would help if staff observed more than one child at a time, perhaps recording conversations and interactions between children?

Lisa: Watching the body language is important too because if they're not actually speaking, they communicate in other ways. We have one child who loves washing up. He's fascinated with washing the dishes. All the dishes go into the sink and there's this big noise and he bashes things around. He doesn't speak to the other children, but he takes the towel across, or goes over to them to get them to come join him. It's hard to communicate with the staff to see that instead of being preoccupied with the noise he was making, I was thinking 'that is how he is communicating, it's good noise'. It's hard to get others to see that as well. It's important to get them to step back and stop observing so much and listen to the children for a while.

Margaret: Well, maybe some people will change their way of thinking now we've all been to the workshop that challenged us to think about art as a way of communicating ideas rather than getting caught up in banal craft activities.

Lisa: Oh, I don't know. The others are asking: 'What is wrong with dish mop painting? It's fun and the kids enjoy it'.

Edith: It's like entertainment. It's as though children have to have fun and the only way to have fun is to provide this kind of stimulation.

Lisa: That's what they are asking me. 'Why shouldn't we? What's wrong with it?' And I know what I feel in my heart, but I don't know how to explain it. I ask: 'Well, what are the children getting out of it?' They say 'It's fun'. Then I say: 'Well okay, what other ways can you think of to have fun with a smaller brush?' I don't how to justify why not to do that. And sometimes they think the children will get bored with just brushes. And maybe they are bored with it and they need to watch the children carefully and get involved—go and read about the issues about how to inspire them and think.

Edith: I've been asked questions like that too and it's been niggling me about why it is a problem. I've been thinking how it may be harder to get in there and investigate something with the children and scaffold their learning. To see where they are up to, and what they are doing and question where they might go next, and what they're trying to find out here and what learning could be in this activity?

That kind of approach is hard work and sometimes it's easier to say, 'If I put the dish mops out for painting, that will be new and that will keep the children busy for a while. The children will be good and I'll go home without a headache.' Sometimes staff may put out an activity because there is a feeling that the children aren't using that area, or they need something new because they're painting rainbows over and over and over again. And I've questioned that too and I've thought 'yes, something more isn't happening in this room'. But it's finding that project and deciding that we're going to go with that idea and take it further. Then the painting is interesting because they are painting an idea or something special; but to get to that stage takes some work.

Alma: There are a couple of issues in there. One is the degree to which we can expect all staff to participate in this conversation. Given the role expectations and the limited pay scales or opportunity for promotion, why should all staff be expected to be keen to look beyond the usual, beyond the expected ways of working?

Edith: I think the parents can be a powerful factor in that. It seems to me that parent expectations get staff motivated more than anything else. If the parents come in and they are happy with what they see, then it's hard to encourage change.

Alma: But the argument might be that if parents feel their child is safe, properly 'looked after', engaged and progressing in some way, they are happy. Perhaps if they haven't had the chance to see some insightful documentation, they are not going to know the difference?

Lisa: That's what I think too. I've got some documentation at home that I've prepared, but I haven't put up yet. I've told parents about it and two parents came up to me after Easter to ask about it. So I've got them waiting to see it. I've been trying to think of ways to get parents noticing and get them involved because this is a new centre and they are not used to coming in and seeing what is happening. I didn't want to put everything up instantly for them.

Margaret: Maybe it's the staff feeling that something like fly swat painting can be seen as having done something—that they've earned their money for the day. Maybe they are more product-minded, because documentation can take months and maybe they think parents will feel the staff are not doing their job if the children don't have something to take home.

Alma: So it's almost time to finish up. Do you see where we might be going with this? If we see pedagogical documentation as a metaphor—a tool to enable people to look at their work differently—it might take us somewhere useful. By taking the potentials of documentation, that puts you into another kind of discussion. It immediately sets up the re-thinking, if not the re-conceptualising of current practice. If you are trying to understand more about what you are trying to do when you document, or if you try to explain to other people, or model for other people or encourage other people to be documentors—just that talking about documentation is the opportunity or the provocation for change.

          To change the way you are observing, the way you organise your room, the way you are looking at your timetable, the links you have with families. It becomes a vehicle for problematising your whole conception of how you teach and what your role is as an adult in children's services. It's a start.

The discussions reported here provide opportunities for exploring contexts for sharing pedagogical inspiration with colleagues. As excerpts from actual conversations, they reflect some of the realities of the unfolding processes involved in thinking through some of these ways of working. Part of the challenge of course, is the role of this conversation in interrupting the discourse about staff roles and planning priorities.

In these conversations, opportunities are presented to consider pedagogical documentation as a vehicle for reconceptualisation. Revisiting existing ways of working may confront established practices and their inherent philosophies. Such things as debates about the positioning of parents as pivotal in shaping centre culture, or a change in ways of visualising important interactions to enable further reflection can be empowering. These ways of working also problematise the entertainment curriculum, asking us to rethink the role of 'having fun' in children's services, not dismissing or diminishing this concept, but perhaps questioning the justification for elements of curriculum decision-making.

Through documentation we can unmask—identify and visualise—the dominant discourses and regimes that exercise power on and through us, and by which we have constructed the child and ourselves as pedagogues. Although, as early childhood professionals, many of us are not used to thinking of ourselves as pedagogues, this European term is useful for causing us to pause to reconsider our roles in relation to the work we do. Related to this rethinking, pedagogical documentation can function as a tool for opening up a critical and reflective practice challenging dominant discourses and constructing 'counter-discourses', through which we can find alternative pedagogies (Dahlberg, Moss & Pence, 1999, p 152). It's this seeking of alternative pedagogies which is the focus of this chapter.

In reflecting on the conversations reported here and trying to consider what might be particular about the philosophies associated with pedagogical documentation, it can be suggested that these ways of working:

- consider multiple rather than singular audiences and purposes;

- have more complex functions of text creation than do either display or plans for teaching, both of which have a tendency to relate primarily to the documents rather than to the additional opportunities being created;

- locate material in an ongoing problematic pedagogical space in which adults are as informed by children's theories and orientations to their experiences as they are by discipline expectations;

- invite more of a sense of possibility about both the unexpected and daily events as sites for closer investigation and richer interaction than predetermined themes and narrowly conceived classroom events;

- enable adult analysis to work with children's analysis to extend the possibilities of experience;

- focus on the individual within the group, a small group that is affected by the actions and insights of its individuals;

- are grounded in the interpretation of focused, personally and culturally relevant experiences; and

- create an integrative approach to pedagogy.

MacNaughton and Dockett (2000, p ii) note that:

> For reconceptualists, the need to 'trouble' our knowledge base remains ever present as new orthodoxies about how young children develop and learn emerge, and as new policies are enacted to respond to and give life to these orthodoxies.

Part of the challenge for those who see potential in pedagogical documentation for interrupting the planning conversation is to keep the procedure from becoming a new orthodoxy. It seems to us that a form of defence against such orthodoxy is to continue to reflect on and make visible the decision-making which contributes to the evolution of professional practice. It is in that context that we offer these conversations.

Reflections on experiences

Several years after the original discussions, the three staff members who had been working together were invited to respond to this account of their conversations. Margaret, Lisa and Edith have moved in different directions and step back from their earlier experiences to offer their current thinking.

Margaret's reflections

When pausing to reflect on the four years that have passed since these conversations took place, I began to realise just how my work has changed. The 'team' no longer exists. We have gone our separate ways. Our lives have changed forever, both personally and professionally. I begin to ponder a number of questions:

- Have I changed? If so, how?

- Have I grown professionally in that time?

- Am I still the facilitator of adult learning as I was back then?

I can answer 'Yes' and 'No' to all questions. As my reflection lingers, I can say that my professional journey took a sharp right hand bend. I moved on to another child care centre. The physical context may have changed—different centre, different staff—but the conversations and pedagogical documentation seemed to be similar. I found myself revisiting my first journey and deconstructing my thoughts, my methods. I knew instinctively that what 'worked' in the first centre would not work in the second. I knew I had to approach the new situation in a distinctly individual way as we do with a new group of children each year.

St Augustine talks about two strong emotions: anger and courage, saying: 'leaders should show anger at the way things are and have the courage to change them'. With these two emotions on board, I began to build a relationship with my new team. As I worked with and beside them I began to realise that this team was feeling confronted and challenged in a very different way than I had experienced with the first team. On reflection, I now realise that both teams were not afraid to embrace the challenge of pedagogical change, but each did so in their own way at their own pace.

My biggest task was to decide on a 'plan of attack'. I thought long and hard. I had a 40-minute drive to and from work each day that proved to be a very productive thinking time. Finally, things began to emerge from my self-conversations.

As a teacher springboards off his/her children, I would springboard off the parents by using the environment as the teacher. As the New South Wales (NSW) Curriculum Framework (2002, p 101) states:

> Human behaviour is influenced greatly by the physical environment…The environment teaches, affords opportunities to make meaning and connections, affects mood, guides children's behaviour, and influences interaction…The physical environment in a children's service is much more than a backdrop for children's experiences. It is a major provider of opportunities and possibilities. More broadly it is a literal depiction of the identity, traditions, priorities, history and vision of the service.

The NSW Curriculum Framework (2002, p 79) clearly emphasises that the family is the most powerful influence on the child's learning and development, and that they are also important members of the children's service community:

> Not only are they welcomed and invited to become involved, but also most importantly they are collaborators with professionals and the child in the provisions made for the children.

I thought an environment that provoked curiosity and questioning would also be tangible and spark conversation between staff and parents, parents and children, staff and staff. It worked. With a focus on revisiting the environment, the collaborations started. Interest was ignited. Our journey had begun.

At my previous centre, the team had travelled the journey together and we had made good progress. We had passed through many stations, including self-doubt. We had engaged reflective practice with both hands. I found this new situation, however, incredibly different and confronting. I was back at the terminus. The passengers weren't even on the train yet.

Staff members were honest in their interactions with me—they weren't ready to deconstruct their methodology. First, they wanted to understand why they should change; second, they wanted to know how they should go about making a change; and third, they were concerned about the amount of time that might be involved in the change. Questions came from every direction. Is it possible for practitioners to learn through pedagogical documentation? It certainly opened up the conversations in the staff room.

This second journey provided me with the opportunity to think more deeply about current practice and justify my own decision-making. This journey was not going to 'de-rail' me. It was noticeable that the room teams became stronger groups as they voiced their opinions and confirmed their beliefs in their daily practices. I was merely coupling up more 'carriages'. It was allowing me to consolidate, research and firmly establish my role as a facilitator of adult learning.

It has been reported that Henry Kissinger once said, 'The task of a leader is to get the team from where they are to where they haven't been.' The new team worked slowly, careful to understand and rationalise each step in the change process. Questioning and collaboration were frequent lunchtime engagements. Dialogue was sometimes heated. The step into the unknown caused anxiety; the parent questioning was daunting. The continual validation of the centre's metamorphosis was taxing yet liberating as each staff member became more confident in the ability to explain changes taking place within the centre and in their own room. Professional growth and peer respect became more evident.

Personally, I have again ventured into new fields. At present, I am not working in a centre environment, but still involved in early childhood education. This momentary move away from face-to-face teaching has provided an opportunity to revisit theory in practice and the philosophies underpinning the emergent curriculum and the NSW Curriculum Framework. An interest has been ignited to investigate further the teachings of Rudolph Steiner. The next journey has just begun.

Edith's reflections

I remember very clearly the day the five of us sat around Margaret's dining table, little tape recorder in the middle, cups of tea all around. I never thought then that our conversations would have such an impact on me now. Four years after those conversations, I received the transcript in the mail with a note asking me if I was 'comfortable' with the chapter and could I please write a reflective response to our conversation. To be truthful, my first response to revisiting the conversations was dismay. I shoved it under a pile of books and decided my response would be 'No, I don't feel comfortable. Please change my name and pretend I wasn't there.' However, a burning sense of curiosity grew. What was different now? Why the feeling of unease? What had changed?

On reflection, what worries me most about our conversation is the tone. There is a definite sense of alienation and separateness, 'us' and 'them'. I look back and realise that the background to the conversation affected its tenor. A lot of the separateness was due to contextual factors.

Margaret, Lisa and myself were all new to the centre. It had just enjoyed seven years of being small and stable with a close-knit staff and community. A period of rapid expansion, however, coincided with our arrival. Two new rooms were added and more new staff came on board. Staff were experiencing a mixed sense of loss while embracing the many changes thrust upon them. In this context, the additional change we aspired to may have been over-optimistic.

Since our conversations, many things have changed—Margaret and Lisa have taken up new positions elsewhere, and many new staff members have joined the team, including a new Director. Our current team consists of 20 extremely committed people all working towards the same goals. We enjoy a strong sense of collegiality and feel supported by each other. Staff meetings provide support, new inspiration and an opportunity for all to have an equal voice. We have many visitors to the centre who come to look at our environment, program and documentation. But first and foremost, I feel that our families are starting to become engaged in the fabric of the centre and its philosophy. How did we get to this point? In reflecting on this, I see many influences, but two features stand out with particular clarity—leadership and community.

Margaret's leadership brought us through the tough logistical challenges of building a bigger centre for the community and laid the groundwork for the dialogue to deepen. The centre's leadership is now all about creating community, nurturing relationships and valuing the other. At the heart of the centre is (Groom 2003):

> ...the need to consider aspects of the environment beyond just the physical to a multi-layered environment that is constructed of meaningful work practices, enriching human interactions and experiences that affirm a worthwhile human existence.

With the wisdom of hindsight, I can now see how easily the 'us and them' mentality can develop. Who can honestly say that they have not at some point or other felt at odds with their colleagues? On reflection, I now understand that this type of impatience with colleagues only serves to alienate them. Alienating colleagues will never allow the discourse to reconstruct.

Effective discourse that is inclusive of all voices is only possible in a group where all members feel equal, respected and valued. If we want to change the early childhood discourse around curriculum decision-making, then I would argue that the starting point has to be the building of relationships for effective discourse. Theobald (as cited in Deveson, 2003, p 71) explains 'fundamental change in thinking isn't triggered intellectually. It's more emotional than that.'

Many visitors to our centre express deep confusion and hopelessness when faced with the pressure to produce multiple panels of documentation detailing extensive investigations. There is a common theme that 'producing good documentation' and having the 'right physical environment' is the magic key that will open all doors to the 'new way of doing things'. When educators feel deskilled, disempowered or operate in an unsustaining environment, then the argument that documentation is the most useful vehicle for reconceptualisation is not valid.

We cannot continue to brush off the outcry from early childhood educators in Australia that we simply 'don't have time' to produce countless beautiful panels of the unfolding of class projects. I used to spend many nights and many a sunny weekend engrossed in documenting all those exciting things the children and I were experiencing together. This level of effort is unsustainable.

With the guidance of an effective and insightful leader, myself, and in fact all of us as a team, have considered what we can reasonably achieve and expect of ourselves. We have discussed how we might be able to build an environment that sustains us as staff as well as the families who use it. As Groom (2003) says, 'Environments must be rich in experiences for human growth, and places to explore personal potentials for learning how to be human.'

I have personally experienced how panels of documentation about projects can be used as a powerful tool for engaging colleagues, and for reflecting on and improving my own practice. However, I have also experienced the intense disappointment when time and again it fails to engage parents and families and even the children. Leading up to our last Accreditation visit, parents filled out the survey provided by the National Accreditation Council. One parent's response read 'I don't know why you do all of this writing, there seems to be more every year. All I'm interested in is my child.' This had never really been said to us so honestly and almost brutally, but it certainly wasn't a surprise or new revelation.

For years we have been getting frustrated about the fact that most parents will only read the bit in the program that directly relates to their child and that they are not interested in documentation unless their child is expressly mentioned. This frustration has been the discussion topic for many a workshop or regional meeting I have attended. Everyone usually leaves these discussions with renewed determination to 'educate the parents'. I can see now that this creates a gap between parents and us, a 'them' and 'us' mentality. If this is what parents are telling us over and over again, why aren't we listening? We are moving towards more respectful relationships with children, listening to and including their voice in pedagogical decision-making. How can we achieve this with parents? How can we blend our own philosophies and educational ideas with what the parents want for their children?

In our centre, we have started to use portfolios as common ground from which to move forward together. As we have poured our energies into children's individual portfolios, they have proven to be the kind of documentation that engages families, children, staff *and* the wider community such as local schools and extended family networks. They have also been the catalyst for the development of skills that are being used in all our documentation modes.

The response from parents to the portfolios is overwhelmingly positive. I guess the image they see reflected in their child's portfolio is the one that they have always had of their child as a complete unique being with many depths and many strengths and many things to love. They have started bringing in photos, stories, bits and pieces from home that reflect this same image. Most importantly, parents and children have taken on a real sense of ownership of the portfolios. We encourage this by asking them to contribute towards the purchase price, by inviting them to decorate the cover together at home, to make entries together, to include photos from home or important events and by encouraging portfolios to travel often to include the absent parent, to meet Nan and Pop or to show teachers at the Big School interview. As educators, we are left with the privilege of making entries into the portfolios and bringing to life current knowledge about how children learn and develop.

The response from staff to the portfolios has been equally positive. Perhaps the main reason for this is that the work that is put into the portfolios is valued by others, such as the individual child and their family members. This fuels our energy for continuously improving and expanding the portfolios and the entries we make. Because the portfolios are valued, read, passed around and discussed, they have become an excellent communication tool that has, for us, accelerated the reconceptualisation process.

Our portfolio entries include many aspects of life at the centre including, for example, samples of children's work, transcripts of conversations, photocopies of the daily record/program, copies of group investigations or excerpts from large extended investigation panels, series of photographs with interpretations attached or records of conversations with parents. The list of possibilities for portfolio entries is forever growing and changing in line with our own research and continual evaluation.

The nature of the entries allows all of us to contribute and participate, regardless of training, experience or ability. We are finding that the varied nature of these entries means that the staff at our centre are able to gradually build skills in the area of documentation. It requires quite complex pedagogical skills to document an in-depth, extended investigation that is undertaken over a period of weeks or months. We have found that portfolio entries provide a gradual, achievable and non-threatening avenue for this. They are a useful vehicle for reconceptualisation, for growth and change, and for building pedagogical skills in a sustainable way.

Lisa's reflections

Since engaging in this project, I have continued my own learning journey. I've moved to a new centre, gained my early childhood qualifications, stepped into the role of teacher and director and entered the exciting world of motherhood. Reflecting on these past experiences, I am thankful for the relationships, discoveries and learning that came with these. These stepping stones have enabled me to have a deeper insight and understanding into team members' diverse skills and the variety of team structures that enhance and help scaffold learning, not only of children but also of colleagues.

After first re-reading this paper, it was interesting to stop and think—I have been documented. I asked myself:

> Are people going to understand what I am saying here? They can't see me, they can't feel my passion, they haven't seen how I relate to my colleagues and attempt to walk alongside children as they learn, they only have words on the page.

This realisation was difficult for me, as I wanted people to have a deeper under-standing of where I was coming from. Everyone interprets things so differently, would they really understand what I meant? This poses the question: How do we show the richness of each child so we don't reduce them to black marks on a page? This whole documented experience reinforces to me how important it is to make sure you can hear children's voices and see through their eyes how they have participated. What have they questioned and which paths have they taken to uncover more questions, answers and learn about relationships with others?

I am also curious about continually exploring ideas to foster and encourage collaboration between colleagues. I am intrigued by the idea of pushing the boundaries of self-expression and discovery to be a better communicator, to entice people to want to learn alongside each other no matter what stage of the journey they are on. Each station has something to offer a traveller. The important thing for me now, is to have everyone embark and share experiences; to join the pictures from everyone's postcards to portray a child's learning journey and paint the 'bigger picture'. I feel that, in the past, I was very focused on my own journey of documentation, and I wasn't bringing together staff teams and appreciating the combination of all types of observations, interpretations, interactions, and sharing the many voices that give a deeper insight into children's learning.

I feel I used to believe documentation was an essential key and everyone should document, but have since experienced that it is important to learn how to be a gatherer. By this I mean a person who can invite all stakeholders' ideas, observations, pictures, and provocations to be shared, to tell a story of the children's questions, discoveries and steps they have taken to uncover new learning experiences together. This may come in the form of posters, portfolios, works collected and displayed for all to see. It has been exciting to share with colleagues the various steps and techniques used to reveal children's thoughts. These processes also enable teachers to learn from each other and discover the different approaches and teaching styles that each individual uses to extend and uncover new ideas from the children. This has highlighted for me how important it is to work in collaboration to bring to light children's ideas and provoke further questioning and learning, discovering deeper relationships with peers and teachers. This depth can be missed if a documentor has to work in isolation. At present, I am finding the idea of using a variety of observers and observations gives the documentation more credibility, displaying the vast relationships children form with others, building a picture of a child from many styles and interpretations.

I have had some fantastic opportunities that have supported my growth in teaching, collaboration and professional skills. I was very fortunate to visit centres in Melbourne (Australia) and share these experiences with a colleague. We then had the opportunity to work together to build on what we had seen. This presented us with new challenges which ensured we were continually reflecting on our practices enabling us to develop and grow as a team of researchers with children and staff. It's great to observe others, absorb this information and then discover for yourself and not duplicate others' work.

I have learnt that you don't have to be the best academic person to share these ideas and influence others to give their best to children. If you believe in the children, promote their capabilities, walk alongside them in their learning discoveries, others soon observe the excitement that's being shared and want to experience it too. Live in the child's moment, and find your inner child to help you work on a level of excitement and wonder, to uncover their amazing curiosity, questioning, and puzzlement about the world around them.

I feel I have learnt so much since the day Alma and Catherine walked through the door of the 0–3 room where I had just begun to explore my understanding of documentation. I remember being challenged by Alma's comment to my work: 'that's not documentation'. To this day, I am very thankful for her honesty as it challenged me to ask more questions, collaborate with other early childhood educators at RE-Search groups, involve families and engage in more meaningful relationships with children. Throughout this process I believe it is important not to judge oneself or others in a destructive manner but understand that moment in time, reflecting on what stage of the journey you were on and how all the different paths you cross with people help you change and grow. Working on each moment-by-moment, striving to be the best we are at the present time, not expecting to be perfect but honest with oneself and others, is fundamental when engaging in pedagogical documentation.

Conclusion

These responses from Margaret, Edith and Lisa reveal some of the complexities and dilemmas of changing practices. There is a sense that at any particular time, one idea or belief may be foregrounded yet it may retreat as the situation changes over time. Change processes are rarely linear or perceived similarly by the people involved; rather they are a maze of circularity and diversions.

Margaret, Edith and Lisa have shown courage in sharing insights into their experiences over time; their thoughts illustrate the rich possibilities of reflecting on daily practices while acknowledging the intricacies and uncertainties of change. While the individuality of these journeys is probably clear, the relation between these ideas and the possibilities for interrupting the dominant discourse may not be. Existing practice and recognised ways of thinking and talking about early childhood work ('the dominant discourse') will always be powerful shapers of action. Attempts to challenge and shift established ways of working in order to create greater possibilities for children, staff and families require on-going conversations, thoughtful reflection and trusting environments. The complexities of relationships between staff need to be interrogated alongside family perceptions and points of view. It can be supposed that both willingness to change and an unwillingness to change are essential ingredients in challenging the dominant discourse—each to unsettle and extend the other. The conversations continue.

References

Cheeseman S and Robertson J (2001, July) *Voices in documentation: A private conversation publicly documented*. Paper presented at the biennial Australian Early Childhood Association Conference. Sydney, Australia.

Dahlberg G, Moss P & Pence A (1999) *Beyond quality in early childhood education and care: Postmodern perspectives*. London: Falmer Press.

Deveson A (2003) *Resilience*. Allen and Unwin: Australia.

Groom S (2003) Presentation to the conference *Unpacking Meaning Making: Provocations from Reggio Emilia in Australia*. North Ryde, NSW: Institute of Early Childhood, Macquarie University.

Hultqvist K & Dahlberg G (2001) *Governing the child in the new millenium*. New York: Routledge Falmer.

Johnson RJ (2001) Epilogue: Reconceptualization as interruption, interrogative punctuation and opening. In JA Jipson & RT Johnson (Eds) *Resistance and representation: Rethinking childhood education*. New York: Peter Lang.

MacNaughton G & Dockett S (2000) Editorial. *Australian Journal of Early Childhood*, 25 (2), ii.

New South Wales Department of Community Services, Office of Child Care (2002) *NSW curriculum framework for children's services: The practice of relationships —Essential provisions for children's services.* Sydney: Office of Child Care.

Robertson J (1997, May) Seeing is believing. In *Unpacking Reggio Emilia: Further implications for Australian early childhood practice.* Conference Proceedings. North Ryde, NSW: Institute of Early Childhood, Macquarie University.

Tobin J (1995) Post-structural research in early childhood education. In JA Hatch (Ed) *Qualitative research in early childhood settings.* Connecticut: Praeger.

Tobin J (2000) *'Good guys don't wear hats': Children's talk about the media.* New York: Teachers College Press.

Note

Parts of this chapter were presented originally as a paper entitled *Readings of the process of constructing Australian pedagogical documentation: Five voices* at the conference Reconceptualising Early Childhood Education: Research, theory and practice 10 years later—What's relevant? (New York City, September, 2001).

Chapter Eighteen

Exhibit-on:
Surprising Site for Conflict and Celebration

Alma Fleet
Janet Robertson

The catalogue for an Australian travelling exhibition that celebrates pedagogical documentation in New South Wales (Australia) lists Alma and Janet as the curators of *Exhibit-on*. The first version of this exhibit has some thirty panels developed into gallery pieces by graphic designer Michelle McDonald, from excerpts of investigations documented by staff in early childhood settings. What is not clear in the public documentation is the angst that shaped the process. As preparation begins for the second version of the exhibition, the issues that arose still generate tension and highlight this arena as a site of ethical debate as well as emotional and intellectual complexity.

The beginnings

This chapter might have been called 'The ethics of an exhibition'. The genesis was an unexpected event that led to an unlikely possibility. The story of that sequence helps to establish a context.

In setting the scene, the reader might note the following definition from the Canadian Museums Association (CMA, 1999, p 3):

> Ethics are based upon the underlying values of honesty, fairness, respect, excellence and accountability which the larger community applies to the rational evaluation of moral issues. The application of these values has changed considerably over time…

This definition arose in the context of ethical debates within the CMA. The relevance will become clear as the chapter unfolds.

The educators of Reggio Emilia have created a travelling exhibition of their work entitled *The hundred languages of children*. Viewing the exhibition in Melbourne in 1993 was the beginning for many Australians of an intellectual and emotional journey into possible ways of reconceptualising their work with young children and their families. This is not surprising as Malaguzzi (cited in Spaggiari, Rinaldi, Filippini & Vecchi, 1996, p 30), foundation philosopher of the project of Reggio Emilia wrote:

> A voyage within a voyage: that is how our experience, as transcribed emblematically in the exhibit, should be understood.

In the intervening years, multiple versions of the Italian exhibition have continued to circulate around the world, energising viewers and inviting educators to see their work through the eyes of these adults and children.

As interest in the ideas from Reggio Emilia expanded, a number of people worked to have the current version of the Italian Exhibition in Australia. By 2001, preparation by Jan Millikan and others resulted in a newer reconfigured version of the *The hundred languages* Exhibition coming to Australia. Efforts to bring the Exhibition to Sydney as part of this collaboration were unsuccessful due to lack of financial support. As host city for the Olympics in 2000, Sydney seemed to have drained its sponsorship dollars. Adding to the stress of this endeavour was the fact that the Sydney team had linked the visit of the Italian Exhibition with the triennial Australian Early Childhood Association conference, scheduled for Sydney in 2001. An exhibition had been promised to the conference organisers. The Italian exhibition was not going to be available. The creation of a local exhibit to fill the void was the only solution.

On one hand, this possibility seemed relatively straightforward in that there were several groups across the state that met fairly regularly to share ideas related to adapting inspirations from Reggio Emilia for local contexts. The participants would have relevant work that could be shared with the larger community. On the other hand, the prospect was daunting. The Italian Exhibition was internationally renowned, reflecting thoughtful work that had been unfolding for decades. The Australian documentors had not had a similar opportunity to be part of an extended debate and peer review. Nevertheless, something had to be done, so the task was undertaken.

Titles: One word matters

Can an exhibit be both a provocation and a celebration of excellence? The word 'exhibition' itself is cause for reflection and, in this case, was seen to potentially misrepresent intent. Certainly something was going to be 'shown' or shared, enabling public viewing, which is the definition of an exhibition; but the term implies excellence and display in a way that seemed inappropriate for the purposes of these selections. By changing the label for this collection of offerings, we hoped that there would be engaging intellectual interaction. The new word 'Exhibit-on' seemed to us to be an active term, one that invoked the respect of an exhibition, but implied an ongoing collection, not finite, moving on, somehow different from a gallery experience in its traditional form. Perhaps the broader term 'presentation' would have been helpful. The CMA (1999, p 4) defines presentations as 'any material or intellectual product which the museum offers to the public in any form'.

There is probably still some element in the label that is missing and which needs to reflect the pedagogical component of a resource collection—a tool for teaching and learning, expanding understanding and provoking growth. Yet there is also the intention to step back from the prosaic, to lift the pragmatic to the level of provocation, to empower as well as inspire, advocate as well as celebrate.

It also seemed important to interrupt any expectation that this presentation might be conceptualised as an exhibit of children's art. Earlier European interpretations of *The hundred languages of children* exhibition were sometimes condensed to a primary focus on children's art, despite its powerful subtitle: *Narrative of the possible* and explanation in the accompanying catalogue (Spaggiari, *et al.*, 1996). An art exhibition would generally have important but different purposes from the NSW process-oriented, multi-faceted exploration of interaction and investigation. The evolving *Exhibit-on* had a fundamental grounding in relationships and unfolding pedagogical insights, seen as often through the nature of the interaction as the physical evidence of creation and meaning making. The difficulty of the label for this collection was addressed partially through the use of multiple subtitles as agreed by the local RE-Search group: *Provocations—clarity and confusion. Unpacking interpretation.*

Part of the intention was to carve a different way of presenting pedagogical documentation. Those known to be using this tool to assist their thinking and their work in advocacy for the collaborations of young children were invited to offer pieces of work for potential inclusion in the unfolding exhibition. As early childhood student teachers at Macquarie University were also learning to use this vehicle in their work, insightful students were invited to submit their work for selection. As time was short, it was not possible to look farther afield for contributions.

The matter of selection

Rather than including complete pieces of pedagogical documentation, we decided to use brief excerpts from various pieces in order to provide more opportunities to promote discussion about multiple interpretations and directions for decision-making. It was also important to highlight work being done across the early childhood age range in a variety of settings. This ensured that babies and toddlers in child care were represented as well as preschool aged children and those in the first years of school. The experiences needed to reflect the public and private sectors as well as a range of topics and ways of approaching representation. Other criteria were also employed—the balancing of indoor and outdoor exploration; a focus on the scientific as well as the artistic; the intellectual and cognitive (how do you count water?); the affective and emotive (hunting spiders seen as exploring fear); the confronting of stereotypes (such as race and gender); as well as exploring important components of community such as friendship and children's secret spaces. Parcels arrived, pages were spread out and the selection process began. The ensuing traumas should have been foreseen. The unchallenged assumptions were breath-taking.

Unintentionally, we found ourselves in a position of identifying pieces for public view, 'naming' excellence as if it were an agreed-upon professional standard. Therein hung the impossibility of the situation. Each of the pieces had its own integrity within each local setting. Staff and student teachers offered their thinking and professional presentation skills, the creativity and curiosity of the children and families with whom they worked, their values, insights and glimpses of their daily lives. Some pieces would go forward for public sharing; some had to be quietly, regretfully returned, unshown, perhaps unsung. In a domain characterised by compassion and collegiality, this discriminating function was discordant.

The original pieces were produced to highlight on-going teaching practice and to help illuminate learning processes, children's curiosities and creativities. They were designed for local discussion rather than public presentation.

In selecting for such a transition, we agreed not to include poor quality (indistinct or blurred) images; we needed quality photographs which captured the essence of a moment. Inevitably, this meant that some pieces could not be included because the core of the experience was not clear to an observer.

There were also difficult decisions related to indefinable judgments such as:

- Is it all right to present adults' and children's work when it is not the best they can do?

- How much relativity do we assign to the construct of 'best'?

- Does excellence mean effectiveness within a particular moment or context or does a piece need to speak to a wider audience in order to be selected for an exhibit?

- Do the criteria vary for individuals at different stages of professional growth?

Others came in to help with the process—the power of selection, even when shared by several people, was humbling. It might seem ludicrous that an apparently pragmatic task for professional people was the source of tears and sleepless nights for the curators, but disagreements were palpable. With deeply felt, powerfully held beliefs and philosophical perspectives, the simple act of disagreeing became difficult to do. As Janet wrote (Robertson, 2001, pp 49–50):

> In the end to preserve our friendship, we had to talk to each other on email about decisions we were making, as we had been bewildered by the gulf that lay between us. Tongue-tied by our need to agree, and by niceness, written words became the way we could express our intimate gaze and agony. One evening's email went like this:
>
> Dear Alma
>
> my personal agony is over our, you and me, own desire to agree...is this a girl thing?...and this fundamental intellectual gulf is perplexing. But actually I think it is very healthy...we each bring a strong personality to the job and a very subjective stance...our interpretations are coloured totally by what we see as the point of the exhibit-on.
>
> Love Janet
>
> Dear Janet
>
> Wanting to agree may be a girl thing...the fundamental need to communicate richly—but in this case, I think it also has a lot to do with the fact that we each have profound respect for each other's intelligence and insight—so when we seem to be seeing different things, it becomes frustrating—terribly un-post-modern of us, not to expect multiple realities and layers of interpretation...
>
> Sleep well
>
> Alma

I don't think our experience is unique. Discussing closely held values and thoughts, and arguing for them within a discussion, is something we can all find prickly and difficult. How do we discuss multiple perspectives without it becoming personal? Seeking ways in which to make clearer what lenses we gaze through is a hallmark of intellectual rigor and transparency. I know both of us are richer for our email experience.

So as an international, intellectual community, what do we take from this situation? Certainly we recognise good intentions, as reflected in the fact that all who offered pieces were recognised in the public listing of the community of documentors. People were asked how they felt about this because there was the possibility that some might have felt embarrassed by being 'unchosen', but no, all were proud to be part of this community of recognised documentors.

More is at stake here than a search for worthwhile projects to pursue with young children, although that in itself is of value. The work matters. The time spent with children matters. Joy and delight are as essential to the enterprise as wrestling with the silences and inequities. The choice to be an early childhood educator includes a responsibility to struggle with 'big ideas' (Oken-Wright & Gravett, 2002).

Design and presentation

Selection issues were not the only source of unease. There was the matter of translation of format for a different genre and audience, the need to display material respectfully. Surely there is not a single format for this kind of provocation; yet there was some specific criticism of the *Exhibit-on* because a different set of design principles were chosen from those in the Italian exhibition. This criticism was unexpected but raised interesting issues about the 'truths' of documentation.

What are the intersections between our subjectivity and design? If work is being re-created for an exhibition, does the final design process help the material lose its pedagogical purpose? Does trying to make it 'presentable' to the public gaze make it lose some of its purity or does this 'presentability' make it more accessible for the public? Is there an ethical slide between the pragmatics of daily presentation and the formalising expected as part of professional regard? Is it a case of metaphorical horses for courses: perhaps one set of re-shaped pedagogical documentation for public viewing, one set of working papers for centre discussion and another even more ephemeral collection of 'bits and pieces' for the documentor? When we re-present an idea, preparing it for a Power Point presentation, for example, are we creating another 'truth'? Is it the raising of the issues themselves that reflects professional behaviour and intellectual integrity?

Somewhere in the process of everyday teaching practice, interactions that are respectfully watched, listened to, thought about and discussed with key players, can become slices of time that are tidied and re-packaged records of events. Perhaps whilst becoming a slice of pedagogical documentation, the subjectivity is made visible—the questions asked, the possibilities proposed, traces of the follow-on decisions that were made. The question becomes one of offering intellectual interactivity between viewer and viewed while acknowledging the tension between raw data, interpretation and presentation.

Disconnected bits of experience and planning become components of collegiality. Having the pieces tabled (or 'walled') creates opportunities for debate and professional reflection. Perhaps the effort of creating *Exhibit-on* is a mega version of why documenting is important on a local scale, as it challenges and supports newer images of educational interactions.

The catalogue

The creation of a catalogue (Fleet and Robertson, 2002) was also an important component of this process. The introduction gave an overview to readers or viewers, including the following (p 1):

> These fragments are visible traces of children's and teachers' lives. They show moments of insight, of conflict, of negotiation, of theory building, of leadership, followship, of thinking, of confusion and clarity, of social construction of knowledge and of powerful capable children as authors of their own learning. These mini narratives come from larger bodies of work carried out by teachers, families and children. Essentially not 'documentation', this *Exhibit-on* tells a partial story derived from a community of thinkers, both adults and children, who are attempting to unpack and re-interpret early education...

The introduction provided a pragmatic and conceptual context for the collection. Having used excerpts from larger pieces, it was important to share a little about the circumstances—as it was often not clear in the printed documentation—perhaps explaining preceding events, or why the documentor chose to notice or be involved in a particular situation. Soja (1996, p 2) in his explanation of the 'tentative and flexible' concept of 'Thirdspace', wrote that:

> Whether in writing the biography of a particular individual or interpreting a momentous event or simply dealing with our everyday lives, the closely associated historical (or temporal) and social (or sociological) imaginations have always been at the forefront of making practical and informative sense of the subject at hand.

For example, in considering an investigation of the experience of rain by the children, Janet commented (Fleet and Robertson, 2002, p 30):

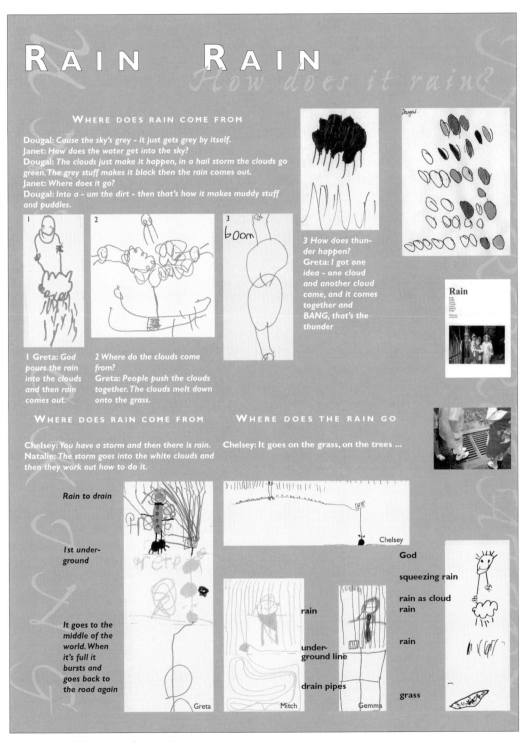

RAIN RAIN

How does it rain?

WHERE DOES RAIN COME FROM

Dougal: *Cause the sky's grey - it just gets grey by itself.*
Janet: *How does the water get into the sky?*
Dougal: *The clouds just make it happen, in a hail storm the clouds go green. The grey stuff makes it black then the rain comes out.*
Janet: *Where does it go?*
Dougal: *Into a - um the dirt - then that's how it makes muddy stuff and puddles.*

boom

3 How does thunder happen?
Greta: I got one idea - one cloud and another cloud came, and it comes together and BANG, that's the thunder

1 Greta: *God pours the rain into the clouds and then rain comes out.*

2 Where do the clouds come from?
Greta: *People push the clouds together. The clouds melt down onto the grass.*

Rain

WHERE DOES RAIN COME FROM

Chelsey: *You have a storm and then there is rain.*
Natalie: *The storm goes into the white clouds and then they work out how to do it.*

WHERE DOES THE RAIN GO

Chelsey: *It goes on the grass, on the trees ...*

Rain to drain

1st underground

It goes to the middle of the world. When it's full it bursts and goes back to the road again

Chelsey

rain

underground line

drain pipes

Greta

Mitch

Gemma

God

squeezing rain

rain as cloud rain

rain

grass

An Exhibit-on *panel: Rain Rain*

What intrigued me with this investigation, were the solutions the children found to depict underground. They usually had to add another page to the one they started to use in order to continue to draw below the ground. I wonder how soon the notion of 'the bottom of the page means the ground' arises in children's graphic representation?

Or acting as an advocate for the reflective role of documenting per se (p 32): 'This experience happened in front of my eyes, and it was only in documenting it and thinking about it later, I realised how powerful their acts were…'

The catalogue also enabled the analysing of key ingredients (p 33):

Looking back on this investigation, the most salient point for me now (a year later) is how important relationships between teacher and children are in gathering this information. We had lived together for three years by the time we worked on this piece. Our personal understandings of each other meant we did not have to take lengthy detours to get to the nub of the matter.

These commentaries intersect with Soja's (1996) dimensions related to time, space and the sociology of experience, and their role in deepening and enriching pedagogical practice. These elements enable us to broaden our understandings of the nature of fruitful analysis.

Reflections

Issues related to the selection and sharing of pieces of pedagogical documentation tumble over each other. Separating out the key ideas feeding into the exhibition becomes problematic. Certainly there is the issue of trying to agree on what is noteworthy in this particular context as distinct from the context in which each piece was created. Related to this challenge is the acknowledgment of the range of forms of useful documentation and curriculum as evidenced at different sites.

As the discussion expands about the value of pedagogical documentation as a tool for reflection, advocacy and professional decision-making, more diverse local strategies are explored for relevant record-keeping. There are dangers in any notion of orthodoxies that assume one right way of 'doing' documentation, which inevitably limits the options available to teachers with young children.

The discussion enables us to reinforce the importance of 'both-and-also' rather than 'either-or' orientations (Soja, 1996) to what is possible, enriching, informative and effective in the realm of pedagogical record-keeping. Rather than implying that something either is or is not within the domain of pedagogical documentation, it is probably more helpful to consider the many possible formats, uses, strategies and intentions of the range of materials that sit under the umbrella of pedagogical documentation. Individual records created for portfolios

WHAT IS IT ABOUT TREES?
A toddler room investigation

Greta 2.10 . Mitchell 2.10 . Tessa 3.9 . Gemma 2.9 . Chris 2.9

THE BEGINNING

In June a passion for trees and forests erupted in the toddler room. After several walks in the copse of trees to the north of the school, small clay forests started to appear in children's clay work. This collective assembly of clay covered sticks remained on the shelf for a month, children looking at it and talking about it, but no further work was done.

REVIVAL

In August several taller trees were made, distinguished by the collaborative nature of their construction. Rather than individual children making single trees, each tree was built by several children.
Possibly responding to the technical challenge of covering the armature (internal support, in this case a cardboard tube) to attain the desired height, Tessa, Mitchell and Chris worked for 30 minutes together. Several technical hitches occurred, (tilting and slipping) which caused hilarity, but did not diminish their desire to 'get it done'.
Two more tall trees were made, the task uniting the children. The language of reciprocity and negotiation occurred. *You hold this - no, more there - I've run out of clay - have mine*, characterised their work.
Branches or leaves? Tessa had made a small tree with a cross branch, and Chris often added small 'leaves' straight on the trunks.
The base of the trees often came alive with holes for creatures to live in, especially snakes, foxes and birds.

THE TALLEST TREE

I decided to give them a serious challenge. I wanted to respond to the 'work' image the children seemed to hold about the construction.
Chris always brings a stick to school, gathering them at the carpark and leaving them at the front door.
Using a 1.5 cm stick I asked Tessa, Mitchell, Chris and Greta if they could use that stick.
They didn't even speak, just opened the clay box and got to work. The adult role then became stick holder, while they organised how to cover the stick.
Mitchell remained in one place, working on a spot just above his eye level, adding small rolls of clay.
Chris worked mostly on the base, adding thoughtful animal houses. Greta and Tessa realised they needed more height and climbed on chairs and eventually the table to accomplish the task. This kerfuffle attracted others ...

An Exhibit-on *panel: What is it about trees?*

may not, however, expand our understanding of processes within the group. Nevertheless, records of events are as useful for some purposes as are critiqued analyses of sequences of experiences. Outside the local context, there may be elements of both in pieces of pedagogical documentation that are noteworthy for promoting discussions with the wider community.

So what sits under this collective umbrella of pedagogical documentation? There is certainly the importance of valuing children's work as well as seeing important threads or patterns in daily events. There is the importance of analytical reflection going beyond display (Forman, 1998) to a sophisticated interweaving of children's and adults' voices in investigations and opportunities that provoke new insights and understandings. Are there some absolutes? Maybe, although the possibility is rather disconcerting. For example, in curating *Exhibit-on*, we disagreed on whether a thoughtful piece by a student teacher should be included. Alma knew how hard the student had worked in an unwelcoming environment to create nurturing possibilities for the children in the centre. Janet, in valuing the importance of outdoor environments, was unwilling to display photographs with a plastic strewn, unkempt playspace in the background.

Ethics of an exhibition

There are tensions in trying to honour the integrity of a piece without being able to include it all, or worrying about revising or deleting material that might be embarrassing to the contributors when seen in another context from that in which it was created. There are issues associated with putting a novice's work on public display for all to see without regarding how vulnerable they are to unthinking critique.

These tensions raise issues regarding the wider sphere of ethics of exhibition selection and presentation, which is a relatively young field. In 1987, Simpson wrote a paper related to conflicts of interest for museums and their employees in which he referred to 'the sensitive youthfulness of museum ethics as an issue in Australia'. While there is more written on the topic in North America, unfortunately, the bulk of the literature relates to such things as tensions associated with questionable sponsorship or the implications of working with private collections or commercial entities (for example: Kennedy, 2004; National Association for Visual Arts, 2004). There is also material written on culturally sensitive collections which tangentially relates to the pedagogical and community issues raised here. A common piece of advice in this literature is that there be written contracts to clearly indicate rights and responsibilities of owners of material (in this case documentors) and the museum mounting the exhibition (in this case, the curators as employees of a university). For *Exhibit-on*, this step was taken with a pro forma contract and advice from a regional gallery director. The literature, however, does not seem to consider the ethical dilemmas embedded in a pedagogical, collegial community such as that described here.

WHAT IS IT ABOUT TREES?
A toddler room investigation

LEAVES

Eventually after 25 minutes, the stick was now a clay tree. The original workers had left and Jeremy, Adam. Jake, Chris and Chelsey came to admire it.
I mentioned there were no leaves and wondered how they could make some. As we had run out of clay, I was hoping they would suggest something else. Jeremy did, running to get card, pen and scissors, he drew a squiggle, cut it out an pushed it into the clay. A flurry of leaf making blew through the room. Again table and chair climbing added a frisson of adventure to the task. For another 20 minutes leaves were made, the orginal workers returned and were once more engaged in the task.

INTERPRETATION

In many ways I think this work is not about trees at all. These young children had found a vehicle in which they could work together on a joint enterprise which matched their differing abilities, utilised each others' skills and had, as it were, an end point.
Too young to really collectively plan ahead, they nonetheless worked as a team, in companionable conversation and with purpose.
The physical nature of the task and its impressive size no doubt added to their sense of engagement as did the technical aspects
I wonder if they will take trees further or will the technical work in clay claim their interest?
We will see...

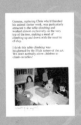

A toddler room investigation: original format included

Bulbach (2002) raises several ethical concerns related to selection of material for exhibition in his rather scathing attack on the approach of art museums to research on contemporary American craft. Some of these concerns relate to the financial ambiguities alluded to above and the absence of appropriate ethical guidelines. He notes that American art museums emphasise 'their traditional roles as research institutions' (p 1). The relevance here is that pedagogical documentation is often seen as an act of cooperative research with adults and children, helping to generate new insights and understandings through processes of analysis and reflection. Bulbach states that (p 3):

> …normal academic research in the arts and sciences enjoys several simple, effective safeguards to help maintain integrity and its accuracy. These safeguards are so simple and effective, that when they are missing, their absence raises suspicions.

He summarises these safeguards as the use of 'open discourse and inquiry about the research' and 'a primary ethical requirement' to have actually examined all material 'leading to a final selection' (p 3). Both of these conditions were met for *Exhibit-on*. He also raises questions about the clarity of definition of the category of material being considered. In the case of our invitation to people for work to be considered for exhibition, a definition of pedagogical documentation was probably implied through a shared community understanding. This book is part of an attempt to refine this vagueness in the future.

An important reference point is, of course, the catalogue associated with *The hundred languages of children* exhibit from Reggio Emilia (Spaggiari *et al.*, 1996). In the introduction to this publication, the Minister of Education from Rome emphasised the role of the exhibit in making visible 'a number of strategic choices' related to the theme of quality in education (Lombardi, in Spaggiari *et al.*, 1996, p 11). The mayor of Reggio Emilia went on in this introduction to write that the 'driving force' behind a new version of the exhibit was 'the courage to bear witness to a way of educating that defends and promotes the rights and potential of children, teachers, and parents' (A Spaggiari in Spaggiari *et al.*, p 13).

Malaguzzi (1996 in Spaggiari *et al.*, p 36) concludes the opening essays with a strong message:

> It is our hope that the subjects and the materials displayed here will be appreciated for what they are, despite the heavy weight of prejudices, myths, exorcisms, sublimations, and also despite the cultural, social and pedagogical policies which blur, elude, accelerate and consume children and childhood. But most of all, we hope that the exhibit will be recognised for the attempt it has made.

One might interpret this summation to say that the ethics of the situation is seen in the persistent and determined insistence on attempting to behave ethically.

343

Conclusion

In considering the ethics of an exhibition, the question is asked, 'How can we engage in this work without making a kind of 'this is how you do it' statement?' Have some people simply missed the idea of what drives the pedagogy in pedagogical documentation, focusing on products or outcomes rather than the 'whole package' of an approach to teaching, a philosophy of learning, a fundamental foundation of relationships? The notion of a 'work-in-progress' is often lost when items are made into something like *Exhibit-on*, as though there were not other paths taken, other things that are equally important that happened but are not recorded in such detail. If we take the stance that pedagogical documentation is about research, about seeking insight and understanding from focused observation, recording and analysis, how can we make that 'research work' accessible to others?

Malaguzzi (in Spaggiari *et al.*, 1996, p 29) tells us to view *The hundred languages* exhibit with optimism, that:

> After all, education must stand on the side of optimism or else it will melt like ice cream in the sun, becoming nothing. It is simply a question of ethics and of culture.

The intention in this case was to offer a discussion starter, a collection of pieces to support and provoke collaborative professional discussion. *Exhibit-on* can walk on its own, being seen and interpreted in multiple ways in a wide range of locations. It has contributed to conference discussions, professional development sessions and backgrounded a state government seminar.

The role of an *Exhibit-on* is neither to instruct nor to show a model of what good pedagogical documentation should look like. It advocates for the creativity, energy, intellect, achievements and relationships of young children and the adults who work with them. It is a component of an intellectually curious and interpersonally respectful professional community. Consideration of the ethics of exhibition adds to discussion around issues associated with different forms and purposes of pedagogical documentation, thereby enriching the debate.

References

Bulbach S (2002) A failure in accuracy and reliability: Art museum research on contemporary American craft. *Organdi Quarterly*, April (No 4). Retrieved 28 September 2004, from <http://www.geocities.com/organdi_revue/April2002/Bulbach01.html>.

Canadian Museums Association (1999) *CMA ethical guidelines*. Victoria: CMA.

Fleet A & Robertson J (2002) Exhibit-on catalogue. *Provocations—clarity and confusion. Unpacking interpretation.* Sydney: Institute of Early Childhood, Macquarie University.

Forman G (1998) Negotiated learning through design, documentation and discourse. In C Edwards, L Gandini & G Forman (Eds) *The hundred languages of children: The Reggio Emilia approach—Advanced reflections* (2nd Ed). (pp 239–60). Connecticut: Ablex.

Kennedy B (n.d/2004) *How much do we care about museum ethics?* Retrieved 28 September 2004 from <http://www.nga.gov.au/Director/musethics.htm>.

National Association for Visual Arts (n.d./2004) *Exhibiting, selling and collecting art and craft*. Retrieved 28 September 2004 from <http://www.visualarts.net.au/practicaladvice/default.asp?page=codeof PracticePart1>.

Oken-Wright P & Gravett M (2002) Big ideas and the essence of intent. In V Fu, A Stremmel & L Hill (Eds) *Teaching and learning: Collaborative exploration of the Reggio Emilia approach*. (pp 197–220). New Jersey: Merrill Prentice-Hall.

Robertson J (2001, July) Unpacking the gaze: shifting lenses. In. *Unpacking interpretation: Deconstructions from Australia, America and Reggio Emilia. Selected papers*. North Ryde, NSW: Institute of Early Childhood, Macquarie University

Robertson J & Fleet A (2001) *The agony of Exhibit-on: emails of confusion and clarity*. Participants' context paper distributed at the Unpacking interpretation: Deconstructions from Australia, America and Reggio Emilia conference held at University of NSW. Sydney. 16–17 July.

Simpson S (1987) Mirror, mirror on the wall: Public museums, employees and conflicts of interest. *Art Monthly*, 3, August.

Soja EW (1996) *Thirdspace. Journeys to Los Angeles and other real-and-imagined places*. Massachusetts: Blackwell.

Spaggiari S, Rinaldi C, Filippini T & Vecchi V (1996) *The hundred languages of children: Narrative of the possible*. Catalogue of the exhibit. Reggio Emilia: Reggio Children.

Response to Part Five

Pulling Together, Reaching Out

Commentator

Sue Groom

Sue's response

Amidst the many positions and possibilities that pedagogical documentation provokes, there appears to be a key one surfacing from the ideas presented in the previous two chapters—pedagogical documentation arouses emotional responses for early childhood educators. These emotions seem to trigger responses such as a feeling of experience or the lack of experience to understand it, time or no time to achieve it, ethical or unethical frameworks to guide it. To address the main ideas raised in the chapters, I will draw together what I detect as the differences between what the 'academy' hopes is achieved through pedagogical documentation, and what I and the other practitioners writing in Chapter Seventeen, have found can be achieved in practice. I hope this will not be interpreted as a negative critique, but one that is from a moment in time and personal experience which, I believe, provides an insight into the complexities of pedagogical documentation. It is a reflection of an Australian experience that can also look to an optimistic future where pedagogical documentation will be a fundamental component of our practice as early childhood educators.

I'm sure many early childhood educators can identify with the experiences of Margaret, Lisa and Edith as they struggled with changes and provocations in their initial experiences of embracing this new approach to curriculum. I wonder, however, whether we should still be dwelling on the struggle for change. I believe we have really moved beyond change to an acceptance of difference in early childhood practices. This includes the maintenance of current practices as well as seeking improvements and a discovery of yet unknown possibilities. We are working within a reconstructed curriculum and we should be focused on the pedagogical processes involved in documentation. In practice, I have found that the challenges no longer lie with a changing curriculum focus, but with helping staff understand the complexities and purposes of pedagogical documentation as a component of this approach to curriculum decision-making.

I believe it will be difficult to prevent pedagogical documentation becoming a new orthodoxy with an esoteric discourse. Creating opportunities for practitioners to develop the understanding of pedagogical documentation is a critical factor. Practitioners are people with many different experiences and levels of training. It is necessary to have frameworks, guidelines, examples to follow and meaningful provocations from the field. In Chapter Seventeen, Alma Fleet suggests that, 'we see pedagogical documentation as a metaphor—as a tool to enable people to look at their work differently'. Before this is possible, before the potentials of documentation can be realised, experience suggests that pedagogical documentation is a whole 'tool box' of ideas, understanding, knowledge and technical skills and that we need to learn how to use the tools. As early childhood educators, I believe we have taken the responsibility to embrace this concept, but the struggle we experienced as we increased our understanding needs to be eased.

I do not want to imply that a definition or formula should be created for pedagogical documentation. I applaud the authors of this book for helping early childhood educators understand this very complex concept. I was surprised but also relieved to read that when the invitations went out for documentation to be considered for 'Exhibit-on' 'the definition of pedagogical documentation was probably implied through a shared community understanding'. No wonder choosing the pieces caused so much angst! I agree that the vagueness for under-standing pedagogical documentation needs to be refined and that possibilities for what is considered documentation should include 'many possible formats, uses and intentions'. In my Australian experience, the important realisation about pedagogical documentation is not about 'what it is'; rather, it is about 'what it does'.

The authors of Chapter Seventeen suggest that these ways of working are grounded in the interpretation of focused, personally and culturally relevant experience, and create an integrative approach to pedagogy. I interpret these ideas to mean that a mature insight into humanity and ways of being human is required to recognise the focus and aims of this pedagogy. In our postmodern practices, not only are we gaining insights into 'children's thinking and ways of being', but pedagogical documentation also has the potential to demonstrate to us our growth as humans, and our own ways of being. Of course, we know from our personal experiences with many different colleagues that we are also as individual as the children we teach. Therefore, good leadership is imperative to achieve a common focus or recognition of a particular philosophy; that is, leadership that expects and includes the participation and the contribution of all, and provides opportunities for all voices to be heard. If this is the experience of the adults in early childhood educational settings, it will also be the experience of the children and parents.

Given the variety of practitioner experiences, perspectives and abilities, it may be difficult to achieve the inclusion of all voices in documentation. Thus, it is important to invite a range of formats and uses of pedagogical documentation.

Extended investigations, although a vital component of new curriculum approaches, require skilled and experienced practitioners. Recording the vitality of the everyday is something everyone can contribute to—it hooks in to the emotions, time is allowed for it to happen, it occurs within the existing relationships, gradual experience creates its understanding and ethical dilemmas can be considered immediately. In Chapter Seventeen, Lisa also comments on her growing insight into 'appreciating the combination of all types of observations, interpretations, interactions, and sharing the many voices that give a deeper insight into children's learning'.

I wonder whether the consideration of 'the many voices' will influence the curators of 'Exhibit-on 2'? Should the variety of types of documentation and practitioners involved in the field be represented? Should practitioners be able to look at the panels and see their current stage of progress reflected? I appreciate the extremely sensitive and difficult task of the curators, but I also believe that all practitioners should be able to connect with and identify in the panels a possibility of self-achievement, balanced with inspiration for greater achievement. The early childhood educational community should feel equal ownership of *Exhibit-on* because it exhibits and celebrates excellent achievement in the Australian context. Even the design and presentation was Australian, unique to our experience and beautiful. It is hoped the curators will be inspired to provide 'Exhibit-on 2, 3, 4-ever'!

Our gradual growth in understanding and use of pedagogical documentation should reflect our Australian experience, especially when the cultural context is a component of a reconceptualised curriculum. The example of portfolios as pedagogical documentation explained by Edith in Chapter Seventeen demonstrates this. The growth of understanding and use of pedagogical documentation in the Australian context may be slow, but this is perhaps because practitioners are exploring their own way of documenting grounded in an Australian pedagogy and culture. I see this as very optimistic as we continue to engage in self-discovery and be reflective practitioners through the use of pedagogical documentation.

The reflections by Margaret, Edith and Lisa show the emotions and the depth of thinking that is influencing practice in the field of early childhood education in Australia. They are describing their use of documentation proudly, skilfully and inclusively in their own contexts to demonstrate a pedagogy that is reconstructing and reconceptualising curriculum. With such reflection and the resulting growth in their professional practice, accountability is obvious; accountability to themselves, to their colleagues, to the children and to parents. I think the discourse has been interrupted!

Each of these practitioners as well as the authors of this book is providing much needed leadership for the field of early childhood education. We don't want to be vague about what it is we are doing; we want clear direction and understanding and even permission to, as Janet said, 'create in unexpected ways'. Early childhood educators do this so well and pedagogical documentation is a wonderful tool to show the world what we are doing. Perhaps the potentials of pedagogical documentation are allowing, and will continue to allow, the many potentials of early childhood educators to become visible.

About Sue Groom

Sue Groom has been working in early childhood education since 1986. Her experience has included early intervention, teaching at the University of Newcastle and working as teacher and Director in community-owned preschools and long day, early childhood education centres. During studies for a Masters degree and following a visit to Reggio Emilia in 1999, Sue was inspired by the challenges presented. She is currently exploring interests in curriculum, leadership and early childhood education centres as family centres, as well as the creation of learning environments that enhance a positive human experience for all involved.

Chapter Nineteen

Conclusion

Alma Fleet
Catherine Patterson
Janet Robertson

Alma, Catherine and Janet have been professional colleagues for more than ten years at Macquarie University in Sydney, Australia. During this time they have had the opportunity to visit Reggio Emilia several times, to visit Scandinavia as part of an international delegation exploring the impact of ideas from Reggio Emilia and to work together in professional contexts.

Arguments about what is appropriate curriculum for young children; ways of interacting with staff and children; ways to record what is worthwhile thinking about; time to ponder things that are important; the risks of undertaking intellectual challenge; the desire to work in ways that lift the profession—these things engage us. The ideas raised in this book can be discussed and interpreted in a wide range of local contexts in all forms of schooling. A prime consideration is the effort by adults to support meaning making, working alongside children in insightful ways. We might say that each of us combines with others to create the foam of local contexts that churns with others in the oceans of possibility, but that definitely stretches the metaphor.

This book has focused on interactions in the early childhood years, including children from 18 months through to those in their fourth year of school, in company with adults who have a range of experience and qualifications. There are fewer examples provided for children younger than 18 months of age. There are, of course, instances of relevant documentation available such as those provided by Gandini and Edwards in *Bambini* (2001). However, in the context of this book, it is more difficult to tease out possibilities for exploring social justice issues with very young children. In themselves, babies may be seen as experiencing inequity from a social justice perspective as they are usually not offered contexts in which funding enables them to have the benefit of growing with fully qualified professionals in children's services.

Documentation and decision-making

This book challenges readers to move beyond the certainties of pre-planned programming. Moving outside these limits also includes redefinition of roles; for example, the prescribed forms of behaviour associated with the role of 'child care worker' or 'teacher', 'practitioner' or 'academic'. Redefined roles would extend beyond qualifications, pay scales and industrial awards, although these elements certainly are important in other circumstances. Narrow role descriptions can limit possibilities of interaction and reflection and can lead to stereotypical expectations. Certainly, job descriptions are necessary to enable individuals to meet their responsibilities and to ensure that all necessary functional aspects of life within a bounded site are acknowledged and addressed. From the perspective of an early childhood discussion, the site in question might be a child care centre, a preschool, a multi-purpose family service, a mobile unit, a junior school or the early years section of a larger school Concerns about role responsibility relate to decision-making by adults, relationships among everyone in the site, and implications for forward thinking.

Procedures such as daily routines can be satisfying. In performing a role that is shaped by routines, you can blinker your perceptions and not be involved in cases of inequity (such as, which children are surviving with minimal positive feedback or encouragement each day?) or aesthetics (what message does our messy environment give about the respect for the work that happens here?) or pedagogy (what could I say in an interaction with a child that could support engagement or investigation?). However, an alternative might be to find approaches which enable all staff voices to be heard.

Participating in pedagogical documentation may provide opportunities for more voices to be heard. Rinaldi (2001) comments that documentation includes 'an element of improvisation, a sort of "playing by ear", an ability to take stock of the situation, to know when to move and when to stay still, that no formula, no general recipe, can replace'. She notes that there are risks with this approach, including the possibility that (p 88):

> Vagueness and superficiality can lead to mistaking a series of images or written notes for documentation which, without the awareness of what one is observing, only creates disorientation and a loss of meaning.

Rinaldi (2001) goes on to say that educators working with young children benefit from a 'broad-based education'. From her description, we would all seek to possess 'the culture of research, of curiosity, of working in a group: the culture of project-based thinking', to participate in the process not only as teachers 'but most of all as people' (p 88). The issue that emerges clearly is that of professional development. Funding, time, and infrastructure configurations need to be addressed to support these challenges.

Documentation and social justice

The possibilities of pedagogical documentation enable social justice issues to become central to the thinking of education professionals. As has been explained in other chapters, there is little consensus on the definitions of social justice. Cannella (1997, pp 168–9) comments that:

> Ultimately we must construct our own views of social justice, our own ways of hearing other human beings, and our own critical dispositions…a professionalism grounded in social justice would welcome controversy and conflict in the name of justice for younger human beings. Actions fostering social justice would be understood as potentially unpopular and threatening to the dominant perspective …Those in the profession would not be those who comply with truth constructed by those in power, but partners with younger human beings in the human struggle.

The inequities and injustices in the world are too stark to be ignored. At a fundamental level, young children are aware of bias and exclusion as these elements appear in such things as choice of playmates. Everyday events (as well as world catastrophes) provide opportunities for engaging children in consideration of 'unfair' practices; local understandings can extend to larger examples of undesirable ways of being. Examples given in this book offer affirmation for those already working in socially just ways to achieve socially just outcomes, as well as introductions for those who are beginning to explore these opportunities.

Looking back

Chapter One included a call of distress from an Australian early childhood educator. On the basis of differing interpretations by staff in her centre of the tensions between privacy legislation and the celebration of children's achievements, she was seeking help with the inclusion of children's names and photographs in centre documentation. The staff in her centre will have been involved in consideration of many of the issues raised throughout the book, in the context of the local curriculum framework (New South Wales Department of Community Services, 2002). Some time later, this teacher wrote again:

> Hi Alma,
> Sorry this has taken me so long to reply. When I became interested in the curriculum framework there was resistance from other staff who I believe perceived that change would somehow reflect negatively on them…By contacting the Department of Community Services, yourself, Office of Childcare etc., we were 'allowed' to document the children's development in a journal. In our room we also changed how we program and as a team designed and implemented our new program format where we are able to add or make changes on a daily basis and have our areas permanently set up. We have also involved parents and through their interest it has been recognised that each room programs differently and there will be ongoing staff meetings to coordinate a consistency throughout the centre. I have been asked to talk to other staff members about the curriculum framework and each room is encouraged to incorporate this into their thinking. Staff have been encouraged to attend courses regarding the curriculum frame-work and we have adopted the terminology eg 'The Thinking Child' and so on. It is still evolving, as is my understanding and that of other members in the centre, for instance adding a daily diary rather than a 'Look what we did today' on a whiteboard (this doubles as our evaluation). Still looking to improve our parent input but we are further down the track than we were in March. Basically a great result!
> Thank you for your support
> Regards
> Briony

The essence of the matter is in the thinking, the wondering, puzzling, exchanging ideas—caring enough to pursue the troublesome topics and to challenge existing practices. This frame of reference (Fleet, 2002) is one which recognises pragmatic constraints but also embraces a sense of curiosity about the range of possible ways to frame a situation, initiate an encounter or series of events, or respond to an unexpected opportunity or confrontation. This orientation also values uncertainty as a necessary component of growth.

Documentation and display

One of the areas where there will continue to be uncertainty is in the area of definition. To some extent, the effort to 'tie down' a definition of pedagogical documentation is less important than the thinking associated with professional development. Nevertheless, although there is a range of processes and products that generally could be recognised as forms of pedagogical documentation, there are forms of recording that probably are not. For example, with the power of the photographic records in Reggio Emilia, many people conclude that it is the photograph which is of the essence, missing the point that it is the thinking, reflecting and analysis of events and experiences that is the essence. Forman and Fyfe (1998, p 241) write that 'The intent of documentation is to explain, not merely to display', and go on to clarify that (p 245):

> The passage from display to documentation travels the path from informing to educating and thereby changes the teacher's perspective from observing children to studying children…display should be converted to documentation by adding interpretation and explanation to the graphics…A set of photographs pasted to a posterboard showing a trip to the farm is a display. A set of photographs captioned with children's words would still be display. The panels need commentary to qualify as documentation…Documentation invites inquiry about children's thinking and invites predictions about effective teaching.

The element of analytical reflection and commentary is essential if photographs or other artefacts are going to contribute to pedagogical decision-making or understanding.

Documentation and community

The use of pedagogical documentation in early childhood services can promote stronger relationships between educators and families. As Katz (1998, p 39), explains:

...documentation makes it possible for parents to become acutely aware of their children's experience in the school...The enthusiasm of the children and the interest of the parents in children's work helps strengthen the involvement of parents in the children's learning, provides a rich basis for parent–child discussion, and deepens parents' understanding of the nature of learning in the early years.

While these ideas focus on the potential of increased involvement of families, pedagogical documentation can offer the possibility to create a new kind of relationship with families—a relationship that centres on shared understandings of children's learning where an 'intellectual partnership' (Forman and Fyfe, 1998, p 252) is formed. This enables 'parents, teachers and children to reflect and search for meaning together' (Fyfe, Hovey and Strange, 2004, p 97).

This concept of the interrelationship between pedagogical documentation and community is explained further by Nimmo (1998, p 297):

The idea of schools as a system of relationships in Reggio Emilia...can be characterized as a true community; a place where collaboration, caring and conflict between adults and children go hand in hand. This sense of community becomes the envelope around the important interactions that occur within each classroom and school.

This transformation to a collaborative relationship can be challenging for both staff and parents. It is important to appreciate that 'not all families have positive attitudes towards or trust educational settings' (Arthur *et al.*, 2005, p 42). It takes time, sensitivity and an appreciation of the diversity of families to create spaces where parents and staff reach a level of engagement that is comfortable for all. Educators must still accept that not all families will engage with pedagogical documentation with the same expectations, willingness or understandings. In addition, with each new school-year intake, comes new children, families and staff requiring us as educators to build on the past and construct anew a culture of democratic engagement.

As MacNaughton and Hughes (2003, p 272) explain, a '...learning community relies on communication between educators, parents and others that creates shared meanings, rather than merely transmitting information.'

Pedagogical documentation can be one of the ways in which educational institutions can create a more democratic engagement with families and communities, building a foundation for such a learning community.

Documentation and assessment

One of the challenges of swimming in a postmodern sea is the avoidance of binaries (Dahlberg, Moss & Pence, 1999); that is, the avoidance of seeing the world in terms of opposites. Instead, this orientation requires that we see divergent constructs as interconnected, or perhaps blurring at the boundaries, enabling things which seem to be fundamentally different to co-exist in an integral fashion. For example, rather than thinking in terms of 'black' and 'white' or 'good' and 'bad' or even 'hot' and 'cold' as mutually exclusive, these apparently contrasting concepts can BOTH be different from each other AND co-exist within the same frame of reference. It is a case of accepting that things that seem to be fundamentally different can sometimes both exist in the same space. This is a useful perspective when considering pedagogical documentation and assessment.

There is a sense of unease around the idea of considering pedagogical documentation as having a role in assessment. This debate has more to do with the definitions of 'assessment' and examples of 'pedagogical documentation' that are being considered, than agreeing or disagreeing with the concept. There are also issues related to questions such as, who is silenced by normative assessment? Whose abilities and potentials are invisible in traditional classrooms? Pedagogical documentation may help to uncover abilities and inabilities in children that have been overlooked or ignored by more traditional methods of assessment.

If an educator is looking for examples of children's increasing sophistication and insight over time, growth can clearly be seen when reading a collection of pedagogical documentation. However, this level of understanding is often not expected or perceived in assessment based on checklists and standardised tests. As Seidel writes (2001, p 304) about the differences between American classrooms and those in Reggio Emilia:

> Indeed, the words at the heart of this conversation—assessment, documentation, teaching, learning, group—are in some cases understood so differently that it is reasonable to wonder how to establish a basis for meaningful conversation.

Therefore, considering pedagogical documentation in the context of assessment is fraught. Forman and Fyfe (1998, p 241) write that:

> Strictly speaking, documentation is not a form of assessment of individual progress, but rather a form of explaining, to the constituents of the school, the depth of children's learning and the educational rationale of activities.

From their perspective, Forman and Fyfe (1998, p 246) go on to note that:

> Documentation presents the wisdom of the teachers who write the explanations and provocations, but documentation is not, by itself, a systematic evaluation of instruction. These two objectives, evaluation and documentation, should be kept separate.

This call for separation is also reflected in the work of Louise Cadwell (2003, p 202), an American who worked as an intern in Reggio Emilia:

> Our dialogue at the St Michael School reveals our current understanding of assessment and documentation as two different worldviews: The first is analytical, reductionist, and decontextualized; the second is holistic, dynamic, and relational. It is hard to accept that these two approaches to learning and the study of learning might be in opposition, but that is what it looks and feels like to us at this point.

On the other hand, from Seidel's (2001, p 304) American perspective:

> In the preschools in Reggio Emilia, documentation is viewed as 'assessment'. As demonstrated in the visual essays…in other books from Reggio, and in the many panels of documentation on the walls of Reggio preschools, documentation is both a product and a process that seeks to represent in words and images, the working, playing, and learning of groups and individuals.

Shifting our understanding of assessment may be possible through consideration over time of individual and group work within pieces of pedagogical documentation. In addition, it is possible that pedagogical documentation could be used as a vehicle for self-assessment of our own teaching. So, by refusing to accept the binary (that assessment and pedagogical documentation must remain at opposite ends of a conceptual chain), these intersections between assessment and pedagogical documentation become valuable topics for discussion. Remember that Briony in her emails, and authors in their chapters, demonstrate that it is possible to pursue ideas related to pedagogical documentation in a context of accountability and government frameworks.

The delicate aspect of this discussion is that there is a danger of moving pedagogical documentation beyond an informative empowering medium to a tool of control. Dahlberg and Moss (2005, p 108) write that:

> It should be admitted that pedagogical documentation carries risks…the child's personality, emotions, creativity, capacity for empathy and co-operation are opened up for judgments and governing…From this perspective, pedagogical documentation can be viewed as a potential act of power and control.

These authors pursue the argument through their understanding of the work in Reggio Emilia (p 109):

> …they have been able to use documentation to resist power, by treating this method as a means to create a space where it is possible to attempt to overcome the techniques of normalisation…That has helped them to refuse to codify children into prefabricated developmental categories, and hence they have been able to transgress the idea of a lacking and needy child.

These arguments about difficulties with defining children in terms of their 'normality' may be unfamiliar to some readers. This is a discussion which is gaining in importance and has been touched on throughout this book.

In closing

This book—perhaps unexpectedly—concerns how we constitute ourselves as members of the early childhood professional community. A new kind of professionalism has been suggested by Cannella (1997, p 168): 'Professionalism would no longer be a way to illustrate for others that we are intelligent and worthy, but a call to action in ways that foster social justice.'

Recognising this vision, the book is definitely an advocacy tool, assisting those who wish to share thinking about pedagogical documentation as a process which recognises children's perspectives and capacities in their learning. It intends to interrupt any discourse which has a 'business as usual' approach to work with young children. It includes both the practicalities and philosophies of intellectual artistry within a context of concern for social justice.

The threads that move through the chapters and responses include:

- the fundamental nature of relationships in pedagogical arenas;
- the centrality of the image of the child held by decision-makers;
- the need to engage with silenced topics that interest and affect children;
- the importance of ongoing teacher growth and thoughtfulness;
- the value of ongoing efforts to evolve pedagogical documentation;
- issues of decision-making seen from the perspective of shared power; and
- the challenges of seeking insights and avoiding orthodoxies.

There are still many questions in this sea of ideas. It is impossible to predict which questions will be the most salient in each situation, but it is inevitable that questions will arise. Ways of working associated with pedagogical documentation may provide a place in which the questions may be asked. The questions may be provoked by a feeling, a snippet of conversation, a pattern of behaviour, a set of photographs, a drawing or a silence. Capturing these moments of uncertainty in visible ways can help focus a particular question and promote further analysis of the data. Pedagogical documentation is the raft on which the ideas, questions and provocations can float for all to see. Once visible, the questions are open to dialogue, community reflection and action.

We do not advocate a movement to newer ways of working simply on the grounds of novelty. Such enthusiasm for 'the new' overlooks the intellectual debts we have to Dewey or Froebel or Vygotsky or others who have preceded us. Indeed, the longevity of Reggio Emilia's 50 years of educational provocation can hardly be considered 'new'. Rather, there is a responsibility to recognise more authentically the rights of children in the worlds they inhabit, to revisit taken-for-granted ways of working with young children, to engage intellectually and sensitively with everyday environments and decisions.

Rather than modernist certainties, a postmodern orientation provides greater complexity, accepts multiple perspectives simultaneously and expects debates about power and silences to be integral to any consideration of pedagogy (Dahlberg and Moss, 2005). The intersection of social justice and pedagogical documentation provides opportunities and responsibilities that cannot be ignored.

References

Arthur L, Beecher B, Death E, Dockett S & Farmer S (2005) *Programming and planning in early childhood settings* (3rd Ed). Victoria: Thomson.

Cadwell L (2003) *Bringing learning to life: The Reggio approach to early childhood education.* New York: Teachers College Press.

Cannella GS (1997) *Deconstructing early childhood education: Social justice and revolution.* New York: Peter Lang.

Dahlberg G, Moss P & Pence A (1999) *Beyond quality in early childhood education and care: Postmodern perspectives.* London: Falmer Press.

Dahlberg G & Moss P (2005) *Ethics and politics in early childhood education.* London: Routledge Falmer.

Fleet A (2002) Revisiting adult work in early childhood settings: Shifting the frame. *Australian Journal of Early Childhood*, 27 (1), 18–23.

Forman G & Fyfe B (1998) Negotiated learning through design, documentation and discourse. In C Edwards, L Gandini & G Forman (Eds) *The hundred languages of children: The Reggio Emilia approach—Advanced reflections* (2nd Ed). (pp 239–60). Greenwich CT: Ablex.

Fyfe B, Hovey S & Strange J (2004) Thinking with parents about learning. In J Hendrick (Ed) *Next steps towards teaching the Reggio way: Accepting the challenge to change* (2nd Ed). (pp 96–105). New Jersey: Pearson Merrill Prentice Hall.

Gandini L & Edwards C (Eds) (2001) *Bambini—The Italian approach to infant/toddler care*. New York: Teachers College Press.

Katz L (1998) What can we learn from Reggio Emilia? In C Edwards, L Gandini & G Forman (Eds) *The hundred languages of children: The Reggio Emilia approach—Advanced reflections* (2nd Ed). (pp 27–45). Greenwich, CT: Ablex.

MacNaughton G & Hughes P (2003) Curriculum contexts: Parents and communities. In G MacNaughton (Ed) *Shaping early childhood: Learners, curriculum and contexts*. (pp 255–81). Berkshire, England: Open University Press.

New South Wales Department of Community Services. Office of Childcare. (2002) *New South Wales Curriculum Framework for children's services: The practice of relationships—Essential provisions for children's services*. Sydney: Office of Childcare.

Nimmo J (1998) The child in community: Constraints from the early childhood lore. In C Edwards, L Gandini & G Forman (Eds) *The hundred languages of children: The Reggio Emilia approach—Advanced reflections* (2nd Ed). (pp 295–312) Greenwich, CT: Ablex.

Rinaldi C (2001) Documentation and assessment: What is the relationship? In C Giudici, C Rinaldi & M Krechevsky (Eds) *Making learning visible: Children as individual and group learners*. (pp 78–89) Reggio Emilia: Reggio Children.

Seidel S (2001) Understanding documentation starts at home. In C Giudici, C Rinaldi & M Krechevsky (Eds) *Making learning visible: Children as individual and group learners*. (pp 304–11) Reggio Emilia: Reggio Children.

Index